QUAKER COMMUNITIES IN
EARLY MODERN WALES

It is suggested that this is a likeness of Thomas Wynne,
the barber-surgeon of Caerwys, and provided in Anon,
Work for a Cooper (1679).

© Library of the Religious Society of Friends, London.

QUAKER COMMUNITIES
IN
EARLY MODERN WALES

From Resistance to Respectability

RICHARD C. ALLEN

UNIVERSITY OF WALES PRESS
CARDIFF
2007

British Library Cataloguing-in-Publication Data.
A catalogue record for this book is available from
the British Library.

ISBN 978-0-7083-2077-8

Published with the financial support of the Marc Fitch Fund
and the Scouloudi Foundation in association with the
Institute of Historical Research.

Printed in Wales by Dinefwr Press, Llandybïe.

For
Thelma, Alfred and Joan Allen

Contents

Abbreviations and Conventions

BBCS	*Bulletin Board of Celtic Studies*
BL	The British Library
CSPD	*Calendar of State Papers (Domestic)*
Extracts	*Christian and Brotherly Advices (The Book of Extracts)*
GAS	Glamorgan Archive Service (formerly Glamorgan Record Office), Cardiff, Glamorgan
GBS	The Great Book of Sufferings
GLH	*Gwent Local History*
GwRO	Gwent Record Office, Cwmbrân, Gwent
HSP	Historical Society of Pennsylvania
Journal	*The Journal of George Fox* (ed. J. L. Nickalls)
JFHS	*Journal of the Friends, Historical Society*
JMHRS	*Journal of the Merioneth Historical and Record Society*
JWEH	*Journal of Welsh Ecclesiastical History*
LSF	Library of the Society of Friends, Friends' House, Euston, London
MC	*The Montgomeryshire Collections. The Journal of the Powysland Club*
NA	The National Archives, London
NLW	National Library of Wales, Aberystwyth, Ceredigion
PMHB	*Pennsylvania Magazine of History and Biography*
P&P	*Past and Present*
QH	*Quaker History*
QS	*Quaker Studies*

SoF	Society of Friends
SPM	*St Peter's Magazine*
TCASFC	*Transactions of the Carmarthenshire Antiquarian Society and Field Club*
TCMD	Testimonies Concerning Ministers Deceased
THSC	*Transcations of the Honorable Society of Cymmrodorion*
THSWW	*Transactions of Historical Society of West Wales*
TRHS	*Transactions of the Royal Historical Society*
WHR	*Welsh History Review*

References and the Quaker Records

Many of Friends' Meeting minutes are not paginated and are referenced by the date when the meeting was held. The calendar was changed in 1752, and this has implications for the dates cited in footnotes. From 1653–1751 the dates adhere to the Quaker custom of beginning the year on 1 March. For example, a meeting dated 28/12/1660, or 28/12/1660–1, should be read as 28 February 1661.

List of Tables and Charts

Tables

Charts

Editor's Foreword

Since its inception in January 1998, the Centre for the Advanced Study of Religion in Wales, located in the School of Theology and Religious Studies, University of Wales, Bangor, has encouraged scholarly research on Welsh religious history and ensured its publication. The Bangor History of Religion series has already contributed towards a stronger and wider understanding of religion among the Welsh people.

Protestant Nonconformity became the dominant tradition in Wales following the Evangelical Revival and maintained its prominence in social life for two centuries. Many of its manifestations have received scholarly treatment in recent years. Yet little has been published chronicling the origins, development, internal organization and significance of the Society of Friends.

Richard C. Allen's volume discusses the Quaker communities in Wales from their inception in Puritan times through the period of their radicalism to the development of quietism and their decline in the nineteenth century. As it does so, it uncovers much that is new and of interest for the history of religion in Wales as well as for the history of the Society of Friends in general.

Geraint Tudor
Centre for the Advanced Study of Religion in Wales
University of Wales, Bangor

Acknowledgments

In preparing this study I have received considerable support from a large number of people. First of all, I would like to thank Geraint H. Jenkins for introducing me to 'this dark corner of the land', as the Quaker Richard Davies called early modern Wales, and for his contribution to my doctoral thesis. I am also grateful to Michael F. Roberts who provided excellent supervision and sound advice which saw me through the final stages. Researchers must always rely heavily upon the expertise and good will of archivists and librarians. I have been particularly fortunate in my searches at Gwent Record Office, Glamorgan Archive Service, Library of the Society of Friends and the National Library of Wales where I have been given generous support and hospitality. I have been helped by Friends in Britain and overseas, notably Jerry Frost, Larry Ingle, Hugh Barbour, Tom Hamm, Ronald Matson, Josef Keith, Tabitha Driver, Chris Densmore, Emma Lapsansky, Dale Johnson, Elizabeth and Harold Rackham, Trevor Macpherson, Howard Gregg, Peter Collins and 'ben' Pink Dandelion.

I have drawn heavily on the friendly advice of Erin Bell and Sheila Wright, and I am eternally grateful to John Graham Jones who read and commented upon earlier drafts of this study. His friendship and that of Alun Howell, Elwyn and Gemma Davies, Robert Tyler, David Evans, Tamsin Gentry, Tim Kirk, Roger Newbrook, Rosie White, Martin Farr, Fergus Campbell, Luc Racaut and Maureen Meikle have kept me going through good times and bad. I have benefited from conversations with colleagues at Durham, Newcastle, Northumbria and Sunderland Universities, and more recently at Westminster College, Fulton, Missouri. My thanks, in particular, go to Norman McCord, Peter Durrans, Peter Waldron, Peter Wilson and Gill Cookson. Owen Ashton and Robert Colls have been stalwart advocates during my search for work: they have encouraged me in all of my endeavours and we have shared many an enjoyable evening together.

I am heavily indebted to Robert Pope at the Centre for Advanced Study of Religion in Wales for his faith in the project, and to the staff of the University of Wales Press who have provided a home for this monograph. This publication has also been made possible by grants from the Marc Fitch Fund and the Scouloudi Foundation in association with the Institute of Historical Research.

I have tested the forbearance of many members of my family while completing this study. My thanks are extended to Gail, Cheryl and Deb and their families, and to Jonathan, Louise and Aled. Without their love, support and patience, I doubt whether this study would have been completed on time. Finally, I owe a very large debt to my wife, Joan, and to my parents. This book is dedicated to them.

Introduction

When I was but very young in years I took my journy into a far Country, where I did wast[e] my goods by riotous living: there were Ringleaders of Wickedness and I took great delight in their companies, then I drank Iniquity as the Ox drinketh water.[1]

These are the words of a little known moralist who concluded his allegory by claiming to be 'one of the People called Quakers'.[2] In 'A Warning for all Youth', Thomas Lewis - described his 'spiritual journey'. In spite of his interest in The Religious Society of Friends (Quakers), he remained in this 'barren land' and did not easily convert:

I found the way very easy into the Country, but to return from thence I could not by my own strength, no more than I could remove mountains; for when I was resolved to forsake the Countrey I could see much Rubbish, and the way very Rough.

This 'pilgrim's' tale, which was one of four papers written by him and transcribed by Monmouthshire members between 1741 and 1742,[3] illuminates Friends' view of themselves as a separate people. By reflecting upon the unpublished papers of Thomas Lewis, who was not a minister or elder of the Society, the reader is introduced to some of the themes covered in this study: the origins of Welsh Quakerism and the search for the inner light; persecution; and the code of discipline.

In any valid history of Wales, or appreciation of the survival of the Welsh language and cultural identity, the impact of Nonconformity is self-evident. The Dissenting tradition dominated the religious landscape, particularly in the eighteenth

1

and nineteenth centuries with the evangelical revivals, and later with disestablishment in 1920. Prior to this date, the Anglican Church 'could hardly have been considered to be a national institution, both because of its claim to be nothing but part of the province of Canterbury and because the vast majority of religious Welsh people attended one or other of the Nonconformist chapels'.[4] The origins and importance of many Welsh Dissenting congregations have been researched and analysed, but, as Geraint Jenkins has noted, a monograph study of Welsh Quakerism has yet to be produced.[5] This is astonishing given the significance of the Quakers in the history of early modern Dissent and the extensive archives that are available. Within the compass of this study, a large percentage of these rich resources have been exploited, Quaker and non-Quaker, and with reference to contemporary and modern analyses. It ought to be pointed out, however, that there are some obstacles which impede the construction of a comprehensive history.

As Adrian Davies and others have found in their work on English Quakerism, the records are far from complete and they have been obliged to draw heavily upon the evidence from particular counties or groups on the grounds that the experiences of Quaker communities were broadly similar.[6] This has been the guiding premise for this work since there is a notable shortfall of documentary evidence for certain Welsh Quaker communities during some of the critical decades. For example, the Carmarthenshire Monthly Meeting minutes cover only thirty-two years, and these all fall between 1724 and 1768.[7] Whereas north Wales is well served in terms of Quarterly Meeting records from the 1660s to the 1790s,[8] there are no minutes for the Montgomeryshire Monthly Meeting for more than a century of its history (1714–1815) and none at all for Merionethshire and Radnorshire.[9] These Welsh Quaker communities shared the same origins and religious principles, and were governed by the same organizational structure and dynamic. Consequently, this history has been constructed using those records which are most plentiful. In this regard, the records from south-east Wales, especially Monmouthshire, have been invaluable. Monmouthshire is extremely well served with primary evidence from the seventeenth to the mid-nineteenth centuries.[10] These important deposits include the minutes, Quaker registers, probates, persecution records and miscellaneous correspondence held at the Library of the Society of Friends, London, Glamorgan Archive Service, Gwent Record Office, the National Library of Wales, and the National Archives at Kew.[11] Nonetheless, key deposits from other important Quaker communities and individuals in north, mid and west Wales have been deployed to test typicality. Quakers also engaged in the burgeoning print culture of the age and produced a vast number of tracts and testimonies. These too have enriched the reconstruction of the Society in its transformation from a radical sect to a respectable denomination.

The history of Quakerism in Britain prior to 1900 was mostly written by antiquarians and enthusiasts who were intent upon providing a heroic account, and who placed great emphasis upon strong leadership and the travails of persecution.[12] There was also a marked tendency to concentrate upon English Quakerism[13] at the expense of a more nuanced reading of the Society's vibrancy in other parts of Britain, most notably Wales. In 1923, Thomas Mardy Rees made the first serious attempt to provide an overview of the Welsh Quaker meetings, their persecution and emigration.[14] This narrative simply catalogued Friends' activities and meetings, and fell short of considering the Society's wider social and cultural impact. Later studies of England,[15] and to a lesser extent Wales,[16] have provided much better insights into both the religious and cultural aspects of the Society over time. Many have explored its origins and early development (c.1650s– 1730s), or focused upon its contemporary presence; others have traced particular aspects of the Society's history, such as theology, demographics, aesthetics, or involvement in business and print culture. There are still some aspects that are under-researched. In August 1997 Larry Ingle, during his presidential address to the Friends' Historical Society at Aberystwyth, elaborated upon a large agenda of work that needed to be undertaken.[17] Furthermore, he urged Quaker historians to liberate themselves from the '"in-group" historiography' which had tended to dominate the published histories. Quaker history, he asserted, would benefit from a more active engagement with other historians and other disciplines.[18] Ingle acknowledged the work of Hugh Barbour, Douglas Gwyn, Rosemary Moore, Geoffrey Nuttall, Christopher Hill and Phyllis Mack – to name but a few – and their attempts to offer a modern re-evaluation. But he felt that this had not gone far enough. Quaker history, he observed, would have to become more critical and raise more questions if it was to make a valid contribution to the history of Dissent and the key role of the Society of Friends.[19] This book has engaged with Ingle's polemic and offers the first scholarly study of Quaker communities in Wales, from their emergence in 1653 to their declining years in the nineteenth century. It aims to provide an analysis of the origins, development and decline of Welsh Quakerism, and then to situate this within its broader context. A comparative approach has been adopted to explore the interaction between Welsh Quaker communities and Friends elsewhere.[20] Such comparisons not only highlight many of the common features of the various communities,[21] but they also enable the distinctive experiences of Welsh Quakerism to be identified. This book seeks to explain how and why Welsh Quakerism was transformed from a persecuted radical religious sect in the pre-Toleration period to a respectable religious denomination in the course of the eighteenth century.

Welsh Quakers built upon the legacy of earlier Dissenters who were active before and during the Civil Wars and Interregnum. The breakdown of Calvinism and the increasing inability of the Established Church to minister to the entire Welsh popultion was the immediate context in which Dissent took hold and Quakerism emerged. Itinerant preachers from Swarthmore Hall in Cumbria travelled widely throughout Wales and converted prominent individuals, who then proselytized the Quaker message and helped to establish nascent communities. Quakers were singled out by a hostile clergy and accused of being a 'deviant' people: papist or radical malcontents, possessed by the devil, witches or mentally unbalanced. The reality was the reverse, for these were serious-minded and devout individuals searching for salvation in an uncertain world. The radical approach of some early Friends to their evangelical work was, nonetheless, controversial and calculated to provoke a strong reaction. Punitive legislation dominated the lives of the early Friends, who were heavily fined, beaten and imprisoned for their beliefs. Welsh Friends responded to this treatment in diverse ways, but overall persecution acted as a strengthening rather than a weakening force upon the existing membership. It made them self-reliant and encouraged them to develop their own alternative community.

A case study of the strength, location and physical composition of early Friends in Monmouthshire has been offered to determine who joined the Society, and what sort of people they were. In addition, an appraisal of the complex meetings structure is provided in a bid to elucidate the decision-making process of these communities. The sheer complexity of the organization, with its overarching London-based management and the multi-layered and gender-differentiated committee system, was both a support network and a constraining mechanism. This unwieldy bureaucracy was increasingly incapable of meeting the challenges of industrial society, and ultimately this contributed to the Society's decline. Even the establishment of the Welsh Yearly Meeting failed to devolve absolute control to Welsh Friends.

The emergence of a code of discipline was an important staging post in the Society's development. Friends were anxious to ensure that members acted responsibly within their meetings and did not undermine the Society's reputation or compromise its principles. In the event, the autonomy of the individual member was subordinated to that of the local meeting. Historians have considered whether the code was a positive development which offered a coherent set of beliefs and helped members to value the Society with its social as well as religious solidarities. This study of Welsh Quaker communities concurs with this assessment, but it remains the case that the code was too intrusive and inflexible. Many members could not conform to its strict rules on plainness and endogamous marriage, and consequently they were forced to withdraw voluntarily or face disownment.

Women had a key role to play in enforcing the code, and also served the Society well as preachers and prophets. The significance of their contribution has been increasingly recognized and some important work has been published.[22]

Until recently their role in Wales has not been fully appreciated or documented.[23] Early female Friends were drawn to the Society because of its egalitarian ethos. As this study will reveal, the equality they sought proved to be somewhat illusory. Family life created its own pressures and women had to make hard choices if they were to involve themselves in the Society. Even though they conducted their own meetings and had administrative responsibilities, most were obliged to accept a lesser, feminized role.

The Society fell into decline after the Act of Toleration in 1689, and competing explanations have been advanced. The final chapter endeavours to view these interpretations in the light of the particular Welsh experience. The interplay of factors which have been cited over the last 150 years can be readily applied to Welsh Quakerism, but some have more significance than others. It has been argued that Quakerism and Welsh cultural life were always strange bedfellows, not least because of the 'English' orientation of the Society, which failed to take sufficient account of the linguistic divide. Emigration, that 'hidden leprosie',[24] offered Welsh Friends an escape: the opportunity to establish a separate community in Pennsylvania – a Holy Christian Community – with their own cultural values and belief system, but their departure decimated the remnant left behind. Given that emigration had more impact on the decline of some Welsh Quaker communities than others,[25] an explanation has to be sought elsewhere. To a large extent, the declining membership must be attributed to the hard line on endogamy and the increasing temptations of consumer society. In the final analysis, did the transformation from radicalism to respectability prove to be the undoing of the Society in Wales?

Chapter 1

'Overcoming the World': *The Origins of the Society of Friends in Wales*

After so many throes and pangs . . . we conceive the great and long desired reformation is neere the birth . . . Oh! my Lord, what are you, that you should be the instrument to translate the nation from oppression to Libertie, from the hands of the corrupt persons to the Saints? And who are we, that we should live to see these dayes, which our fathers longed to see, and reape the harvest of their hopes.[1]

Thus wrote Morgan Watkins and other Friends from Herefordshire to Oliver Cromwell in May 1653. It was a testimony of the millenarian expectations of a 'Parliament of Saints'[2] as well as signalling the arrival of Quakerism on the Welsh borders. But to what extent was there an identifiable Quaker community before 1661 with a coherent and distinctive set of beliefs?[3] As the Society of Friends was a diverse movement, encompassing Seekers, Independents and Baptists, there may have been more than one form of early 'Quakerism'.[4] David Scott has also questioned the assumption that at this stage it combined a coherent radical ideology with an inflexible militancy, and argued that the portrayal of an early Quaker as 'a radical religious activist, a social revolutionary, and an ecstatic visionary' primarily relates to 'public' Friends. Most Friends, he claims, would have found it difficult to reconcile such radicalism with their respectable role in the community.[5] Nevertheless, while many Friends were able to balance their daily business with their Quaker beliefs, others concentrated on 'overcoming the world': they abandoned their responsibilities and even their families in order to become Quaker missionaries. For example, Richard Davies of

7

Cloddiau Cochion, Montgomeryshire, recalled his own conversion experience in the mid-1650s and the impact that this had on his relationship with his family, friends and his employer, Evan Jones of Llanfair Caereinion:

> it was the great talk of the country that I was become a Quaker. My parents were much concerned about me. I was informed that the priest of Welch-pool, W. Longford, went to them and told them, that I was gone distracted, and that they should see for some learned men to come and restore me to my senses . . . My father soon turned his back on me. I had heard of his displeasure, and that he had said, he would leave me nothing . . . At length my mother came tenderly to me, and took a view of me, looking on my face, and she saw that . . . I was not, as they said, bewitched or transformed into some other likeness.[6]

With the growth of religious diversity in the sixteenth century, the Established Church came under threat from a new religious movement: Puritanism. In general, two broad categories of Puritans can be identified: 'church types' and 'sect types'.[7] Even though they sought the reform of Protestant society and liturgy, 'church types' were committed to the Established Church and expected universal conformity; 'sect types', to which the later development of Quakerism belongs, rejected the precepts of the Church, and sought to establish an independent godly community of worshippers. It has been asserted that Friends were 'a by-product' of the religious and social dislocation of the Puritan revolution. The conflict of ideas between Presbyterians, Anglicans and Independents divided Protestant orthodoxy, and led to the creation of new religious movements.[8]

In the 1630s, Puritans reacted strongly against Archbishop Laud's efforts to impose uniformity. Many felt that his religious policies, with their Arminian emphasis, were thinly veiled attempts to restore Catholicism. Furthermore, Laud's use of diocesan church courts, the Court of High Commission and the Star Chamber, alarmed many who believed this to be a deliberate attempt to usurp the authority of the judiciary. Laud's determination to enforce the *Book of Common Prayer* and the *Thirty-Nine Articles*, as well as the restoration of church property and tithes impropriated by laymen, also raised fears that government would be controlled by bishops who would reinforce Charles I's 'Personal Rule'.[9] After 1640, the aim of many Puritans was to exorcise the Church of Laudianism and of his 'scandalous ministers'.[10]

During the upheavals of the 1640s and 1650s, a further redefinition of religious worship was prompted by the growth of printing and itinerant preaching. Radical religious doctrines were proselytized via tracts and pamphlets, and by zealots holding impromptu services and debates in market squares, waste grounds and churchyards. In response to the radicalism of the Civil War years and the Interregnum, dissenting groups proliferated and new leaders emerged.[11] George Fox, a weaver's son from Fenny Drayton in Leicestershire, envisaged a new community of believers and found willing converts to his ideas.[12] In Wales, converts to Quakerism in the 1650s abandoned the parish churches which had so conspicuously failed to meet their spiritual needs. They rejected Calvinist orthodoxy, particularly the doctrine of predestination, and instead sought the 'inner light'.[13] The possibility of salvation for all and the idea of human 'perfectibility' proved to be highly seductive.[14] Thomas Wynne from Caerwys, Flintshire, was one of the first in Wales to convert to this new religious movement, and left behind a full account of his convincement and that of many others:

> I could find neither Bishop, Doctor, Prebend, Vicar nor Curat, to look after my soul . . . and this was the time . . . that the Almighty God . . . did break in upon my soul by his Everlasting Light, and discovered to me the emptiness of all those great Professions, who talked Largely and Eloquently of God and Christ, and of Religion . . . And it was at this time that the Lord raised many Witnesses . . . and made them exceedingly to Tremble.

Wynne's extravagant description typically exaggerates the physical as well as the spiritual effects of the conversion process which

> wounded as a Sword, it smote like a Hammer . . . in my Bowels it burned like Fire, yea, so dreadfully it burned, that it made my Bowels boyl . . . And then the Pangs of Death I felt in my Members which did make me to roar, yea, and to Quake and Tremble.[15]

Like their co-religionists elsewhere in Britain and Ireland, Welsh Quakers wanted a faith based upon simplicity and plainness, and upon their own spiritual experiences rather than unquestioned reliance upon the Scriptures. They wanted to revert to the precepts of primitive Christianity, which recognized their personal and direct relationship with God; like the first Christians, they believed that the Holy Spirit would lead them to 'Truth'.[16] Thus Walter Jenkins, an early Welsh Quaker, observed that God was the 'author and finisher of the Salvation of every one that believes in him'. As for the clergy, he was scathing, and suggested that they did not set a good example to their parishioners.[17] Friends' beliefs challenged the religious and social traditions of their communities. They did not value consecrated buildings or a professional ministry; they refused to swear oaths, pay tithes or maintain the parish church; they declined to remove their hats to social superiors; and adopted the arcane 'thee' and 'thou' as the preferred means of address. This provocative stance led to persecution, but Friends were prepared to endure physical suffering rather than recant.

The development of the Quaker movement in the mid-seventeenth century is especially distinctive in the history of Welsh Protestant Nonconformity because of the speed with which it expanded. This is partly attributable to the apocalyptic preachers who visited Wales in the early days of Quakerism. These charismatic individuals soon established active 'cells' throughout Wales. Even so, it is debatable whether preachers such John ap John, a yeoman from Ruabon, and the English Quaker missionaries Thomas and Elizabeth Holme were solely responsible for the progress of Welsh Quakerism for they were most successful in areas where Dissenting traditions were already well established. As James Maclear has observed, the Quaker movement 'dwelt in the same atmosphere of breakdown in political, social, and religious relations which produced the "gathered churches"'.[18] In 1779, Edmund Jones, an Independent minister, recalled the conversion of a gentleman, and this illuminates the fluidity of religious belief after the Civil Wars. John James Watkin had sought to kill the Baptist preacher of Llanddeti, Jenkin Jones, but was converted 'and the Grace of God made him a Soldier of Jesus Christ'. Watkin became a prominent member of the Pen-Maen (Monmouthshire) Independent congregation and together with Edmund Rosser of Bedwellte[19] and John Rosser of Trefddyn parish he visited Morgan Llwyd, the millenarian minister of the Congregational Church at Wrexham. Llwyd promised to 'make Ship-wreck' of Edmund Rosser's faith, and told John Rosser that 'there are a people called Quakers risen up here, they will come down to your parts'.[20] What this illustrates is that there was a 'window of opportunity' for the Welsh people to identify those groups whose faith most accorded with their religious convictions. The intention here is to locate Quakerism within a Dissenting tradition, and consider the extent to which it constituted a viable religious alternative.

In the eighteenth century, William Williams (Pantycelyn) denounced the Anglican Church in Wales for its

> spiritual death, love of the world, arid disputations, self-regard . . . Ministers without talent, with no experience of grace, without simplicity, without a contrite heart, without faith . . . crawling like tail-wriggling serpents into houses, that is to say churches, for gain, for profit or bodily sustenance, feeding on the fleece of the flock, with no care for the souls.21

There were allegations of corruption, negligence and the failure to deliver the Reformation. Chief Justice Lewknor noted in 1601 that there was 'great backsliding in religion . . . [especially in] Monmouth, Hereford and Shropshire, and the skirts of the shires of Wales bordering upon them'.[22] When summoned by Archbishop Laud for itinerant preaching in the 1630s, William Wroth of Llanfaches claimed that there were 'thousands of immortal souls around me, thronging to perdition'.[23] By July 1646, Walter Cradock, the Independent preacher from Trefela, Monmouthshire, advised the House of Commons that in the thirteen shires there were not 'thirteene conscientious ministers who preached profitably in the Welsh Language twice every Lord's Day'.[24] In Merionethshire, Dolgellau was believed to be a veritable Sodom and Gormorrah, Llanrwst, 'a town of harlotry', and Colonel John Jones of Maesgarnedd wrote in December 1651: 'Where is there more sinne to encounter with, more ignorance, where more hatred to the people of God . . . than in Merionethshire?'[25]

The underlying poverty constrained the work of the clergy and this was further hindered by the impropriation of church livings. On 18 December 1603, the returns of Bishop Goodwin of Llandaff revealed that as many as 105 (61.5 per cent) church livings had been impropriated, and these were parishes where both Roman Catholicism (and later Quakerism) had taken root. This can be compared with impropriations in three other dioceses: Durham, 64 per cent; Bangor, 62 per cent; and York, 58 per cent.[26] As clergymen shunned unattractive parishes, they were impropriated by laymen and this helped to foster religious pluralism. Yet there is evidence that the quality of the clergy was improving at the beginning of the seventeenth century.[27]

Progress was undermined by the difficult terrain, poorly maintained roads and the disinterest of the industrious 'middling sorts'. In addition, there was a paucity of Protestant literature produced in the vernacular and low literacy levels.[28] On the eve of the Civil Wars, the vast majority of monoglot Welsh men and women remained superstitious and ignorant of religion.[29] The impact of the Reformation was relatively limited and recusancy thrived.[30] As Catholicism revived there were also indications, particularly along the Welsh border, that Puritan cells were being established.[31] On the eastern fringes of Wales improved communications and an easier terrain assisted the work of itinerant preachers.[32] Furthermore, the proximity to Bristol and to London where Puritan ideas proliferated, was bound to have an influence on these outlying regions. Monmouthshire, as Brynmor Jones has suggested, was

> a natural bridge across which new ideas and new movements could travel as freely as new fashions . . . Some came from Bristol City via New Passage and Chepstow; some came from London and Oxford via Gloucester and Monmouth; some from Chester and the north through Leominster to Hay and Abergavenny.[33]

The growth of Welsh radical Dissent can be linked to the pioneering efforts of William Wroth,[34] William Erbery,[35] Walter Cradock,[36] Morgan Llwyd,[37] Vavasor Powell,[38] Henry Walter and Richard Symonds. Indeed, it has been argued that 'several of the early Quaker communities in

Wales were connected with districts where . . . Llwyd, Powell and Cradock laboured . . . The early publishers of *Truth* did not labour in a field that had been absolutely unprepared for them by others.'[39] Naturally, the activities of Catholics, separatists and sectaries must be investigated, and their views analysed to establish whether there was a causal link between the growth of religious nonconformity and Quakerism. The paucity of seventeenth-century Church and Quarter Session records,[40] however, poses significant difficulties for any analysis of Welsh Nonconformity before 1642. There is little evidence of those who appeared before the Church courts in the 1630s, or why they absented themselves from church.

The existence of recusants in parts of Wales before the outbreak of the Civil Wars indicates that some still clung to the 'old faith',[41] even though they were persecuted and there were very few missionary priests. From 1603 to the outbreak of hostilities in 1642, there were 3,649 convictions for recusancy in Monmouthshire.[42] Furthermore, the influence of the powerful Catholic Marquis of Worcester at Raglan Castle intensified speculation that there was a potential 'Welsh Popish Army'.[43] By the early 1640s the political situation had deteriorated. In a letter dated 19 April 1640, John Wellch, the overseer of the workhouse in Newport (Monmouthshire), complained of 'pernitious bookes wch are now spread abroad . . . [in support of] Romish articles against the church of God and Supremacy of our Souveraine'. He added: 'these bookes doe much blind the eyes of the simple . . . soe that many are drawne away from . . . the love of there owne countrey & therefore become an enemy of the State'.[44] The Irish Rebellion, especially the massacre of Irish Protestants in the late autumn of 1641, further intensified fear of a Catholic invasion.[45] The evidence for a significant Catholic population was demonstrated when the Exchequer reviewed the convictions for recusancy between 1625 and 1641. The 963 convictions in Monmouthshire between 1641 and 1642 was the largest single number of convictions in the first half of the seventeenth century, and this was exceeded only by the 1,305 convictions transcribed in the 1679 recusant roll at the height of the 'Popish Plot'.[46]

13

Robert Matthews has noted that missionary priests 'launched a tradition of separatism'.[47] Consequently, the authorities argued that Wales was a breeding ground for Catholics and in desperate need of a religious awakening. The Recusancy Rolls for the period c.1625–42 documented the scale of absenteeism.[48] For the remainder of the 1640s and the early years of the Interregnum there are no surviving recusancy rolls. In 1655, however, a further 320 recusants were investigated.[49] Overall, the recusancy rolls for the period c.1603–55 suggest several possibilities. The tradition of recusancy in parts of Wales and the border areas and the challenge this posed to the Established Church may have encouraged further dissent.[50] The outbreak of the Civil Wars hampered the prosecution of recusants and undermined episcopal authority, leading to 'a climate of greater freedom of conscience'.[51] It is noticeable that Friends at Ross-on-Wye 'had for some time separated ymselves from ye Publicke worship of ye world, who did see ye End of ye priests Teachings, who did often meet together by ymselves, and would many times sitt in silence'.[52] Their meetings were held at the home of James Merrick, a tanner,[53] who later became a Quaker minister at the Pant Meeting in Monmouthshire.[54] There is evidence to suggest that itinerant preachers from the Ross area and from across the Bristol Channel were holding open-air meetings in Wales during the 1650s and 1660s.[55] In September 1655, two important Elizabethan recusancy laws were repealed,[56] protecting not only large numbers of Catholics but also Protestant Dissenters. Nevertheless, Dissenters were thereafter forced to swear oaths to the state authorities, a practice which was widely resented by Catholics and Dissenters alike.

The unwillingness of some Puritan ministers in the 1630s to use the *Book of Common Prayer* or to perform church services according to Arminian guidelines suggests widespread dissatisfaction with the policies of Archbishop Laud. Bishop Murray of Llandaff, an avid supporter of Laudianism, complained in January 1634 that he had found William Erbery, the vicar of St Mary's in Cardiff, and his curate, Walter Cradock, preaching schismatically.[57] In the following January he protested against the malign influence of Wroth and Erbery, and in 1635 both men were cited in the Court of High Commission for, among other things, failing to read from the *Book of Sports*, which Charles had issued to the clergy in October 1633.[58] They had also refused to wear appropriate clerical attire.[59] By 1638, Erbery had resigned,[60] and Wroth had reached an accommodation with the Court of High Commission. In November 1639, the first Dissenting congregation in Wales was established at Llanfaches in Monmouthshire.[61] The mixed congregation of Independents and Baptists at Llanfaches was sponsored by Sir Edward Lewis of Y Fan, near Caerffili, and led by William Wroth. Although Llanfaches remained within the Established Church, it gained a reputation for being 'Antioch, the mother church in that Gentile country',[62] and Wroth was hailed as 'the Apostle of Wales'.[63]

The influence of the Llanfaches congregation was so significant that in 1639 the bishop of Hereford wrote to Archbishop Laud claiming 'dangerous errors' were being preached by Dissenters on the Welsh borders. The bishop was infuriated that whenever any inquiry was instigated the offenders would 'slip over the border to another diocese'.[64] As opposition to Laudianism grew, Welsh Dissent became more confident. In 1641, Edward Harris unequivocally condemned the activities of Baptists and other sectaries:

> they perswade their auditory to condemne the prayers of the Church, and Preachers of the Gospell ... By which lewd perswasion of theirs they have drawne divers honest mens wives in the night times to frequent their Assemblies, and to become of most loose and wicked conversation, and likewise many chast Virgins to become harlots, and the mothers of bastards; holding it no sinne for a brother to lye with a brothers wife; as also a virgin gotton with childe by a brother not to be the worse.[65]

Outraged Welsh Puritans lobbied Parliament for religious reform, and a petition was presented to the House of Commons in June 1641 calling for preachers to be sent to Wales.[66] An attack on church rites, particularly baptism, was also recorded by the diarist Walter Powell of Llandeilo Gresynni who noted in 1642 that the 'ffont was abused wth foule water'.[67]

The lack of good preaching meant that many sought guidance directly from the Scriptures, and inevitably they were drawn to movements that emphasized personal religious experience. The Church authorities tried to counter this dissidence by arguing that only ordained ministers could interpret the Bible accurately. The impact of the Civil Wars and the collapse of episcopal authority signalled the end of Laudianism, but for those who preached the gospel in Wales the risks were great.[68] Vavasor Powell in Breconshire was attacked in the early 1640s and the Llanfaches congregation was forced to relocate to Bristol,[69] and later to London.[70] Walter Cradock, Jenkin Jones, Morgan Llwyd, Henry Maurice and Anthony Thomas were all denied permission to preach at Aberystruth. Ambrose Mostyn, the itinerant Denbighshire preacher, tried to give a sermon in the parish church but was denied access. He then attempted to preach in the churchyard, but was pelted with dead hedgehogs, and taunted about his preaching which, it was claimed, taught the people nothing new.[71]

In 1646, the House of Commons approved the recommendations of the Westminster Assembly of Divines,[72] and began to eject unsuitable clergymen from their livings. Among those who lost their livings for drunkenness, immorality or their inability to preach, was Henry Vaughan of Pant-Teg, a parish which became a Quaker stronghold.[73] The Committee for Plundered Ministers (CPM) appointed, amongst others, George White who was installed at Llanfihangel Ystern Llywern parish before turning to Quakerism.[74] Nevertheless, the influx of new clergymen did not lead to a reformed ministry. A significant number of the new appointments made between 1644 and 1649 were offered to those whose primary motive was allegedly financial rather than spiritual.[75] Inevitably, there was a backlash. After Wroth's death in 1641, his followers sought independence from the church authorities and argued for religious tolerance to deliver a more effective reformation. Radical Congregationalists condemned Presbyterian reforms as the work of the anti-Christ, disrupted public worship and had their views represented by Cradock and Llwyd, who suggested that 'mechanic preachers' ought to be allowed.[76] Cradock observed that in Breconshire and Monmouthshire there were 'eight hundred godly people' who were taught by itinerant preachers and ought to be praised for their efforts.[77] The maintenance of preachers and attendance at parish services were hotly debated issues.[78] Morgan Llwyd called for an exodus from 'parish palaces' and 'rotten churches'.[79] He argued for free communion, questioned whether baptism with water and oil was essential, and maintained that a barn, if used appropriately, was as holy as any church.

A combination of the breakdown of religious authority and the emergence of alternative forms of religion encouraged people to challenge the normal patterns of worship. As Elizabeth Quine has observed, 'a holy community of Gospel Christians could only exist in congregations gathered from the general community, by the spontaneous and willing adhesion of the few, who responsibly recognised the preaching of the pure Word or were led by the guiding of the Spirit'.[80] Before the Restoration, radical sects and visionaries seized the initiative. Quakerism figured largely in these religious developments, and those who were drawn to the early Quaker movement appear to have experimented initially with a number of religious alternatives. Furthermore, considering the amorphous nature of early Quakerism, and the diverse responses it provoked, including the ecstatic, almost ranter-like, behaviour of some Friends in Cardiff in 1657,[81] it is evident that Welsh Quakers made a distinctive contribution to the Society.

Quakers had been initially drawn to a range of Dissenting movements. Although separatists and sectaries were doctrinally at odds with each other, they all sought to revert to the practices of the early church. The emergence of the Independents, especially at Llanfaches, their opposition to the Presbyterian Church reform programme, and rejection of external authority, led to the creation of autonomous parish churches. The Congregationalists chose to remain within the Established Church, but insisted upon the independence of their own ministers. In contrast, the Seekers gathered in silent contemplation, patiently waiting for the time when God would constitute a new church and call upon them to be the apostles.[82]

The establishment of Baptist meetings throughout Wales during the late 1640s and early 1650s under the leadership of John Miles was an intrinsic element of this religious pluralism.[83] Such developments assumed greater significance given the number of prominent Welsh gentry converts, most notably the Parliamentary Commissioner, Colonel Edward Prichard of Llancaeach Fawr and William Blethin of Mathern.[84] With many others they proselytized the Baptist message of salvation for all as well as proclaiming the forthcoming millennium. One of the most extreme movements which surfaced between 1649 and 1651 was led by the Ranters.[85] They were deeply influenced by the work of Joachim of Fiore, a twelfth-century Cistercian monk, who believed that, as God was manifest in all creatures, man could not sin. According to their critics, the Ranters took this sinless ideology to extremes, and their excesses were curtailed only by the introduction of the Blasphemy Act of 1650 and the stiff penalties which it imposed. The currency of millenarian ideas during the Civil Wars gave rise to another radical movement, the Fifth Monarchists. They were convinced that the world would soon end. It was their duty to prepare for this and ensure that 'the godly' constituted a 'parliament of saints' in order to guarantee the coming of 'King Jesus'. Morgan Llwyd and Vavasor Powell, who both expressed millenarian views, believed that they were entitled to challenge ecclesiastical power and advocated fundamental political and religious restructuring.[86]

With the defeat of the Royalist forces in 1648 and the execution of Charles I in 1649, it seemed as if the political hopes and religious aspirations of the Fifth Monarchists might be realized. Both Llwyd and Powell devised a programme of evangelization in Wales as preparation for Christ's return. Although the introduction of the Act for the Better Propagation and Preaching of the Gospel in Wales in February 1650 aimed to rid the ministry of delinquent clergymen, it nevertheless failed to deliver the required reforms.[87] Until 1649, the gulf between the demands of the radicals, especially millenarians, and the Presbyterian elements in the Long Parliament was unbridgeable. Initially, the Presbyterians resisted reforms, but with the execution of

Charles I the radicals were able to exert maximum pressure upon the Rump Parliament and the army leadership to endorse the evangelization of Wales. The combination of seventy-one Commissioners, led by the Fifth Monarchist, Colonel Thomas Harrison, and a smaller body of twenty-five Approvers still failed to meet the spiritual needs of Wales – a situation made even more acute by the ejection of 278 delinquent clergymen.[88] In March 1651, the *Humble Petition from Wales and Monmouthshire* was signed by 15,000 people protesting against the dearth of regular preaching.[89] Unfortunately, trained clergymen were in short supply, and the Approvers had to rely upon a large number of inexperienced itinerant preachers.[90] Some Welsh parishes were fortunate and benefited from the services of qualified preachers, including Charles Edwards in north Wales, Henry Walter of Newport and Captain Jenkin Jones of Llanddeti, as well as the occasional sermon given by Wroth Rogers, the governor of Hereford.[91] However, the growth in the number of sects provoked widespread fear that radical sectarianism would lead to anarchy. The enforcement of the Propagation Act, coupled with inadequate clerical support and allegations of corruption and maladministration by the Propagation Commissioners, aroused considerable resentment.[92] The Anglo-Welsh poet Henry Vaughan complained in the 1650s about the usurpation of the Church by radical Puritans, and wrote: 'The Ministers are trodden down, and the basest of people are set up in the holy place.'[93] The Propagation Act was judged to have failed. When its three-year term expired in April 1653 it was not renewed.

Conflict over the way the Church was administered and how society was being governed was the context in which Quakerism emerged, yet this did not lead to a rapid rise in separatism or sectarian worship, or indeed to widespread acceptance of Quakerism.[94] It is possible that general dissatisfaction was simply a reaction to the grievances outlined above and was not typical of those parishioners who sought independence from the Anglican Church. The Dissenters were deeply at odds with one another, and theological disputes were commonplace.[95] Such wranglings warrant careful analysis, especially to determine whether they had any direct

19

impact upon the fledgling Quaker movement. The growth in the number of Baptist congregations in Wales certainly led to a break with ecclesiastical authority, not least over the vexed question of infant baptism and baptism by water. Some such as Walter Cradock and the early Independents opposed all forms of baptism; others did not. Vavasor Powell outrageously declared that he would rather offer a child as a sacrifice to Moloch than witness a baptism. Yet later he advocated a 'believers' baptism.[96] John Miles believed that without baptism there was no church,[97] while Jenkin Jones rejected infant baptism and sought to baptise adults by immersion. In 1650, in the light of conflicting baptismal rites practised by different Baptist congregations, Jones engaged Miles in a lengthy dispute in a bid to reach some kind of resolution.[98]

As Quakers did not believe in baptism, other than that effected by the 'inner light',[99] it is likely that some Baptists found this more straightforward approach appealing.[100] Quaker preachers certainly exploited these doctrinal differences and, as Fay Williams suggests, 'the split between strict and free Baptists on fundamental issues laid them all the more open to Quaker proselytising'.[101] The hostility between the Baptist and Quaker congregations is also apparent in the pamphlet war of the 1650s and in disputations at each other's meetings.[102] For example, in 1658 the Quaker Meredith Edward of Breconshire was 'much abused' by Jenkin Jones when he attempted to dispute theological issues with the minister in Faenor parish church.[103]

One of the most fundamental and damaging divisions in the ministry in the mid-1650s was that between Morgan Llwyd and Vavasor Powell. If Powell was disappointed at the failure to extend the Propagation Act in 1653, he was even more incensed by Cromwell's assumption of power the - following December.[104] From this period onwards a breach in the ranks of the 'Welsh Saints' is visible. Between 1653 and 1656 those who later became Friends were divided into pro- and anti-Cromwellian camps. In 1655, among the 322 names appended to Powell's *A Word for God* there were a number of early Quakers from north, mid and west Wales who cited Cromwellian rule as a key factor.[105] On 23 February 1654, Philip Rogers wrote to Llwyd stating bluntly that the 'question is not so much now who is Independent, Anabaptist, Seeker etc., as who is for Ct [Christ] & who for Crom[well]'.[106] Conversely, there were many early Quakers in south Wales among the 762 signatures appended to Walter Cradock's *The Humble Representation and Address . . . of several Churches and Christians in South Wales and Monmouthshire* who supported Cromwell in 1656.[107]

The disagreements between Llwyd and Powell, which gradually surfaced, not only illustrate the fragility of their millenarian aspirations, but also reveal their fundamentally different political and religious perspectives. While both men resented the dissolution of the Barebones Parliament in 1653, and the end to their millenarian hopes, their reactions diverged. Even though Llwyd's name was appended to Powell's *A Word for God*, together with some members of his congregation, he was fearful that civil war would resurface, and so he cooperated with the Protectorate authorities until another millenarian government could be installed. His refusal to add his name to Powell's letter, condemning Cradock's pro-Cromwellian *Humble Representation*, was an important staging-post in their increasingly fraught relationship.[108] Further division occurred over state maintenance of the clergy which Llwyd, unlike Powell, was prepared to accept,[109] and the collection of the tithe to fund such payments. The breach with Powell was never healed and consequently Llwyd began to show more interest in the Friends.[110]

In the second half of 1653, Llwyd was in correspondence with George Fox and, according to Geoffrey Nuttall, may have undergone a Quaker 'convincement'.[111] A 'conviction under judgement' was effected in October 1653 when two leading Quaker itinerants, John Lawson and Richard Hubberthorne, met Llwyd at Wrexham. Correspondence between Lawson and Margaret Fell notes that during this meeting 'the prist was silent, Richard [Hubberthorne] layd more judgm^t on him, the priest sat sobin'.[112] Afterwards Llwyd wrote to George Fox referring to himself as 'a child & a foole . . . dung & dirt'.[113] Further correspondence followed but, in spite of his apparent convincement, at the time of his death in 1659 he was still undecided.[114] Nevertheless,

between 1654 and 1657 he continued to show an interest in
the Friends, believing that they 'seeme at least to be more pure
than the rest'[115] – sentiments of which Richard Baxter, the
Kidderminster divine and critic of the Quaker movement,
complained.[116]

Why did Llwyd find Quakerism so appealing? Like many
of the early Quakers, he sought a simple but lasting religion.
Llwyd, it is said,

> gathered his flour from many mills, but baked his bread in the
> glowing furnace of his own experience. He learned from Jacob
> Boehme, from Peter Sterry, from John Saltmarsh, from Erbury
> and from the Quakers. He leaned on the Cambridge Platonists
> and on Richard Baxter. He was acquainted with the views of Fifth
> Monarchy Men and Levellers. He knew his Calvin and, like all
> the Puritans, he was above all steeped in his Bible . . . His way
> was not so much to borrow as to assimilate.[117]

In a letter to William Erbery in June 1652, he longed 'to
become a little child again, willing to learn my A.B.C. anew,
if my once dear Schoolmaster Erbury can teach it me . . . I am
daily longing to withdraw into the inner world.' With some
humility, in May 1653, he wrote 'let me be a private seeker,
lest I should be spiritually a loser, and seem more than I am',
and later at the time of his alleged convincement, Llwyd
wrote to Erbery about his spiritual turmoil, 'forget not your
poor, tryed, tempted, tyred, and through mercy sustained and
renewed Lover and Brother'.[118] If there were many aspects of
Quakerism which Llwyd found attractive,[119] Powell had no
such affinity.[120] The disintegration of the millenarian cause
led many who were racked with 'guilt, torment, resentment
and disillusionment' to turn to alternative religious groups
such as the Quakers during the mid-1650s and early
1660s.[121]

Although the introduction of the Propagation Act increased
the number of open-air meetings, and of meeting places later
recorded as conventicles, the programme of itinerant preaching could not meet the spiritual needs of the Welsh people.
The failure to provide a comprehensive network of preachers,
especially those with a command of the Welsh language, was

a particular obstacle. Quakers demonstrated that, although the foundations of institutional worship were being recast, it was still possible for people, whatever their social status or gender, to find true Christian values in their meetings. Friends, along with other Dissenters, continued to attack a Church based on an ordained and educated ministry supported by tithes. Walter Jenkins, a Welsh Quaker, appealed to

> people of all sorts and sexes, and degrees, come, Why will you die, Why will you die? Oh come and delay not, lest it be too late for you, and then your cry will be great and sore, and you shall seek, but shall not be able to find.[122]

The early Quaker leaders were drawn from various religious backgrounds, including churchgoers and separatists.[123] They attacked the beliefs of Independent ministers and occasionally secured the conversion of their adversaries, such as George White.[124] Ministers, like White, did not automatically bring their congregations with them into the Quaker movement. White's presence may have influenced Walter Jenkins, the owner of the early meeting house in Llanfihangel Ystum Llywern, though his conversion actually took place at Whetstone in Leicestershire.[125] Furthermore, it was John ap John's missionary work rather than George White's preaching which encouraged men like Jenkins to turn to Quakerism.

The question is whether Quakerism offered a radically new solution to the religious problems of the age. Calvinism, as a cohesive religious phenomenon, had broken down well before the mid-seventeenth century with various religious groups taking up different positions on predestination.[126] The Society of Friends emerged from this ideological conflict, and began to regard themselves as a separate religious community. Indeed, Richard Price of Llanfor and Owen Lewis of Tyddyn-y-garreg would later describe themselves as 'true and reall' Protestants and Christians. For them, there was 'no Pope nor false Christian'.[127] The theological foundations upon which Fox based his views contrasted with contemporary Calvinist beliefs in the nature of humanity and man's relationship with God. Calvinism held that only a predestined elect would secure eternal salvation, and this depended upon leading a virtuous life. Fox maintained that regeneration would only take place when an individual accepted the 'inner light' of Christ and encouraged that belief to flourish.[128] Baptists and other Dissenters who attacked Quaker ideology were condemned by Friends as 'pleaders for sin',[129] while Morgan Watkins criticized Vavasor Powell in the following terms: 'O, thy sottish blindness makes thee grope at noon day, strain at a gnat and swallow a camel. Why dost thou pray against sin, while thou believest thou cannot be delivered from it on earth?'[130]

Historians have noted that many of Fox's ideas were not original.[131] Fox's contemporary William Erbery had already mooted the idea of an 'inner light' before it appeared in his ministry. Thomas Rees observed that Erbery's religious beliefs shared characteristics with that of Friends, and indeed Erbery's declaration that 'all men are in God, and God in them and they his offspring' could as easily have been spoken by Fox.[132] The acceptance of the 'perfectibility of man' and the guidance of the Holy Spirit were not new ideas,[133] and neither were the principles of faith which Friends were encouraged to follow.[134] Fox's refutation of seventeenth-century conventions were also expressed by the Baptists,[135] and his critics were quick to highlight the similarities between the two sects. Their attacks upon social status, wealth and authority led people to believe that both the Baptists and the Quakers were revolutionaries. In 1659, in response to the activities of Captain Jenkin Jones and his armed followers in Brecon, an anonymous tract alleged that the Baptists plan 'not onely to destroy the Ministry, but also the Magistracy, that none may be left to preserve publick interest'.[136] For Richard Baxter, Baptists and Quakers were equally abhorrent. The Baptists, he said, were 'zealots' and 'opinionists, who all hasted directly to enthusiasm and subdivisions, and brought forth the horrid sects of Ranters, Seekers and Quakers'.[137] Nevertheless, Fox's originality derived from his charismatic personality and ability to recruit people to his message of 'truth'. He offered these 'gathered churches' a new beginning.

Quaker itinerant preachers and their 'gathered' meetings attracted many during the Commonwealth period. Yet, unlike many similar movements at that time, Friends survived the Interregnum and Restoration. As Edward Milligan has commented, early Friends 'gathered for worship without liturgy or pre-arrangement of any kind, or any appointed preacher, believing that out of an energetic and expectant silence God might use any one of the worshippers as a minister'.[138] As some have suggested,

> with the relative decline in importance of Scripture went a complete disavowal of the necessity for the ordinances. Friends were particularly anxious to prove the fallaciousness of baptism by water, arguing that it could only be by the Holy Spirit and with fire. Nor was the Lord's Supper to be continued as an outward ordinance 'for Christ had appointed it only until He came again'.[139]

Christopher Hill has argued, however, that the success of Quakerism turned more upon Fox's ability to exploit the situation than upon the benefits of a new religious ideology.[140] Complaints against the payment of tithes were never far from the surface of Welsh affairs. Money provided under the terms of the Propagation Act to pay for ministers and lecturers was drawn from the sequestered livings of the Church, and ultimately from the tithe.[141] This was more acceptable to conservative religious groups, such as the Presbyterians and moderate Baptists, than it was to radical Dissenters.[142] William Erbery who accepted £200 a year in maintenance between 1650 and 1651, thereafter complained that God was beginning to 'rot in his soul'.[143] In a letter written in April 1652 Erbery observed that a 'worthy Gentleman from England' complained about the Commissioners of Monmouthshire who were exacting excessive tithes.[144] Vavasor Powell, the staunchest critic of them all, wrote in April 1657 to Morgan Llwyd that to accept a salary was to 'wrest it out of ye bowells of ye poore'.[145] Furthermore, Powell, along with other 'Saints', condemned Walter Cradock for his *Humble Representation* to the Protector, and questioned why he had changed his mind about state maintenance and the collection of tithes: 'How also did you preach & pray against parishwayes & tythes etc, and yet since you have had your hand in upholding them?'[146]

The most sustained resistance against the tithe in this period was that organized by the Friends.[147] They not only refused to pay tithes, but encouraged non-members to do likewise. The Quaker movement, whose early development depended upon itinerant preaching, rejected the idea of a paid ministry. They were supported by former parliamentarian soldiers who sought religious liberty and freedom from the tithe. Nevertheless, such opposition remained a matter of individual conscience and Quaker policy did not become codified until after the Restoration. It is possible that the flexible nature of the early Society allowed people to join in fellowship with the movement and gradually absorb its principles. By extension, therefore, it was not incompatible for Friends to pay tithes or to own them. Even among Welsh Friends, there were or had been lay impropriators of tithes, such as Major John Gawler of St Fagans who in 1648 rented a tithe barn in Whitchurch in Glamorgan and in 1652 rented glebe land in the same parish.[148] Yet it is worthwhile noting that those Friends who had been tithe-farmers later came to accept the Society's anti-tithe position.

In their opposition to tithe payments and 'hireling' ministers, Friends had adopted the radicalism formerly associated with the Baptists, and were critical of their failure to stand firm. Friends abhorred their acceptance of 'benefices' and ministers who 'read sermons which they finished at appointed times, rather than preaching as the Spirit moved them'.[149] In Wales, Friends persuaded some Baptists to reconsider their allegiance and even to join the Quakers. For example, in Radnorshire Quaker missionaries soon found a ready congregation among former Baptists. This process was confirmed by Thomas Holme who observed that there were 'divers meetings wher many ar Convinced of the truth, of that peopell called babtis; many of ther Churches ar broken in peeses'.[150] Their success soon made Friends the target of criticism. Among the first to condemn the Quakers was John Miles who called for 'An antidote against the infection of the times'.[151]

John ap John was one of the first Welshmen to have any formal association with Quakerism when he was sent by Morgan Llwyd to visit George Fox at Swarthmore Hall in

Cumbria in 1653.[152] John was soon converted to Quakerism and became a renowned preacher in Wales,[153] along with the Westmoreland weaver-preacher, Thomas Holme. While the date of Holme's first Welsh preaching tour is uncertain,[154] between 1653 and 1654, Fox despatched him and other missionaries from Cumbria to the Welsh borders.[155] Great efforts were now made to proselytize throughout Wales. In 1653, Richard Hubberthorne was at Wrexham, and called on Margaret Fell to direct letters, books or printed papers to him there.[156] In May 1654, John Audland sent a progress report to Fox, observing that there was 'a deadnesse over that countrey'. Together with John Ayrey, he travelled to Wrexham and held meetings at Trefor in Denbighshire.[157] In December 1654, Holme's wife, Elizabeth, and Alice Birkett travelled over a hundred miles throughout Wales, while John ap John had also been preaching before his arrest and imprisonment at Cardiff.[158] In February 1655, Holme reported that he had held a meeting at a magistrate's house in Montgomeryshire, preached to some soldiers and held a meeting in Radnorshire before travelling south. He held two meetings at Abergavenny: the first at an inn and the second in the market place where he 'drew the peopell into A convenient place & spok A prety time to them'.[159] Holme was satisfied that 'the Lord is gathering A peopell in Monmuthshir & Glamorgenshir'. Additional meetings were held in Chepstow, Newport and '6 mils beyond Cardife at the seeasid'.[160] In a further letter to Margaret Fell in August 1655, Holme stated that three Friends, Thomas Hills, Richard Millner and Alice Birkett, had 'come out of Ireland', Birkett travelling southwards to rendezvous with Elizabeth Holme.[161] By April 1656, Margaret Fell was informed that at least ten meetings were being held in Monmouthshire and Glamorgan on a regular basis.[162] By the mid-1650s, therefore, Quaker groups had emerged throughout Wales and formed the nucleus of an alternative community.

With the assistance of his wife, Alice Birkett, John ap John and other Quaker missionaries, Holme organized further meetings throughout Wales. Among the first attenders were Walter Jenkins, a magistrate of Monmouthshire,[163] and

Robert Owen of Dolserau in Merionethshire, the son-in-law of Robert Vaughan of Hengwrt, who had served on various committees in the county. In later testimonies, Owen and his wife, Jane, were the first to open 'the door for a reformation in the country where they lived, after the Civil War', and 'zealously devoted to religion . . . being one of the first in our parts who sought after it [Quakerism]'. By 1660, Owen was denounced by his opponents as 'dangerous and in actual disturbance of the peace'.[164] More conversions followed and Fox convinced another magistrate, Major John Gawler, while he was in Cardiff in 1657, and possibly Owen Humphrey and Lewis Owen during his visit to Merionethshire.[165] These gatherings increased in size until Holme was able to organize small communities of worshippers to meet regularly in family homes or other suitable venues. For example, in Monmouthshire small groups of Quakers came together in the rural parishes between Abergavenny and Monmouth, as well as at Pontypool, St Mellons and in the parishes east of Newport including Caldicot and Shirenewton. In Merionethshire, Quaker farmsteads were clustered around the market towns of Bala and Dolgellau. These close-knit groups developed a strong sense of community and included Quaker families of wealth and influence. The location of these meetings often determined whether Friends faced local hostility or tolerance. Violent clashes were much more likely in urban areas, which early Friends regarded as 'bastions of institutionalised religion, lavish ceremonies, jealously guarded privilege'.[166] Law enforcement by churchwardens and constables in rural parishes was at best ad hoc, and most sought compromise to avoid interference by the diocesan and civil authorities. For example, rural Quakers in south-east Wales were more protected than their co-religionists in Cardiff, Swansea and Welshpool. Large numbers of Quakers were imprisoned in east Glamorgan and Cardiff, and it is noticeable that the Cardiff Friends declined in numbers in contrast to those in the Monmouthshire meetings.

Notwithstanding such hostilities, Welsh and English Quaker preachers were highly successful. Throughout south Wales 'gatherings' of Friends were convened by itinerant preachers and recent converts included Edward Edwards of

Denbighshire and Thomas Ellis, a former member of Vavasor Powell's congregation.[167] In north and mid Wales, Quakers were also gathering in parishes near Dolgellau, Welshpool and Wrexham, while in 1656 Richard Davies, formerly an Independent, recorded that his ministers accused Friends of being 'false prophets' who denied the Scriptures and the existence of Christ. They were judged to be 'a dangerous sort of people', and 'we were afraid of any one who had the name of a Quaker, lest we should be deceived by them'.[168] Encouraged by Morgan Evan, a Quaker preacher from Radnorshire, Davies, along with other Independents, turned to the Friends.[169]

Other Friends throughout Wales hosted their own meetings and provided burial grounds.[170] The success in recruiting members from other separatist groups was soon recognized. In 1657, leading Friends, including George Fox, travelled to Wales to support them in their missionary work. Holding meetings near Caerwent, Cardiff and Swansea,[171] he ventured to Brecon with Thomas Holme and John ap John where the town was 'in an uproar'. The magistrates incited the crowds to attack them and, as Fox recalled, 'if the Lord's power had not prevented them they might have plucked down the house and us to pieces'.[172] Thereafter several large meetings were held in Monmouthshire, Montgomeryshire and Radnorshire.[173] John ap John spoke to the people in Welsh, while Fox 'stood-a-top of a chair about three hours . . . and many people sat a horseback . . . And many were turned that day to the Lord Jesus Christ.'[174] Accompanied by John ap John and Edward Edwards, Fox held further meetings in west and mid Wales before preaching throughout north Wales.[175] Meetings were held in Pembroke, Haverfordwest and Tenby,[176] but in Carmarthen John ap John was briefly imprisoned after he had preached in the streets. Fox intervened and reproved the magistrates of this 'very wicked town':

I showed them how unchristian their carriage was to travellers and strangers . . . and what an unworthy thing it was to hinder us in our journey . . . And the Lord's power came over them, they were so ashamed, but I could not get a word from them in answer. So I warned them to repent and to turn to the Lord.[177]

Further meetings in Cardiganshire produced equally hostile receptions at Cardigan and Lampeter where the crowd was 'exceeding rude'.[178] At Aberystwyth, John ap John again preached in the streets, while Fox was accosted by a 'great man' on the road to Machynlleth.[179] In Merionethshire, they held an impromptu meeting at Dolgellau where John ap John 'declared through the streets' and later spoke to them in Welsh. Fox recalled that 'many people accompanied us to our inn, and rejoiced in the Truth that had been declared unto them'.[180] They held meetings in Caernarfon where they gathered a crowd and a clergyman challenged them before Fox 'declared the word of life amongst them'. Although there was some resistance to the Quakers, there was a reluctance to persecute or abuse them.[181] Before travelling to north-east Wales, John ap John spoke at Beaumaris but was promptly arrested. Fox was threatened by an innkeeper's wife with the same treatment, but he reproved the local townspeople for the 'uncivil and unchristian thing they had done in casting John in prison'.[182] They later had a large meeting in Denbighshire, before passing into Flintshire. At Wrexham, they were met by many members of Morgan Llwyd's congregation who were 'very rude [and] wild', and a woman asked for a lock of Fox's hair.[183] About this time, Richard Davies first encountered John ap John at a meeting in Shrewsbury and found his 'words so sound and piercing' that he established a small meeting of Friends in Montgomeryshire. As Davies later wrote, 'we all agreed to meet together, but none of us had a house of his own to meet in. We determined therefore to meet upon a hill in a common, as near as we could for the conveniency of each other . . . in silence.'[184]

Although Davies briefly left Montgomeryshire to look for work in London and complained that he tried to shut out thoughts of Wales because it was 'barren and uninhabited with Friends and Truth',[185] these early 'threshing' meetings aroused the wrath of the civil authorities who began to take more notice of this vociferous group. Irrational fears of the Quakers provoked alarm and the scale of the response far outweighed the actual strength of the movement. The tendency of Friends to adopt prophetic speech or to identify themselves as 'children of Christ' provoked the authorities, especially as they were so critical of the magistracy and ministry. Opponents drew attention to Quaker blasphemies, or dangerous and fanatical behaviour.[186] Many Friends were treated as vagrants and roughly manhandled or imprisoned by constables, watchmen and churchwardens. During the 1660s, Friends developed strategies to counter this prejudice, particularly accusations that they were insane or practised witchcraft. When Richard Davies was brought before the magistrates at Welshpool in 1660, he was asked why he supported a 'strange religion'. He replied that it was 'the good old way', but this brought forth accusations that he was mad and suggestions that he ought to be whipped.[187] In 1661, Merionethshire Quakers personally delivered a petition to the king and Parliament outlining the vicious attack upon them by Alban Vaughan and several others. Apart from being dragged out of their meeting house and physically abused, they had been accused of witchcraft. It was alleged that they had a witches' familiar, 'a little dog that followed them', and this served 'to be the spirit which led them in the way of worship'.[188] That accusations such as these caused some concern at this time is clear in a letter from Francis Gawler to George Fox. Gawler complained that Mary Chapman, a member of the St Melons Meeting, 'hath Refused to pay Aney Contrybeution and latly shee and hear servants did winow corne in the barne on the first day of the weeke'. As winnowing corn was commonly held to be a sign of witchcraft, Gawler was concerned that her behaviour might provoke hostility from the local community. He believed that her actions were not the 'le[a]dings of the spirite of truth'.[189] The code of discipline established by Fox in the post-Restoration period was not just calculated to reform Friends' behaviour, but also to instil a clear set of values and ideologies.

Friends' readiness to hold open-air meetings remained crucial to the early development and success of the Quaker communities in Wales, but they were high-risk events. The publication of meetings and tracts, especially in the years of severe persecution, risked not only the censure of the local authorities but imprisonment. Quakers saw these meetings as serving a dual purpose: they were a powerful recruitment tool and the means of saving lost souls. In a letter from Thomas

Holme to George Fox in 1657, he reported that there had been several meetings, including two meetings 'in the hills . . . wher noe meeting was befor, wher many was convinced'.[190] In the same year, Richard Davies went to a gathered meeting at Llanfyllin to listen to an Irish Quaker preacher,[191] while in 1659, Walter Jenkins, Edward Edwards, Elizabeth Holme and Francis Gawler were all arrested at Shirenewton and brought before the magistrates. They had been repeatedly warned that they were not to meet near the church, but they argued that the law provided 'liberty to all for to meet together in the faith of Christ'.[192]

The years of missionary work as well as several periods of imprisonment took its toll on the early pioneers. In March 1663, Holme informed Fox that his wife was ill and 'trubled with the rising of the mother [panic or hysteria] in one side, & the splin in the other, besid the ston doth muche Anoy hire besides sume other destempers, soe Hir body is all out of order'.[193] Two years later, Elizabeth died at Kendal,[194] closely followed by her husband in October 1666.[195] Thereafter, Welsh Friends had to rely on their own ministers to develop and support the Society. Between 1667 and 1668, Fox once again intervened personally by touring Wales to support the cause and establish a system of Monthly Meetings. He addressed gatherings in many places, including Denbighshire, Merionethshire and at Dolobran, the home of Charles Lloyd, where a General Men's Meeting was held. After leaving Radnorshire, Fox and his colleagues were violently attacked on the roadside.[196] In Monmouthshire, Fox visited the Pant and held a large meeting where 'four priests [were] convinced'. Fox, however, noted that these meetings were not safe havens for Quakers as a 'drunken bailiff' had entered the meeting in 1663 and 'the country was in a great rage . . . some rude people came and shot a musket against the house'.[197] Later in 1668, Fox returned to south Wales and held meetings at Pont-y-Moel, Quakers Yard, Swansea, Tenby, Haverfordwest and 'many other places where the Monthly Meetings were settled in the gospel order'. As before, they were threatened by 'some rude gentry' on the outskirts of Mumbles, and narrowly avoided arrest at Chepstow before returning to England.[198]

In the years after 1660 Royalist reprisals, legislative change and petty malice against Dissenters all created problems for the Quakers. It was certainly no time for the faint-hearted, and many were imprisoned in damp, squalid conditions. Gradually meetings were established throughout Wales, which 'turned many people from their loose lives' and made 'a great reformation amongst people'.[199] In spite of all their hardships, Friends were occasionally able to take advantage of political change. The Declaration of Indulgence in 1672 allowed Friends, along with other Dissenters, to register their meeting houses. Similar concessions were made in 1687 and 1688, making it easier for the Society to grow. There were some significant converts to Quakerism during this period, notably, in 1675, Rowland Ellis, a twenty-five-year-old landowner of the Bryn Mawr estate in Merionethshire.[200] Indeed, the Welsh Yearly Meeting at Haverfordwest in April 1688 was able to record that 'things are well wth friends in the severall Counties of Wales & unity & prosperity among them in a great measure . . . meetings increase (rath[r] than diminish) & things are on a growing rather than declining hand'.[201]

Chapter 2

'A gathered people': *A Case Study of the Distribution and Social Composition of Monmouthshire Friends*

In his study *Protestant Dissenters in Wales*, Geraint Jenkins raised important questions about Quakerism: Who were the Friends? What sort of people were they?[1] The answers are complex, and have provoked considerable research, particularly studies of the demographic patterns of English and Irish Quakerism conducted by Richard Vann and David Eversley.[2] Nevertheless, little has been written about the social origins and membership profile of early Welsh Quakerism. This is not surprising given the relatively small numbers involved and the dearth of available registers. Comparisons between meetings in Wales cannot easily be made for some registers are missing, notably Cardiff and many of those relating to mid and north Wales.[3] This study proposes to address the problem by offering a case study of Friends in Monmouthshire, for whom good records survive, and whose community can be regarded as broadly similar to other Welsh Quaker communities. It will draw pertinent comparisons with another persecuted community in the county, the Roman Catholics, and an attempt will be made to delineate the distribution and social composition of Friends from the seventeenth century onwards.

The limited coverage and questionable reliability of Friends' registers, coupled with the instability of parish registers for this period, must hamper the construction of a demographic analysis. Nevertheless, a meaningful assessment is possible if we draw upon data which shows *c.*1600 Monmouthshire had a population of at least 24,000 inhabitants,[4] and between 1655 and 1676 a Quaker community of approximately 200 (0.8 per cent). The Quaker population at the Restoration has been estimated at 30,000–60,000,[5] and Monmouthshire Quakers constituted a very small percentage of this. The case study assumes that if the head of the family was a member of the Society, and his children appear in the records, they too can be identified as Quakers. Divisions between Quaker and non-Quaker family members were a commonplace and due caution must be exercised in any estimate of numerical strength. As the figures below indicate, Monmouthshire Quakers were a very peripheral group in comparison with English meetings, such as Essex, where the Quaker population was over one thousand strong between 1655 and 1664.[6] Before attention is given to the evidence from the local registers, the data on Quaker conventicles supplied in the 1669 ecclesiastical returns and the 1676 Bishop Compton census on Nonconformity must be examined. The list of Dissenting congregations compiled by Dr John Evans, a London Presbyterian minister, and several others in the early eighteenth century will also be consulted.

It had been hoped that the Clarendon Code would curtail the growth of Quakerism, but this was not to be. In June 1669, Archbishop Gilbert Sheldon ordered a survey to be made of the location, relative strength and leadership of Dissenting congregations.[7] In the event, the low figures and inaccuracies of the returns demonstrate the limited knowledge of Quakers and other Dissenters in Wales. The Monmouthshire returns specifically recorded two Quaker teachers, five meeting places, four conventicles and thirty-five 'conventiclers',[8] and this probably underestimated their strength. Quakers in the Pontypool area met at Richard Hanbury's house where between forty and sixty, and 'sometimes more', Quakers gathered.[9] At the Pant, between thirty and forty members gathered to listen to James Merrick, a tanner from Ross-on-Wye, and George White. These Friends could muster at least sixty members, especially when they heard an 'eminent seducing teacher'.[10] At Shirenewton and Wilcrick, the homes of Robert Jones, George Phillip and John Jones appear in the records, along with Edward Webley, an 'entertainer' of the Quakers.[11]

Conventicles were convened at the homes of David Robert, John William Morgan, weaver, and Thomas William, tailor, in Llanwenarth.[12] At these conventicles between eighty and one hundred people, described as 'tradesmen, and most women and maidens' gathered to hear preachers such as Morgan Evan. Various analyses of these Llandaff returns have questioned whether these conventicles were Quaker meetings, especially those in the Llanwenarth and Shirenewton parishes. Thomas Rees believed that the congregation at Llanwenarth were Anabaptists,[13] but Thomas Richards claimed that they were Quakers, arguing that Morgan Evan was probably the same man who converted Richard Davies of Cloddiau Cochion, Montgomeryshire.[14] There is always the possibility that Quaker listings for Llanwenarth were inaccurately transcribed; if the words 'weaver' and 'taylor' denoted occupations rather than surnames it is possible to identify the Quaker weaver, John William Morgan.[15] David Robert and Thomas William 'taylor' have not been found in Welsh Quaker registers, but this may reflect their role as itinerant preachers. The Shirenewton returns are also problematic. Richards suggested that there was only one Quaker conventicle, and according to Friends' registers this was held at George Phillip's house.[16] The alleged conventicle at Robert Jones's house[17] can be discounted as his name appears in the returns as a non-Quaker 'repetitioner' at Netherwent and Llan-Gwm.[18] Although there are no references to the Monmouthshire meetings at St Mellons and Castleton, the returns for Glamorgan list a meeting in Marshfield at the house of Jane Reynolds.[19] However, the presence of the Baptist preacher, Thomas Quarrell, casts doubt on its provenance. Another Quaker meeting was held at the home of William Williams of Canton (Cardiff), where James Adams of Bristol and Francis Gawler were preachers and which attracted between forty and one hundred Quakers.[20] Fortunately, it is possible to cross-reference the 1669 returns with official Quaker records. The Society recognized four meeting places (c.1668): Castleton (St Mellons); the Pant; Llanfihangel Pont-y-Moel; and Shirenewton.

Elsewhere in Wales, the returns were equally poorly attested. In Glamorgan, apart from the return for Canton, Quakers were among the hundreds of 'mixd Rabble' at Merthyr Tydfil, and met at the homes of Jenkin Thomas, Harry Thomas and Lewis Becke. At Cadoxton, near Neath, Mary Prichard's house was also a conventicle for an unspecified number of Friends, while it is less likely that Friends were counted among the Dissenters of 'mean qualitie' at Llanedeyrn or the unspecified congregation at Eglwysilan, both of which were led by the Baptist minsters, Thomas Quarrell and John Powell.[21] In Montgomeryshire, meeting places, 'abettors' and members were recorded at Llanwddyn at the home of John Thomas, and at Meifod at the home of Charles Lloyd.[22] Although no Quakers were recorded in the Bangor and St David's Dioceses, a year later Richard Habberley, the vicar of Talgarth, was censured at the Brecon Consistory Court for his failure to employ a suitable curate. This, it was alleged by the churchwardens, had caused an increase in the number of Dissenters as Habberley had 'not used any lawful means to reclaim them from their errors'. In his defence, the vicar claimed that the churchwardens had not brought any proceedings against the conventiclers in the civil courts.[23] By February 1673, Bishop Lucy of St David's expressed concern to Archbishop Sheldon that there were a number of unlicensed schoolteachers in his diocese, including James Picton, a Quaker from Carmarthen who had been excommunicated by the church courts. He was imprisoned but freed after a writ of *de homine Replegiando* was accepted, and thereafter taught '70 or 80 scholars'.[24] It is, however, clear that there were many other Quaker teachers and meeting places throughout Wales. Thus, in Pembrokeshire by 1663 Friends had acquired a burial ground at Trewern in Llanddewi Felffre, and in Glamorgan, Quakers Yard was visited by George Fox in 1668 on his way from Pontypool to Swansea:

> We passed over the hills declaring the Truth to people and visiting Friends, and came to another widow woman's house where we had a meeting. But the woman could not speak one word of English but praised the Lord that he should send me over those hills to come and visit them.25

A second ecclesiastical survey conducted in April and May 1676,[26] although still flawed, provides more information.[27] For various reasons, the census taken in the four Welsh dioceses[28] is a gross underestimation of the strength of Protestant Dissent. Geraint Jenkins highlights the difficulty of identifying Dissenters and suggests that clergymen may have wanted to avoid drawing attention to their numerical strength.[29] Anne Whiteman's critique of the 1676 returns concludes that the aggregate total of Dissenters for Wales was 4,196,[30] a little over 1 per cent of the total population of around 371,000.[31] The estimated Dissenting population for the Llandaff diocese was 905 or 2.4 per cent of the total population (37,100). Thus, Dissenters represented an extremely small percentage and Quakers an even smaller minority. In the areas where there were known Quaker meetings, the census again underestimates the strength of the Friends. For example, in Monmouthshire the numbers of Dissenters were: Marshfield/St Mellons (18), Shirenewton (7), Llanfihangel Ystum Llywern (4), Llanwenarth (27) and Llanfihangel Pont-y-Moel (12), while in Meifod in Montgomeryshire only 14 Dissenters were recorded.[32] Again, a number of Welsh Quaker meeting places and their congregations seem to have been ignored. At Swansea, a meeting house was built in 1674, and the Tref-y-Rhyg meeting was established by John ap Evan (Bevan) in 1675. In Radnorshire, the Pales meeting had been in existence from at least 1663, and in Montgomeryshire, Merionethshire, Denbighshire and Flintshire there were sizeable meetings at Llanwddyn; Dolobran; Esgairgoch; Cloddiau Cochion; Tyddyn-y-garreg; Llwyndu; Dolserau; Penllyn; Trefor; and Wrexham.[33] On balance then the percentage of Quakers in the population was much greater than the official surveys would suggest.

Between 1715 and 1718, Dr John Evans compiled lists of Dissenting congregations in order to lobby for an end to the 1714 Schism Act.[34] Unfortunately, the Quaker community was not large enough to warrant specific scrutiny, and historians have had to rely upon the contemporary evidence of Friends and modern analyses.[35] Michael Watts calculated that in c.1715 there were 696 Quaker congregations in England and Wales.[36] The Quaker population for England, including Monmouthshire, stood at 39,510[37] and, of that number, membership of the four Quaker meetings in Monmouthshire was 90 (see table 2.1). For Wales, including Monmouthshire, the estimated total of 750 members suggests that Monmouthshire supplied at least 12 per cent of the overall Quaker population, and 2.69 per cent of the Dissenting population which stood at 3,350. There were only two Welsh

Table 2.1. Estimates of Dissenting Congregations (with known Quaker populations) in Wales and the border counties c.1715[1]

County	pop	Q cong/no	%	P cong/no	%	I cong/no	%	PB cong/no	%	Totals cong/no	%
Monmouthshire	29200	4/90	0.31	-/-	-	9/1180	4.04	7/2,080	7.12	20/3350	11.5
Breconshire	26700	1/50?	0.19?	1/150	0.56	4/1200	4.49	1/400	1.50	7/1800?	9.99?
Cardiganshire	18020	1/?	?	1/250	1.39	2/1000	5.55	1/?	?	5/?	?
Carmarthenshire	34430	4/200?	0.58?	17/4750	13.8	2/1350	3.92	3/900	2.61	26/7200?	20.9?
Denbighshire	38670	1/20	0.05	2/285	0.74	-/-	-	1/150	0.39	4/455	1.18
Glamorganshire	43400	2/?	?	1/?	?	6/2060	4.75	5/1600	3.69	14/4500	10.37
Merionethshire	17450	3/150?	0.86?	-/-	-	1/150	0.86	-/-	-	4/300	1.72
Montgomeryshire	28650	6/?	?	1/120	0.42	3/300	1.05	-/-	-	10/?	?
Pembrokeshire	29860	4/70	0.23	1/500	1.67	3/480	1.61	1/450?	1.51?	9/1500?	5.02?
Radnorshire	14660	2/40	0.27	-/-	-	3/850	5.80	2/1,000	6.82	7/1890	12.89
Total	272040	28/750?	0.28?	24/6975?	2.56?	33/8550?	3.14?	21/6300?	2.32?	106/22575?	8.30?
Herefordshire	71440	5/120	0.17	7/1190	1.67	1/200	0.28	1/200	0.28	14/1710	2.39
Gloucestershire	137790	22/960	0.7	16/4,360	3.16	9/1660	1.20	13/2400	1.74	60/9380	6.81

Key: Q (Quakers); P (Presbyterians); I (Independents); PB (Particular Baptists)

[1] Extracted from M. Watts, *The Dissenters: From the Reformation to the French Revolution* (Oxford, 1978), pp. 509–10 (tables XII–XIII); P. Jenkins, *A History of Modern Wales 1536–1990* (London, 1992), p. 146 (table 8.1) who supplies additional estimates for the Quaker population or a total estimate for Dissent from which the Quaker population can be deduced.

counties which had more members: the four Carmarthenshire meetings had approximately 200 members and the three Merionethshire meetings had approximately 150. The only other sizeable Quaker community would have been those comprising the six meetings in Montgomeryshire, but the number of adherents is not known. The Monmouthshire meetings were only slightly smaller than their co-religionists in Herefordshire (90:120), but they represented a higher percentage of the total county population than their English counterparts. Moreover, the twenty-two meetings in Gloucestershire, although they could command at least 960 adherents, represented less than 1 per cent of that county's population.[38]

Assessing the numerical strength and composition of Welsh Quakers in the seventeenth century is far from easy. Even in the case of Monmouthshire, the historian is hindered by a lack of primary material, and that which has survived is not wholly reliable: the minute books for Monmouthshire cover only the post-Toleration period, and the registers of births, marriages and burials are not exhaustive;[39] birth and marriage registers cannot confirm lifelong loyalty, while a considerable number of Quaker children appear on burial registers but are not recorded in the births register. The problem is compounded by a lack of Church and Quarter Session records which would have provided valuable information on early Friends. Yet the available evidence, if treated with care, can yield interesting data. The statistics presented here will be supported by qualitative analysis to indicate the fluctuating pace of marriages and births which mirrored the shifting fortunes of the Society.[40]

Between c.1650 and 1830 there were 331 children born to Quaker families in Monmouthshire (see table 2.2). During the first forty years, 93 births were recorded and this trend showed a steady if unspectacular rise. As table 2.2 shows, a sharp decline followed the passage of the 1689 Toleration Act when only 13 births were registered, and then gradually births returned to their earlier strength. Indeed, the 1710s and 1730s were the decades with the greatest number of Quaker births, and this represented over 22 per cent of the total number of Monmouthshire Friends born in the period. After

1740 this tailed off and, aside from a small increase in the 1760s, thereafter there were fewer than 10 births per decade. The ratio of male to female births was 170:158, revealing near parity between the sexes. Yet, because of the low birth rate, small fluctuations in the gender balance may have contributed to late marriage patterns and explain the increase in exogamous marriages.

Table 2.2. Monmouthshire Births c.1650–c.1830

Decade	Male	Female	Total
1650s	7	9	16
1660s	12	11	23
1670s	11	18	29
1680s	13	12	25
1690s	5	8	13
1700s	14	9	23
1710s	18	19	37
1720s	16	10	26
1730s	23	15	38
1740s	15	9	24
1750s	7	7	15*
1760s	10	10	21*
1770s	4	4	9*
1780s	0	2	2
1790s	3	5	8
1800s	4	2	6
1810s	3	4	7
1820s	3	1	4
1830s	2	3	5
Total	170	158	331

*Includes one child whose gender was not specified.

The most surprising statistic, however, is that between c.1650 and c.1830 only 75 marriages were recorded in the registers, and a further 7 reported in the minutes of the Quarterly or Monthly Meetings (table 2.3). Although the number of marriages was low, there was an increase in the number of Quaker births c.1700–39. During this period at least a third of the births and nearly half of the marriages took place in the county.[41] After 1770s there was a noticeable decline in both births and marriages, with only 41 births between 1770 and 1830 and 9 marriages between 1770 and 1820. It is evident, however, that many of the marriages of Monmouthshire Quakers were not recorded and, of those marriages that were noted, at least one-third involved members from elsewhere in Wales and England.

Table 2.3. Monmouthshire
Marriages c.1650–c.1820

Decade	Total
1650s	1
1660s	9
1670s	4
1680s	5
1690s	4
1700s	8
1710s	6
1720s	11
1730s	9
1740s	5
1750s	6
1760s	5
1770s	1
1780s	0
1790s	1
1800s	4
1810s	1
1820s	2
Total	82

Quaker marriage registers show that just over 7 per cent of marriage partners were widows or widowers. Seventy-five per cent of second marriages occurred between 1710 and 1734 and, of these, two-thirds were widows. Indeed, Rachel Cooper of Pontypool was married three times, to John David of Marshfield in 1707, Joshua Phillips of Castleton in 1710 and finally, in 1722, to Evan Thomas of Aberdare.[42] This example also highlights the inadequacies of the registers as remarriages were not always recorded in the registers.

Throughout the lifetime of the Monmouthshire Society burial registers show that deaths outnumbered births by 549:331. In only two decades were the number of births greater (table 2.4). The problem was particularly acute in the 1670s, 1690s, 1720s and between the 1750s and 1780s. In the 1670s a substantial contingent of the early adherents to Quakerism died. The slight increase in births between the 1650s and the 1680s represented an upward trend, but the progress that this presaged was negated by the large number of deaths in the same period. As table 2.4 indicates, recruitment was not keeping pace with natural loss. By the turn of the nineteenth century the decline in the Society was all too evident with no more than 10 births or deaths for the remainder of the period under review.

Table 2.4. Monmouthshire Burials *c.*1660–*c.*1830

Decade	Male	Female	Total	Cf. Births
1650s	?	?	?	−16
1660s	17	15	32	+9
1670s	34	29	63	+34
1680s	16	8	24	−1
1690s	14	18	32	+19
1700s	16	17	33	+10
1710s	30	20	50	+13
1720s	32	30	62	+36
1730s	21	23	44	+7
1740s	18	12	30	+6
1750s	14	17	31	+16
1760s	25	24	50*	+29
1770s	16	12	31**	+22
1780s	12	8	20	+18
1790s	8	8	16	+8
1800s	4	3	7	+1
1810s	4	6	10	+3
1820s	5	4	9	+5
1830s	1	3	4	−1
Total	287	257	548	+218

Includes one burial where gender was not specified.
**Includes three burials where gender was not specified.*

As with the birth data there was near parity in the burials of male and female members (table 2.4), but there were occasions when there was a small imbalance and this may have affected the equilibrium of the local meeting. For example, in the 1670s, 1680s, 1710s and 1740s more men than women died. The resulting gender imbalance may have obliged Friends to seek partners elsewhere, to accept that early marriage was unlikely, or relinquish their membership by marrying non-Quakers. Despite the limitations of the registers, they can support an investigation that reaches beyond a simple statistical analysis. Monmouthshire Friends were never more than a small religious clique, but they did manage to secure a distinct role, and it is as an 'alternative community' that they have left their mark. It is to the wider interpretation of the registers that attention now turns.

The registers provide valuable information about the origins, development and longevity of the Society. They also shed further light upon membership, especially those individuals who are absent from other Quaker records. The keeping of registers gave Friends a sense of their own identity as a separate and vibrant community within Monmouthshire. The birth registers, for instance, include several children born to Friends in the period before 1655 and prior to the establishment of the Monmouthshire meetings. Possibly these retrospective entries reflect a desire to affirm the longevity of the Society, but it may also have been part of their long-term strategy to augment their numerical strength. Sometimes it is the *absence* of information in the registers which most illuminates the history of Monmouthshire Quakers. For example, the eighteenth-century Monthly Meeting minutes suggest that Friends in St Mellons and Castleton attended their meetings irregularly, but they do not offer any helpful explanation. It is likely that the number of Friends at St Mellons was small, and was not sufficient to warrant the building of a meeting house. For its part, the Monmouthshire Quarterly Meeting recognized St Mellons as falling within its own jurisdiction but closer proximity to the Cardiff meeting would doubtless have been a decisive factor.[43] In the event, it is not too surprising that when the Cardiff Meeting went into decline after the deaths of its leading spokespeople,[44] so too did the St Mellons community. Furthermore, the children of Friends in this area who were recorded in the births registers,[45] or noted in probate documents,[46] were not specified as having retained membership. It is possible that some members migrated to other areas, but it is more likely that, as the initial burst of enthusiasm waned and the ravages of persecution and distraint took hold, the second generation did not retain their allegiance to the Society in any significant numbers.

As already noted the marriage entries are not entirely reliable. By cross-referencing the marriage records with information about Quaker parentage contained in the registers, it is possible to build a more accurate view of the number of married couples. In addition, material taken from meeting minutes from the 1690s, probate records, land deeds and accounts of sufferings can be used to corroborate the findings. For the purposes of this study evidence related to Monmouthshire Quaker 'family groupings' has been collated over a fifty-year period, c.1650–1700. This family unit includes information about husbands and wives; their domicile; dates of birth, marriage, death/burial or association with the Society; occupations; and their children.[47] While this is not an entirely foolproof method,[48] it does give a fair indication of the number of married Friends in the period, the longevity of some marriages and a rough estimate of the size of the Monmouthshire Quaker community.

During the period between c.1650 and 1700 the registers list 23 marriages. A closer examination suggests that there were at least 115 'family groupings', including second or third marriages, and a further 73 Friends who were not listed as married. From this cohort, members who married Friends from other counties and migrated to other parishes, along with other anomalies, have been discounted. Yet there are still far more Quaker couples than the marriage registers indicate. The 111 couples who remained in Monmouthshire had at least 224 children prior to 1700, which suggests that relatively small families were the norm and possibly reflects high infant and child mortality rates. Allowing for certain exclusions, the Monmouthshire cohort consisted of 295 adults and 224 children, thus giving an estimated Quaker population of 519. The estimate does not include the presence

of a non-Quaker mother or father, or loss because of emigration, migration, resignation or disownment. The registers and
the compilation of 'family groupings' for the remainder of the
period under review also provides helpful insights into the
lives of Friends. Sometimes the records give the time as well
as the date of birth, as in the case of Basil, the third son of
Richard and Mary Hanbury.[49] Similarly, the registers provide
details about other Friends such as midwives and Quaker witnesses who were present at the birth and naming of the
child.[50] Occasionally, the marriage registers give the occupational status of the bride and groom, as well as details of sets
of parents and witnesses.[51]

It is often possible, especially from the late seventeenth century onwards, to calculate the age at which some Friends
married and the period for which such marriages survived.
Jenkinson Beadles, the son of John Beadles of the Pant,
married Grace Brace of Bromsgrove in 1689. Jenkinson was
aged twenty-one and his bride eighteen.[52] Their marriage was
short-lived as he died in 1695.[53] In August 1699, Grace
married another prominent Monmouthshire Quaker, Charles
Hanbury,[54] and during this second marriage six children were
born. Other marriages were more enduring; some lasted more
than twenty years,[55] but only in a small fraction of cases were
the dates of both partners specified.[56]

Stillbirths and infant mortality were inescapable features of
early modern society.[57] Instances of death in childbirth punc-
tuate the registers. In the eighteenth century there are far
more cases of the mother and child dying in childbirth as well
as cases of infant mortality than in the previous century. In
1746 Mary, the wife of Nathaniel Beadles, died in childbirth
along with 'a still born son'.[58] This would have been her
seventh child of whom three had died in infancy.[59] The life
expectancy of adults in the early modern period was also
compromised by ill health and epidemics.[60] In 1681, the
White family of Pontypool suffered great personal loss when
three generations (mother, son and grandson) died within
three months of each other.[61] Again, in 1708, epidemic was
the most likely cause of the death of Samuel Lewis, a yeoman
of Llanfihangel Ystum Llywern, Jane, his sixteen-year-old
daughter and his aunt, Jane Lewis senior.[62] Apart from

natural causes, the Quaker community was depleted by occasional fatal accidents. Handley, the young son of Elisha and Anne Beadles, was drowned while returning from America in December 1728,[63] while in July 1731 Peter Evans, the son of David Evans of Llanofer, 'lost his life in ye river Usk near Newbridge'.[64]

Some, of course, lived a rich and long life in contrast to many of their contemporaries.[65] John Beadles of the Pant was sixty-one when he died in 1699 and his wife, Elizabeth, was over eighty when she died in 1732.[66] Richard Hanbury II of Pont-y-Moel was sixty-seven at his death in 1714, and his sons, Charles and Capel, were fifty-eight and sixty-two respectively at the time of their deaths in 1735 and 1740.[67] In some cases the burial registers include valedictory statements, testifying to a member's good character, generosity and integrity. Occasionally, more personal detail is offered as in the case of William Waters of Rhisga who died in 1727 at the great age of eighty-six. It was said that he was 'a zealous and honest Friend'.[68] Roger Jenkin of Llanfrechfa, who had been a minister for twenty-six years, was described as a 'worthy Friend and valiant in our Israel . . . a notable minister tho' blind for several years' at his death in 1728.[69] In 1777, John Jones, also of Llanfrechfa, was interred at Pen-y-Garn burial ground and was reputedly 'exemplary in conduct, had a small share in ye ministry & of good report . . . of innocent conversation in ye world & universally beloved'.[70]

As already shown, the numerical strength of the Quaker community was, in comparison to the fear they aroused, rather small. It was also a community which had a wide geographical base, stretching from St Mellons parish in the south-west to the market towns of Abergavenny and Pontypool, and a scattering of members along the main trade routes in the south and north-east of the county. To what extent were Friends a rural or urban community, and how does the geographical distribution of Friends compare with that of another persecuted community in Monmouthshire – the Roman Catholics? Statistical evidence from these two communities will be examined, notably Quaker 'family groupings' and information extracted from the Recusancy Rolls.

Quaker historians and demographers have disagreed over whether seventeenth-century Friends were predominantly rural or urban dwellers.[71] Agriculture was naturally important to the economy of Monmouthshire, but there were a number of small urban centres which functioned as markets for the exchange of goods and services. Friends mostly clustered around four parishes linked to the market town of Pontypool[72] with 196 Friends of all ages living within close proximity of the Pont-y-Moel meeting house. An additional fifty Friends came from other parishes that were market towns or small urban centres, such as Abergavenny, Chepstow, Newport, Monmouth and Usk.[73] Many of these Friends were employed in agriculture or came from a rural part of the parish, but some were incorrectly recorded as members of a particular meeting while living in an adjacent or nearby parish. Further complications arise because on twenty-six separate occasions members were allocated to two parishes. A final anomaly is that of the eighteen Friends for whom no parish has been specified in the meeting minutes and registers, wills or property and land deeds.

The location of Friends in rural parishes near other meeting places show that the Quaker community in the vicinity of the Pant Meeting numbered 110, the Shirenewton Meeting numbered 50 and there were 44 Friends in the St Mellons/ Castleton Meeting. How should this data be interpreted? It is possible that the Hanbury family at Pontypool encouraged family members, neighbours and business associates to become Friends, as well as acting as an inspiration for those living in parishes close to Pontypool. For example, members of the Hanbury, Handley and Lewis families were involved in the development of the ironworks at Pontypool,[74] and it has been suggested that during the early 1660s Richard Hanbury brought Thomas Allgood, a fellow Quaker from Northampton, to Monmouthshire to work as his manager.[75] Furthermore, as respectable members of the Monmouthshire business community, the Hanburys may have helped local Quakers, especially in terms of providing protection from the civil authorities during periods of persecution. Equally, their social position, which was dependent upon local, financial and social networks, may well have meant that the Hanburys and other Friends in Pontypool had to avoid any provocative activity. Significantly, there are very few instances of Pont-y-Moel Friends having their meetings interrupted or reports that members were arrested. At the same time, there is little evidence to suggest that the local clergy had their services disrupted by either itinerant preachers or local members. Even so, by the late 1670s the local authorities were sufficiently worried by the presence of Friends at the Pont-y-Moel Meeting to fine members, including the Hanbury family, for recusancy.

The number of rural Friends ought not to be ignored as many Friends either lived or were employed in rural parishes during the first fifty years of the Monmouthshire Society's existence. They were strongly influenced by gentry families, notably the Jenkins and Beadles families in Llanfihangel Ystum Llywern, while the development of Friends' organization and code of conduct helped the Society to consolidate a following in rural areas among those who had already separated from the Established Church. From the above analysis of Quaker 'family groupings' it can be shown that Friends clustered around urban centres, particularly Pontypool and other market towns, but they had a noticeable presence in rural areas.

There were several parishes in Monmouthshire in the early seventeenth century where Catholicism was particularly strong, namely Abergavenny, Caerleon, Llandeilo-Gresynni, Pen-Rhos, Llantarnam, Llanfrechfa, Monmouth and Raglan. It is also noticeable that in the prominent Protestant Dissenting parish of Llanfaches only one recusant was ever recorded, and that was at the beginning of the seventeenth century.[76] This would suggest that the recusancy law for the majority of the seventeenth century was, in this parish at least, directed against Catholics rather than Dissenters. Robert Matthews's study of Roman Catholic recusancy has shown that 'places with consistently high numbers of convicted recusants are invariably places where significant Catholic populations are revealed by extraneous evidence, whilst areas of strong Protestant nonconformity appear in the Recusant Rolls hardly or not at all'. Indeed, he argues that Protestant Dissenters rarely feature in the Recusancy Rolls because they were more likely to be punished under the Conventicle Acts, for the non-payment of tithes, or for causing a public disturbance.[77] Yet it is still possible to find some Quakers on the Recusancy Rolls because they were regarded as ideologically similar to Catholics.[78] The classification of recusants depended upon how the local authorities interpreted the law. In 1679, at the time of the Popish Plot, anyone who acted subversively or against the interests of the establishment would have been punished. Nevertheless, financial gain was a prime motive for implementation of the recusancy law.

Using the Monmouthshire Recusancy Rolls it is possible to determine the geographical distribution and morphology of the Catholic community during the seventeenth century.[79] Matthews's research shows that recusancy was concentrated in north-east Monmouthshire and 'north of a notional line from the parish of Usk to that of Dixton on the English border'. Here, between 1603 and 1689, 2,962 of the 5,218 convicted Monmouthshire recusants lived.[80] An attempt will be made to analyse a sample number of parishes where Quakers and Catholics coexisted, and consider whether or not Monmouthshire Friends avoided the worst excesses of persecution, such as during the early and late-1670s and the early-1680s, as a consequence of this coexistence. In the seventeenth century, Abergavenny had more than one hundred known Catholics at a time when only two Quaker families are thought to have lived there. The 1655 Recusancy Rolls indicate that 45 Catholics were presented for non-attendance at church services, rising to 106 in 1675 and then fluctuating between 54 and 8 presentments for the next three years, before reaching a peak of 113 presentments in 1684.[81] Well-attended clandestine gatherings of Catholics to receive communion at the Gunter household in the town may well have prompted reprisals from Anglican ministers fearful of the growth of popery.[82] Even though the authorities were zealous in their pursuit of errant Catholics, they seemed less eager to prosecute Quakers in the area.

Llanfihangel-Llantarnam and Caerleon were also important Catholic centres in the first half of the seventeenth century with as many as one hundred papists attending Mass in the 1640s.[83] According to Matthews's statistics there were at least 194 Catholics in these two parishes during the seventeenth century,[84] while the total Quaker population consisted of just 4 Friends from the early 1650s onwards. As in Abergavenny, large numbers of Catholics were prosecuted,[85] but no Quakers appeared on the Recusancy Rolls between 1655 and 1684. They were more likely to be prosecuted for the non-payment of tithes. In 1659, Arnold Thomas of Llanfihangel-Llantarnam was distrained of his goods by Arnold Williams, a Catholic, who had impropriated the parish tithe.[86] Compared with the apparent threat posed by Catholic recusancy between 1655 and 1684, the few Quakers in these parishes, who lacked either a Quaker meeting house or identifiable conventicle, were a less pressing concern. In contrast, both communities were recorded as recusants in the parishes near the Pont-y-Moel Meeting and at the Pant Meeting. The statistics indicate that, although Friends appeared on the Recusancy Rolls, they were largely concentrated in the period c.1679–84. Furthermore, many of those Friends who appeared on these lists were high-profile figures, notably members of the Hanbury, Beadles and Handley families, and this may reflect an attempt to make an example of them, especially as there were fears that they were in league with local Catholics.[87]

The Recusancy Rolls show that in Shirenewton and Marshfield parishes, where Friends had other established meeting places, the overall presentments for recusancy were again extremely low. For example, at Shirenewton one recusant was recorded during the 1670s and 1680s, while at Marshfield, where the Castleton Meeting was located, only sixteen recusants were presented between 1679 and 1684.[88] In the parishes in and around Mitcheltroy and Wonastow there were a number of Quaker families. Henry Milborne, a Protestant magistrate from Llanrhyddol in Herefordshire, owned land in the area and, before 1679, had sufficient influence to shelter both the Catholic and Quaker communities from prosecution. It was suggested by John Arnold, the chief Monmouthshire informant during the Popish Plot, that Milborne had used his influence to dissuade constables from enforcing the recusancy laws. His intervention may have inadvertently protected Friends from the recusancy laws,[89] but it certainly did not shield them from other forms of persecution. In the 1660s, two Monmouthshire Friends, Phillip and John Williams of Cwmcarfan parish, were arrested and imprisoned several times for refusing to swear oaths of allegiance, or had their goods seized for defaulting on the required tithe. There were no Friends among the lists of recusants during the late 1670s and early 1680s. This may indicate that old scores were being settled between Arnold, a zealous anti-papist, and his Catholic neighbours rather than an attempt to prosecute Dissenters.

The presence of a Catholic constable and churchwarden in Llangatwg Feibion Afel parish, who allegedly failed to return recusancy lists in 1679, meant that both Catholics and Quakers in this area were temporarily spared punishment or fines.[90] Nevertheless, although there were individual cases where Catholics were protected, either by their own or sympathetic Protestant gentry[91] and parish constables, in most cases they did not escape due legal process. Both Catholic and Quaker communities of whatever social standing could be prosecuted for recusancy or for breaking the penal laws.[92]

An analysis of the origins of Monmouthshire Quakers not only provides an insight into their early years but also reveals biographical information about some of the members. Similarly, an examination of their later records helps to identify patterns of change in the social composition of the Society. Since Alan Cole first investigated the social origins of Friends in 1955,[93] several more analyses have been produced. They have ranged from Cole's hypothesis that Friends were drawn from the petite bourgeoisie, to Richard Vann's conclusion that members were yeoman and traders, and then to David Scott and Adrian Davies's analyses which suggest that Friends were composed of both the upper and petite bourgeoisie.[94]

For the reasons already given, the available evidence of the social origins of Monmouthshire Friends has to be treated with caution. The registers do not yield the occupational details of all Friends,[95] while probate records often give a misleading picture. The absence of meeting minutes, parochial and court records for this period makes it difficult to clarify anomalies that creep in if Friends are crudely classified as 'yeomen'. Nonetheless, it has been possible to identify the occupational status of 94 male Friends, and this reveals that the vast majority were involved in agriculture[96] (table 2.5 and chart 2.1). Pinning down the social status of Friends is further complicated by the use of different descriptors.[97] For example, Richard Hanbury I and II and Charles Hanbury, who were of gentry stock, were frequently referred to as 'yeoman'. Conversely, a very high proportion of Friends, who were referred to as 'gentleman', were nonetheless yeomen.[98] Among yeoman stock, the terms 'yeoman' and 'husbandman' were synonymous. For example, Roger Jenkin of Llanfrechfa is designated in one document as a yeoman and in another as a husbandman.[99] Other Friends were defined as 'yeoman/tailor' or 'yeoman/potter' and even as 'yeoman/blacksmith'. Of the small number of Friends involved in medicine, one is classified as a doctor while the other three were 'doctor/apothecary'; 'apothecary/mercer'; and a 'practitioner of physick/tailor'. Edward Webley offers a good example of the complexity of defining social status with any precision. In 1674, Webley, a tanner from Shirenewton who ought to be identified as petite bourgeoisie, left goods appraised in his will at £260.[100] In comparison, George White of Llanfihangel y Gofion, who was referred to in his 1698 will as a yeoman and represented the lesser 'middling sorts', had his goods valued at a mere £49 18s 4d.[101]

Table 2.5. Comparative Table of the Occupational Status of Monmouthshire and Gloucestershire/Wiltshire Quakers c.1655–1700

Occupations	Monm.	%	Occupations	Glos/ Wilts	%
Gentleman	20	21.3	Gentleman		
Agriculture	34	36.1	*Agriculture*	24	25.5
Yeomen	26		Yeomen		
Husbandmen	4		Husbandmen		
Farmer (Other)	4				
Professional	5	5.3	*Professional*		
Doctors/Surgeons/ Apothecaries	4				
Schoolteacher/					

continued

former Lawyer 1

Occupations	Monm.	%	Occupations	Glos/Wilts	%
Manufacturers	3	3.2	Manufacturers		
Commerce, Food and			*Commerce, Food and*		
Consumption Goods	4	4.3	*Consumption Goods*	8	8.5
Merchant			Merchant		
Baker			Baker		
Chandler			Chandler		
Butcher	1				
Grocer	1				
Shopkeeper/					
Haberdasher	2				
Clothing Trades	19	20.2	*Clothing Trades*	37	39.4
Mercer	3		Mercer		
Draper			Draper		
Clothier			Clothier		
Clothworker			Clothworker		
Fuller			Fuller		
Weaver/Tailor	8		Weaver		
Woolcomber			Woolcomber		
Cordwainer or			Cordwainer or		
shoemaker	7		shoemaker		
Glover	1				
'Mechanic' Trades	6	6.4	*'Mechanic' Trades*	23	24.5
Smith			Smith		
Blacksmith	1		Blacksmith		
Saddler			Saddler		
Saddle-tree-maker			Saddle-tree-maker		
tanner	3		tanner		
Cardmaker			Cardmaker		
Cooper			Cooper		
Carpenter/Nailer	1		Carpenter		
free-mason			free-mason		
mason			mason		
thatcher			thatcher		
mariner			mariner		
Carrier			Carrier		
Potter	1				
Servants/Receiving					
relief	3	3.2	Servants	2	2.1
	94	100		94	100

Chart 2.1. The Social Composition of Monmouthshire Quakers *c*.1655–1700

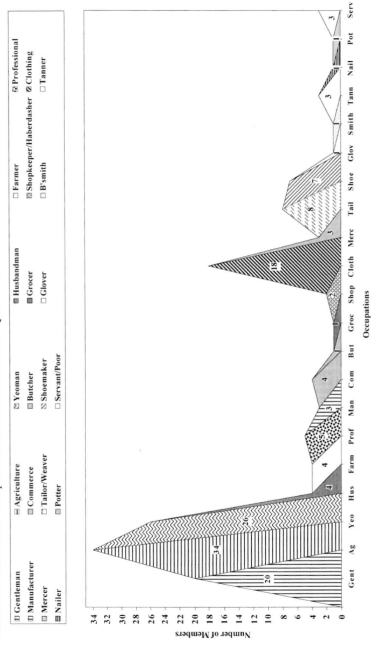

During the first fifty years of the Society's existence in Monmouthshire, a number of wealthy citizens converted to Quakerism, including those of good social standing such as the Hanbury family of Pont-y-Moel, the Beadles family of the Pant,[102] John Handley, a gentleman from Worcestershire who had settled in Pontypool,[103] Richard Clarke, the squire of Parc Gras Dieu Estate in Treworgan, and the Allgood family who were Japanware manufacturers at Pontypool. Others came from agricultural backgrounds such as yeomen or well-to-do craftsmen. Hugh Barbour notes that 'early Friends were, in general, farm people or town craftsmen . . . few were either outright proletarians or gentry'.[104] This is partially substantiated by a comparison with other areas of Wales. Early Quaker converts came from among the squirearchy,[105] yeomanry and craftsmen in Carmarthenshire, Glamorganshire, Pembrokeshire, Merionethshire, Montgomeryshire and Radnorshire, as well as from 'middling sorts' in the towns of Dolgellau, Bala, Carmarthen, Haverfordwest, Swansea and Wrexham. When Edward Evans was arrested in Montgomeryshire in 1657 it was recorded that he was 'an honest and substantial man', while other members who were arrested at the same time were described as 'substantial freeholders'.[106] Geraint Jenkins has also observed that many Friends at the Meifod meeting in 1669 were described as 'well-horsed',[107] and a number of leading Merionethshire Quakers, after their emigration to Pennsylvania, provided evidence of their high social status.[108] In his testimony to Robert Owen, Rowland Ellis, a substantial landowner, wrote that Owen had 'a competent inheritance' and was 'descended of a very ancient family'. His wife, Jane, was also of gentry status, but significantly, as Ellis observed, Owen was 'of the rank next Justices of Peace'.[109] All things considered, it is clear that yeoman and craftsman dominated Welsh Quakerism.[110] For example, in 1669, Lewis Owen of Tyddyn-y-garreg left £95 in his will in corn, sheep and cattle; his son, Lewis Owen II provided £150 for his daughter and £79 for his son in 1686; and John Thomas of Llaithgwm, who styled himself a gentleman, was listed in the Philadelphia Deed Book as a yeoman.[111] As J. Gwynn Williams points out, twelve of the seventeen Penllyn Friends who purchased land in Pennsylvania in 1683 were yeoman. Barry

Levy has, however, observed that most Merionethshire and Montgomeryshire Quakers lived in one-hearth houses and cottages, with an average holding of £18 between 1662 and 1681.[112] This assessment is corroborated by the 1686 will of Richard Price, a husbandman of Nantlleidiog, who bequeathed little more than £20 in crops and livestock, and the relatively lowly status of Ellis Pugh of Garthgynfor who was counted among the poor inhabitants of Dolgellau in 1670.[113]

Notwithstanding the occasional conversion of landed gentry, most Monmouthshire Quakers were yeomen; at least thirty-four of the ninety-four Friends identified were involved in agriculture, with the majority classified as yeomen (76.5 per cent).[114] This is not altogether surprising as Monmouthshire had few towns and little in the way of industrial development. The county was dominated by its pastoral economy and by yeoman who took advantage of the

> flaws in the parochial structure of the Church in rural areas in the impecunious dioceses of Llandaff and St David's, especially where lack of pastoral supervision and infrequent sermons prompted disgruntled church-goers to throw in their lot with Dissent. Wherever there were large parishes where people were poorly served by underpaid or non-resident or lazy pastors, Dissenting conventicles were at hand to fulfil their spiritual needs.[115]

In the seventeenth century there were seven towns in the county. Abergavenny, Caerleon, Chepstow, Newport, Usk and Monmouth were all fairly modest settlements, while Pontypool was described as 'a small town . . . noted for its iron mills'.[116] By the end of the eighteenth century the town of Caerleon had not significantly developed and was often compared unfavourably with its ancient past.[117] The 127 parishes in the county contained a large rural population, and even the urban areas bore scant resemblance to urban centres in England at that time.

It is clear that, although the Monmouthshire meetings did not have many very wealthy Friends, they were not an impoverished community; just over 21 per cent were styled as 'gentleman'. Further information derived from property deeds for the counties of Monmouthshire, Glamorganshire and Breconshire underlines the importance of yeomen in the Society.[118] However, other occupations were represented: Elisha Beadles, an apothecary and mercer; Daniel David, a mercer; John Barrow, a cooper; Thomas Wisdom, a potter; Isaac Morgan, William Cooper and Roger Phillips, shoemakers; and Joseph John and William Walter, farmers/agricultural workers. The evidence for Monmouthshire provides little information about early Friends who were petite bourgeoisie, and clearly skilled artisans are under-represented. The data provided in table 2.5 lists 7 tailors, 1 weaver, 3 mercers, 3 tanners and 7 shoemakers, while only small numbers appear to have been employed as shopkeepers, grocers, butchers, haberdashers, glovers, blacksmiths, potters and nailers. Yet evidence from other parts of Wales where Quakerism had taken root indicates that many of those Friends who appeared before magistrates were skilled artisans. These included the hat-maker, Francis Gawler of Cardiff; Richard Davies, the feltmaker of Cloddiau Cochion; the mercer, William Bateman who held a conventicle at his Haverfordwest home; and Bryan Sixsmith, a draper, who disseminated Quaker publications in the Wrexham area.[119]

Finally, it is worth considering how this study of the social composition of Friends compares with Quaker communities in the neighbouring English counties of Gloucestershire and Wiltshire between 1656 and 1688. Alan Cole analysed the details of 94 Friends in these two counties and found a high percentage of members in the clothing trades (39.4 per cent) and 'mechanic' trades (24.5 per cent), while yeomen/husbandmen accounted for 25.5 per cent of the Quaker population.[120] Whereas Cole found little evidence that 'gentlemen' attended Quaker meetings, they constituted a high percentage in Monmouthshire (21.3 per cent). Such findings may well reflect the arbitrary use of the term 'gentleman' when, in a number of cases, yeoman would have been more appropriate. Whatever the case, Monmouthshire Friends involved in agriculture accounted for at least 36 per cent of the Quaker population, and if the propertied 'gentlemen' are included then this figure is nearer 60 per cent, a finding which is broadly in line with Barry Reay's research.[121]

As shown above, Friends in Monmouthshire were a small and distinct community of believers who, although never numerous, continued to hold a separate Monthly Meeting until the mid-1830s. Yet, as the statistics show, for most decades there were far more deaths than births, which would suggest that the Society was in decline rather than prospering. By 1813 this small community had only 28 adherents.[122] Close examination of Friends' registers demonstrates that statistical analysis does not provide an entirely accurate picture of the Quaker community. A more meaningful insight into this community has been gained by scrutinizing Quaker 'family groupings'. This allows for a wider interpretation of the registers, including an insight into Friends' lives, their community and coexistence with other religious communities. The evidence shows that in the seventeenth century Monmouthshire Friends mainly belonged to the 'middling sorts' as well as having several fairly wealthy, propertied and respected members among their community. The findings for the county also line up with those for other areas where agriculture was dominant, and where 'yeoman-gentlemen' were strongly represented. Yet it is interesting that skilled artisans should be so under-represented in the early registers. The references to Friends who were involved in the clothing trade and in manufacturing clearly show that not all members were involved in agriculture. During the eighteenth century, when there is far more extant evidence applicable to a study of social composition, it is possible to identify a larger number of skilled artisans among the Monmouthshire Quaker community. However, this was paralleled by a gradual decline in the number of wealthy or propertied Friends. This tendency was not reversed until the last quarter of the eighteenth century with the migration of the Harford family into Monmouthshire and the establishment of the ironworks at Ebbw Vale.[123] By the early decades of the nineteenth century the occupational spread of Friends is more balanced, but by then the Society had declined dramatically.

Chapter 3
'A Divine democracy'? *The Organization of the Society*

> The Society was . . . in thought and purpose a Divine democracy, a real communion of Saints . . . It had no constitution, no creed, no sacraments, no clergy, no ordained officials, no infallibilities, except the infallibility of the guiding spirit.[1]

Following Fox's evangelizing visit in the mid-1650s, Welsh Friends began to formalize the organization of their meetings. As already suggested, early Friends attempted to create a new society, an 'alternative community', based upon well-regulated and ordered meetings. Accordingly, leading Friends put in place a raft of meetings for both worship and the conduct of the Society's business. This structure was essentially hierarchical with lines of authority which saw individual meetings look to the London Yearly Meeting for guidance and discipline.[2] Over time, the Welsh Yearly Meeting assumed some of these responsibilities (table 3.1). The aim of this chapter is to appraise the organisational and developmental strategies of Friends in Wales, and consider what impact this had upon the long-term stability of the Society. As before, the substantial records of Monmouthshire Friends will be used to demonstrate the overarching organisational framework.

Although Swarthmore Hall in Cumbria was the spiritual home of Quakerism,[3] it was London Friends who developed the complex and hierarchical organization of the Society in the seventeenth century. Meetings which were begun in the mid-1650s, such as the Two Weeks Meetings, provided leadership and dealt with evangelization, financial matters and the imprisonment of Friends. The Yearly Meeting, which had formerly been held in Skipton and Barlby in Yorkshire,

Table 3.1. Quaker Organization[4]

London Yearly Meeting (1668)
↓
London Meetings:

Two Weeks Meeting (1656)
*Separate meetings for men and women; financial matters,
especially poor relief*

Morning Meeting of Ministers (1670)
Weekly meeting; ministry and distribution of literature

Six Weeks Meeting (1671)
*Supported the London Meetings; assisted cases of imprisonment
and distributed relief to persecuted members*

Meeting of Twelve (1673)
Quarterly meeting; financial matters and assisted imprisoned Friends

Meeting for Sufferings (1676)
*Weekly meeting; documented cases of persecution in the
British Isles and Overseas*

Welsh Meetings:

The Welsh Yearly Meeting (1682)
↓
The Welsh Women's Yearly Meeting
↓
Welsh Ministers' and Elders' Yearly Meeting
↓
Welsh Men's Half-Yearly Meeting
↓
Welsh Women's Half-Yearly Meeting
↓
Welsh Ministers' and Elders' Half-Yearly Meeting
↓
Quarterly Meeting
↓
Men's Monthly Meeting
Women's Monthly Meeting
↓
Preparative Meeting
↓
Meeting for Worship (open) Meeting for Worship (Silent)

---

was transferred to London in 1668, and Quarterly Meetings appointed their own representatives. Delegates would report instances of persecution and the strength of their meetings and donate funds for poor relief or to travelling ministers. By the early 1670s, other London meetings dealt with poor relief and the discipline of the Society.[5] Propaganda became increasingly important and more sophisticated in line with developments in print culture.[6] From 1673 the Morning Meetings of 'Public Friends' were responsible for publishing Quaker tracts and managing the network of preachers who ministered throughout Britain and Ireland. In the same year the Meeting of Twelve was established. This committee drew representatives from the six London Meetings, and offered poor relief and legal assistance.[7] Three years later the Meeting for Sufferings was inaugurated to lobby the government on behalf of Friends who were persecuted.[8] It consisted of ministers, elders and other invited representatives of the Welsh Yearly Meetings. Welsh representatives in the late seventeenth century included James Picton, James Lewis, Charles Lloyd, William Fell, Phillip Leonard, Richard Aubrey, Peregrine Musgrave, Thomas Ellis, John ap John and Richard Davies.[9] The Meeting for Sufferings was designed to help Friends negotiate the legal complexities and assist members who were financially ruined by the courts. Its members gave explicit legal advice, and suggested ways in which the Society could appeal against both legal and illegal actions.[10] The clerk kept detailed accounts of persecution, including fines or terms of imprisonment. With the implementation of the Toleration Act (1689) this meeting became a Standing Committee which managed the business of the Society when the Yearly Meeting was in recess,[11] and continued to give much needed support to those who were persecuted for the non-payment of tithes.

The earliest Welsh Quaker meetings were held out of doors and the Quaker message was proselytized to anyone who registered an interest.[12] Inevitably, such meetings were the occasion of both negative and positive responses. The hostility and prejudice encountered by many early Friends convinced Fox that for the movement to survive it needed the cohesion of a network of meetings. These were gradually developed in all areas to provide a vital support system, and so assist the creation of a lasting Quaker community.[13] Quakers believed that there were times when Friends should gather publicly to proclaim their faith, and others when silent contemplation was more appropriate. Their adopted system of meetings reflected this rationale. At public gatherings,[14] they would listen to sermons, read the scriptures, pray and explore the meaning of their faith. At weekly meetings,[15] both men and women reflected upon their lives, waiting until 'the evil in me being weakened and the good built up'.[16] Times could vary; thus in 1695 the 'first day meeting' at the Pant was held at 11 o'clock in the morning,[17] and this remained a typical pattern of worship until July 1706 when the Pont-y-Moel Meeting decided to experiment by holding two first day meetings during the summer months.[18] The Shropshire and Montgomeryshire Monthly Meeting in 1698 expected members 'to com in time to their week, and first day meeting at ii in the forenoon'. Occasionally, when it was more convenient meetings were held the day before.[19] In general, however, a significant decline in attendance is discernible from the late seventeenth century onwards, and this is reflected in the constant exhortations to Friends to be more diligent in attending their meetings. In 1693, Pembrokeshire and Glamorganshire Friends were censured for not attending their Quarterly Meetings; north Wales Friends were admonished in August 1695 for failing to attend their monthly business meetings; and members of Pant Meeting were called to account by their Quarterly Meeting in October 1696, and again in 1708, along with the members of the Castleton Meeting.[20] By 1710, the Quarterly Meeting for Monmouthshire and east Glamorgan observed that both meetings for worship and business were poorly attended, and Friends were asked to 'stirre up & remind Friends of their duty therein, that we may as many Members in one body be servicable in other places, to ye comfort & advantage of one another'.[21] These admonishments did not have the desired effect as subsequent minutes continued to note 'backwardness', or 'remissness', in attendance.[22]

Absenteeism was symptomatic of the general decline in membership in the post-Revolution era and the failure of Friends to negotiate the temptations of the eighteenth century.

Nevertheless, accounts of meetings held at Trosnant in the early nineteenth century provide insights into gatherings and the pleasure Friends derived from them: 'The meeting for Worship began at 11 o'clock, there was but 19 persons in all there besides my companions & myself. I felt very low & poor in mind but best help being near, it proved a remarkable time of favour.'[23] An interesting account of a 'silent meeting' in Rhaeadr is provided by the Revd James Plumptre in 1799 who recorded:

I found the room filled with chairs set round and in rows. Two farthing Candles were set upon the chimney piece with black tea boards as reflectors . . . The lady, who I found was to preach, was seated on a chair on one side, her head leaning on her hand and shaded by her bonnet. The men sat on each side of her. The room soon filled, and after waiting about a quarter of an hour, the lady arose. She began by only half sentences, in apology for her calling the meeting and for a weak woman preaching . . . She then recommended silent devotion, after which she sat down again, and in a few minutes more began preaching.[24]

Monthly Meetings managed vast geographical areas and increased in size as local groups amalgamated after 1700. In the seventeenth century, Monthly Meetings were more ad hoc and held wherever Friends could gather in conventicles. For example, in 1695 the Monmouthshire Quarterly Meeting allowed Castleton Friends to hold a Monthly Meeting 'every last first day of each mo'th'.[25] By the early eighteenth century, however, representatives from every Quaker meeting in the county[26] held prearranged meetings. The Monthly Meeting in Monmouthshire was normally held at Pont-y-Moel until 1729 and, thereafter, at Pont-y-Moel and Shirenewton.[27]

Before conducting their business, Friends would sit in silence to compose their thoughts and seek divine guidance. Representatives would then consider the appointment of overseers or elders, the admission of new members and the granting of removal certificates. They managed the local Society's financial, legal and property transactions, including the provision of poor relief and education, and enforced the code of discipline. George Fox set out the responsibilities of such meetings in detail:

Where two or three are gathered together in Truth, there the Church is, and if one of the Meeting would dishonour God let him be waited upon and admonished. Care must be taken in business that the demeanour be honest and straightforward. Widows and children must be cared for. Couples must not go to Baal's priest to be married, for their hands are bloodstained, having driven their brethren away to strange lands. 'The rotten religion of the Ranters' (*Crefydd pwdwr y Ranters*) must be shunned. In courtship there must be no flitting in mind from one woman to another or guidance cannot be discovered. Any dispute to be settled at once. The instruction of children [is] important. Must have own burial ground, like Abraham of old. Records must be kept, and for this end suitable books to be purchased.[28]

Occasionally, meetings were adjourned because of inclement weather, impassable roads,[29] or more often the insufficient numbers present,[30] but most attended when called upon, and even those who infringed the code of discipline rarely refused to appear.

The Quarterly Meetings, which were established in England and Wales in the period between 1666 and 1668, received and deliberated upon the minutes of the Monthly Meetings. In conjunction with the Monthly Meetings they implemented the Quaker code of conduct, especially where disciplinary matters needed a firm hand. If disputes arose between individuals or Monthly Meetings, the Quarterly Meeting would also act as a mediating body. As the Quarterly Meetings helped to coordinate many of the local Society's financial affairs they levied a charge on the constituent Monthly Meetings. From 1668 the north Wales Quarterly Meeting consisted of representatives from mid Wales and the northern counties as well as Shropshire, while in west Wales representatives at their Quarterly Meeting were drawn from Carmarthenshire, Cardiganshire, Pembrokeshire and West Glamorganshire. In Monmouthshire, the several Monthly Meetings combined to form the Quarterly Meeting until the early years of the eighteenth century. By 1707 a decline in membership, especially at the Tref-y-Rhyg Meeting in Glamorganshire,[31] forced Monmouthshire Friends to reconsider whether or not they should support two Quarterly Meetings. After lengthy negotiations, in 1708 they decided to amalgamate the two meetings. In the interests of good relations it was also decided that two Quarterly Meetings should be held at Tref-y-Rhyg and two at Pont-y-Moel.[32]

Monmouthshire Quarterly Meeting minutes have survived from 1692, but a rare testimony from 1668[33] suggests that minutes were kept at an earlier date. This was true for north Wales and Pembrokeshire for whom some records begin in the 1660s. Minutes for the Men's Meeting at Bristol were originally written on loose papers and then transferred in order to safeguard records during times of persecution. It is likely that this practice was followed in Wales, and this would explain why loose paper testimonies sometimes appear in the Monmouthshire records.[34] After 1692 the minutes contain attendance lists, and such detailed information clarifies the relationship between various sections of the Society. Occasionally, they reveal something of the cordial relations which prevailed between the constituent Welsh Quarterly Meetings. In 1697, ten years before the east Glamorganshire and Monmouthshire Quarterly Meetings amalgamated, it was agreed that the respective Monthly Meetings would send two representatives each to their Quarterly Meetings.[35]

In view of the persecution meted out to them in the early 1680s, Friends looked for ways to promote the well-being of the Society and decided to introduce a Preparatory Meeting of Ministers and Elders. This was effectively a subcommittee of the Monthly and Quarterly Meetings.[36] In 1720, Shirenewton Friends were required 'to hold a Conference one with another before every Monthly Meeting that their representatives may be furnished to give a full account of ye state of their Meeting'.[37] There is evidence of Preparative Meetings being held between 1737 and 1769,[38] but very few minutes have survived and those that have relate to the closing years of the eighteenth century. For instance, records show that the Monthly Meeting of Ministers and Elders[39] responded to enquiries from the Quarterly Meeting about the condition of Friends. Occasionally, the clerk recorded the appointment of new elders[40] and the presence of visiting ministers and elders from England.[41] These minutes are at best infrequently recorded and end abruptly on 7 August 1804. There is no record of the meeting being discontinued after this date, and it is probable, therefore, that some formal gathering was still held before the men's and women's meetings.

The Quarterly Preparative Meetings were formally instituted in the last quarter of the eighteenth century and were held at Pont-y-Moel and at Rees Bowen's house in Radnorshire.[42] Ministers and elders were appointed to deal with enquiries from the Yearly Meeting (see table 3.2), and to refer any pressing matters to the Quarterly Meetings. This meeting was open to men and women, and attended by visitors from a wide geographical radius. Visiting Friends included Martha Williams and Joseph Cowles from Neath, Thomas Waring from Leominster, Rebecca Jones, Zachariah Dicks and Rebecca Wright from America, William Simmons from Northamptonshire, Samuel Smith from Philadelphia, Edward Hatten from Cork and James Harford from Bristol.[43] In 1791, the meeting was reconstituted as a 'Select Meeting' of Ministers and Elders and represented the whole of south Wales.[44] This meeting took over the functions of Monmouthshire, Radnorshire, Carmarthenshire and Glamorganshire Quarterly Meetings. The records disappear between February 1797 and 1806, but this does not mean that the meetings were abandoned; the Meetings of Ministers and Elders were held twice yearly between 1806 and 1832.[45] Preparative Meetings suffered from the same sporadic attendance which undermined other constituent meetings, and they frequently had to be rescheduled. Business pressures at busy times of the year, especially the timing of local fairs or markets caused meetings to be postponed. Despite organizational difficulties, meetings were beneficial to the Quaker community in affording a 'general sphere of oversight . . . the preparation and revision of papers of advice, and . . . an occasion for elders and ministers to consider the state of the ministry'.[46]

The success of the London Yearly Meeting prompted a call for provincial Yearly Meetings, and Richard Davies moved to establish an annual Welsh assembly in 1681.[47] London Friends readily approved on the grounds that a Welsh Meeting would help to develop those leadership qualities which would take Welsh Quakerism into the eighteenth century:

Table 3.2. List of Enquiries c.1789[48]

---

1 Do no Publick Ffriends travel in the work of Ministry without the approbation of the Monthly Meeting they belong to and a certificate thereof or against ye advice of said meeting?

2 Are Ministers and Elders careful, diligently to attend their Meetings for Worship and Discipline and in bringing with them as many of their families as they can?

3 Do none over charge themselves wth Business to the hinderance of their service?

4 Are they in love and unity one with another, Harmoniously labouring for the advancement of Truth, and care taken tenderly to admonish such as appears Inconsistent therewith in ministry and conduct?

5 Are they careful diligently to rule their own Houses well, bringing up their families in plainness of Dress, Language and in True moderation, and are they good examples in these respects themselves?

6 Are the advices of 1775 read at least once in every year in your Monthly and Quarterly Meetings and are they under Ffriends care?

---

haveing a sense of the Remotness of Wales and of the conveniency of a Yearly Meeting for the publique friends of the same, and for the County friends to have their business and concernes in part done, transacted and ordered there, & what may not be concluded by them there, the same may be soe methodized and digested that they may be transferred thence to be perused & determined by the Yearly Meeting at London.[49]

In 1682, the Welsh Yearly Meeting was inaugurated and was held continuously until 1797 in places as diverse as Wrexham, Brecon, Haverfordwest, Llanidloes and Chepstow. Meetings were usually held in April and, on average, lasted three days. Many were held in areas where there were no established meetings or where Friends were few. The intention, it seems, was to proselytize and widen the circle of Welsh Friends; at times this was quite successful. In 1724, John Kelsall recorded that the Monmouth Yearly Meeting attracted 1,500 people who 'behaved themselves civilly . . . it was a brave comfortable meeting'.[50] Four years later, the

Meeting held at Brecon was attended by 'a great Appearance of People of other Professions . . . and Friends had a good Opportunity to declare the way of Truth to them'.[51] The Cardiff Yearly Meeting in 1753 was a great family gathering with a large number of children, 'the noise of who's [sic] feet made a great sound in so large a room'.[52]

Welsh Yearly Meetings, especially in the seventeenth century, were held in private dwellings such as the homes of John ap John in Denbighshire (1693), Roger Hughes in Radnorshire (1695) and Robert Evans of Llanidloes (1697).[53] Attendance at the business part of the meeting was limited at these early assemblies, but at least twenty-one Friends attended the meeting held at the Pont-y-Moel meeting house in 1696.[54] Those who attended had often travelled long distances. In 1695, it was suggested that accommodation ought to be secured by the constituent Quarterly Meetings before the Yearly Meeting took place 'to prevent the Charge and trouble, that did usually fall upon one particular house'.[55] Undoubtedly, this was a great assistance to the Hanbury family in arranging the Pont-y-Moel meeting the following year. From 1699 to 1704 the Yearly Meeting was held in Llanidloes, and Robert Evans, a former mayor of the town, provided accommodation, a barn and stables. He also had to find enough seats and benches for the meeting and for his trouble Evans was paid £15.[56] Between 1701 and 1704, Friends attempted to hold the annual meeting in Llanidloes Town Hall, but permission was denied, and they continued to rely upon Evans' hospitality.[57] The accommodation problem proved intractable as the example of John Goodwin of Esgaircoch, Montgomeryshire, shows. In the 1720s, when he and his wife hosted a meeting they were obliged to give up their own bed and sleep in the stable.[58]

Initially all decisions were taken by the London Yearly Meeting but, with the establishment of their own Yearly Meeting, Welsh Friends assumed greater control of their own affairs. Delegates from the Welsh counties were able to impose their own authority upon members, particularly in matters of finance and discipline. Accordingly, representatives made a financial contribution to the Yearly Meeting in order to offset the costs of travelling missionaries and poor relief, and to provide assistance to those who had been heavily distrained for non-payment of tithes. When Carmarthenshire Friends suffered losses because of the Poll Rate in 1691, the constituent Welsh meetings approved a sum of money for their relief. At the other end of the spectrum, in April 1694 Richard Davies of Radnorshire was given £1. 4s. by the Yearly Meeting after his house burned down.[59] Other financial commitments ranged from the hiring of barns, inns and town halls[60] to the seating arrangements at meetings. The Yearly Meeting was fully alive to the temptations inherent in the rise of consumer society, and to that effect in April 1697 the Llanidloes Yearly Meeting warned Friends against 'running forth wth great earnestness into great trade and business, letting their hearts into the things of the world'.[61] Welsh delegates took responsibility for disciplinary matters. They counselled members to avoid inappropriate marriages, to attend meetings regularly and to keep faith with the practice of non-payment of tithes. Many of these instructions were taken directly from the epistles of the London Yearly Meeting, demonstrating that, despite the apparent devolution of power, the influence of London Friends remained significant. This advice was disseminated to all constituent meetings in a circular letter, and ministering Friends were encouraged to travel widely to ensure that Quaker families were visited and kept informed of developments. Thus, in 1706, the Llanidloes Yearly Meeting selected suitable members to visit families in outlying regions.[62] This work was very important in keeping the Society together as demonstrated by the testimony given to the Pont-y-Moel Yearly Meeting in 1716. Friends observed that they were 'much refreshed' by the visits.[63] The Yearly Meeting also arbitrated whenever there were disputes between Friends or constituent meetings, and heard appeals from disgruntled members.

By the middle of the eighteenth century, however, the Welsh Yearly Meeting was in marked decline as an epistle from the annual assembly at Chepstow in April 1758 indicates. The clerk called on Friends to 'exert themselves that there may be an enlargement in Christian Liberty'.[64] By 1780 the situation had worsened. The Yearly Meeting at Usk was 'slenderly attended',[65] and at the Rhaeadr meeting in May 1784 the clerk observed that 'our numbers in this Principality is much decreased and the concern for the prosperity of truth thro' indifferency and lukewarmness much abated'.[66] Eventually, these difficulties were brought to the attention of London Friends who decided to suspend the Welsh Yearly Meeting.[67] The last Welsh Yearly Meeting was held in Welshpool in 1797 and thereafter their business was conducted by a Half-Yearly Meeting.

George Fox and other leading members believed that women should participate in the day-to-day management of the movement by holding their own meetings.[68] Quaker women played an important part in imposing the code of discipline upon female members and in coordinating charitable activity. A London Women's Committee was convened in 1658 and after 1668 women's meetings were formally established. Although the earliest surviving records of Welsh Women's meetings date from c.1747,[69] evidence suggests that separate gatherings were held much earlier. In November 1693, both men's and women's monthly meetings were held at Cloddiau Cochion,[70] and the Montgomeryshire men's meeting referred a young couple who intended to marry to the women's meeting.[71] It may be that a Women's Quarterly Meeting was held in tandem with the Men's Meeting, and either minutes were not taken or they have simply been lost. Nevertheless, later minutes constitute a useful adjunct to the Men's Meeting and provide an insight into the activities of women Friends during the mid-eighteenth century. These well-attended meetings demonstrate that they were valued by female Quakers. They include regular references to the reading of epistles from London. These letters kept the local meeting informed of developments and enabled Quaker women to implement their recommendations. The establishment of women's meetings was controversial, not least because it empowered them in ways that were not entirely acceptable to everyone. For women, networking with London Friends and others gave them a greater awareness of their own contribution to the Society.

As an independent Dissenting community which sought to avoid interment in churchyards, procuring land for burials was a high priority.[72] At the Skipton Conference in 1653, Fox recommended that meetings acquire burial plots as 'a testimony against the superstitious idolising of those places called holy ground'.[73] Little has been written about Welsh Quaker burial practices, but there is plenty of evidence of how Welsh Friends acquired these plots and used them. For example, in opposition to the established practices of the time, Owen Humphrey of Bryn Tallwyn, Llwyngwril, in Merionethshire, buried his twin sons in February 1654 on his own land, and would later provide this plot of land for the benefit of other Friends.[74] Two years later, William Bevan provided a burial ground in Swansea, and Friends in the area acquired an additional plot at Loughor in 1659.[75] In Radnorshire, a burial ground at Lower Cilgu, Llanyre, was provided by Goley Morris in 1656, and another burial ground at Llanoley was available from the early 1660s, while the 'Quakers Yard' enclosure at Dolserau, Merionethshire, was both a meeting place and burial ground. In 1665, Owen Lewis of Tyddyn-y-garreg also gave the Friends some land to bury their dead after his convincement, and Mary Erbery of Cardiff and Richard Davies of Cloddiau Cochion in Montgomeryshire provided burial grounds near their homes. This generosity was continued by the Lloyd family at Dolobran Hall at the end of the seventeenth century.[76]

The rich deposits for Monmouthshire explain how these sites were usually managed. The Pant, 'a square plot of ground of eight or ten perches' in an orchard was used for burials in the late 1650s.[77] It was protected on all sides by a brick wall, probably to avoid detection or intrusion by non-Quakers. According to Francis Gawler in 1663, however, Friends built and enclosed their properties also to keep out 'Swine [that] have been seen in some of your [church] yards in this County.'[78] The property remained in the hands of Friends and, by the end of the seventeenth century, the Pant burial ground was formally preserved under the bequest of Richard Clarke, the owner of the Parc Gras Dieu Estate. In his will of 1697, Clarke left an annuity of £2. 10s. for the maintenance of the site.[79] The registration and maintenance of the Pant burial ground was kept up throughout the seventeenth century, and in 1712 an indenture was signed by

Elisha Beadles and William Cooper of Pontypool; Roger and Thomas Jenkin of Llanfrechfa; Isaac Morgan of Mamheilad; Joseph John of Trefddyn; and Jonathan Barrow of Monmouth. The indenture enshrined the rights of Friends to

> bury or interre their dead therein and that wee should permit & suffer them so to doe when & as often as they should have occasion to make that use thereof for and during such time or times as the civil magistrates should permitt and suffer them peaceably to Bury or Interre their dead therein.[80]

Friends struggled to maintain the burial ground and constantly had to make running repairs to the door and the walls.[81] In spite of the problems, burials were still conducted at the Pant, with the last interment in 1771.[82]

Another small plot of land was purchased as a burial ground at Pen-y-Garn in Trefddyn parish in 1660. The original deed noted that twelve Friends paid 20s. to John Rosser of Trefddyn Parish for the 'Newgarden'. These twelve leading Friends included Richard Hanbury and Walter Jenkins, as well as John Jones of Llanfrechfa; William Howell of Llanfihangel Pont-y-Moel; John Griffiths of Pant-Teg; George White and John Woodland, both of Llanfihangel Ystum Llywern. The enclosed plot stood on land on the road from Pontypool to Abergavenny and was restricted to the use of 'their successors in the faith . . . [who] . . . bear the reproachful name of Quakers or have deserted or borne their testimony against the false prophets hireling priests and idol temples'.[83] Thus, only seven years after the Quaker message had been proclaimed in the county, and while persecution was still rife, Friends had acquired their own burial yards. One of the earliest interments was that of the Quaker missionary Thomas Holme who was buried in the Newgarden on 4 October 1666.[84] The last recorded burial took place on 7 July 1777 when John Jones of Blaenbrane (*sic* Cwmbrân) was interred,[85] and the property was held for another sixty years before it was sold for £20 in 1840 to Capel Hanbury.[86]

It was not uncommon for burial plots to be bought in cojunction with the purchase of meeting houses. This was the case with the Pont-y-Moel burial plot which was purchased in early 1677. Many influential Quakers in and around Pontypool were interred there, including Richard Hanbury's immediate family as well as Thomas Allgood who was buried in 1716.[87] Friends used the site for 135 years and the last recorded burial was that of Hannah Jones, a widow of Pant-Teg, in April 1817.[88] Monmouthshire minutes carry regular references to the practicalities of managing burial grounds. In January 1699, Richard Hanbury was instructed to 'take care to gett ye writings of ye burying place made secure and sound as soon as they may be';[89] in April 1704, the responsibility for safeguarding the keys and tools belonging to the burial ground was entrusted to William Cooper, a cordwainer of Pontypool, who was 'to be carefull that none are buryed there contrary to the order of Friends';[90] three years later, the Quarterly Meeting relaxed its regulations and allowed 'as many as have a mind to be buried in this meeting house yard may do it without any molestation'.[91] In 1715, after the death of an infant, Ruth Hanbury, a children's or 'lesser bodies' burial plot was designated,[92] and in 1856, the property was sold for £21. 6s. 8d. along with the meeting house.[93]

The records for Trosnant burial ground which date from the beginning of the nineteenth century reveal that this was located in 'a 'slummy' neighbourhood', and linked to the meeting house by a passage. The burial ground itself measured roughly 20 yards by 9 yards and had a separate entrance to the road. It had eleven mounds but in accordance with Quaker protocols there were no gravestones, and this was common well into the nineteenth century.[94] Surviving correspondence shows that at least twenty-four burials had been conducted there between 1810 and 1831 in only nine graves. Friends were not only laid to rest with their kinsfolk, but also with their co-religionists and the young with the old.[95] The last Quaker burial was that of Margaret Edwards, a spinster of Llanddewi Court, in April 1870, and the last recorded burial was that of a non-member, James Lewis Williams, a farmer of Llanddewi Court, in 1873.[96] Reginald Nichols noted that the site was subsequently rented for 1s. a year as a vegetable garden.[97]

Just occasionally the acquisition of a burial ground preceded the establishment of a meeting place. Shirenewton

Friends had their own burial ground more than fifty years before they secured a permanent meeting house.[98] The quarterly minutes from October 1700 show that at that date the deeds were held by Richard Hanbury.[99] The 120-year lease noted that a 'new burying place conteyning by estimacon one halfe quarter of an acrě', along with an adjoining plot of land, had been purchased from John Walter of St Bride's Netherwent and William Walter of Shirenewton for 20s. Rent was fixed at 1d, but Friends were allowed to erect a meeting house for an annual rental of 1s.[100] The additional plot of ground was the same size as the existing burial ground. Friends held the lease throughout the eighteenth century, but the meeting house was built on another plot. Indentures show that, as was usual elsewhere, Shirenewton Friends retained control of the burial ground and regularly updated their leases by appointing new trustees.[101] The last recorded interment at Shirenewton was that of Ann Giles, a widow of Penhŵ, on 10 January 1836.[102] The Shirenewton meeting house was sold, but the lease of the burial ground was retained.[103]

The establishment of meeting houses was crucial to the development of the Quaker community. It provided Friends with a dedicated space in which to gather and worship, and afforded them an identifiable presence in Welsh parishes. Of course, meeting houses were not established everywhere. Acquiring a property was not always a viable proposition, especially in rural areas where Friends lived at great distances from one another. The cost of purchasing land and materials could be prohibitive, and the upkeep of a meeting house was often beyond the means of less wealthy members. As Davies suggests in his study of English Quakers, Friends were dependent upon the goodwill of members to offer their homes for meetings.[104] The journal of Richard Davies documents the establishment of various meetings in Montgomeryshire in 1662. The first was at the home of Cadwallader Edwards, who lived near Dolobran. This was attended by Charles Lloyd and several of 'his well-meaning neighbours', and a further meeting was held at Dolobran. When Edward Lord Herbert, Baron Cherbury, heard about the meeting he feared that 'most of that side of the country were turned Quakers' and quickly had the Friends arrested.[105] A further meeting was 'settled' at Cloddiau Cochion, formerly an Independent conventicle, which became an established meeting place for Friends after the convincement of William and Margaret Lewis in the mid-1650s. Richard Davies was also instrumental in establishing a meeting at Penllyn, and visited the homes of Owen Lewis at Tyddyn-y-garreg, near Dolgellau, Robert Owen at Dolserau and Owen Humphrey at Llwyngwril. Here they kept meetings, and 'many were gathered to the Lord among the rocks and mountains in those parts'.[106] Other meetings were held in Friends' houses throughout Wales, but where no communal site was obtained the local Quaker meeting was likely to flounder.[107]

The development of meeting houses was encouraged by Fox who visited Wales in 1668 and made great efforts to unite the scattered worshippers into Quaker communities.[108] Afterwards, these places were recognized as official meeting houses by Friends. In Monmouthshire, the Pant was duly recognized until 1756 and thereafter used as an occasional meeting place.[109] In contrast, the Llanwenarth community declined because they were unable to secure a meeting house after the death of John William Morgan in 1685,[110] while in Breconshire, where there were early converts, there does not seem to have been a permanently settled meeting place until late in the seventeenth century. It is very likely that earlier meetings were held at the home of William and Elizabeth Aubrey at Llanelyw.[111] In 1688, the Yearly Meeting at Pont-y-Moel was attended by at least three Breconshire Friends, Richard Aubrey, the son of William, Richard Walter and William David who reported that 'things are very well, trueth of a good report, one meeting added and a meeting had in Brecknock Town . . . William Ffell kept that meeting upon the Cross in the said town.'[112] The Yearly Meeting at Dolobran in 1694 noted that a meeting was held at the home of Richard Aubrey, a gentleman from Llanelyw, and a 'constant first day meeting' was to be held at Llwyfen, near Blwch. Moreover, Friends in that county were encouraged to establish their own monthly meetings and weekday gatherings, or at least to 'resort to some of the next county weekday meetings'.[113]

Other meeting places were adapted by Friends, notably at Pont-y-Moel and Tyddyn-y-garreg, and in the first quarter of the eighteenth century Monmouthshire Friends erected a purpose-built dwelling house and meeting place at Shirenewton. During the same period, Friends erected a meeting house at Esgairgôch in Montgomeryshire.[114] A later tenement in Trosnant, Pontypool, was converted into a meeting place at the turn of the nineteenth century. The development of such establishments did not, however, contradict the ethos of the Society. The meeting place, unlike the parish church, was not regarded as having any special importance other than as a convenient location for Friends to meet. This fact can be illustrated by their simple construction, the spartan interior and in the alternative functions of the buildings. For example, the meeting house was occasionally used as temporary accommodation for elderly, poor or infirm Friends.[115] Yet, over time, Friends began to conduct rites of passage ceremonies normally associated with the Established Church. In usurping the traditional role of the Church and its paid ministry, the local Quaker meeting began to create a new community of believers.

A better understanding of the changes which occurred in the establishment of meeting houses can be gathered from the evidence from Monmouthshire. The first reference to the purchase of a suitable meeting house at Shirenewton can be found in a minute from December 1723.[116] The Welsh Yearly Meeting at Monmouth was consulted in 1724 and, following the necessary approvals, financial support from other Welsh meetings was requested.[117] A lease from Francis Roberts of Elberton in Gloucestershire and William Roberts of Magwyr, innkeeper, stipulated that one dwelling house, stable and garden would be granted for Friends 'to teach, preach, pray, worship and serve God and also bury or interre their dead'.[118] Patrick Waters and John Richards of Shirenewton, John Biggam and Charles Howell of Newchurch, Thomas Ridley of Marshfield and Evan Thomas of Castleton all helped with the conversion and oversaw the work. The initial purchase money was £26 and the total amount expended was £204. 18s. 8d., with Shirenewton Friends receiving in total £237. 7d. from Welsh and English Friends. The donations included £20 from

Radnorshire, Shropshire, Montgomeryshire, Pembrokeshire and Swansea Friends.[119] The inventory reveals that Friends and their relatives provided labour and supplies which helped to reduce the costs. Such investment demonstrates the importance Friends attached to the provision of meeting houses. Many members were willing to assist in their construction, or offer financial support. Although the Welsh Yearly Meeting acted as guarantor and covered the expenses of the constituent meetings, some meetings fell into arrears or found the payments difficult to meet. The Yearly Meeting at Whitchurch in 1737 recorded that Pembrokeshire owed £6. 15s; Swansea £3. 8s; Montgomeryshire £2; Shropshire £2. 8s; and Carmarthenshire £1. 9s. 1d.[120] Nevertheless, the Shirenewton meeting house was completed and continued to be used until it was sold in 1823 to the Methodists.

As noted, the Pont-y-Moel Friends first met for worship in the house of Richard Hanbury. In 1677, however, they bought land for a meeting house. John Handley, a wealthy Quaker landowner from Pontypool, sold 48 square feet of land to John Jones, a doctor and a Quaker minister of Llanfrechfa parish, for 40s. and an annual quit rent of one penny. Two years later he entrusted the plot to the Society, and a meeting house was erected.[121] The title deed stated that Friends were

> to suffer the new tenement or house to remain and continue for ever thereafter for a house and place of teaching, prayer, worship, and service of God . . . for all and every person that should be thereafter named or reputed or commonly called or distinguished by the name of Quaker . . . or any of their wives or children or servants that shall profess their religion.[122]

The Pont-y-Moel meeting house served the community until 1800 by which time it was 'very much out of repair and the yard very full',[123] and a new one was built at Trosnant, Pontypool.[124] John Rudhall, a Bristol Quaker printer, offered a building, and on 17 March 1800 Richard Summers Harford purchased the copyhold tenement, garden, stable and land for £90.[125] This meeting house was registered at the Quarter Sessions at Usk Guildhall on 13 July 1803.[126] A reconstruction programme was begun almost immediately and by 1806 a new building had been erected on the site at a cost of £803. 15s. 9d.[127] This sum was offset by numerous donations, including those of the Harford family, the Frys of Bristol and David Barclay.[128]

The puzzling question is: why did Friends, whose numbers had dramatically fallen after 1750, erect a new meeting house? The answer must lie in the renewed confidence engendered by individuals, such as the Quaker industrialists John and Richard Summers Harford, who were stalwarts of the Monmouthshire Society from the 1790s until the middle of the nineteenth century. In April 1818, they established an additional week day meeting at the Ebbw Vale ironworks,[129] and in 1823 a Newport Meeting. Yet, in spite of their efforts, the Society continued to decline with the closure of the Trosnant Meeting in 1835.[130] Thereafter the members came under the jurisdiction of the South Wales Monthly Meeting. Six years later (c.1841)[131] the Ebbw Vale and the Newport Meetings were also discontinued.[132]

Friends ensured that they possessed legal rights to their burial grounds and meeting houses, and new trustees were regularly appointed. Their refusal to swear oaths, however, left them vulnerable to unscrupulous people who sought to take advantage. To make sure that Friends shared this responsibility and to guarantee impartiality over the funding of repairs, trustees were drawn from all the constituent meetings. For example, the title deed for the Shirenewton burial ground (c.1700) shows that only two of the six trustees came from the Shirenewton Meeting.[133] Friends were reluctant to replace such trustees, and in practice many of them remained in post until they died.[134] Monmouthshire Friends were also responsible for properties held outside of the county, notably the Sowdrey (Cardiff) burial ground, Tref-y-Rhyg meeting house and burial ground, and Merthyr burial ground. In a deed of ownership for the Sowdrey burial ground (c.1695), Tobias Hodges, the last of the original trustees,[135] granted ownership to twelve new trustees. Of these, six were from Monmouthshire,[136] while in 1743 another four Friends from the county were appointed.[137] These protocols were applied to other Glamorgan trusts. In Merthyr, the burial ground was originally entrusted to the safe keeping of five Glamorgan Friends. By 1746, Daniel Thomas was the only trustee from the Merthyr area, while there were three Friends from other meetings in Glamorganshire and five from Monmouthshire.[138] Similarly, the cottage and burial ground at Llwyfen in Breconshire were administered by Friends from other counties. In 1705, six trustees were appointed: two each from Breconshire, Monmouthshire and Radnorshire,[139] and this balance was maintained each time a new board was constituted.[140] Monmouthshire Friends also had an interest in the meeting house at Llwyfen. Although indigenous Friends had long since died or emigrated, the visiting Monmouthshire Friends were greeted with 'great tenderness among the people about Llwyfan . . . shewn extraordinary love and affection', and were asked to return more often.[141]

As with other property, Welsh Friends were regularly appointed to tend the various plots.[142] Occasionally, the Monthly Meeting appealed to London Friends for assistance, as in 1749 when repairs had to be made to the Pont-y-Moel meeting house.[143] Even after meetings had closed in the nineteenth century, Welsh Friends continued to maintain their properties.[144] Sometimes arrangements were made to repair Friends' properties without the agreement of the local meetings and such interventions were criticized. For example, in September 1713 a general warning was given to Monmouthshire Friends not to take on responsibilities without the consent of the meeting.[145] In June 1745, Seth Waters and George Window were censured by Friends for arranging repairs to the graveyard at Shirenewton without official approval. The meeting required them 'not to meddle any more in it'.[146] Such incidents reveal the extraordinary control exercised by their bureaucratic system of meetings.

The difficulties of financing local meetings often meant that individual Friends, especially the more prosperous members, shouldered most of the burden. They provided funds for repairs, travelling costs, lawsuits and for good causes.[147] From time to time, legacies were bequeathed by Friends for the maintenance of meeting houses and burial grounds. In 1709, Richard Lewis of Llanhilledd ordered that his executors should pay the Pont-y-Moel Meeting 'three pounds towards the reparacon of the meeting house at Pontymoïle'.[148] Throughout the eighteenth century, the Parc Gras Dieu legacy assisted Monmouthshire Friends in the provision of poor relief and other financial matters.[149] By the nineteenth century, however, Friends were having difficulty in accessing the fund,[150] and in December 1820 Friends sought legal advice when Thomas Sanders, the current owner, failed to pay the arrears of the annuity. Their claim was upheld, but it took fourteen months for the arrears to be paid in full.[151] In January 1822, Sanders paid £40 which amounted to eight years of arrears.[152] Five months later, Richard Summers Harford reported that he had received a further £35 for the period c.1806–12.[153] Negotiating a further eight years' arrears was protracted and ended in a civil suit at Chancery.[154]

In the absence of their own property, Welsh Friends rented premises to hold meetings. In January 1702, the half-yearly rent for a meeting place in Chepstow was 15s,[155] and the following year Thomas Wisdom of Malpas was delegated to visit Chepstow to negotiate a lower rent.[156] This was successful and the rent was reduced to 10s.[157] By July 1704, Monmouthshire Friends were considering whether to purchase a meeting house in the town. With the encouragement of Friends from Gloucestershire and Bristol, they pursued the matter and a £10 donation was approved by the Monmouthshire meeting.[158] However, some Friends questioned whether the numbers were sufficient to warrant such an outlay.[159] In December 1706, Monmouthshire Friends paid £10 deposit, only to discover that Bristol Friends, who had undertaken the negotiations, could 'make no good title' upon the property and the idea was abandoned.[160] Monmouthshire Friends continued to rent a room in the town, but as the costs were prohibitive they gave notice to quit the premises the following Midsummer unless the landlord lowered the rent.[161] After this date there are no further references to meetings in Chepstow. By 1781 the only Quaker in the town was a widow who kept a grocery store.[162]

Poor or old Friends were sometimes allowed to live in the meeting houses for a nominal rent. In 1727, Lewis Hughes of Pont-y-Moel rented the meeting house,[163] and later, in 1770, Benjamin James of Shirenewton occupied the dwelling part of the meeting house for 19s. a year.[164] The finances of Quaker communities were often precarious and occasionally they rented their property to raise additional revenue. When the new meeting house was erected at Trosnant, the other property at Pont-y-Moel was rented to John Probert, the Anglican curate of Pant-Teg church at an unusually high rent of £3. a year.[165] By 1813, John Lewis of the Pont-y-Moel Meeting was using it as a school room and was charged a rent of ½d. per week. Roger Merrefield and Thomas Hughes were asked to estimate the cost of converting the property into dwelling houses and the rent that could be obtained.[166] Shortly afterwards, Capel Hanbury Leigh, Walter George and Robert Smith applied for a lease to set up a Lancastrian School.[167] The meeting was inclined to give its approval, as

> such an object would be nearer to the original View of the Grantor of the premises . . . keeping closely in mind if it be not let to those persons that it is to be confined to Education alone and that no creeds or Catechism be introduced and nothing but simply reading and writing and arithmetic as recommended by Joseph Lancaster to be taught.[168]

The strictures proved too exacting for Hanbury Leigh and his associates but, undaunted, they applied to convert the property into a dwelling house.[169] This plan also failed as Friends imposed other restrictions, especially the selling of alcohol,[170] and Robert Smith protested that 'the conditions introduced are I believe quite unusual between Landlord & Tenant inasmuch as we cannot subscribe to'.[171] A general survey of all the properties held by Friends in south Wales was undertaken in 1840 and the Pont-y-Moel meeting house was described as being in state of disrepair. It was eventually sold in 1856.[172] As Nonconformists became more respectable and relations between them improved, they assisted each other. The Trosnant meeting house was rented in the nineteenth century to a Baptist congregation until they were able to build their own chapel in 1846.[173]

Apart from their attendance at meetings and their responsibility for managing Friends' property, leading members of the Society acted as spiritual and moral overseers. It was the duty of the clerk, treasurer, ministers and elders to ensure the general well-being of Friends. The important positions of clerk[174] and treasurer were often filled by one person.[175] There is little detailed information about these posts, but anecdotal evidence can be extracted from the meeting minutes. For example, William Cooper, a shoemaker of Pontypool, may have acted as pro-tem clerk between 1696 and 1704 as well as holding the position of treasurer at Pont-y-Moel.[176] It is likely that the official clerk at this time was Elisha Beadles as he signed transactions on behalf of the Monmouthshire meetings.[177] It was a position that could be both mentally and financially demanding. Decisions involved full consultation with members, but depended thereafter upon the clerk's 'sense of the meeting'.[178] If he failed to reach a decision a committee would be set up to investigate the matter. If no acceptable solution was arrived at the matter would be reconsidered, or referred to a higher meeting. There are various examples of meetings being adjourned to decide upon matters such as the suitability of marriage partners, members' behaviour and business transactions. In 1710, Monmouthshire Friends discussed whether to continue to include east Glamorgan Friends in their Quarterly Meeting. It had been proposed that the Tref-y-Rhyg Meeting could amalgamate with Friends in Swansea, and thereafter constitute the Quarterly Meeting for Glamorganshire. The clerk suggested that 'the matter being a thing of moment, it is desired that Friends take it into their weighty consideration'. After lengthy deliberations, Friends agreed that east Glamorganshire should remain part of their Quarterly Meeting.[179] The clerk was expected to exercise impartiality and act as a calming influence upon the meeting. If difficulties arose he would call for a period of silence to restore order.

Financial contributions were collected by the treasurer who managed the accounts and ensured that the necessary proprieties were observed. The accounts were regularly audited and large payments were authorized only after the local meeting had ratified the expenditure.[180] In the early years of the Society, preachers were directly assisted by Swarthmore Hall. The financial statements of George Taylor and Thomas Willan, of Kendal, between 1655 and 1656, allow valuable insights into fund-raising activities and how these funds were distributed to itinerant preachers in England and Wales.[181] In 1654, Welsh Friends received 12s, a further £1 for their missionary work and 8s. for those who were imprisoned. In some cases, money was given to individuals to buy clothes and basic essentials. Thomas Holme was given 10s. 6d. for a pair of britches and shoes, and Alice Birkett received 2s. 6d. to buy footwear.[182] Even during the worse years of persecution the London Yearly Meeting collected 'stock' for Quaker missionaries, and was never in debt or short of funds.[183] By July 1695 a fixed, monthly collection was introduced in Wales and the funds were later transferred to the Yearly Meeting.[184] This measure regulated the extent to which Friends were expected to defray the costs of their meetings. In the early years of the Society, before the creation of the meeting system, their financial affairs were less bureaucratic. Those who took on the responsibilities of treasurer did so voluntarily and occupied a position of trust. It was not until later that the position of treasurer was formally recognized.[185] As the Society developed, the treasurer became more important to the administration of finances. Although there are references to particular financial transactions, there are no detailed financial accounts for any Welsh meeting before c.1803.[186]

With the death of the first generation of Friends it was important for the Society to ensure continuity of ministry, and so the constituent meetings in England and Wales appointed a 'hierarchy' of ministers and elders for each Quarterly Meeting. The creation of such a powerful body within the Society was initially viewed by some members with apprehension. They argued that the establishment of 'spiritual overseers' ran counter to the spirit of the early Quakers, who believed that individuals should control their own path to salvation. They were also concerned that more assertive members might monopolize the meetings while other members sat in silence, and such fears were exacerbated by the privileged seating arrangements for ministers and elders.[187] It was the duty of these leading Friends to organize the Society: discuss matters of contention; examine any disputes; and enrich the spiritual life of the Quaker community by providing wise and impartial advice. Elders and overseers mediated the views of the Welsh Yearly

Meeting to their Quarterly Meetings, and ensured that Friends were well informed about major developments. For example, elders who attended the Yearly Meeting at Tenby in 1743 were asked to encourage their members to keep 'children to a reasonable & orderly frequenting of week day, as well as of first day, Meetings, instructing them to have their minds stayed in the Divine Gift'.[188]

Ministers and elders were responsible for organizing regular family visits.[189] Women elders were also encouraged to visit families, and the minutes of their own Yearly Meetings demonstrate their commitment to this policy. The 1713 Yearly Meeting at Newtown expressed concern that some Friends were remiss in visiting families, but acknowledged that leading Friends had difficulty reconciling the demands of the Society with their own personal and spiritual needs.[190] Ministers who secured permission to travel to other areas were provided with a letter of introduction by the clerk. This ministry was further regulated by a letter of approval issued by the clerk of the host meeting, which normally confirmed the integrity of the guest.[191] The issue of certificates was strictly monitored and Friends without the correct documentation were admonished. In January 1706, Walter Heathcott was chastised for 'roaming abroad wthout a certificate', and the Monmouthshire Quarterly Meeting requested him to return home.[192] Typically, ministers travelled in pairs on horseback over great distances.[193] For example, the journey north to meetings held at Dolobran, via Welshpool, Newtown, Llanidloes, Rhayader, Builth, Abergavenny and Pontypool, was a distance of at least 100 miles.[194] In 1720, Roger Jenkin of Llanfrechfa and Ann Rosser of Trefddyn were allowed to travel together to north Wales. This was unusual as the Society normally discouraged male and female ministers from travelling together to avoid accusations of impropriety.[195] The journal of Rebecca Jones of Pennsylvania, written in 1786, gives a vivid picture of the Welsh countryside, the people and the difficulty of travel. She found the journey exhausting due to the rugged terrain:

> The roads are in general sound and hard; but we were comparatively like a ship on the ocean, continually ascending or descending, and the steps very great, with a deep precipice at the

side for miles together; so that yesterday morning a very high wind taking us on the tops of the mountains, the probability of being overturned was very alarming.

As she recalled, 'the Welch people are an industrious, hardy, plain people, and there are a few precious Friends worth visiting. I have a secret hope that there will be a revival in Wales.'[196]
Such visits provided members with an opportunity to hold impromptu meetings and to discuss more intimately their religious beliefs. For their part, Friends were able to keep the costs of travelling to a minimum and, to speed the journey of the traveller, the meeting would appoint a guide to take them to the next place on the itinerary. In April 1699, the Monmouthshire Quarterly Meeting agreed that Friends should provide guides and accompany visitors at least as far as Haverfordwest. Later in the year an official list was drawn up of designated guides, and it was agreed that 'dilligence and care may be taken in offering this matter that soe no ffriends travailing on the account of truth may be at a loss for want of a guide, but when a friend comes every one may know his place and turne'.[197] In 1714, Francis Jenkin was criticized for failing to guide 'strange friends' around the country. Thereafter, the Monthly Meeting called upon volunteers to 'be carefull to discharge that duty'.[198]
   In constructing such a complex organization, the Society of Friends was reacting to the difficulties of the years in which they were persecuted as a malevolent, destabilizing force. The bureaucracy they put in place to defend themselves delivered essential leadership to a movement that was initially amorphous and vulnerable. This unifying process created local and national solidarities that provided strength in numbers, an efficient administration, and ultimately created a recognizable community of believers. For Wales, with its predominantly rural landscape, where Friends were often scattered in remote and isolated places, the connection with this overarching organization was arguably crucial. As it developed, however, the negative aspects of Quaker bureaucracy became increasingly problematic. Decision-making shifted away from the individual to a corporate body that was, at times, aloof from its membership. The meeting

system could be expensive and cumbersome, and not all Quakers wanted to formalize their gatherings, especially as this appeared to imitate rituals associated with orthodoxy. As Friends gradually turned their back upon radical activity and their meetings dwindled, the unwieldy bureaucracy was increasingly unable to meet the changing needs of its members in an industrial age. The organizational structure which had nurtured the infant Society in the end was part of the reason for its decline.

Chapter 4

'Snares to catch the Innocent and faithfull servants of the Lord':
The Persecution and Tolerance of Friends

> The rage and mallice of the Men of this generation being exceed-
> ing greate the Innocent are daily made a prey to the wicked &
> laws that were first made against or for discovery of such as were
> suspected to bee Treacherous to the King, are now turned into
> snares to catch the Innocent & faithfull servants of the Lord when
> nothing can be proved thats evill donne by them against any man
> nor any . . . cause of suspition found by them.[1]

The persecution which Friends endured in their long struggle
for civil and religious freedom exemplifies the fortitude which
distinguished Dissenters. The intolerance of the Church and
the secular authorities changed in line with external forces,
and this was reflected in the diverse ways in which Dissenters
were persecuted. Quakers responded differentially to their persecution over time, and in the past this has not always been
fully appreciated by historians of the Society of Friends.[2]
Annette Hampshire and James Beckford claimed that sects,
like minority groups, were regarded as deviant whenever
public hostility was aroused by their activities.[3] While studies
of these religious groups have tracked the transformation from
sect to denomination, they make only passing reference to
the notion of deviancy. Indeed, they concentrate on the
change from radicalism to acceptability, but not upon those
influences which may have prompted such a shift. This chapter
will outline the reasons for persecution, focusing upon the
perceived deviancy of Quakers, as well as the challenges which
they posed to the authorities after 1660. This appraisal will
offer an analysis of the different methods of persecution
deployed, including the actions taken against Friends, and a

consideration of how sanctions were enforced. It will explore the way that Quakers responded to persecution, whether it afforded a legacy of suffering to which they could refer, and how this affected their relationship with the Established Church and the state. Finally, the changing attitudes of Friends will be examined in a bid to explain the rejection of radicalism in favour of less provocative forms of dissent.

Accusations of deviant behaviour in Wales are evident both before and contemporaneous with the emergence of Quakerism. The growth of radicalism and sectarian worship worried propertied Welshmen and clergymen alike. Quakers were seen as the purveyors of dangerous and schismatic policies and described as 'infectious and contagious'; 'a strange, growing faction', or 'vipers' that 'crept into the bowels of your Commonwealth'.[4] On 16 December 1653, Oliver Cromwell had permitted 'liberty of conscience' to those religious groups of a puritanical persuasion. Nevertheless, the Commonwealth and Restoration periods were challenging times for those with tender consciences. Friends were resented and taunted by their neighbours and harshly dealt with by the authorities who believed they were subversives. Although Friends were a small minority, their evangelicalism and harassment of the clergy and magistrates made them objects of hostility. The authorities believed that society was being destabilized by the behaviour of deviants and fanatics. Moreover, as Philip Jenkins has observed, Quakers were doubly unpopular: they had ranter characteristics, and some of their members were ex-soldiers who, it was alleged, had yet to abjure militarism.[5]

Even when liberty was granted it did not constitute a significant advance in religious freedom. The considerable growth of Quakerism which, by 1655, had been transformed from a local nuisance to a public concern preoccupied both churchmen and magistrates. According to the parliamentarian William Prynne it seemed that the biblical prophecy of Jeremiah 1: 14 would be fulfilled and that 'out of the North an evil shall break forth upon all the inhabitants of the land'.[6] Cromwell, disturbed by threats to peace and order, issued a proclamation on 15 February 1655 against those who disrupted 'public and private meetings',[7] stating that if Quakers persisted they would be treated as disturbers of the peace and liable to prosecution.

It has been argued that Quaker 'threshing meetings' and public disputations were intentionally orchestrated to arouse a reaction, and that much of the persecution of the early Quakers was prompted by their over-exuberance and provocative actions.[8] In 1655, Joshua Miller, the incumbent of St Andrews in the Vale of Glamorgan, stated that the intruders were

> sometimes like the Swine, looking and bending to the earth, then staring and raving like the men in Bedlam, anon they go with bended back, arms unfolded, thus mocking the Lord their maker . . . Sometimes they weep and howl Pharisee like to be heard of men. As if they were in Hell already, for Christ tells us the damned shall so do.[9]

If the accounts of Miller and other clergymen are to be believed, then it is not surprising that Quakers were ostracized by local communities. Fay Williams has argued that in the Commonwealth period the Glamorganshire Quakers were punished as disturbers of the peace and not for advocating radical doctrines. She claims that Friends were allowed to hold their meetings in peace and were chastised only when they threatened general disorder.[10] Parliamentarians were disturbed by the Quakers and complained bitterly. Miller, whose prejudice is clear, called upon the authorities to act:

> O! Ye Magistrates, can you see Christ bleeding a fresh every day in City, Town, Village, Country, speared by Oaths, Lying, Drunkenesse, Prophanation of the Lords day, Whoredomes, Blasphemies? Are you Christian Magistrates and will not step in to punish such offenders?[11]

In spite of the prejudice they aroused, or perhaps because of it, Friends proclaimed their belief by dressing in sackcloth or appearing 'naked as a sign'.[12] According to Norman Penney, such conduct was not frowned upon by leading Friends,[13] and George Fox believed that such actions were signs that Friends were 'moved of the Lord'.[14] Between 1653 and 1655, Thomas

Holme and his future wife, Elizabeth Leavens, both tramped naked through some prominent English towns.[15] In Chester in August 1655 Holme was attacked for his behaviour but he remained unapologetic, stating that, 'I am clear in my obedience to the lord'.[16] These 'signs and wonders' are said to have reached their height in the early years of the Society between 1652 and 1656, and again in the last years of the Protectorate when Millenarian hopes intensified.[17] It was during this later period that Thomas Briggs of Lancashire walked naked through the streets of Cardiff:

> I got up in the Morning and went out of a Friends House, with my Coat upon me till I came into the Street, and when I came there, I let my Coat fall down, and so went naked up and down through the Streets; and this was the Message that the Lord put into my Mouth . . . *Thus must you be stripped of all your Profession, that are not found in the Life of Righteousness.*[18]

Briggs disrupted a church service, and reputedly appeared naked elsewhere in Wales.[19] Friends apparently found this liberating, but others regarded it as a sign of their deviancy. By 1656 the spread of deviancy led the Baptist preacher of Ilston, John Miles, to pen a condemnation in which he reviled the growth of Quaker delinquency as follows: 'Seekers, Quakers, Ranters, Familists, yea, and profest Infidels, &c. Yea there are many railing Rabshakehs who (to her greatest grief) never cease to blasphem the name, wayes, and precious Ministers of the Lord.'[20] The James Nayler affair in autumn 1656 divided the Quakers into ranters and others who preferred more conventional means of proclaiming their message.[21] In 1657, George Fox specifically admonished those Cardiff Quakers who associated themselves with Nayler's extremism, notably Dorcas Erbery who claimed that Nayler raised her from the dead while imprisoned in Exeter.[22] Thomas Holme wrote to Margaret Fell in April 1657 and criticized Friends who constantly prostrated themselves in religious fervour, wildly sang the praises of God during meetings, or who attended meetings dressed in sackcloth and ashes, and 'acted in all maner of decept & Imagination, being full of confusion in ther words'.[23]

The debates precipitated by Nayler's activities damaged the reputation of Friends and raised doubts about their beliefs. On the one hand, they were linked with extreme radicals and, on the other, with devil worshippers.[24] Richard Davies observed that people in Montgomeryshire 'look'd upon us as Witches, and would go away from us, some crossing themselves, with their Hands about their Fore-heads and Faces'.[25] The shaking and trembling of Quakers caused people to assume that they were possessed by an evil spirit. As Joshua Miller said,

> I have heard them hum like a swarm of Bees, as if Beezlebub, the God of the Flies was there. Well dear Christians some of you have read the life of Kilpin a great Quaker, but lately brought back to Christ. How he manifests that he was often possessed with the Divel. As also you have heard of the fly that came to two men in a Bed at Wrexham.[26]

In 1659, when Henry Walter, the Independent minister of Newport, believed Francis Gawler was possessed he had him removed from church fearing that he would bewitch him.[27] Walter Cradock also remonstrated with Gawler at Newport in June 1660: 'Get thee behind me Satan, I have hearkened to thee, but now do deny thee, thou dost torment me day and night. I speak not to thee Gawler, but to the divell in thee.'[28]

The restoration of the monarchy in 1660 did not allay the fear of social anarchy, and rumours abounded that former republicans were prepared to take up arms.[29] Friends' involvement in the army during the Civil Wars and the enforced ejection of clergymen from their livings produced a 'spirit of vengeance' against those who had wielded pikes and muskets. The Welsh royalist, Arise Evans, wrote in 1660, 'the Quakers give out forsooth, that they will not rebel nor fight, when indeed . . . the Army was full of them'.[30] The previous year, in response to Booth's rebellion, Robert Owen of Dolserau, was requested to raise a troop although this was countermanded by the Committee of Safety.[31] A few months later he was suspected of instigating a conspiracy in north Wales to undermine the restoration of the king and the elections to the Convention Parliament.[32] In his journal in May 1660, Richard Davies referred to the arrest of various former

Roundheads in Montgomeryshire, including himself. Although he had never taken up arms, he was forcibly taken from his home by a solider who brandished a pistol and 'naked sword'.[33] When Walter Jenkins of Llanfihangel Ystum Llywern was arrested in January 1661, the soldiers 'broke open the coffers and trunks under pretence of searching for arms'.[34] That same year, Fox decided that it was better to adopt pacifist principles in order to protect Quakers from such attacks. Henceforth, Friends became a pacifist movement, refusing to take up arms, pay military subscriptions or placate the militia by sending replacements. Extolling the virtues of spiritual weapons they were advised to 'love your enemies' and 'do good to them that hate you'.[35]

Another reason why Quakers were persecuted was their refusal to take an oath or pronounce their allegiance to the king.[36] This led their enemies to equate the Society with papists and their meetings as breeding grounds for Catholicism.[37] In July 1660, many Merionethshire Quakers were attacked by a mob who 'did lug them out of their beds, wounding, beating and bruising several of them'. The group, which included the elderly, women and children, were marched 20 miles to the Quarter Sessions at Bala. Four Friends refused to swear the Oath of Allegiance even though the magistrate insisted that: 'You are to swear faithfulnesse or obedience not to your heavenly King, but to our earthly King.' Subsequently, they were forced to walk an additional 12 miles in irons to another prison where they were incarcerated for four months.[38] Shortly before the publication of Walter Jenkins's tract, *The Law given forth out of Sion* (1661), he had been arrested and imprisoned for his refusal to swear an oath.[39] This refusal was judged to be treasonable. Earlier, in 1655, William Prynne condemned Quakers as 'the Spawn of Romish frogs, Jesuits, and Franciscan Fryers, sent from Rome to seduce the intoxicated Giddy-headed'.[40] To be branded as a secret Catholic organization was a commonplace, for most sects at some stage were suspected of plotting to undermine Church and state. Moreover, the Quaker doctrine of inner light was regarded as a thinly disguised version of the Catholic dogma of grace.[41] Their fasting and recording of visions implied that they were influenced by the Jesuits.[42]

Some believed that Quakerism was a ruse to deceive the Established Church into allowing Roman Catholic practices. In 1655, Joshua Miller argued that their plain attire imitated 'the monks of Rome', noting that they 'rise oft in the night to Prayers, go barefoot, sometimes in hair-cloth many a mile in cold weather'.[43] Miller also questioned Friends' salvationist ideology, arguing that there was little difference between their doctrines and those of the Catholic Church; in their denial of the gospel ministry of the Church of England, they were in full accord with the Catholics.[44] Moreover, the attack upon Henry Walter and other Puritan ministers at Llanfihangel-Llantarnam on 12 July 1660 by the local Catholic community[45] was mirrored by that of Monmouthshire Friends during the Interregnum and early years of the Restoration. In an attempt to prove that Quakers were not crypto-papists, Francis Gawler quoted the example of Arnold Thomas of Llanfihangel-Llantarnam. Thomas had goods distrained in 1659 by Arnold Williams, a farmer, and William Davy, a bailiff, both of whom were Catholics. Gawler, full of righteous indignation, wrote: 'now let the priests be ashamed to accuse us to be Papists, and they one with the Papists in their practices, and taking away our goods'.[46] In 1663, Morgan Watkins of Radnor argued that in burying their dead in their own simple way, Quakers were testifying against 'Popish consecrations'.[47] Yet, such unfounded accusations continued until well into the 1680s.

As already discussed, before the 'Popish Plot' there were rumours that Catholicism was on the increase, and Quakerism was thought to be part of this phenomenon. As Monmouthshire was the most notable Welsh Catholic stronghold, this may have given the rumours added credence.[48] Like their Catholic neighbours, they were accused of sheltering itinerant preacers.[49] The rise in the number of Dissenting meetings, and the frequency of Catholic services held in secret locations in Monmouthshire,[50] augmented the number of prosecutions for recusancy. As Robert Matthews suggests, popery was always seen as 'expansive, conspiratorial and dangerous'.[51] Popular anxiety underpinned the reports produced in 1679 suggesting that more people attended covert Catholic services in Abergavenny than at the Anglican Church.[52] The same argument was used against Friends at Pont-y-Moel. Consequently, Friends whose religious beliefs were remote from Catholic dogma became embroiled in the complex religious divisions of the time. The situation was 'magnified by factional and economic conflicts that provided a backdrop against which the numerical strength of local Catholicism could spark the traditional tinder of anti-Popery'.[53]

Mid-seventeenth-century Catholicism and its adherence to the 'old faith' was representative of an older religious tradition, whereas Quakerism was a new form of dissent. In periods of heightened tension they were persecuted along with their Catholic neighbours for a number of reasons. Not only were their theological foundations viewed as similar and sinister, but their economic strength and patronage was considered threatening. In addition, in swelling the numbers of recusants in Monmouthshire, they were considered a destabilizing force. It is possible that this analysis makes too much of the view that rank-and-file Catholics and Quakers were ungovernable because of their nonconformity. David Scott has argued that the pejorative reputation of early Friends rests upon the 'uncompromising militancy' of itinerant preachers and the peaceful role of the majority of the movement in the 1650s and 1660s has been largely ignored.[54] This argument could be applied to the Catholic population too, where greater attention has been paid to the Catholic gentry, Jesuit priests and martyrs than to the laity. Both communities faced a dilemma – some members were able to 'overcome the world' and abandon their families and livelihoods, but many others arrived at a compromise with society. As Scott noted, only a minority 'were likely to display a total disregard for contemporary social standards'.[55]

Apart from legal disabilities, the Quakers' dealings with the Established Church also led to their persecution. The clergy feared that the growth of the sect would lead to a decline in standards of worship. The greater religious toleration of the 1650s enabled Quakers to challenge many of the tenets of orthodoxy and refute the authority of the 'Visible Church'.[56] Clergymen felt challenged by these religious zealots who dismissed the view that membership of the Established Church equated to political loyalty. The Friends' call for a ministry who spoke simply, unlike the university-trained clerics, aroused deep suspicion. Elizabeth Holme, Edward Edwards and Francis Gawler were brought before the magistrates at Shirenewton in 1659 and asked by Justice Robert Jones why they denounced the clergy as deceivers and hirelings. Friends argued that the clergy had 'the mark of the Beast in their fore-heads, and they were those that upheld the worship of the Beast in the Idols Temples, where the beast is now worshipped in this generation, by which mark the false prophets are known to be deceivers'.[57]

The handbill of a Quaker meeting issued by Richard Hanbury of the Pont-y-Moel Meeting further illustrates their hostility towards such issues as tithes, rates and the Church's status as a Christian institution. Hanbury was scathing in his condemnation, claiming that the clergy were 'half protestants and half papists' as they used popish rituals in their services to demand tithes.[58] The clergy were denounced by Friends as the oppressors of the poor. According to Francis Gawler, they were 'fighters and strikers, false accusers, pullers by the hair of the head, evil speakers', who secured their livings by underhand methods or by the taking of tithes from the destitute.[59] Campaigns against the payment of tithes were a direct challenge to the Church and local government. In November 1658, when John Hardwick, vicar of Mitcheltroy and Cwmcarfan, prosecuted Charles Jenkins for non-payment of tithe, the Exchequer was informed that his refusal meant the loss of four lambs worth 3s. each and a tenth of the produce from 4 acres of oats, 10 of wheat and 40 bushells of apples.[60] In the same year, Hardwick also prosecuted Jane Edmonds, a widow, and James ap John, both of Cwmcarfan, for their refusal to pay tithes worth £6.[61] In 1659, Gawler condemned the way that non-Quakers were allowed to break the law without punishment and cited the case of Griffith David of Gelligaer, who had allegedly marked his neighbour's sheep. In spite of being found guilty, he had been released unpunished 'lest the rest of the Trade should come to shame'.[62] The enforced payment of church maintenance provoked Friends to call for its abolition. George Fox argued that it was the responsibility of the clergy to maintain themselves, for God had neither ordained tithes, 'Easter reckonings, and mid-summer dues', nor called for the imprisonment of people who refused to pay.[63]

There is some truth in the assertion that opposition to the tithe had biblical roots, but there were also economic and social grievances. Stephen Roberts has noted that for the majority of parishioners the tithe was 'at best a perennial irritation and at worst a disincentive to agrarian progress and a moral iniquity'.[64] Some historians have observed that in south Wales during the early 1650s preaching and profiteering 'often went hand in hand'.[65] In a lawsuit from Bassaleg brought before the Exchequer in January 1662, the rector, George Watkin, and a number of Puritan lay officials, were prosecuted for having impropriated the tithes of the bishop and chapter of Llandaff during the Interregnum.[66] In the same year, William Matthew, a yeoman of Porthsgiwed, was charged by the local vicar with having received tithes between 1650 and 1659 as well as occupying the parsonage house and glebe lands worth £60.[67]

The attacks upon tithe payments underlined the antipathy not only to the social hierarchy, but to the impositions of the clergy and lay impropriators. The disproportionate distribution of wealth sharpened the divide between rich and poor, and urban and rural areas. This served to aggravate the situation for the burden of payment fell mostly on the rural and poorer sections of Welsh society. The tithe question became a matter of conscience for the individual or for the community, as well as an economic concern for rich and poor. In some areas there were tithe strikes, such as Glamorgan in 1651, and in Porthsgiwed and Llanfihangel-Roggiet in 1652 where 'none would ingage' in the collection of tithes worth £30.[68] In 1655, lay impropriators for the parishes of Llandeilo Gresynni, Pen-Rhos, Dingestow, Tre'r-Gaer and Llan-Arth in Monmouthshire pursued their claims for tithe payments in the Exchequer against various defaulters, while Matthew Herbert of Llangatwg in Breconshire also prosecuted some of his parishioners.[69]

After the fall of the Barebones Parliament, the refusal to pay tithe was widespread. Justification ranged from the claim that payment would impede the Second Coming of Christ to the allegation that payments satisfied the clergyman's god – 'their bellies'.[70] In one instance, Walter Watkins of Shirenewton was distrained of his goods by the parish constable who seized two saddles for a 3s. demand.[71] On 27 June 1659, Friends issued a petition containing 15,000 signatures, which stated 'woe unto them that make the gospel chargeable, it being the free gospel of peace'.[72] In a supplementary petition signed by 7,000 female members in 1659, 245 names appear from members in Wales and Herefordshire.[73] Many leading churchmen were quick to pen damning tracts. Friends' opposition pitched them against both clergymen and landowners, for their refusal to pay lay impropriators was an attack upon property. Furthermore, the non-payment of tithes by well-connected Friends infuriated the authorities who feared it would encourage others to default. Such fears were not unfounded. It is likely that in 1659 non-payment by the Hanbury family influenced their non-Quaker kinsman, Capel Hanbury of Pontypool, to refuse to pay a £60 tithe.[74] Capel Hanbury was again cited in the Exchequer in 1682 for his refusal to pay tithes to Walter Rogers, the rector of Llantrisaint Fawr, for wood cut down in the parish. In his defence the Quaker John Handley informed the bench that, although Hanbury had indeed cut down wood between 1660 and 1662, no wood had been cut down for thirty years previously and so no tithe was due.[75] The attacks on the Church prompted a backlash from disgruntled clergymen who sought to eradicate malcontents and enforce attendance at church services. Friends, such as Charles Jenkins and his wife, Gwenllian, who had been excommunicated by Llandaff Consistory Court in March 1663, were barred from proving wills and acting as jurors, and were unable to testify in courts.[76] Unfortunately, the loss of many of the Llandaff church court records frustrates the attempt to precisely document persecution cases in this part of Wales. Most of the evidence for persecution in south-east Wales necessarily derives from Quaker sources and has to be treated with due caution.[77]

Welsh Quakers refused to attend any service within the confines of the parish church in spite of the insistence of the clergy. Non-attendance led to frequent court appearances, and by the late 1650s and early 1660 attacks on Quakers had become so vicious that 'the very Name of a Quaker exposed a Man to the Loss of his Liberty'.[78] As the presence of Quakers could stir up a vehement reaction, holding a meeting must have been a courageous act. In February 1660, Friends at Wrexham were attacked by an Irish brigade wielding

> staves and crab-tree cudgels, and thrust and pusht one another upon Friends . . . and forced them out of the meeting place, striking them with their staves . . . [and] they drove some Friends into the water, and one they pusht down in the water, and bruised him so that the Blood ran down, another mans head was broken and his blood shed in the street.[79]

In the same year, Glamorgan Friends were 'forcibly removed' while holding a meeting,[80] and in a letter sent by Thomas Holme to Fox in March 1660 he described the disruption of Quaker meetings. An armed militia broke up a meeting held at Pont-y-Moel 'with much villence and threatened to pistoll on[e] or two of us'. Thirty Quakers were later imprisoned in the 'steeple-house' before being brought before the magistrates the following day. Nineteen Friends were then gaoled in Usk prison for five days.[81] In Radnorshire in February 1660/1, various meetings were violently disrupted by soldiers, and twenty-three Friends were imprisoned for their refusal to swear the oath of allegiance. The following year they were fined £5 each at the Sessions court.[82] By 1663 the situation had become perilous, and Holme reported to Fox that six Breconshire members had been imprisoned, while in Monmouthshire he had been threatened by 'one great man of that county' who stated that 'if I kept meetings and preatched to the peopell hee would take mee up and prison me'.[83] In an effort to stem the growth of sectarian worship, particularly Quakerism, such meetings were criminalized under the Conventicle Acts of 1664 and 1670. The prevalence of conventicles in 1669, both Quaker and non-Quaker, however, bears testimony to the intransigence of Welsh Dissenters.[84]

The Quakers drew the hostility of prosperous members of the community. Complaints that the Quakers were contemptuous of the authorities are common throughout the period. Even Baptists, such as John Miles, spoke out against the attacks on the magistracy, suggesting that such contempt was promoted by those who 'despise government . . . they are not afraid to speak evil of dignities'.[85] The refusal to defer to the wealthy and swear the oath of allegiance exposed them to the malicious power of the magistrates, and this led to the imprisonment of many Friends. All those who would not swear the Oaths of Allegiance and Supremacy were presumed to be political malcontents, or papists. As Geraint Jenkins has remarked, Friends

> aroused more hostility and fear than any other radical sect in this period. Their inflammatory language, outrageous codes of behaviour and bellicose postures made them much more than simply squalid nuisances. Churchmen and Puritans closed ranks against them because they feared that such dangerous malcontents would never rest until the world was well and truly turned upside down.[86]

The Quakers tried hard to dispel such fears. In 1662, Welshpool Quakers had their meeting broken up by the magistrates who suspected them of plotting against Charles II. As the names of Friends were being taken, the wife of Richard Davies held out her three-month-old baby, but was told that the child was too young to be included. She retorted that: 'We are all as innocent from plotting and contriving, or thinking any harm to any Man, as this little child.'[87]

Inherent in the Quaker code of conduct was the assertion that all were equal in the sight of God, and this underpinned Friends' refusal to defer to authority. They refused to 'hat-honour' social superiors or refer to them by their titles. This stance, as the following Welsh ballad shows, was not confined to Friends, but was one of the methods adopted by them to distinguish between the honour accorded to God and that which men had usurped:

> One day a learned bishop,
> In measured voice and deep,
> Pronounced the benediction
> Above his gathered sheep;
> And listening with attention
> To what his Lordship said,
> He noticed there a peasant
> His hat upon his head.

The Bishop when he saw him,
In anger did cry out,
'Now there, while I am speaking,
Take off thy hat, thou lout!'
'I won't' the peasant answered,
'The merit must be small
Of words that will not enter
The brain through hat and all.[88]

The refusal to remove hats is well documented. In 1659, Francis Gawler refused to take off his hat before the magistrates in Cardiff, and consequently was threatened with a fine for contempt.[89] Other affronted gentlemen responded more violently. In 1661, James Lewis of Carmarthenshire was severely beaten with a stick, and had his hat knocked off his head and thrown down a hill.[90] An interesting account of hat-honour was provided in 1741 by Thomas Lewis:

I was to appear before one of the Rulers of yt Country . . . and the custom of this countrey was to bow unto Idols, which I was not to do. Then he was in a rage, and thought to compel me; but thro' mercy I feared him not which could kill the body. When he saw that he could not prevail over me, he compelled the people to take off my hat . . . afterwards I did talk with that same Ruler several times without any more reverence than Mordecay gave unto Hamar, and within his own private chamber where I drank without any bowing or crouching.[91]

Quakers adopted the use of 'thee' and 'thou' when they addressed others, and this aroused considerable antagonism.[92] In 1659, the sister of the Quaker Lieutenant-Colonel Bowen of the Gower was denounced in Swansea by Revd John Robert for 'theeing and thouing him'.[93] Richard Davies recalled that, when he used the terms 'thee' and 'thou' to his employer, 'she took a stick and gave me such a blow upon my bare head, that made it swell and sore for a considerable time; she was so disturbed at it, that she swore she would kill me, though she would be hanged'.[94]

Ostentatious displays of wealth and status were also frowned upon by Friends as they were viewed as morally indefensible. Walter Jenkins maintained that deference to magistrates who placed a 'great store of Ribbons . . . Silver Buttons, and Tassels in [their] Hats' was misplaced.[95] A pre-occupation with finery among the upper orders was thought to distract the faithful away from devotion to God. Strange though it may seem, Friends' code on plainness, especially the adoption of a dress code, was viewed as threatening behaviour. Quaker deviance and radicalism did not warrant the outlandish accusations made against them.[96] By 1659, to be a Quaker was to be a miscreant, whether the individual was law-abiding or not. For some, defaming Friends and turning them into outcasts was justified on the grounds that this would rid the land of God's enemies.[97] In return, God's favour would be bestowed and, by the same token, He would exact retribution on those who harboured delinquents. Furthermore, it can be argued that Quakers were despised for their rejection of those rituals associated with birth, marriage and death for, in doing so, they flouted the social conventions.

To many Friends, the law was used to exploit the poor, while protecting the interests of the property-owning classes. Walter Jenkins of the Pant wrote that lawyers and magistrates were getting rich at the expense of the lower orders for they were 'greedy after men's estates'.[98] There were at least seventeen separate Acts under which a Quaker could be charged and punished. Friends were subjected to crippling fines, public whippings, verbal abuse and imprisonment in dreadful conditions.[99] After the Restoration in 1660, the Clarendon Code was used to punish the disaffected and empower magistrates and clergymen who wished to outlaw Dissent. Many members faced considerable financial losses from distraint of land, produce and personal items, and even imprisonment if they failed to comply with the new laws. The Quaker records of distraint, especially for tithes, provide historians with valuable insights into Quaker households. Yet these records represent only a partial view, privileging wealthier Friends; rank-and-file members were also fined, imprisoned or distrained, along with their prosperous co-religionists, mainly for not attending church or meeting in conventicles.

The first action taken against Dissenters was the implementation of the Corporation Act of December 1661. This measure barred any person from municipal office unless they were prepared to swear the oath of allegiance and receive the sacrament in Anglican services. On 2 May 1662, specific clauses in the Quaker Act outlawed their meetings.[100] In 1664 and 1670, life was made even more difficult by the Conventicle Acts and the use of paid informers.[101] Known informers included Robert Sowtrell who actively pursued Friends in mid Wales; Edward Harris, 'the Grand Informer' of Pembrokeshire; John David alias Pugh of Welshpool; and David Maurice of Penybont, Denbighshire, who Richard Davies claimed was 'a great persecutor, not only of our Friends, but of other Dissenters also'.[102] In March 1674, Maurice was instrumental in disrupting a Quaker meeting at Cloddiau Cochion. It was alleged that Thomas Lloyd of Dolobran had preached a sermon about 'the Nature of True Religion and Worship' and was subsequently fined £20 for contravening the penal laws.[103] Two years later, in August 1676, nine Merionethshire Friends, including Elizabeth Williams, were imprisoned after being indicted for recusancy. Among those charged were Rowland Ellis and Cadwallader Thomas. At the ensuing Bala Assizes, the magistrates, Kenrick Eyton and Thomas Walcott, were prepared to execute the nine Quakers for failing to attend the Established Church and, more significantly, for refusing to swear the necessary oaths. Although the Quakers had declared their loyalty to the crown they would not take the oath. Subsequently, Walcott tried to revive the heresy laws passed against the Lollards in 1399 and other similar statutes. He warned the Friends that they could be tried for treason. The men would be hanged and quartered, while the women would be burned. At their second court appearance in September they once again refused to comply and were imprisoned as traitors. They were denied any materials to light a fire, and an elderly Quaker, Edward Rice, was 'unable to bear the severity of the cold' and died that winter. The House of Commons later reprieved the others, and Walcott was censured for his harshness.[104] Quakers were even barred from office holding. The Test Act of 1673 stipulated that Crown appointments would only be available to known Anglicans who swore allegiance to the king. Thus, throughout the first three decades of their existence, Quakers and other Dissenters were pursued within their communities and in their daily lives.

In the 1650s, several Marian and Elizabethan laws were resurrected. As already noted, the provocative way in which Quakers interrupted church services was confrontational. Friends who were convicted of maliciously disrupting church service could be imprisoned for up to three months.[105] One of the first Friends to be imprisoned for such acts was John ap John who in the mid-1650s was roughly manhandled and imprisoned at Swansea; Margaret and Rebecca Thomas were also accused of the same offence.[106] Early Welsh Friends often entered into disputation with ministers, especially in Glamorganshire and Monmouthshire.[107] In a clash between Gawler and Joshua Miller two different accounts of what ensued have survived.[108] In autumn 1655, Gawler was challenged by Miller and another Puritan minister, Edmund Ellis, to engage in a public debate. Gawler interrupted Miller while he was delivering his sermon at St Andrew's Church in Cardiff. Miller bade him sarcastically to 'Go stitch thy hats',[109] and left the pulpit. The following day, Gawler was summoned before the local magistrates, but was acquitted on the grounds that Miller had issued the challenge in public. The acquittal provoked Miller's fervent condemnation of the Quakers in his tract, *Antichrist in Man: The Quaker's Idol*, which claimed that as an outsider in Wales he had become a prime target. In September 1655, he had argued with Gawler about Christ's ascension into Heaven and again over whether a man-made ministry was a legitimate Christian institution. Miller publicly criticized Gawler for his abuse of the church and its ministers. Later, when Gawler tried to enter into a correspondence with Miller on the subject of Quaker theology, his challenge was rejected. Each disputant viewed the situation from their own self-interested position and the differences between them were irreconcilable.

Friends continued to disrupt church services in Wales throughout the 1650s. According to Thomas Holme's account, there were 'few dayes but wee have meetings in on[e] place ore outher which is a torment to the prestes & makes them mad'.[110] In 1658, Revd Jenkin Jones of Faenor was disturbed by Meredith Edward who was pulled out of the church by the congregation,[111] and John Brown was imprisoned for disturbing a clergyman after a 'threshing' meeting at Caerwent in 1658 with Thomas Holme. He was soon joined in prison by Holme, and upon their release they were both escorted from the county by several constables.[112] On several occasions local mobs, or 'rude people',[113] were instructed by clergymen and magistrates to restrict the movement of Friends or attack them. In 1657, George Fox met with 'rude treatment' during a visit to Brecon when the townsfolk, urged on by the magistrates, 'gathered up the town so that for about two hours together there was such noise as the like we had not heard'.[114] In 1658, Meredith Edward was arrested as he attempted to testify against Revd Henry Morgan of Trefddyn. He was assaulted by Thomas Jones who 'strook him athwart the face' and brought him before the magistrate at Abergavenny. He spent five weeks in Usk gaol before being released by the Quarter Sessions.[115] Later on, Edward was charged with disrupting a church service in Glamorgan and calling the vicar 'a thief and hireling'. The magistrate ignored his protestations, tried to 'stop his mouth with a handkerchief, and took him by the throat' before committing him to Bridewell Prison where he was flogged. He was eventually reprieved by Major John Gawler, the Quaker magistrate.[116] In the same year, Francis Gawler was attacked by 'drunkards, swearers and scolding women', and those who had been in 'arms against the Commonwealth'.[117] In the final year of the Commonwealth, Elizabeth Holme and Alice Birkett repeatedly harassed the clergy. At the funeral of Henry Walter's wife in Newport, Walter Cradock condemned such behaviour and objected to the provocative presence of Holme and Birkett. The Friends had little sympathy for him and judged him to be 'a wicked man'.[118]

Quakers were also punished under the Vagrancy Act,[119] which was an established mechanism for moving on troublesome citizens. As Friends recorded in the Great Book of Sufferings,

Such was the rage & envy of this generation against an Innocent People that neither age or sex could be exempted from their cruelty . . . [they] deprived them of liberty of travelling from one pish to another or to abide peaceably in their owne habitations.[120]

In 1659, Elizabeth Holme and Alice Birkett were charged with vagrancy.[121] The issuing of warrants in 1660 by magistrates in Wales to 'cause a sufficient watch within your parish both day and night' encouraged the judiciary to detain Friends on flimsy evidence. Watchmen and constables were informed that Quakers and Anabaptists should not be

> suffered to goe from one pish to another, or to gather together to any meeting or conventicle . . . [and to] . . . have a speciall care to ensure all the Quakers within your pish untill you receive further order from the justices. Whereof faile you not at your p[er]ill.[122]

In June 1660, three Merionethshire Friends were violently beaten, forced to walk 3 miles and placed in the stocks. Their assailant, Alban Vaughan, later seized one of their horses and riding equipment as well as the goods they had been carrying.[123] In another case, the authorities in south Wales pursued Elizabeth Holme as she travelled from Monmouthshire to Cardiff in the early months of 1661. The magistrates made arrangements to have her arrested quickly. A serving maid, who was suspected of being in league with Friends, was arrested as was the town watchman for allowing Holme to enter Cardiff. The magistrates seized her horse, and imprisoned her groomsman. Afterwards, Holme tried to reclaim her property, but was imprisoned along with her husband.[124] Also, in 1661 several Carmarthenshire Quakers were attacked while travelling through the county and, in May 1679, Phillip Leonard and Howell Jones were brought before the Carmarthen Assizes under the vagrancy laws, and for being 'disaffected to the present government of this realm and the protestant religion'. At their trial they refused to tender the oaths, and were imprisoned along with James Picton, a Quaker schoolmaster from Tenby.[125] Picton had already spent 'above nine years' in prison (c.1663–72) on a charge of praemunire.[126]

In 1658, John Thomas of Goldcliffe refused to accept the position of constable because he would be required to take an oath. For his trouble, he was sentenced to four months' imprisonment at Usk, 'greatly to the hurt and suffering of his family'.[127] The punishment did not act as a deterrent for he later condemned the payment of tithes.[128] In similar cases throughout the seventeenth and eighteenth centuries, Quakers were selected as constables and sheriffs only to be fined for their refusal to serve. This abuse was finally brought to an end in 1734.[129] In October 1660, twenty south Wales Quakers were sent to Cardiff gaol for their refusal to tender the oaths.[130] Following the abortive uprising of Thomas Venner's Fifth Monarchists in January 1661, church ministers lived in constant fear of a resurgence of the 'Good Old Cause', and their panic helps to explain the virulent persecution of Friends in this period.[131] John Husband, a shoemaker from Carmarthenshire, was viciously attacked while visiting Whitland fair, and nearly had his nose cut off.[132] Several Friends were apprehended by the 'watch' while travelling around Monmouthshire and taken before the magistrates where they were interrogated. They were imprisoned for refusing to swear allegiance to the king. Even when Friends professed themselves to be loyal subjects, it availed them nothing. On 31 January 1661, Walter Jenkins, Charles Jenkins, a yeoman of Wonastow, and John and Phillip Williams, of Cwmcarfan parish, were forced to walk through 'dirt and mire more like cattle to a market or sheep to the slaughter than like men, not suffering them to go the footway which was by the horseway, using many opprobrious reproachfull and provoking words, yea such was their malice and cruelty', and were imprisoned in Monmouth gaol. At the Sessions court, they were treated viciously by the mayor who beat one of the Quakers and tugged at his beard more 'like an Egyptian taskmaster than a Christian magistrate'.[133]

Punitive measures were put in place to ensure that the population attended church on Sundays and feast days, and to curtail the activities of itinerant Quakers. Travel on Sundays had been limited by an ordinance of 1644 to those who could show just cause. The penalty for disobedience was a 5s fine or three hours in the stocks. In 1656, an *Act for the better observation of the Lord's Day* forbade the opening of shops on holy days. In January 1661, three Monmouthshire Quakers were charged with vagrancy on the Sabbath.[134] Quakers were prosecuted for opening shops on Christmas Day. As they believed that Christmas Day encouraged idleness, Friends continued to keep their shops open until evening. In 1668, William Dawson was told to close his shop as a mark of respect for the Christian celebration, or face having his goods seized. Furthermore, the town clerk encouraged 'a company of boyes' to threaten both Dawson and Roger Scudamore. Dawson was infuriated by the vengeful nature of his adversaries, expecting 'no justice nor equity from them'.[135] Friends had good reason to believe that they were 'brutalized by law-enforcement officers, informers, and the militia, and that they were victimised by unethical and illegal tactics',[136] but in this instance the refusal to close their shops on Christmas Day displayed a blatant disregard for the religious sensibilities of others and is difficult to defend. It was hardly likely to endear them to their neighbours.

Many clergymen forbade Quakers to bury their dead in churchyards and so they were forced to acquire their own burial plots. It is then all the more extraordinary that some Friends were prosecuted for burying their dead outside church grounds. In 1666, Phillip Williams of Cwmcarfan and William David from Talgarth, Breconshire, were imprisoned for burying a fellow member in unconsecrated ground.[137] The reason for such punitive action seems to be more prosaic than pious: although there was no legal requirement, traditionally a fee was paid to both parson and churchwarden. If it could be proven that the incumbents were being deprived of their dues, Friends could be prosecuted under common law.[138] The refusal of Friends to engage ministers for religious ceremonies caused great resentment since it deprived the clergy of a lucrative source of revenue. William David's letter to Fox sheds additional light upon the circumstances of his imprisonment for thirty-six days 'without bed or soo much as a little straw'. His prolonged incarceration owed much to the malign intervention of Lewis Morgan, who was an attorney to Charles II. Morgan lived near the Quaker burial ground and had ordered the bodies to be exhumed. George Fox, while travelling through Wales in 1668, discovered that Williams and David were held under an order of *excommunicato capiendo* which allowed sheriffs to detain Friends until they acknowledged their guilt, paid their legal costs and agreed to abide by the court's ruling.[139] The expense and complexities involved in enforcing such edicts usually deterred magistrates, and probably saved many Dissenters from longer spells of imprisonment.

Studies of Quaker persecution have shown that attacks on members were sporadic; they turned upon the whim of local magistrates and mostly coincided with periods of acute political turmoil. There is evidence to suggest that some magistrates exercised tolerance provided that Quakers posed no threat. When Elizabeth Holme was brought before the magistrates in May 1659 for disturbing Walter Cradock in Newport, they refused to prosecute her.[140] Bailiffs and constables could also exercise leniency. John ap John was freed by the bailiff, Roger Sheares, in Cardiff because he had 'little desire to persecute him'.[141] In 1659, Alice Birkett was brought before a constable in Haverfordwest for being a vagabond, but he 'having less enmity, and more wisdom then the magistrates', released her.[142] The pre-Restoration correspondence of Thomas Holme and Francis Gawler suggests that even those who held high office could be won over. In 1656, Holme wrote that Major-General James Berry had

> spoken much in the be halfe of frinds which keeps down the per[se]cuting spirits in theas parts, and we heard he impresoned t[w]o beadles for putting t[w]o frinds out of the town of Monmouth, and he reproved the maire sharply which hath given a great dash in thease parts to the percuting spirits.[143]

There is evidence too that Quakers and the authorities could occasionally cooperate with each other. Francis Gawler asked Fox in 1660 whether his brother, John, ought to accept a commission as Lieutenant-Colonel in the Glamorgan militia as Bussy Mansel, the high sheriff of Glamorgan, was keen to include Quakers in his forces.[144] Francis Gawler acknowledged the reservations the Society had about military activity, but added that Matthew Gibbon had 'partly Ingaged to bee A Captan And A nother a privat souldger'. At this early stage the Society was prepared to allow John Gawler to take up his commission, along with other Quakers from mid and north Wales.[145] In March that same year, Thomas Holme recalled that nineteen Pont-y-Moel Friends were released from gaol by two gentlemen who 'apeared very modest to us and did not soe much as reugier [require] any one to put of[f] a hat'.[146] Equally, Richard Davies acknowledged that the Montgomeryshire high sheriff 'continued loving and kind to Friends', and this was mirrored by his deputy and several local magistrates. Similar beneficence was apparent in Cardiganshire where the deputy sheriff and high constable treated Friends 'very civilly' and turned to Quakerism themselves.[147] On a visit to London in the mid-1670s, Davies visited Lord Powis and his wife, for they were 'particular friends' who were prepared to write to the Duke of Beaufort, the Lord-President of Wales, to 'stop the rage and ruin against Friends in that country'.[148] However, in 1675, the behaviour of Merioneth Quakers, who stood in the market 'like fooles in Bedlam', prompted Robert Wynne of Gwnnodl Glyndyfrdwy to insist that magistrates and constables prosecute Friends according to the law.[149] In the same year, Rondl Davies, the vicar of Meifod, published *Profiad yr Ysprydion, neu Ddatcuddiad Gau Athrawon, a rhybudd iw gochelyd* (A Tryall of the Spirits or a Discovery of the false Prophets, and a Caveat to beware of them), against the Lloyd family of Dolobran, and in the early 1680s called on William Lloyd, bishop of St Asaph to prosecute Friends.[150]

In periods of heightened political tension, notably 1660–7, 1670–2, 1679–83 and 1685–6, magistrates were more likely to move against clandestine assemblies and recusants. Hugh Roberts believed that 1672 was 'the hottest time of persecution that ever we underwent in that part of the country. The chief Informer being a cunning subtill man.'[151] Between 1673 and 1680, Thomas Wynne frequently appeared before the Court of Great Sessions for different infringements of the penal laws, including 'following [his] own sensuality', persuading his neighbours to 'desist from the true Protestant Religion' and for simply 'being a quaker'.[152] In the early years of the 1680s, Richard Davies stated that persecution in Wales was 'very sharp and severe', and in 1685, upon the accession of James II, remarked that the recusancy laws were more strictly applied to Friends.[153] Yet, as Friends adopted a less militant approach, they began to influence politicians and local authorities. Consequently, magistrates and some church leaders exercised their power more judiciously. In the early 1680s, Bishop Lloyd of St Asaph summoned 'all sorts of dissenters to discourse with him', especially Thomas Wynne,[154] Thomas and Charles Lloyd, and Richard Davies.[155] In April 1685, the Welsh Yearly Meeting noted that Friends in Monmouthshire were 'kept out of their meeting house',[156] but by the beginning of 1686 relations were more 'peaceable'.[157] Although Friends in north Wales could not secure the release of a prisoner in Caernarfon, they noted that the magistrates were again 'pretty loving' towards Friends.[158] This may have been in response to the appeals made by George Whitehead and Richard Davies to Lord Powis the previous year.[159]

Every village was responsible for the welfare of its inhabitants, and local people acted as the guardians of the common good. It was socially and financially important to secure the good regard of the local community and few would have willingly chosen to be outcasts. Despite the prevailing fear that Quakers were 'a dangerous sort of People', they were sometimes protected by their neighbours and non-Quaker relatives.[160] The influence of Quaker gentry families, such as the Lloyds of Dolobran, was a significant factor, and it has been claimed that if moderate Dissenters were 'well-regarded and decent neighbours . . . [they] were allowed to live almost as normally as members of the church'.[161] Yet, social status afforded little protection to those who resisted payment of the tithe, or who displayed recusant or Quaker proclivities, for any infringement was likely to attract heavy fines or imprisonment.[162] Robert Owen of Dolserau's prominent position in county politics engendered a certain amount of jealousy, and his role as sequestrator of estates in 1651 created a number of enemies. His conversion to Quakerism provided his opponents with the opportunity to settle long-standing grievances. A forged letter in December 1662 implicated him in a rebellion against the recently restored monarchy, leading Friends to record that 'the Divell inventeth one snare after another to entrapp and catch the Innocent Lambs of Christ'.[163] Influential Quakers also appear on the recusancy lists, particularly from Montgomeryshire from the early 1660s onwards.[164] In south Wales, the

Hanbury family dominated the Monmouthshire lists throughout the 1680s.[165] Richard Hanbury and his wife, Elizabeth were both fined £11 in 1686 for non-attendance at church services while living in Bristol.[166] It was sometimes the case that poorer members who were fined for attending Quaker conventicles had their fines paid by other members. For example, in 1688 Ann Hugh of Mamheilad had her £1, recusancy fine paid by William Ridley.[167] The refusal to pay left many Friends vulnerable to abuse by the church or court officials. If successful lawsuits were brought against Quakers the impropriator could claim damages which effectively trebled the original demand. This often warranted seizure of property and produce far in excess of the tithe, and caused great hardship.[168] William Roberts, a poor man of Llanfair Isgoed, was distrained of all of his goods in 1682 for meeting at a conventicle, a much larger penalty than the original fine.[169] Poor Quaker families, who could hardly cope with the loss of one pot or pan, let alone the distraint of farm produce, were often left to survive at subsistence level.

Many Friends were prepared to go to prison rather than pay such fines. The length of imprisonment varied enormously from a few days to a few years. For example, Robert Owen of Dolserau was imprisoned for five and a half years.[170] Prison conditions were appalling; prisoners were kept in foul-smelling and disease-ridden pits or dungeons.[171] Twenty-one Quakers died while imprisoned in the years leading up to 1659, and an estimated three hundred or more Friends died between 1659 and May 1660.[172] Only rarely were Friends given access to the upper levels of gaols where the air was fresher; more often than not such requests were denied. In 1657, the excrement of 'felons and other malefactors' fell upon several unfortunate Montgomeryshire Quaker freeholders who were housed in the chamber below.[173] Four years later, three Glamorganshire Quakers were imprisoned in a cellar for between four and five months 'without the Common Benefit of air allow'd to Felons', and another four Friends were incarcerated in a cellar in Merthyr Tydfil without fresh air or any visitors.[174] The conditions were so bad in Usk gaol in January 1661 that the gaoler took several sick Quakers to his own house.[175] In the same year, a petition to the king and Parliament was sent from Welsh Friends who gave a graphic account of their treatment. In Pembrokeshire, eighteen Friends were committed to a 'nasty, stinking, cold Place'. Radnorshire and Merionethshire Friends were threatened with swords, and one of the assailants in the latter county 'threatened to knock them on the head with an Ax'. In Montgomeryshire, eight Friends were imprisoned and often denied water or food, and were forced 'to lay six nights on the bare boards without straw . . . and not suffered to ease themselves, but are forced to do it where they lodge'.[176] Shortly afterwards, ten Montgomeryshire Friends complained to the magistrates that their co-religionists were denied visitors while in prison, 'though drunkards, liars, thieves and robbers' were allowed them.[177]

It has been suggested that in the post-Restoration period only five Welsh Friends died in prison while the penal code was in operation.[178] Among them were Edward Evans of Montgomeryshire who died in 1664 after being imprisoned for eighteen months for refusing to swear the oath of allegiance, and the following year Humphrey Wilson died 'of a Distemper contracted thro the coldness and unwholsomness' of his prison. Another Friend from the same county, Thomas Hammond, died while imprisoned in 1674.[179] Little account was taken of gender, age, or infirmity when Quakers were imprisoned. The incarceration of Elizabeth Holme and Alice Birkett in 1659 at Haverfordwest was made all the more unpleasant by the gaoler's constant threats to have them clapped in irons.[180] In 1660 David Jones, 'a very aged man', was imprisoned at Cardiff for refusing to swear the oath of allegiance,[181] and in 1661 a poor Glamorganshire woman and her blind husband were imprisoned for several weeks in 'a nasty stinking cocks loft'.[182] In March 1665, Phillip Williams was imprisoned for a very paltry sum owed to John Hardwicke of Mitchel Troy. He was held prisoner for over two years in spite of being a widower with three small children.[183]

In the early years of the movement, Friends' attachment to millenarianism helped them to cope with the worst ravages of persecution.[184] The conviction that the imminent coming of Christ would end their suffering gave them courage to

113

face imprisonment and other forms of persecution. In 1659, Francis Gawler attested that it was 'a great joy . . . to suffer for righteousness sake, and in so doing we have peace and joy which no man can take away'.[185] Friends likened their suffering to that of the early Christians who chose to suffer rather than deny their faith.[186] Richard Davies wrote that it was better 'to suffer affliction with the people of God, than to enjoy the pleasures of sin for a season'.[187] They believed that, as they were fighting the Lamb's War, suffering had to be borne patiently and without complaint. Friends were nevertheless keen to testify to their tribulations as their numerous tracts and epistles demonstrate. Francis Gawler's 1659 testimony, *A Record of some persecutions*, is important as is the travelogue of Thomas Briggs, *An Account of Some of the Travels and Sufferings of that Faithful Servant of the Lord*.[188] During his visit to south Wales in 1657, George Fox had earlier compared the hostility of the Brecon mob to that which attacked St Paul at Ephesus, and had 'the Lord's power not prevented them they might have plucked down the house and us to pieces'.[189] The Welsh Yearly Meeting address in April 1688 asked that Friends

> be not dismayed or discouraged, by reason of stormes & tempests, even if the proud waves of the sea should yet happen to arise, or be lifted up against you, may appear terrible & formidable, yet the Lord our God is able by the arme of his great powr to altr & change the purposes of the ungodly, & to bring stillness, calmness and quietness.[190]

Friends believed that God directly intervened in their lives. One of the most interesting examples of this occurred in 1663 when Frances Bowen, a poor widow from Llanfihangel-Roggiet, was distrained of her property for non-payment of tithes between November 1662 and February 1663. The bailiff, who was acting on the orders of Revd Morgan Jones, took away two cows and a horse valued at £3. for a 2s. tithe. After the second distraint, the widow called upon God to judge between her and the priest. A fellow Quaker proclaimed that Jones's action was against God's law and he would be punished. Ten days later, 'to the amazemt of all yt did heare, & understand', the clergyman died and the poor widow claimed that this was divine retribution.[191] Likewise, Friends drew their own conclusions when the tormentor of John Humphrey of Merionethshire died from 'a sore Distemper in his Limbs' shortly after mocking him, and after John Swayn, who had persecuted Thomas Ellis of Is Cregennan, was 'struck dead on the highway in a most strange and terrable manner'.[192]

By the mid-1660s the Society had, however, become less vociferous, and their meetings were far removed from the antagonistic 'gatherings' of the Interregnum. Many Quakers now viewed their own sufferings as a test of loyalty to God and an ordeal that had to be endured with patience. The earlier resolve to challenge their persecutors gave way to a determination to outwit their adversaries. Friends poured over legal texts in order to find ways of avoiding detention by constables and magistrates. Even in the pre-Restoration period they used the law as a weapon against their opponents. For example, in 1659 Friends argued that some Quakers who were detained for disturbing clergymen were illegally prosecuted. The law stated that Friends had to be seen to have a malicious intent in disturbing ministers during the service. When Francis Gawler was brought to trial he said: 'You have asked us many questions and you cannot say that you are dissatisfied in any one in particular.' His offence was preaching in the vicinity of the church and disturbing the congregation. But it is likely that the magistrates were incensed that the Quakers had engaged the interest of the people who 'came forth of the Steeple-house to our meeting'. Gawler and his fellow Quakers asserted that they had not broken any law or caused a disturbance as they had not come 'wilfully, maliciously, and of set purpose so as to make disturbance'. Their confinement was short-lived, and they were soon at liberty, holding an impromptu meeting in a local inn where a large crowd gathered.[193] The establishment of Monthly and Quarterly Meetings, coupled with the recommendations of the leadership, led to the reconstitution of the Quaker movement. From this point onwards, the Elders of the Society exerted greater authority and imposed a code of conduct that was based on 'approved practices and principles'.[194] J. F. MacGregor has argued that with the Restoration the leading

Quakers diverted their efforts from proselytizing to a consolidation of the Society. He suggests that this was achieved by 'subordinating the liberty of individual inspiration to the charismatic monopoly of Fox and the so-called weighty Friends'.[195] Deviant or ranting activities which had provoked widespread hostility were no longer accepted by the Society. Moreover, the adoption of the Quaker code of conduct led to a movement away from ranterism. Unfortunately, many of the schisms within the movement during the remainder of the seventeenth century were a direct response to this change in emphasis and opposition to members who displayed ranter characteristics. Richard Davies recalled that John Perrot caused an upheaval in 1660s, and, at a meeting at Welshpool, John Whitehouse, a follower of Perrot, had 'sown an evil seed . . . which led them to have a light esteem of their brethren'. This included Cadwalader Edwards who was testified against in 1668.[196]

By voicing their collective disapproval of the church and tithes, and their preparedness to suffer for their beliefs, Friends established a tight-knit community. In October 1683, Monmouthshire Friends sought assistance from the Meeting for Sufferings against charges of recusancy, a demand of 20s. a month and their presentment before the sheriff. Friends were advised to appear before the court 'and save their being taken', or to seek advice from the sheriff two or three days before the court appearance.[197] The rationale was quite clear. They recognized that non-attendance prevented Friends from presenting their case and defending their beliefs, while compliance with the law would serve to reduce the antagonism with the civil and church authorities. Friends were called upon to petition local dignitaries and to persuade judges, magistrates and juries to exercise leniency.[198] In their appeals, they explained that presentments stemmed from matters of conscience rather than obstinacy or a desire to cause offence to the authorities.[199] Later on, the Meeting for Sufferings offered advice on the proving of wills,[200] spoke on behalf of Friends to their persecutors,[201] and provided money for the dependants of imprisoned Friends.[202]

Although the fiercest periods of persecution were over by the accession of William and Mary, discrimination did not entirely cease.[203] Many Friends still suffered under the penal code, especially by having to prove their loyalty to the king and his government by signing a document, witnessed by six Quakers. Friends also had to bear the burden of tithes throughout the eighteenth century and beyond. The long years of persecution had, however, hampered the progress of the Quaker movement. The frequent imprisonment of Quaker leaders obstructed the spread of Quaker ideology, while excessive fines and tithe distraint acted as financial deterrents to possible converts. Nonetheless, Friends were now free to hold meetings for worship, albeit on condition that their gatherings were not held in secret or behind closed doors.

For many years after 1689, Quakers were excommunicated for non-attendance, harassed by the clergy and the courts, as well as imprisoned for their refusal to pay tithes or supply the militia with substitutes. The provocative actions of Friends still rankled in the minds of clergyman. The very presence of Friends could arouse hostility,[204] and accusations of deviancy were still made despite their newly found respectability. Thus, in 1690, when Carmarthenshire Quakers objected to the excessive demands of the Poll tax, Roger Manwaring, a Llandovery magistrate, wanted them to be hanged.[205] Some members continued to behave like ranters. For example, William Jenkins of Goetre was condemned for his 'very pre-sumptuous blasphemous Ranting spirit'.[206] Although Friends were tolerant, his behaviour reflected badly upon the Society.[207] On 24 July 1707, the Society for the Promotion of Christian Knowledge (SPCK) commented on the growth of the Quaker community at Llantrisaint in Glamorgan follow-ing the return of John Bevan from America. Revd Richard Harris complained, and as a result the SPCK agreed 'to putt some of the Tracts agt the Quakers in to the next packet that shall be sent to him'.[208]

Friend's determination to hold outdoor or 'gathered' meet-ings throughout Wales aggravated the situation. In 1707, the Revd Thomas Andrews of Trefddyn objected that

for some weeks past [Friends had] taken a very Riotous Liberty of assembling in the open streets ... they invidiously and falsly reproach'd our Establish'd Worship, as Anti-Scriptural and Carnal; Our Ecclesiastical Discipline, as Tyrannical and Ungodly; and the Ministers of Religion, as Mercenary and Hypocritical, regarding more the handfulls of Barley, than the Good of Souls.[209]

He condemned their visit to a sick clergyman's wife, Barbara James, which he claimed left her ranting for several days.[210] The virulence of his attack clearly shows the antipathy towards Quakers in certain parts of Wales. In the same year, Roger Jenkin of Monmouthshire and several Glamorganshire Friends were indicted 'for a Ryot' at Cowbridge. They were accused of not subscribing to the Declaration of Allegiance, holding an unlicensed meeting and conducting an assembly on the common.[211] The Friends were denied a copy of the indictment 'unless they appeared in court and demanded it'.[212] The disruption of church services had not ceased either. Revd Andrews insisted that, 'for all their pretended meekness in turning t'other cheek upon an Inquiry, they can yet (occasionally) give me first blow, and, without any provocation, fly in the face even of the Constitution itself'.[213] He claimed that on 22 January 1707 his service in Trefddyn was disrupted by Christopher Meidel, a Norwegian Quaker.[214] Andrews felt that the Quakers had 'insulted the Constitution' and, although toleration had been granted, the government should not countenance any challenge to the church's authority.[215] In their defence, Friends argued that the accusation of riotous assembly could not be substantiated as the Society 'neither use force nor Arms, nor had any other Intent than to worship the Lord'.[216]

The reluctance of Quakers to close their premises on Sundays or holy days led to the appearance of two Pontypool Friends at the Llandaff bishop's court. Elisha Beadles and Mary Rosser were finally excommunicated in 1706 for having acted inappropriately on Good Friday. They appealed to the archbishop of Canterbury to lift the excommunication order as they had been illegally cited to appear before Llandaff ecclesiastical court. This was important because the excommunication order damaged their trade. Many people capitalized on the situation and sought to avoid paying their debts. For their part, the Friends were unable to prosecute their debtors until the excommunication order was lifted.[217] The London correspondents defended the Pontypool Friends by pointing out that two markets had been held on Good Friday, and that the evidence supplied by the two informants was contradictory. They suggested that opening shops on Good Friday was no worse than allowing people to play nine-pins, and for Revd Andrews 'to play with them (as reported) after he comes from saying or reading his service'.[218]

After the early decades of the eighteenth century, relations gradually improved. In 1743, the Welsh Yearly Meeting called upon members to be more circumspect in their relations with the authorities: 'In all manner of conversation let none be rash and forward in entering into disputes with any (preachers or others) . . . Other wise you may do harm.'[219] In 1746, Joseph Rule, a Quaker gentleman from Llanfair Isgoed, proposed a preaching tour throughout the 'West Country'. Friends refused his request because it might bring them 'to blame by disturbing ye National way of Worship under whose mild Government we enjoy such liberty'.[220] They were anxious not to annoy the more influen-tial sections of the community as this would have jeopardized the cordial arrangements that existed between them. Even so, in the post-Toleration years, Quakers were still punished for non-payment of the tithe.[221] A damning critique of the clergy and the tithes was written in 1741 by Thomas Lewis of Shirenewton who stated that:

> If a poor man have a few goats upon a free common they claim a share in them, if a poor widow have a couple of ewes and lambs they likewise claim a share in them, but if a weak one or Fatherless that lie upon a Bed of Straw perhaps with hungry Bellies . . . and any of them happen to meet any such poor Fatherlesss or any weak old Body in the way, it is much if they open their mouths unto them much less give them any Advice concerning their latter end.[222]

Quaker farmers continued to lose their most valuable crops and the tradespeople their most expensive cloth and groceries, while poorer Friends, such as widows, were distrained even of their kitchen utensils. Between 1690 and 1736, an estimated 1,100 Friends were prosecuted in the Exchequer court for non-payment of tithes, and between 1700 and 1740 more than £167,000 had been taken in fines.[223]

One well-documented case concerns the prosecution of Joshua Williams in the court of the Exchequer in August 1705 for a 40s. tithe.[224] William Ketchmay, along with his attorney and a bailiff, seized 'all ye corn he had in the world' and two cows to the value of £30. The following month, Ketchmay returned and sequestered hay and straw, leaving Williams with nothing.[225] The Ketchmay family expressed their intention of making a 'Sacrifice of one of the Quakers'. Yet, in spite of being financially ruined, Joshua Williams was steadfast and he issued this challenge to the clergyman:

> if he [Ketchmay] can clear himself from being Unmerciful, Covetous or being an Extortioner, let him . . . and prove by the Holy Scripture, whether his Demands, Practice and Conversation, are like to a Minister of Christ, who said . . ., *Freely ye have received, freely give*; but never sent his Ministers to Ruine honest and industrious People, for Non-payment of Tythes.[226]

The burden of distraint and subsequent subpoenas and imprisonment naturally bore hard upon Quakers and many chose to emigrate to America as a means of escape. In 1711, Joshua Williams requested a certificate of removal and joined many other Quakers who had left Wales for Pennsylvania.[227]

Friends made an unsuccessful appeal to Parliament in 1735 against Exchequer and consistory court proceedings,[228] but at the local level many authorities were less zealous in their pursuit of the non-payment of tithes. This change in attitude partly reflected greater acceptance of Friends among the wider community. When the apothecary Elisha Beadles was distrained of his goods in 1733, the magistrates were reluctant to grant the warrant or add further costs, not least because several customers 'seem'd very much concern'd at it'.[229] In 1734, Jonathan Barrow reported that 'one Parson Holland never troubled him for any of his demands'.[230]

It would seem that the transition of Friends from a radical sect into a quietist denomination and an awareness of their 'good neighbourliness' and philanthropic work had made them more acceptable to the local community. Although tithes were still extracted as a matter of course, they were less likely to be accompanied by the heavy-handed tactics of the past. Family and communal ties between Quakers and non-Quaker families which had been severed during the formative years of the Society were gradually re-established. The entrepreneurial skills of leading Friends provided work for the local community, while other members played a greater role in community affairs. There is evidence too which suggests that the payment of tithes by some Friends was not as onerous as some commentators have suggested. The minutes of Welsh meetings reflect the inability of members to adhere to the Society's rules.[231] Between 1688 and 1691, north Wales Friends were told to observe their testimony against tithes, while in the 1690s several Welsh Yearly Meetings noted 'a slackness' against resisting tithe payments.[232] At the Yearly Meeting at Builth in 1705, Quaker elders urged members to remember the 'former dayes in which you . . . were mocked, scoffed, persecuted and made a gazeing stock'. They castigated those who, 'instead of being good examples to others', persuaded neighbours and relatives to pay the tithe on their behalf.[233] In 1712, the Welsh Yearly Meeting warned Friends of the consequences if their instructions were not followed:

> their collections shall be refused by ye Frds of this Meeting & they not admitted to Meetings for Business, and if after all this they shall persist in such their unfaithfulness and opposition, that then this Meeting may further proceed to give judgment for ye clearing of ye truth.[234]

Yet even the threat of disownment did not have the desired effect. In 1746, the Welsh Yearly Meeting at Builth felt that it was necessary to testify against underhand methods of payment and evasive actions.[235] Nineteen years later, the Welsh Yearly Meeting at Hay noted that some Friends were still circumventing the rules.[236]

By examining the statistics of those who opposed tithe payment in Wales between 1682 and 1791 it is evident that this downward trajectory reflected a deeper malaise. In comparison with English counties, the distraint for non-payment in Wales was not substantial (see tables 4.1 and 4.2). For example, between 1720 and 1729, Monmouthshire Friends were distrained on average £7 per year[237] in comparison with Lancashire (£279), Lincolnshire (£391. 8s) and Somersetshire (£210).[238] The amount distrained was consistent with that taken in the 1690s and the early eighteenth century. There are gaps in the information, but nevertheless it is clear that in most years Pembrokeshire, Montgomeryshire and Radnorshire were more committed to the rule on non-payment of tithes than other Welsh counties. The limited number of distraints would suggest that only the more prosperous members were paying tithes, and Quakerism was judged to be less of a threat. The period between 1730 and 1739 has the same contrasting profile (Lancashire, £212. 8s; Lincolnshire, £219; Somersetshire, £220. 7s).[239] This evidence needs to be viewed with caution, for with a decreasing Quaker population there would naturally be fewer recorded cases of distraint.

Post-1689, Friends were also not free from abuse or imprisonment. Admittedly the cases were fewer, but some of the lengths of imprisonment reveal a deep-rooted desire by the clergy to punish Quakers. The death of John Merrick in Abergavenny gaol in 1700[240] illustrates this point as does the imprisonment of an eighty-year-old man, John Bevan of the Tref-y-Rhyg Meeting. He was imprisoned in 1720 for non-attendance at church.[241] The lengthy periods of imprisonment of both Roger and Thomas Jenkin in the early eighteenth century also shows the extent to which imprisonment was still being used to punish Friends for their refusal to pay tithes.[242] Occasionally, Quakers were punished for refusing to serve in the militia, provide a suitable replacement, or take up civil offices. In January 1707, James Lewis of Pembrokeshire was fined 40s. for refusing to serve as a high constable or supply a deputy.[243] In 1745, Nathaniel Beadles restated Friends' position on the militia: 'we ye Society of People called Quakers do not by any means take up arms'.[244] This was endorsed by the London Yearly Meeting and in their exchanges with the authorities in 1759 and 1778.[245] Two cases illustrate how Friends responded to the 'call to arms' and what punishments were exacted. In 1760 Samuel Richards, a labourer from Llanfrechfa, refused to serve in

Table 4.1. Tithe Distraints of Friends in Wales c.1720–1729

	Carms	Denb	Merion	Mon	Pembs	Rad	Shrop	Flint	Glam	Montg
1720	£7-16	£3-14	£12	£8-8-10	£45-2-2	£22-12	£10-19-6	–	–	–
1721	–	–	–	–	–	–	–	–	–	–
1722	–	–	–	–	–	–	–	–	–	–
1723	£11-7	£9-11-6	£7-15-10	£7-10	£55-14-5	£25-11	–	£3-14-3	£13-13	27-17-7
1724	£10-7-6	£18-1-0	£3-12-2	£5-14-10	–	£12-7-6	£6-5-00	£7-6-2½	£7-10-0	–
1725	£11-10	£20-19-3	£5-4-6	£17-3-	–	–	–	–	£4	–
1726	–	£14-14-0	–	£5-11-	–	–	–	–	–	–
1727	–	–	£5-19-8	£11-9-10	–	£7-00-0	£5-2-4	–	–	–
1728	–	–	–	£10-8-6	–	–	–	–	–	–
1729	–	–	–	£8-11-	–	–	–	–	–	–

QUAKER COMMUNITIES IN EARLY MODERN WALES

Table 4.2. Tithe Distraints of Friends in Wales c.1730–1739

	Carms	Denb	Merion	Mon	Pembs	Rad	Shrop	Flint	Glam	Montg
1730	–	–	–	–	–	–	–	–	–	–
1731	–	–	–	–	–	–	–	–	–	–
1732	–	–	–	–	–	–	–	–	–	–
1733	–	–	–	–	–	–	–	–	–	£14-4-3
1734	–	–	–	£13-16–	–	–	–	–	–	–
1735	£15-6–	–	£6-18-2	£1-3-6	£43-2–	£14-3–	–	–	–	£15-9-11
1736	–	–	£5-13–	£2-12-6	–	£46-5-6	–	–	£7-18-8	£12-2-7
1737	–	–	£6-4-2	£5-17-2	£39-9–	£19-14-6	£13-15–	–	£6-8-6	£10-3-6
1738	£15-19–	–	£6-11–	£-6-2	£22-16-4	£7-19–	£14-15–	–	£6-1-6	£8-00-9
1739	–	–	£7-16-6	–	£35-19–	£7-3–	£14-13–	–	–	£10-1-9

the local militia. As he had no property to distrain, he was imprisoned for three months. Ambrose Williams of Pontypool advised the Meeting for Sufferings that Richards's term of imprisonment was not onerous for he was not closely confined.[246] In 1767, Henry Powell, a grocer from Chepstow, also refused to serve in the militia or supply a replacement, and was fined three guineas; four loaves of sugar worth £3. 15s. were distrained from his shop.[247]

At the turn of the eighteenth century local attitudes changed perceptibly. There was a growing acceptance that persecution had not forced Dissenters to recant, and many acknowledged that the Quaker movement had retreated from its earlier radical position. On 10 January 1702 two Monmouthshire Friends, Thomas Wisdom and John Harris, warned the Crown of an imminent Jacobite invasion. They reported that a former footman of James II had revealed plans for 'a sudden invasion' to restore the Stuart monarchy.[248] Such overt displays of loyalty would have been unthinkable in the pre-Toleration years and its significance would have registered with the authorities. In his journal, Hugh Roberts, who had returned from Pennsylvania to Wales (c.1698), commented that in south Wales there was 'a great tenderness... amongst Friends and the world's people and some Presbyterians'.[249] Friends could now depend upon the assistance of influential members of the community in times of difficulty.[250] Following the imprisonment of John Richards and James Lewis of Shirenewton in 1731, Colonel Morgan of Tredegar and members of the Hanbury family intervened, and the two Friends were released in 1732.[251]

The Society became determined to preserve their respectability and standing in the community. They looked after their own poor and provided education for their children. The development of the certificate of removal and travel system meant that Friends were no longer subject to classification as vagrants and strangers. Such was the growing acceptance of Friends that in October 1735, a Monmouthshire Quarterly Meeting minute stated that 'we are really much indebted to the Lord for this Peaceable Time, when we may meet together... and none do molest us'.[252] When Evan Morgan, a yeoman of Langstone, died in January 1758, apart from the normal respect of members, it was said that he was 'well beloved by his neighbours'.[253] References to Friends in the eighteenth-century diary of William Thomas of Michaelston-Super-Ely registered the changed attitude towards Friends. Thomas observed that Evan Evans of Tref-y-Rhyg, who was buried in 1767, was 'a very Quiet sober man', and William Rees of Caerffili was 'a Civil, Innocent man, and one that leaded a strict life'.[254] Respectability rather than denomination was now the criteria for acceptance. By 1803, an application for a licence for a Quaker meeting house had become a formality.[255]

Chapter 5
'Faithful labourers in God's vineyard':
The Quaker Code of Discipline

The Quakers, as everybody knows, differ more than even many foreigners do, from their own countrymen. They adopt a singular mode of language. Their domestic customs are peculiar . . . They are distinguished from all other islanders by their dress. The differences are great and striking.[1]

While given to radical and unusual behaviour, membership of a meeting required a willingness to submit to a rigorous discipline in order to ensure that no member brought shame upon the Society. Friends advocated a rigid code of conduct which ensured that all aspects of life were controlled, and this strict adherence to a set of regulations distinguished them as a 'Peculiar People'.[2] This chapter will consider the extent to which Friends set themselves apart as a community in Wales by analysing the methods adopted to regulate the Society. It will also determine whether this code of conduct was specially chosen, or if it originated in earlier traditions. Tracts advocating a well-ordered life and identifying the pitfalls that could befall members were important. In the first of his four papers, Thomas Lewis of Shirenewton gave his own assessment of how to achieve salvation:

Thy Kingdom come; I doubt there is a great number of people that knows not where his kingdom should come; but fornicators, adulterers, thieves, and robbers, common drunkards and such as can call for damnation upon their brethren and fellow creatures, except they repent, his kingdom will not come; his kingdom will not come into an old nasty bottle: for new wine must be put into new bottles.[3]

Friends believed that salvation was open to everyone rather than to an elect,[4] as the will of Edward Webley of Shirenewton in 1674 shows:

> I commend my soule to Almighty God my Creator, assuredly believing That I shall receive full pardon and free Remission of all my sins, and that at the day of the Resurrection of the dead my soule to be saved by the precious death & meritts of my blessed Saviour and Redeemer Christ Jesus.[5]

Statements such as these were common in Quaker wills in this period.

As salvation rested upon leading a conspicuously virtuous life,[6] various protocols were put in place by Friends to regulate conduct. Leading members from within their own Monthly Meetings and from other Welsh meetings were called upon to examine Friends' behaviour and to dispense counsel to those who were found wanting.[7] These appointees or overseers would endeavour to reform those who had strayed by allowing them to explain the reasons for their failings. Periodically, Friends were warned to be diligent at prayer meetings and avoid drowsiness. Between 1695 and 1706, two Friends were appointed to 'admonish, exhort and reprove all yt are heavy, drowsy and sleepy, in or att meeting time'.[8] In 1753, John Churchman of Nottingham commented that at two meetings at Pontypool there was a 'want of order among them'.[9] The 'pernicious practice of sleeping' in meetings and frequenting taverns and alehouses were major concerns raised at the Welsh Yearly Meeting in Newtown in 1773.[10] Friends were constantly counselled and reproved for neglecting meetings, both individually and collectively. Absenteeism was usually linked to other misdemeanours such as fraternization with non-members, or other infringement of the code of conduct. If a member refused to condemn their behaviour and repent they were publicly exposed in the meeting. A copy of the testimony would be sent to the member, and it would also be declared at the Meeting for Discipline. If no reform was apparent, the meeting would draw up a paper of disownment which barred the offender from membership of the Society. Disownment protocols were a familiar mode of Puritan discipline and similar methods were employed by

Baptists and Independents. It was not a measure that Friends took lightly, but was regarded as a last resort after counselling. According to Richard Vann, however, the primary purpose of the disciplinary process was not to reform those who erred, but rather to protect the reputation of the Society as a virtuous and godly community.[11]

Tight controls were imposed on Friends. In their rejection of many traditional customs associated with the rites of passage, Friends set themselves apart from their neighbours. The individual's relationship with non-Quaker family members and neighbours was subject to the Society's approval and could be questioned. At all times the good of the Society assumed precedence. Quaker midwives were specially appointed to ensure that there was no contamination with 'the world's people', and to circumvent any surreptitious attempt to baptise the child, especially if the newborn was gravely ill. Thus, the Society intruded in aspects of life that would normally have been outside of their jurisdiction. On the rare occasions when a suitable midwife could not be found, as in the years between 1738 and 1742 in Pont-y-Moel, a non-Quaker midwife was allowed to attend the confinements of Mary Beadles, but several Quaker women were also present to ensure that the proprieties were upheld.[12] In the mid-nineteenth century, Quakers in south Wales sponsored a scheme for the provision of midwives for the poor.[13] The birth of a child into a Quaker family was a source of joy, but not a time for excessive celebration. The registration of the birth of an infant was conducted as if a business transaction had been made and no formal baptismal ceremony was held.[14] Quaker mothers refused to be 'churched' as this was regarded as a superstitious practice that had no scriptural justification. In 1723, John Kelsall of Montgomeryshire dreamt that a Friend was going to be 'churched' and in his dream he counselled the woman against such an action.[15] It is also noticeable that the Puritan trait of bestowing virtuous names upon children was quite rare. Quakers were more likely to choose biblical names.[16]

Friends valued education and endeavoured to give their offspring a good start in life.[17] Quaker parents were expected to bring up their children in a temperate manner which would ultimately lead to their 'convincement' in adulthood when they were admitted to full membership. It was accepted that much of this formative education was the mother's responsibility. The role of the father was to lead a family timetable of prayers, to impose discipline and inculcate Quaker values.[18] Friends chose to educate their children within the Society in order to avoid any corruption of their faith by outside influences, but detailed information about Welsh Quaker education is limited. In 1673, Bishop Lucy of St David's wrote to the archbishop of Canterbury protesting that James Picton of Carmarthen was keeping school for seventy or eighty scholars and thereby disseminating Quaker ideology.[19] After the Toleration Act, the Society began to establish schools based on a practical curriculum.[20] Parents and Quaker employers were encouraged to assist with the education of fellow members and they privileged literacy as a key skill. There were no purpose-built Quaker schools in Wales until a 'poor children's school' was established in 1793 at Llandiloes with one schoolmaster and one schoolmistress.[21] However, Friends' journals and meeting minutes give insights into the ad hoc provision that many communities put in place.

In 1701, the Dolobran meeting house in Montgomeryshire was used by John Kelsall as a school, and by 1703 there were fifty scholars.[22] At the same time, Pembrokeshire Friends had established a school at Haverfordwest.[23] In August 1709, Monmouthshire Friends acknowledged that they had failed to provide education,[24] and again in 1719 it was noted that 'at Pontymoile such [poor] children are far from ye school and so are yet unprovided'.[25] Individuals, such as John Burge of Haverfordwest and Thomas Jenkin of Llanfrechfa provided for their own children, but this did not address the problem of the poor.[26] Some schooling was provided for children at the Castleton Meeting in 1721,[27] but it was not until June 1725 that the Pont-y-Moel Monthly Meeting made their own arrangements.[28] Prominent well-educated Quakers were active in Wales in promoting educational initiatives. In the 1730s, Evan Bevan, an Oxford-educated Quaker, set up a school within the confines of the Pont-y-Moel meeting house. According to an extant testimony by Evan Rees,[29] Bevan kept a school for about thirty-five years.[30] A few children attended as boarders and 'a general day school' was held in the meeting house.[31] Bevan, it is said, 'would not teach any of the Heathenish Authors', but Quaker children acquired a knowledge of 'the useful parts of Literature, as Latin, Greek and Geography, with the various Branches of the Mathematicks'.[32] After Bevan's death in April 1746, the majority of children were educated locally. In 1747, Monmouthshire Friends produced a report stating that their children were being educated, but from 1748 the minutes show that the small numbers of children were too few to warrant specific provision.[33] Considerable emphasis was placed upon providing spiritual and moral guidance. The memoirs of John Fothergill, a Quaker doctor from London, are indicative of the pedagogical rationale employed by Friends in England and Wales. Friends' children were 'taught habits of regularity, of decency, and respectful subordination to their superiors, of forbearance, affection, and kindness towards each other; and of religious reverence towards their maker'.[34] In addition, they were instructed in the necessity for simple attire, obedience to the code of conduct and the avoidance of self-indulgence.

Such moralizing was dispensed alongside a standard basic education. In 1710, Elizabeth Lewis, a Glamorgan Quaker, provided for her daughter to attend school 'to learn to write and to learn plaine worke'.[35] In the 1734 pre-nuptial settlement of Barbara Howell of Pontypool specific allowance of £50 was made for each of her two children's education, 'together with a trade upon the son'.[36] Although there was no shortage of applicants for the position of teacher, many were rejected for being inadequate or non-members. Owen Bowen, a Carmarthenshire Friend, was offered the position of teacher at Pont-y-Moel in 1746 on condition that he reformed his behaviour.[37] The following year, William Tate of Pontypool, was ruled ineligible because he was not a Quaker.[38] In 1762, John Binns was appointed to teach at Pont-y-Moel meeting house,[39] and the following year he was succeeded by John Townsend, who proposed the setting up of a school in the Pontypool district.[40] In 1763, the Welsh Yearly Meeting at Presteigne recommended that the education of Friends ought to be a priority, especially as 'Divers of Friends Children are not taught to Read and Write'.[41] Wealthy Quaker parents were able to send their children to the English Quaker schools in Yorkshire and Somerset. John Forthergill bought an old hospital in 1778 for £7,000 and converted it into what became Ackworth School, where more than three hundred Quaker children were educated at a cost of eight guineas per year.[42] In 1808, Welsh Friends raised a subscription to set up Sidcot School in Somerset.[43] Despite the enormous fees imposed in such schools, the regime is said to have been harsh, though this was not unusual for the time.[44]

The dramatic increase in the population of south Wales not only created new social problems, but also ushered in an age where educational provision was seen as the optimum means of alleviating poverty and preventing disorder.[45] The Harford family were at the forefront of educational provision at the turn of the nineteenth century. In 1786, Edward Williams, a schoolmaster, was the first signatory on the register of Harford's Melingriffith Tinworks Benefit Club, Whitchurch, and funds were used to repair the school. In October 1807, John Harford invited Joseph Lancaster to give a lecture on the importance of education at a meeting at Melingriffith. As a consequence a committee was set up and £53 3s 3d was raised to establish a new works' school.[46] Sixty-two children from Whitchurch, Eglwysilan and Pentyrch attended the school in 1809.[47] Unfortunately the Melingriffith school declined rapidly after the Harfords left the area at the end of the decade.[48] A similar initiative was taken by the Swansea Quaker philanthropist, Richard Phillips, who founded two Lancastrian-type schools in Swansea.[49] In 1812, John and Richard Summers Harford provided rudimentary education for workers and their children at the Ebbw Vale works.[50] They built a new ironworks, school at Nant-y-glo in 1836 and a year later the school was enlarged.[51] By September 1841, however, a survey of education for children employed in mines and ironworks in the Ebbw Vale district concluded that 'the extensive and populous neighbourhood of Ebbw Vale remains destitute of almost every educational resource, excepting that of inferior Sunday Schools at the sectarian chapels, where large numbers attended but few teachers were forthcoming'.[52]

The decision to promote literacy was based on the belief that this would help secure suitable employment as well as enable Friends to be conversant with biblical texts. Friends made ample provision for their offspring and the children of poorer Friends, not least by allowing poor families access to books from the meeting house.[53] It is difficult to ascertain the impact of Friends' educational initiatives or assess levels of literacy. In the middle of the seventeenth century, it has been estimated that at least 70 per cent of Englishmen were unable to read fluently.[54] The marriage registers show that some Friends were sufficiently educated to be able to record their own names, but as an indicator of literacy this is not necessarily helpful. The couple intending to marry may not have signed their names; the clerk of the meeting may have done so on their behalf. The marriage of John Corbyn and Candia Handley in 1696 is a case in point for their signatures are written by the same hand.[55] Nevertheless, a general survey indicates that literacy was not the preserve of the wealthy, and many Quakers could read and/or write. Others, for example, Thomas Wisdom, a potter from Malpas parish, in 1709, and Evan Morgan, a labourer from Langstone, in 1758, were at least able to sign their wills.[56]

The Quakers believed that diligence was essential for any successful career and strove to direct their children towards a respectable profession. Young Friends were apprenticed to other members, especially in the ironworks established by Quaker entrepreneurs such as the Lloyd and Harford families, or to local Quaker blacksmiths and wheelwrights. Young women Friends were also taken into service by the more prosperous members of the Society. In 1703, west Wales Friends enquired whether members would offer a position to a young girl, and in 1742 the Monmouthshire Friends received the certificate of removal of Elinor Thomas of Carmarthenshire who had been taken into service by Nathaniel Beadles.[57] Apprentices not only learned a trade but were given instruction in their faith. George Harris, a Quaker doctor from Christchurch, bequeathed £10 to his nephew John Harris 'to put him to apprentice to learn the art or mystery of physick or chyrurgery' in 1709.[58] Richard Clarke left a legacy of £30 for the 'placing forth of six poor boys apprentice to some handy craft trades, in some market towns to be nominated in Herefordshire'.[59] In the mid-eighteenth century, the Richard Clarke legacy paid for two apprenticeships: William Bevan of Llandenni was apprenticed to a shoemaker and Henry Lewis of Shirenewton was apprenticed to a wheelwright.[60] Young apprentices were carefully monitored, but there were occasions when they were ill-treated by their employers or work associates. Christopher Herbert of Abergavenny admitted assaulting 'his fellow servant' in October 1708.[61] In March 1748, Samuel Biggam of Caerleon was accused of abusing his apprentice, William Evans, but an investigation revealed otherwise – even though he had prevented Evans from attending meetings. Eventually he was reprimanded for showing 'a bad example to his "prentice"'.[62]

Quaker businessmen were warned against extravagance and taught to be prudent. In 1742, Jane Evan of the Pont-y-Moel Meeting was advised to give up her farm as it was becoming 'burdensome' to Friends.[63] In 1819, the Yearly Meeting advised Friends to protect their business interests, especially as trade was depressed. It encouraged those in financial difficulties to seek assistance for this would 'often save the representation of individuals, call forth the respect and compassion of their creditors, prevent the keen sufferings of tender wives and innocent children'.[64] Those who became bankrupt were assisted provided that they were not demonstrably culpable. The assistance given to William Roberts of Llanfair Iscoed who was imprisoned for a debt in 1704[65] can be compared with Charles Lloyd III of Dolobran who grossly mismanaged his affairs in 1727, and was eventually testified against by the Welsh Yearly Meeting at Rhaedr in 1730. He was called upon to make restitution to his creditors and reconciled with Friends in 1742.[66] In the nineteenth century, Charles Napper of Newport who went into business with his father without realizing that the company was in grave difficulties was dealt with sympathetically by the Society.[67] Robert Hayward, a hill farmer of Abercarn, was less fortunate. He borrowed money for supplies, but as he was unable to meet the repayments he had his stock seized. He continued to make bond agreements even though he knew he could not honour them. The meeting duly disowned him for his ill-conceived business dealings, and he was imprisoned in 1823 after falling into debt.[68] Relatively few Welsh Friends are recorded as debtors, which may indicate that they were chary of taking risks or entering into partnerships without formal verification. Friends who transferred to other meetings had to produce a statement of their finances.[69] Financial difficulties were usually linked to either a family bereavement or the ravages of tithe imprisonment and sequestration of goods. To avert misfortune and assist those Quakers who were trying to construct their own businesses, Friends regularly intervened and offered financial support.[70]

Disputes between members, although rare, also fell within the remit of the code of conduct. At the Skipton Conference in 1653, George Fox advised Friends how to deal with differences of opinion.[71] Friends were expected to bring individual grievances before the Meeting for Discipline, and not to involve outsiders or the courts. When a dispute occurred overseers were appointed to arbitrate in order to effect a reconciliation.[72] Occasionally, however, Friends did resort to outside arbitration. In March 1713, in a dispute between Charles Hanbury of Pont-y-Moel and David Price of the Pant Meeting, both men agreed to the arbitration of Thomas Evan, Esquire, of Llangadog.[73] Unusually, in the early 1760s Friends were unable to reconcile Thomas Lewis and his sister-in-law, Elizabeth Lewis, both from Shirenewton; Thomas was disowned and Elizabeth admitted she was at fault.[74]

In conflicts of interest between the Monthly and Quarterly Meetings, the judgment of the latter took precedence. Appeals could also be made to the Yearly Meeting whenever necessary.[75] Most meetings worked together cooperatively, especially in defraying the expenses of poor members,[76] sharing the costs of meeting houses and locating displaced or errant Friends. Thus, the Pont-y-Moel meeting asked Glamorgan Friends for help in locating William Rowe, a known alcoholic. After evading censure for many years, he was testified against in 1800 for excessive drinking.[77] International cooperation was also strong, as illustrated by the various certificates issued by the Welsh Meetings for those

Friends who settled in Pennsylvania after 1682. For example, in the preamble to the certificate of Evan ap William Powell of Llanfachreth, Merionethshire, it was recorded that these documents were in response to 'many [who] have been known to transport themselves, or were transported upon the acc[oun]t of their Evill doeings, as theft, murther, Debts or running away in passionate discontentedness wth parents, wives or the like.' Powell's certificate stated that he been a Quaker for thirty years and was 'an [h]onest plain man, fearing god, and zealous of good works, not given to covetousness, inclinable to deeds of charity'.[78] The certificate of John Roberts of Penllyn in July 1683 similarly recorded that he had been a Friend for six years and was 'blameless in his conversation'.[79] A few years later, the certificate for Ellis and Sinai Pugh, formerly of Brithdir, stated that Ellis was

> greatly beloved of all honest, good, rational people ... His wife Sina we know her in her place as a good, careful, industrious woman in things relating to the poor, small children and family, wise, discreat & circumspect in her dealings and doings.[80]

These testimonies and certificates of removal served a dual purpose. Not only did they give an account of a worthy minister or Friend but they also provided examples of how members ought to conduct themselves privately and in public. Equally, meetings in Britain and Ireland exchanged information about errant or dishonest individuals who might try to abuse the hospitality and support of Friends, and bring the Society into disrepute. For example, in 1741 the Meeting for Sufferings warned Welsh Friends about the activities of George Cawdry who had cheated several meetings and their members for many years.[81]

Extravagance and high living were firmly denounced in accordance with the precepts of the 1689 Yearly Meeting in Breconshire.[82] Friends who infringed the code risked admonishment and possible disownment. They were required to be correct, 'holy and unblameable' in their conversation, 'as becomes the gospel of Jesus Christ'.[83] Testimonies by leading Friends were widely circulated to encourage members to observe the regulations on plainness.[84] The exemplary conduct of Barbara Bevan of the Tref-y-Rhyg Meeting was used as a model in the testimony of Elisha Beadles of how to foreswear worldly pleasures, to spend more time on the Bible and less on 'over curious dressing or decking of themselves at their mirror'.[85] Friends found such strictures difficult, and their preference for knee breeches, white bibs and traditional wide-brimmed hats set them apart from society.[86] Their puritanical attitude to dress was also applied to children at Quaker schools, such as Sidcot in 1809.[87]

Inevitably, some Friends did not abide by the regulations on dress.[88] The inventories that accompanied many wills demonstrate that wealthy Friends owned luxury goods and jewellery, as in the case of John Burge, a clothier for Haverfordwest, who in 1685 bequeathed a silver tankard, silver cup and silver spoons,[89] or John Richard, a tailor-doctor of Newport, who left a silver watch worth 15s in 1693.[90] John Beadles of the Pant went even further. In 1683, he entered his own family pedigree at the Herald's Visitation.[91] Friends' houses contained little in the way of decoration, for there were normally no pictures or portraits. However, a study of over one hundred Monmouthshire Quaker wills and administrations revealed items such as clocks, watches, gold plate, silver cutlery and jewellery as well as expensive clothing. For example, Edward Webley, a tanner from Shirenewton, left thirty pewter dishes, £5 in clothes and four brass kettles at his death in 1674,[92] and five years later his widow left six silver spoons, a clock and £8 in clothes.[93] The will of the Quaker doctor, John Jones of Llanfrechfa, bequeathed his silver plate and £21 in gold as well as a further £8 in clothes.[94] One interesting aspect of the dress code which has engaged Quaker historians is the ruling on the wearing of wigs.[95] Although this fashion was ubiquitous in the seventeenth and eighteenth centuries, there is little evidence to suggest that this unduly exercised Welsh Friends. On the contrary, Evan Bevan, the aged teacher of Pont-y-Moel, wore one in 1737 in order 'to defend his ears from the cold' and this attracted no criticism.[96]

Concerns about observing the code were regularly raised at the Welsh Yearly Meeting,[97] but featured only rarely in the constituent meeting minutes, implying that the code was instigated by the leadership rather than embraced by the ordinary members. In 1705, west Wales Friends endorsed the recommendations of London Yearly Meeting concerning the deportment and behaviour of Friends. At the following meeting members were warned to avoid 'the fashions & customs of the World ... in speach, apparell, furniture of houses & all super-fluities, so that we may all show forth the vertue of our holy profession in our vertious lives'.[98] The code nevertheless became more relaxed by the end of the eighteenth century, and Welsh Friends were prepared to modify their customs and dress.[99] Barry Reay appraised this aspect of the code,[100] and claimed that, as many members could not comply, this created a clash between indulgent popular culture and Quaker 'godly subculture'.[101] Arguably, the Welsh Yearly Meeting pronounce-ments were calculated to raise awareness of the dangers of worldly values. Change was inevitable, especially as Friends were increasingly accepted by their local communities. As a consequence, the use of broad brims and drab habiliments fell out of favour. The original code was undoubtedly a means of protecting Friends from the vanities of Restoration society. John Wesley was deeply critical and questioned the way that Friends focused on the cut of the clothes rather than the cost of the material: 'Do you testify against the *costliness* of their apparel, however plain and grave it may be? Against the *price* of the velvet, the linen, the silk, or raiment of whatever kind?'[102] By the late nineteenth century, John Howells was moved to observe that the poke bonnet and the broad brims were not only anachronistic, but tended to foster 'the pride that apes humility'.[103] It is quite feasible that such progressive views were held by Welsh Friends much earlier, and this may help to explain the lack of censure in the minutes. On the other hand, the pressures were not the same for everyone. Friends who lived at a greater distance from centres of commerce were bound to be less susceptible to the temptations of the new con-sumer society.[104] Proximity to the Welsh–English border pro-duced other pressures. Fashionable Bath and Bristol exerted their own gravitational pull, and this may well have exercised wealthy Friends in south Wales rather more than those who lived in the rural heartlands. In 1716, the Irish Quaker, Joseph Pike, highlighted the extravagant behaviour of Bristol women Friends who wore 'the finest of silks and laced shoes, and when they went to Bath made as fine a show as any'.[105]

In conjunction with their adherence to 'plainness' of dress and speech, Friends sought to uphold the New Testament precept on swearing oaths even though this prevented them from taking an active part in civil, municipal or political life.[106] Prior to the 1696 Affirmation Act it must have been difficult for Quakers to execute probates in ecclesiastical courts.[107] Both Helen Forde and Adrian Davies have suggested that before this date, English Friends appointed non-Quaker relatives or neighbours to act as executors or surrogates in order to avoid contravening the Quaker code.[108] Friends were often named as executors in Welsh wills as the following examples from Monmouthshire show. In 1669, the will of David Jones, a yeoman of St Bride's Wentloog, was attested to by David Price, an appointed 'surrogate'.[109] Similarly, in 1677 John Thomas, a yeoman from Goldcliffe, clearly nominated two non-Quakers to act as his executors instead of his Quaker relatives or neighbours.[110] In 1692 Margaret Morgan, a widow from Llangybi, called upon a fellow Quaker to act as her executor, and yet the will was proved by the surrogate, J. Francklyn.[111]

The various forms of affirmation available to Friends from 1689 to 1722 were not acceptable to all members; some claimed it was just an oath in another guise. In Wales, this seems to have been less of an issue and only a few examples have been found of the 'affirmation controversy'. In 1711, the North Wales Quarterly Meeting allowed Friends to debate the issue, and in 1713 the Montgomeryshire Monthly Meeting called upon the Welsh Yearly Meeting to 'sollicite the Government for an Affirmation that may be *satisfactory* to the whole body of Friends'.[112] In December 1723, Lewis Lewis and Henry William were censured by the Pont-y-Moel Meeting for having taken the affirmation, which would indicate some uneasiness about the issue.[113] While this would seem to indicate that many Welsh Friends, like 'metropolitan' Friends, and in marked contrast to Lancashire Friends, were prepared to reach an accommodation with the authorities this does not mean that they were prepared to sacrifice their beliefs for financial gain.[114] Unfortunately, the lack of government records and other documents, to which Friends would have affirmed, make it difficult to draw any firm conclusions. It is possible, as David Scott has suggested for York Friends, that Welsh members accepted the affirmation not from 'a desire for social respectability or growing affluence', but from 'the sense of obligation they felt as members of a community in which many of their neighbours, trading partners and social peers shared essentially the same pious principles'.[115]

Cursing was particularly frowned upon and great efforts were made to encourage offenders to reform. In 1707, a Welsh translation of John Kelsall's *Testimony* (1682) was circulated to dissuade Friends from 'calling upon God to damn them'. John Barcroft's *Faithful Warning to the Inhabitants of Great Britain and Ireland* (1720) was published for the same purpose.[116] Similarly, in December 1730 Evan Bevan proposed that his tract against *Profane swearing and cursing and taking ye Lords name in vain* be printed. It was agreed that it should be inserted in the *Gloster Journal* in 1734.[117] Prophetic utterances were permitted[118] but the foretelling of doom or destruction was frowned upon, especially after the Toleration Act and the trend towards quietism. Therefore, Friends who brought the Society into disrepute by their ranting behaviour were censured or expelled. For example, Thomas Goodwin of Llanidloes was censured in 1705 for his unsanctioned preaching.[119] These could have been examples of the schism that existed among Quakers over the apostate George Keith. This is referred to by Hugh Roberts of Pennsylvania.[120] The Keith affair had reverberations throughout Wales. In July 1694, a Quarterly Meeting held at Llan-Llwch in Carmarthenshire recalled Keith's publications and curtailed their circulation.[121] The Society for Promoting Christian Knowledge, on the other hand, actively distributed Keith's works which vindicated Anglicanism, and James Harries, the vicar of Llantrisant, claimed in April 1701 that 'many of the Quaker's Eyes have been open'd'.[122]

Offenders were openly shamed into rejecting their errant behaviour, and forced to humble themselves to the satisfaction of the meeting. For example, between 1711 and 1736 Nathaniel Phillips, a yeoman of Pen-Rhos, was frequently taken to task for being 'a recalcitrant member', and Friends repeatedly deprived him of a legacy bestowed in 1697 by Richard Clarke.[123] There were, however, occasions when even disownment proved insufficient. In the early eighteenth century, Pembrokeshire Friends were forced to disown one of their older members, Edward Lord of Haverfordwest, for refusing to submit to their judgment over a disputed sum of money. Lord appealed to the Swansea Quarterly Meeting in 1702, but failed to overturn the earlier decision. Undaunted he continued to attend and disrupt meetings for the next two years, and in 1708 he attempted to seek redress in the Court of Great Sessions. Again he failed, but Friends were forced to publicly condemn his actions 'for the satisfaction of the world'.[124]

Specific rules governed courtship and matrimony, and the advice of all parties was sought.[125] Friends were above all else concerned to ensure that marriages were based on sobriety, compatibility and financial security.[126] There was to be 'no fickleness in courtship: the mind must not be allowed to flit from this woman to another woman' (nid oes gwamalu i fod mewn cariad: nid yw'r meddwl i hedeg oddiwrth y ddynes hon at ddynes arall).[127] While employed as a felt-maker in Southwark between 1658 and 1659, Richard Davies fell ill and became convinced that he should return to Wales and proselytize the Quaker message. He also became committed to taking a wife who could support him in his missionary work. As he recorded in his journal,

> the Lord . . . provided a help-meet for me . . . for it was not yet manifest to me where she was, or who she was. But one time, as I was at Horselydown meeting in Southwark, I heard a woman Friend open her mouth, by way of testimony against an evil ranting spirit that did oppose Friends much in those days. It came to me from the Lord that the woman was to be my wife, and to go with me to the country, and to be an helpmeet for me.

Fortunately for Davies, his chosen wife was receptive to this rather strange courtship:

> We waiting upon the Lord together, she arose, and declared before me . . . that in the name and power of God she consented to be my wife, and to go along with me, whither the Lord should order us; and I said, in the fear of the Lord, I receive thee as the gift of God to me.[128]

Once an engagement was entered into, only death or impropriety could make it void. On 28 November 1688, William David of Talgarth committed suicide after his proposed marriage was prevented. He was subsequently buried in Glasbury churchyard 'where noe good Xtians are buried'.[129] Any ill-conceived alliance was either prohibited outright or referred to the local meeting. However, there were cases when unsuitable marriages were inadvertently approved. In 1741, Monmouthshire Friends allowed Isaac Evans of Llandeilo Gresynni to marry, but they later discovered that he had 'kept company wth the young woman who is now [his] wife for upwards of 12 months before she came to our meetings'. Worse still was the knowledge that he had attempted to seduce other women with offers of 'a pretty handsome ffortune & he as we found afterwards worse than nothing'. Steps were immediately taken to disown his 'subtle cunning & loose conduct'.[130]

George Fox formulated the basic foundations of Quaker marriages[131] which were modified by Friends when new legislation made a reappraisal necessary.[132] After formally obtaining parental consent, the two contracting Friends had to declare their intentions to their local meeting. If the parents were deceased, other family members, guardians, or well-esteemed Friends could act as proxy. This was also the case for servants and apprentices. Where the male Friend belonged to another meeting, he had to make a declaration to his fiancée's meeting and provide a certificate of approval from his parents and his own meeting. Thereafter, two Friends were appointed to institute checks.[133] In 1704, this proce-dure was strengthened by the appointment of two male and two female representatives.[134] The Society was naturally keen to see engagements result in marriage, but would not 'unequally yoke' a couple where love had waned, or where the couple were judged to be incompatible. In 1700, the engagement between Richard Dalton of Carmarthenshire and Mary Wilcox from Bristol was allowed to proceed even though Bristol Friends believed that the engagement was ill-advised. Preventing the marriage, it was thought, would have more serious consequences.[135] The period between the proposal of marriage and its approval usually gave couples enough time to test their compatibility. In 1774, David Williams of Pembrokeshire took this too far. He failed to inform Friends of his decision to break off his engagement and several years passed before the truth was eventually discovered.[136] On most occasions, however, once the certificate of 'clearness' was acknowledged, the intended marriage was announced. Finally, a note of approval was recorded in the minutes.

After the contracting parties had submitted a second declaration to the Monthly Meeting, they were 'given liberty' to proceed with their marriage preparations. Occasionally a delay was required, pending further investigations. In March 1739, Roger Hughes of Mamheilad was obliged to delay marrying Mary Ballard of Posset until attempts to discredit him had been officially dismissed.[137] More seriously, in 1752 Roger Jones, a shoemaker of Pontypool, had his marriage to Hannah Biggam of Llangadog delayed because of his reputed gambling. The marriage was subsequently approved, but less than a year later both were accused of 'bringing reproach upon Truth and Friends'.[138] Further restrictions applied to proposals of marriage which were deemed too precipitate following the death of a spouse.

Weddings were usually held in conjunction with the Meeting for Worship, and the ceremony was performed at the bride's meeting after a period of silent meditation and worship. During the ceremony representatives were appointed to ensure that due propriety was observed during the ceremony. Unlike the procedure followed by most denominations, the bride gave herself away and the ceremony involved a mutual contract between the bride and groom, transacted in a solemn, almost clinical fashion.[139] The clerk of the meeting acted as registrar, and all present were named as witnesses on the wedding certificate. The witnessing of a marriage by the assembled congregation symbolized the firm and lasting bond between Friends and their community of believers.[140] It also made it decidedly more difficult for the authorities to distinguish a Quaker from a non-Quaker. Extravagance at weddings was strictly avoided. The Welsh Yearly Meeting at Rhayader in April 1697 emphasized that 'extravagant extraordinary excessive provisions' should not be made at weddings or burials.[141] This view was endorsed by the Women's Yearly Meeting in 1749 when Friends were advised to avoid 'extravagant Feasts at marriages and the births of their children'.[142]

Marriage to a non-member was permissible, though disapproved of, in the seventeenth century. By the eighteenth century, however, the regulations had been tightened and such relationships were prohibited. Mixed marriages, in the earlier period, were allowed to go ahead on condition that children were given a Quaker upbringing. It is notable too that Friends were prepared to allow non-Quaker marriages to be held according to their rules, but in such circumstances no testimony of the wedding appeared in their registers. Many Friends who chose non-Quaker partners elected, however, to marry outside of the Society. In such cases, the meeting would counsel the estranged Friend, explaining that unless they annulled the relationship they risked disownment. In October 1701, Howell Thomas, a hosier from Glamorgan, was condemned by the Quarterly Meeting for marrying 'a woman of an unclean and unhonest conversation who had severall bastards'. The testimony also commented that he had married the woman 'by his own lustfull desire' despite being warned that he would be disowned. Friends disowned him, specifying that they had 'no hatred to his person but do desire & heartily pray yt appeal of repentance'. Barely four months later, Thomas duly repented of his actions.[143]

The Monmouthshire Monthly Meeting in August 1712 recorded that Charles Hanbury, along with his wife Candia, admitted that they had been married in a church, and yet their confession was accepted and they were allowed to continue as members.[144] By 1718, however, Hanbury was again censured for acting contrary to the Quaker code and falling into 'a disorderly life'.[145] Friends failed to persuade him to reform and give up his 'disorderly walking', and concern was expressed that the Society's reputation would be irreversibly damaged by the 'unjust scandal we lie under'.[146] It would seem, however, that Hanbury was readmitted for he was interred at Pont-y-Moel burial ground in 1735.[147] In 1754, in contrast to the leniency Friends had shown Charles Hanbury, Nathaniel Beadles was disowned.[148] These examples clearly show the collective will of the Society being exerted over the wishes of individual members on marriage proposals, and the resort to disownment when no change could be affected.

The Welsh Yearly Meeting's enquiry into the state of Friends' marriages in Monmouthshire in 1711 contained the following terse remark: 'some are too likely to be ensnared in running against ye consent of Friends for husbands and wives'.[149] The decision to disown Friends for marrying outside the Society led to an exodus from the Society in the eighteenth and nineteenth centuries. It was this, more than any other breach in the Quaker code, which led to the decline of the Society. The unwillingness to relax their rules and accept 'mixed marriages' had a twofold effect: it deprived the Society of the infusion of young people and severely undermined its longevity. In a list of disownments drawn up by the Monmouthshire Monthly Meeting in 1786, seventeen Friends out of thirty-three were disowned for marrying outside the Society, while a further fourteen Friends were recorded as having left the Society without reason (see chart 5.1). The other two were disowned for misconduct, debt and excessive drunkenness.[150] Friends who were disowned by the Society often retained a strong attachment to Quakerism, and some even continued to attend meetings. In August 1746, Friends began an enquiry into the conduct of Eleanor Thomas who had been 'keeping company wth a man who is no ffrd' and her attendance at Blaenafon Chapel. She denied the affair, but admitted that she been to the chapel. A further investigation proved that she had been involved with a non-member, and was 'with child by him tho' not married'.[151] She was disowned, but readmitted fifteen years later when it was accepted that she was 'a true penitent'.[152] This was also the case for Nathaniel Beadles, who had been disowned in 1754, and was allowed to rejoin ten years later.[153]

As was usual in the early modern period, separation or divorce among Quakers was quite rare. This was partly because strenuous efforts were made to reconcile the two parties; occasionally this involved delicate negotiations between two meetings. Between c.September 1673 and May 1681, Pont-y-Moel and Bristol Friends sought to reconcile Richard Hanbury II and his wife, Katherine, who had

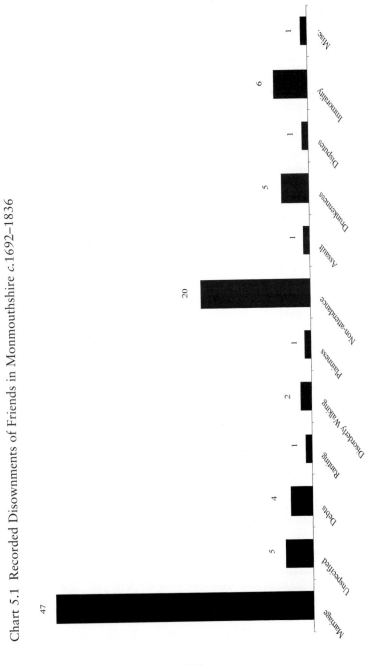

Chart 5.1 Recorded Disownments of Friends in Monmouthshire c.1692–1836

separated.[154] Extensive correspondence was conducted, but to no avail. By May 1681 it was accepted that the breakdown was irreparable and the couple were testified against. Presumably Hanbury acknowledged his guilt as he remained a member until his death in 1714. The relatively low numbers of cases of separation or divorce may be taken as an indication that many Quaker marriages were loving relationships, but pressure to conform was significant and only those prepared to relinquish their faith would challenge the code in this way.[155] In any case, evidence that love was the primary factor in any marriage, Quaker or otherwise, must inevitably be questionable. In his journal, John Bevan of Tref-y-Rhyg acknowledged that his marriage prospered with the passing of time, 'our love is rather more now towards one another than at the beginning'.[156] The courtship and marriage rituals with their formal expressions of devotion, and the terms of endearment in probates,[157] do not of themselves prove that such relationships were built upon mutual affection. In 1654, after his marriage to Elizabeth Leavens, Thomas Holme stated: 'I was emedeatly comanded of the Lord to take hir to wife that day . . . Soe in obedience to thee Comand of the Lord I tooke hir to wife contrary to my will.'[158] Despite such inauspicious beginnings, it was noted that the first year of their married life was 'an idyll of mutual help and childlike happiness'.[159] However, as the couple frequently did not live together because of their missionary work, their compatibility was never fully tested.[160]

Some cases of immorality were dealt with by the Welsh meetings. In 1692, Edward John of Coedcernyw was condemned for committing adultery with his sister-in-law and fathering her child. Friends tried to persuade him to repent, but he refused to be parted from the woman.[161] In 1701, Friends had more success with Richard Lewis of Llanhiledd who had committed adultery with his neighbour's wife. Following his confession, Lewis was allowed to retain his membership.[162] In 1703, John Howell of Haverfordwest was disowned for refusing to end his relationship with 'a strumpet', while in 1705 Lewis Hughes of Pont-y-Moel was censured along with 'those that he takes to lye with him'. He was not, however, disowned and in 1729 he was interred in Friends' burial yard.[163] Friends were often left with little choice but to issue a testimony against fellow members for their immorality. Such accusations were levelled against Thomas Evans of Llanfrechfa who had 'left a bastard [at] the parish and ran away to shun punishment and charges' in 1738.[164] In most cases of this kind, Friends pointed out that immorality was related to excessive consumption of alcohol.

Illegitimate births were denounced by Friends, and where the pregnancy of a servant girl was discovered then her Quaker employer's immorality was exposed. In 1760, the pregnant maid of William Davies of Pontypool ran off to London where she insisted that he was the father of her child. Although Davies vigorously denied her accusation, her story was substantiated and he was duly expelled.[165] Friends were prepared to take action against those who brought shame upon their Society, even if they were attenders rather than members. William Walters of Mamheilad and his pregnant servant, Amy James, were both condemned in 1775 for compromising Friends' reputation.[166] Merry Wiesner has drawn attention to the difficulties faced by many female servants. Apart from being vulnerable to the advances of her employer or his son(s), a young woman often worked unsupervised with men. However, she has also shown that pregnancies outside marriage were very common, and estimated that between one-fifth and one-third of brides in England were pregnant before the marriage ceremony in the sixteenth and seventeenth centuries, while in the eighteenth century this figure was nearly one-half. Local customs, such as the practice of 'bundling' in Wales, also informed popular attitudes.[167] In this case, an 'engaged' couple would be allowed to share a bed overnight to ensure compatibility.[168] Michael Mullett claims that Friends' attempt to distance themselves from their radical past helps to explain their attitude towards sex and marriage, and suggests that this was 'a defensive reaction to old charges of Ranter irregularity and their attempts to live down the slur of antinomianism'.[169] Evan Bevan's public confession in 1712 illustrates this point. He recalled that five years earlier he was guilty of immorality ('O filthy sin'), but since that time, 'with God's grace' and the support of the

Society, he had been able to resist 'carnal temptations'.[170] By admitting his wrongdoing in such a public forum he was openly disassociating himself from such behaviour as well as promoting the advantages of membership.

The Welsh meetings denounced those aspects of everyday life which they considered to be frivolous, immoral or simply unnecessary. George Fox had already warned innkeepers to discourage drunkenness, and testified against wakes or feasts, May-games, sports, plays and shows, which, he believed, 'trained up people to vanity and looseness'.[171] It could be argued, however, that such puritanical views denied Friends the pleasures of music, drama, politics and sport,[172] and, more importantly, made them appear disagreeable neighbours. Thomas and Elizabeth Holme would sing religious songs,[173] but such activities had their critics. In her tract, Margaret Fell wrote that hymn-singing as practised in the Anglican Church was 'more like May-gaming than the worshipping of God'.[174] Equally, in 1657 Richard Davies warned a 'company of people' at Llanfair Caereinion who had 'met to dance and to play, at that they called a *merry night*', and he 'declared the Word of the Lord among them'.[175] In 1701, north Wales Friends translated into Welsh John Kelsall Snr's *Testimony against Gaming, Musick, Dancing, Singing, Swearing and People calling upon God to Damn them. As also against drinking to excess, Whoring, Lying and Cheating . . .* (1682) to strengthen Friends' resolve. Five hundred copies of the translation were produced and distributed.[176] Barry Reay has argued that, as Quakers accepted the principles of the 'reformation of manners' and developed 'a serious culture', many Friends were admonished or expelled for enjoying popular pastimes.[177] According to Mullett, Friends' reluctance to engage in community events was rooted in their fraught relationship with their neighbours. Even in the post-Toleration period, Friends recalled the years of persecution and chose to remain outside the world, believing that their neighbours, and especially the clergy, were still full of animosity and spitefulness.[178] This attempted reformation of manners was never achieved as the Society constantly had to remind the constituent meetings to be vigilant, especially in their relations with the 'world's people'.

The clash between popular culture and reformed behaviour, as shown earlier in the problems associated with plainness, led many Friends to challenge the tenets of the Society. Indeed, as Reay demonstrates, many rank-and-file Quakers were just as attracted to social pursuits as others.[179]

Friends' abhorrence of self-indulgent pleasure, such as frequenting inns or cockfighting arenas, led them to challenge some popular social activities. The diaries of John Kelsall Jnr are full of scathing attacks upon popular pastimes. In May 1722, he complained of the wickedness of the townspeople of Oswestry who were 'drinking swearing', and the following month at Llanfyllin, he commented upon the disturbance made by 'rude company all night long'.[180] Kelsall's views were reinforced by Evan Bevan who published an article in the *Gloster Journal* in 1731, entitled *Of the evils of Cockfighting*. This paper condemned the inherent debasement of God's creation 'to gratify the Lust of depraved Nature'. This stinging rebuke stated that cockfighting led to 'Covetousness and Idleness, and lays a Snare before Multitudes to do Evil'.[181] As Thomas Lewis observed in 1741,

> There were such idleness as Cock fighting, and a great number of those Country people did flock into it. Some did curse, and some did swear; some did hoop, and some did quarrel; there was such idleness as dancing, singing of ungodly books, and Ballads; there was likewise such idleness of Gamings as Balls, Bowls and Pins, Cards and shuffleboards; and a great many of that Country people took much delight in them both old & young.[182]

Some Friends sought to distance themselves from temptation. In 1746, when the school teacher of the Pont-y-Moel meeting was asked to explain why he had vacated the premises without notifying Friends, he replied that on one side of the meeting house was a cockfighting arena and on the other a skittle ground, the 'noise of which he could not bear'.[183]

Friends issued strong warnings against excessive drinking because of the way it contaminated mind and soul. Alcohol abuse, throughout the period under study, was a serious problem and was justifiably condemned as leading to idleness.[184] In 1693, the Yearly Meeting at Coed Cristionydd,

Denbighshire, warned against the evils of excessive drinking, especially when travelling or residing at inns.[185] In 1706, Humphrey Williams 'sottishness' provoked west Wales Friends to withhold the allowance they usually gave him.[186] Likewise, John David, a tailor of Castleton, was condemned for his 'excessive' drinking and 'sitting up late' in 1706 and 1707,[187] and these habits may well have hastened his death in 1709.[188] This sorry tale is made more poignant with the knowledge that he had reformed his 'ill course of life'[189] and been married less than two years before he died.

Friends were concerned not merely to restrict the harmful effects of alcohol abuse, or to preserve their growing respectability. By attacking excess, they were attempting to limit the consequences of such behaviour, and avert the dangers posed to family life and economic prosperity. In 1775, in the testimony against Owen Edwards of Pontypool it is clear that as a consequence of his heavy drinking his business had collapsed, leaving his wife helpless.[190] Quaker industrialists ensured that strict controls on alcohol consumption were in place in their businesses.[191] These warnings did not forbid drinking in moderation. In April 1796, John Harford relaxed his conditions on alcohol when Jenkin Griffith was contracted to refurbish a boiler for £2. 2s. and was to be provided with 2s. 6d. 'to drink if he makes a good job of it'.[192] Astonishingly, at least three Monmouthshire Friends were publicans in the eighteenth century, namely Jonathan Barrow of Monmouth, Samuel Thomas of Caldicot and Charles Chambers of Newport.

Bad company was to be avoided at all times and the reading of trivial or 'immoral' literature was frowned upon. Prose, plays and poetry were all deemed unsuitable for younger Friends.[193] From the earliest years of the movement, Friends had used the printing press to spread their message and educate their members. Tracts written in newspapers and the purchase of works written by leading members helped Friends to consolidate their views.[194] The spread of Quaker beliefs through their own publications was a serious enough matter for the authorities to warrant seizure of any tracts written by them. This was especially true of the period before the limited toleration afforded to Dissenting sects in the late

151

1650s and early 1660s.[195] Often the publication of tracts was designed to counter the spread of anti-Quakerism,[196] or to educate the population in the principles of the movement. Ownership of Quaker publications does not seem to have been a particularly high priority, yet there were obvious exceptions.[197] Members were encouraged to borrow publications from the meeting and from one another.[198] The circulation of Quaker publications was normally conducted through the local meeting. In their registers, Monmouthshire Friends recorded lists of books that were purchased and loaned to members.[199] Some texts were specifically kept as handbooks for errant Friends, most notably in 1738 Michel Evans was required to read Thomas Bayly, *The Serious Reading and Comfort of Holy Scripture Recommended* (London, 1714) and Joshua Middleton, *A Tender and Compassionate call to Profane Swearers, and Takers of the Holy Name of God in Vain* (London, 1707).[200]

Matters concerning disease and death were never far away from the minds of Friends.[201] Particularly interesting is the response of Friends towards the mentally ill. The prevailing attitude of Friends was one of sympathy and a willingness to help the afflicted.[202] Edward John of Coedcernyw, who had been disowned in 1693 for immorality, became mentally ill. In a short testimony, written after his death, it was noted that John had been 'so grievously beset at times that he was tempted to destroy himself . . . under some anxious thoughts that his heavenly maker had turned his back upon him'.[203] He was readmitted and buried at Tref-y-Rhyg. Indeed, an awareness of their mortality made Friends conscious that they should live virtuously and prepare for death. Friends were urged to provide for their wives and families.[204] Any bequeathed land or property was given to the spouse or to their children. In some cases the testator indicated that the beneficiaries of the will would be responsible for the remaining parent or support a near relative. If such offspring were minors then the remaining partner would be expected to act as overseer for any inheritance and any interest on the bequest would be used to pay for the child's education needs or apprenticeship. In 1695, John Beadles bequeathed property and money to his wife and children. In the case of his eldest daughter, Tabitha Beadles, he left a marriage dowry on condition that 'she marry with her mothers consent'. If Tabitha married against 'her consent and good likeing', then the £170 payable under the terms of the will would be bequeathed elsewhere.[205]

Friends were careful to appoint guardians for their children.[206] These arrangements had clearly to be arranged well in advance in order to avoid misunderstandings or possible disputes with non-Quaker relatives over the custody of children. The choice of Quaker executors also helped to guarantee a settlement that would respect the wishes of the deceased Friend. By implementing these measures, however, Friends were again displacing non-Quaker relatives or members of the local community by placing their trust in their co-religionists. Yet this is not to suggest that non-Quaker kin were ignored altogether in Quaker wills, for there are numerous references to near and distant relatives, or non-Quaker neighbours, receiving land, furniture, clothes and other bequests.

Quaker burials were conducted 'according to the scriptures and not according to the custom of the heathen'.[207] Occasionally, the non-Quaker relatives of deceased Friends tried to dictate the final resting place. On 11 September 1694, the body of Rachel Bowen was 'stolen from Friends' and buried contrary to the Society's wishes in Llandeilo Parish Church.[208] Rather than resort to conventional church funerals, Friends were prepared to make use of Quaker burial grounds at a great distance from the meeting,[209] or simply to inter the dead in their own gardens. The funeral service did not follow the rituals of the Established Church.[210] Friends also ignored contemporary mourning dress and observed the code on plainness.[211] Outsiders were critical of the perceived lack of respect to the dead. It was said that Quaker burials were conducted as if burying dogs.[212] Fox was contemptuous of such criticism, arguing that

we have not superfluous and needless things upon our coffin and a white and black cloth with scutcheons and do not go in black and hang scarfs upon our hats and white scarfs over our shoulder and give gold rings and have sprigs of rosemary in our hands and ring the bells.[213]

In 1663, Morgan Watkin of Radnor insisted that Friends bore 'testimony against the idolatry and superstition of hallowed ground . . . and vain traditions'.[214] In the wills of Friends this intention is standard, and reflects a common Puritan orthodoxy among the sects. In 1722, the Pont-y-Moel Friends complained that the burial regulations were being flaunted, and sought to prohibit such impropriety. They reaffirmed that Friends should not 'come with a Black Cloth over a corpse to be buried in Friends graveyards. For it has been a burden to some, and our testimony is against the use of it amongst us.'[215] Many Friends made specific requests for a Quaker burial, whereas others simply asked to be buried in a 'decent manner' as the executor 'shall think fit' or 'in the place appointed'.

Friends' scruples also meant that gravestones were regarded as an unwarranted extravagance. The Quarterly Meeting at Dolobran in 1695 recorded that 'such things have been superstitiously abused by some, neither is there any such thing used and practised or allowed by the people of God'. A year later, the Welsh Yearly Meeting at Pont-y-Moel in April 1696 agreed that gravestones 'ought not to be used . . . and where they are it is desired they may be taken away'.[216] This view was endorsed by the Welsh Yearly Meeting at Llanidloes in 1701 which resolved that 'gravestones may be put down and taken away to avoid giving occasion to say that the relics of popery is among us'.[217] The following year, Monmouthshire Friends ordered all Friends to be 'buried orderly side by side, as ye manner of ffriends in England is, & yt no tombes nor stones shall be layed upon ye graves'.[218] They were concerned that headstones might privilege wealth and status, and commented: 'how can we by our profession honour the rich more than the poor, the high more than the low'.[219] Subsequently, in 1704, seven Friends were appointed to remove the stones.[220] Evidence from 1715 suggests that some stones had been replaced by flat stones bearing only the name of the deceased and the dates of birth and death.[221]

After the funeral, Friends held a silent meeting in honour of the deceased and contemplated their own mortality. In 1700, Pembrokeshire Friends complained that wine and food provided at funerals was contrary to their beliefs and recommended that 'friends should fore beare ye use of wine

& cake & any other unnecessary things at buryalls'.[222] At a later public meeting, the normal practice was for the clerk or another elder to give a eulogy which commented on the life of the deceased and his/her relationship with God.[223] In the testimony to John Bevan of Tref-y-Rhyg in 1727, the clerk stated that Bevan's name should be 'transmitted to posterity among ye Faithful labourers in God's vineyard'.[224] In 1747, Bevan's kinsman, Evan Bevan of Pontypool, was also held up as a model for Friends, who were told that he had been 'clothed with the Spirit of Meekness and Patience, he would condescend to the weakest Member in Charity, Goodwill and pure Love . . . Yea, a noble Pattern and Example was he: His Conduct kept pace with his Doctrine, and with the Principles.'[225] Such sombre occasions were also used to warn 'backsliders' to repent before it was too late.

As noted at the outset, Friends recourse to the code of discipline distinguished them as an identifiable community. Inevitably, this required Quakers to withdraw from the company of their neighbours and non-Quaker relatives. Michael Mullett defines this as 'a surrogate form of kinship control', whereby Quaker communities acted as 'large and censorious families', protecting Quakers from the temptations of early modern consumer society.[226] This level of control, however exacting, was never entirely complete; human relations being what they are, there were bound to be occasions when members had to cooperate with their non-Quaker relatives and near neighbours.[227] This isolationist position was not based solely upon the code of conduct, or Friends' objections to church-based rituals, rather, it stemmed from their belief that, as a persecuted community, they had to be self-reliant. Other than being disowned for marrying out, which did so much to undermine the Society, members largely adhered to the code. Although Welsh Friends struggled to keep the precepts on plain living, and were prepared to take advantage of the Affirmation Acts, evidence suggests that many held fast to the code. Their stoicism can be attributed to the manner in which the code was inculcated, and also the way in which it was enforced.

The code of discipline was both strength and weakness. It offered members a coherent value system which shaped their everyday lives and unified a far-flung community of believers in keeping with the Fox's vision of a company of saints. Later generations of Friends increasingly found the code too inflexible, particularly in the light of eighteenth-century developments. Ironically, the stress on collective responsibility ruled out the very individualism upon which the Society was founded.

Chapter 6

'Be plaine and desent in your habitts': *Women Friends and their Role in the Quaker Community*

I heare of a sect of woemen . . . come from beyond the Sea called Quakers and these . . . begin to preache what hath bin delivered to them by the spirit.[1]

It is widely acknowledged that women played a crucial role in the foundation and survival of the Society of Friends.[2] Jane, the wife of Robert Owen of Dolserau, was

a woman rarely endow'd with many natural gifts; unto her husband in her exercise a meet help, in her deportmt solid & stated . . . And in all their exercise together for ye trueth sake they did not shrink, nor give way for fear or flatter, their house & hearts were open unto all . . . & [were] much beloved in their country.[3]

That being said, any analysis of the role of women Friends must be viewed from the wider context of seventeenth-century attitudes to women, and the impact of the Civil Wars. Naturally, the surviving testimonies of leading women Quakers warrant particular attention for their influence on the movement was so significant, but in doing so the contribution of other women must not be overlooked. Historians have tended to emphasize the uniquely democratic character of Quakerism which empowered women in ways that were completely at variance with early modern society.[4] This study will test the extent to which this egalitarian ethos was sustained, for evidence suggests that the position of women in the Society changed over time.

In the uncertain world of the seventeenth century, the family unit was regarded as a stabilizing force with distinct roles allotted to husbands and wives. As the head of the household, the

157

husband imposed discipline while, in theory, the wife was expected to be passive, humble, chaste and frugal.[5] As Keith Thomas observed, 'woman's destiny was marriage . . . and then the hazards of continual childbearing. She was allowed a voice in neither Church nor State . . . her chief ornament was silence, and her sole duty obedience to her husband under God.'[6] The duties of women obviously depended upon their status, but they were expected to manage the household, provide food and control the behaviour of any children or servants.[7] Wealthy women often had more licence, involving themselves in the family business and in charitable endeavours.[8] Yet, in matters of religion, women were subordinate. In the 1630s, and especially during the Civil Wars, these tenets of female subservience were increasingly challenged.[9] Disillusioned by the failure of the Church to meet their spiritual needs, women turned to Dissenting preachers or became separatists.[10] The relaxation of the censorship laws allowed men and women to express views that were normally suppressed,[11] and so women from across the social strata became active preachers. Others became prophets,[12] and were encouraged by leading Quakers, such as George Keith who wrote that a Quaker women's preaching was 'of the Lord alone', whereas the Anglican clergy was self-interested and corrupt.[13] The acceptance of women as preachers and prophets was thought to threaten to traditional values, and some believed that the world was indeed being turned upside down.[14] Consequently, such women were often portrayed by their critics as witches, sexual deviants and lunatics.[15]

That Quakerism appealed to women is clear from an analysis of those who joined the early movement. The Puritan intellectual, Richard Baxter, wrote in 1657 that early Quaker meetings were composed of 'ignorant, ungrounded people, young raw professors and women'.[16] Many women who were attracted to the movement followed in the footsteps of Civil War Dissenters who had 'harangued prelates and country priests'. They used 'their pens to defend their doctrinal beliefs' and propagandize their spiritual awakening.[17] Other female members may have been drawn to the Society by the declarations of equality for Quaker women. According to Hugh Barbour, Quakerism appealed to women because they were accepted as equal members. This view is persuasive given that most women at the time were valued for their potential wealth, childbearing capabilities and domesticity.[18] An open letter written by Lancaster Women Friends between 1675 and 1680 noted that God made 'no difference in the seed, between the male and female . . . so here in the power and spirit, of the Lord God, women comes to be coheires, and fellow labourers'.[19]

Christine Trevett claims that women also sought social equality.[20] Quaker marriages reflected the egalitarian message of the Society as well as the importance of women to their meetings. Friends stressed that both partners shared responsibility for the physical and spiritual well-being of the family, and mutual cooperation was essential to the growth of the Quaker community. Yet for some women, whether married or single, preaching was an affirmation of their independence and their determination to occupy an equal role in the development of the Quaker community. The road to independence was by no means straightforward. Sometimes a woman's familial role collided with her vocation as a Quaker preacher, forcing her to choose. Marriage in 1654 between two of the movement's earliest preachers, Thomas Holme and Elizabeth Leavens, and Elizabeth's pregnancy in 1656, raised difficult issues. When Margaret Fell questioned whether Elizabeth should be allowed to impose herself on Cardiff Friends during her pregnancy,[21] Thomas argued that 'the Lord hath provyded a chamber for hir in Cardife, wher she labores with hir hands, & is not chargable, & as much as in hir lyes shee will keep from being borthensome ore chargable to any'.[22] More controversy arose when Elizabeth returned to her preaching mission only fifteen days after the birth of her first child, giving credence to rumours that she had deliberately abandoned her child. Once again Thomas sprang to his wife's defence, insisting that

For the charge & borthen thou compleanse of consarning our child it is yeat to come, & if our goeing together be the ground of what is against us, the ground shall be removed, & the ocction of ofence shall be taken away, for we had both of us determined long befor thy leter came to keep asunder.[23]

The matter did not conclude there. After consulting George Fox, Thomas informed Margaret Fell in June 1656 that Elizabeth would 'give up hire child to the frind [in Cardiff] which soe long befor had desiared hire'.[24] Further correspondence in April 1657 illuminates the struggles of all concerned to reconcile their spiritual and temporal needs:

> as for hire ministring a brod, if shee could be clear befor god in silence, I could be well contented, & be at more ease, thou might let hir alone shee suffereth all & replyes not . . . the Lord judg be twixt you, have I dishonred thee . . . ney I love thee the more & am pla[i]n harted towards thee as thou alsoe towards mee . . . I love thee noe lese tho: I have writen thous to thee, for give mee I pray thee I fear to ofend thee the Lord knows.[25]

Holme regarded Elizabeth as his equal, and could not understand why Margaret Fell thought that he could command his wife to give up her mission. This kind of conflict threw into sharp relief the tension between egalitarian principles and the realities of married life and motherhood. The Quaker movement nonetheless emphasized that female members had an equal share in the propagation and development of the Society – a fact which is often borne out in the testimonies to women Friends. When Esther Richards of Llanfrechfa died in 1764, she was described as a 'publick Friend and of good report among her neighbours'.[26] Equally, in 1788 the Yearly Meeting at Hay extolled the long marriage of Martha and Ambrose Williams of Pontypool: 'they were true help meets to each other in the promotion of Truth, giving up each other freely to the Service'.[27]

Those outside of the Society were deeply critical. In 1655, Joshua Miller voiced his contempt for women preachers, claiming that this 'monstrous doctrine' was unnatural.[28] Clergymen cited Biblical texts such as I Timothy 2: 12 which stated: 'I suffer not a woman to teach, nor to usurp authority over the man, but to be in silence.' The readiness of George Fox and others to redress the inequalities between women and men helped to fuel the attacks upon this Pauline injunction. Fox, did not, however, intend that women should share the administration of the religious community, but rather he emphasized their role as preachers.[29] In 1647, in response to earlier critics who argued that 'women have no souls . . . no more than a goose', Fox demonstrated the significance of women to the Christian religion by using scriptural evidence.[30] The equality of women was endorsed by John Banks of Pardshaw Meeting in Cumberland who wrote in 1674:

> God . . . said not unto man in the beginning, thou art righteous, and to woman, thou art not so, neither to the man, I have ordered thee of use to work, and not the woman, but he put them both in the Garden together to dress and keep it.[31]

Phyllis Mack has explored the reasons why women felt the urge to preach, and questioned whether they were motivated by personal, social or economic deprivation. Many women prophets, Mack concluded, admitted their inability to control their emotions, but insisted that their actions were not based upon an arrogant self-importance.[32] Geoffrey Nuttall agrees, citing Elizabeth Holme who, he suggests, had 'a peculiarly emotional temperament, given to visions'.[33] It has been argued that many Quaker women felt compelled to add their own distinctive interpretation of social changes and to preach accordingly, but they were the exception rather than the rule.[34] Many women visionaries were well-established members who were prepared to conduct the daily business of the meeting as well as to make public pronouncements. The prophetic statements of women ministers rarely mention gender issues, and this runs counter to the argument that they were primarily expressing their own sexual or social frustrations. Moreover, as Mack has noted, most women preachers travelled together in groups or in pairs, and 'welcomed the liberation from repeated pregnancies that itinerant preaching gave them'.[35]

Notwithstanding the many dangers and hardships they faced, women preachers in Wales believed that divine inspiration compelled them to defy the conventions of the period and preach as freely as any man. They travelled long distances and preached to small and large gatherings, bore testimony against tithes, oaths and the clergy, and published their innermost thoughts. Barry Reay has estimated that of the 360 Quakers who were recorded as disputants with church ministers between 1654 and 1659 just over one third (34 per cent) were women.[36] Many Quaker evangelists, as already noted, encountered powerful opposition but this rarely deterred them. It has been argued that women prophets and preachers seemed more credible if they appeared dressed in sackcloth and made prophetic statements, rather than simply condemning ministers or engaging in theological debates.[37] While demonstrations of ecstatic behaviour helped to reinforce the notion that they were visionaries, conversely, it enabled their critics to attribute their behaviour to female irrationality and hysteria, madness or witchcraft.[38] In turn, the same rationale was used by civil and ecclesiastical authorities to justify the persecution of Quaker women.[39]

The courage and determination of women preachers such as Dorcas Erbery, Alice Birkett, Elizabeth Holme and Elizabeth Richard enraged church ministers and magistrates. The controversial re-enactment in 1656 by James Nayler of Christ's entry into Jerusalem, in which Dorcas Erbery took a leading role, heightened already inflamed sensitivities. During the ensuing blasphemy trial at Bristol, Erbery not only insisted that Nayler had raised her from the dead, but claimed that he 'shall sit at the right hand of the Father' - an outburst which merely confirmed rumours that she was bewitched, especially when she joined Martha Simmonds and Hannah Stranger near the pilloried Nayler, in dramatic emulation of the crucifixion of Christ.[40] Undaunted by the ridicule heaped upon her, Erbery remained a committed Quaker and was frequently incarcerated in Welsh and English gaols.[41] The influence of her parents, William and Mary, inevitably dictated her extreme zealotry.[42] On the one hand, early Welsh Quakerism benefited from the intrepid missionary activities of women such as Mary and Dorcas, but on the other hand there is little doubt that such extremism provoked a backlash in which the Society began to discipline those judged to be a disruptive influence.[43]

Dorcas Erbery was certainly not alone in suffering for her faith. In 1658, after attempting to disrupt Henry Walter's sermon, Alice Birkett and Elizabeth Holme were incarcerated on Newport bridge.[44] Later in the same year, Birkett was stabbed in the arm by William Williams of Newport, possibly in an attempt to ward off evil spirits,[45] and on Easter Monday in the same year, she was stoned in Llandaff churchyard and stripped naked for challenging Revd Benjamin Flower.[46] Mary Moss of Penarth and Mary Richard of Cardiff were similarly manhandled in 1658 as they were beaten, dragged up a flight of stairs and locked in the stocks without being charged. Their 'crime' had been to reprove the minister, John Catts of Sully.[47] During her missionary work that same year, Elizabeth Holme was imprisoned for disturbing a Swansea clergyman. In the 'dark house', she was 'chained by the leg' and allowed no visitors, and 'through a hole of the door with a cane she sucked some bear'.[48] In 1694, the imprisonment of Ann Thomas, an eighty-year-old widow of Llanyre, Radnorshire, was recorded in the Welsh Yearly Meeting minutes at Dolobran.[49] By such action, women Friends demonstrated their commitment to their faith, and this distinguished them from many other women in the parish.[50] It is inordinately difficult to ascertain which women were punished for non-payment of tithes. If the husband was alive his name would normally be appended to the distraint, even if he was absent or imprisoned. Furthermore, in the early years, female members married to non-Quakers must have struggled to uphold their testimony against tithes.[51] The distraint of goods impinged upon the whole family, and for the poor the loss of farm produce or livestock was a incalculable hardship.

At the end of the seventeenth century, women preachers were still a common sight throughout Wales. Of the six full testimonials in the Welsh Yearly Meeting minutes to leading Friends, four related to women. When Martha Williams died in 1788, after a fifty-year ministry,[52] she was memorialized as

truly a mother in Israel, a great encourager of the weak, a Seeker after the Scattered & a Sympathizer with the afflicted . . . her engaging chearful condescention gained her a near place in the affections of many of the youth, who were particularly the objects of her tender care, & her advice hath often proved effecatious in Drawing them nearer to the pure witness within.[53]

Other testimonials related to Mary Goodwin of Montgomeryshire (1778), Dorothy Owen of Tyddyn-y-garreg (1794), and Abiah Darby of Coalbrookdale in Shropshire (1795).[54] Such women were highly esteemed and took a prominent role in the Society's meetings. It is curious, therefore, that the women's desire to hold their own meetings was not universally welcomed, and, even when this hurdle was overcome and separate meetings were established, limitations were still imposed to preserve the overarching authority of male members.[55]

Various dates have been mooted for the development of women's meetings in London, but some time between 1656 and 1660 they were inaugurated.[56] Initially, shared meetings were the norm, but Quakers such as John Banks of Cumberland were aware that women might be overshadowed by the men. He observed in 1674 that some women 'quenched the notion of the good in themselves by looking out at the men' and, therefore, he advocated separate meetings.[57] The debate continued throughout the late seventeenth century.[58] In 1675, James Lancaster of Walney Island wrote:

> You that stumble at Women's Meetings and thinks yourselves sufficient as being men: What was and is it that makes thee sufficient? Is it not the grace of God, and hath not that appeared to all men and to all women? . . . Must they not give an account to God who is a spirit, as well as men, of their stewardship being stewards of the same? Thus being members of the Church, Christ Jesus being the head, male and female all one in him; therefore, dismember not the Body . . . look on them [women] to be meet helps.[59]

It was agreed that these meetings would work towards mutual goals, and this guaranteed women an administrative role in the Society.[60]

In the course of the eighteenth century, however, the Society became increasingly bureaucratic and the role of women more circumscribed.[61] The efforts of women were being redirected into traditionally feminine roles and responsibilities, effectively reversing the progress that had been made in the early years. As Trevett observes, 'while women imposed some discipline, they did not make it'.[62] Their account books were overseen by the men's meetings, and women ministers were required to be more circumspect in central (London) meetings. They were warned to avoid monopolizing meetings at the expense of other male speakers, and their contribution was further delimited by the requirement to register their intention to speak beforehand.[63] The attempt to establish a separate meeting for women ministers was firmly rejected by the Second Day Morning Meeting in London in 1701 on the grounds that

> They do not understand that ever this meeting gave direction for the setting up the said meeting; neither do they judge there is any necessity for it or service in the continuance thereof . . . it is a hurt to Truth for women Friends to take up too much time, as some do in our public meetings, when several public and serviceable men Friends are present and are by them prevented in their serving.[64]

This refusal may have arisen because of fears that if women were allowed to exert more authority, they might ultimately influence the entire Quaker community.[65] Limited finances undoubtedly constrained the missionary work of female preachers, but the Society's move towards greater respectability is a more likely explanation. For both men and women Friends, conformity not individualism was the new orthodoxy. Testimonies to women Friends in the eighteenth century stressed qualities such as understanding and hospitality,[66] while Mary Beadles was praised for having been 'circumspect and innocent in her conversation'.[67] Charles Cherry has observed that, 'Quakers ceased to indulge in miracles or even discuss them, the individualistic appeal was de-emphasised, organisation and discipline received more emphasis'.[68] Quaker women who went against this new protocol faced the censure of their own meeting for acting contrary to its wishes. In August 1752, the Monmouthshire Quarterly Meeting read aloud letters from the Sticklepath Meeting in Devon in which two women Friends repudiated their earlier 'outgoings and publishing [of] erronious papers'.[69] Clearly, this was intended to persuade other women to remodel their behaviour.

Despite the shift in attitudes noted above, there is evidence to suggest that not all eighteenth-century Welsh women Friends were submissive and unwilling to undertake missionary work. Indeed, the ministry of Martha Williams was much vaunted:

> Under this Devoutedness of mind she was frequently concerned to leave her near connections in the Service of Truth & several times Friends in most parts of England & Wales, & twice in Ireland being frequently engaged in visiting families which service she was peculiarly favoured in.[70]

The clerk acknowledged the personal difficulties that she had overcome in order to serve the Society. Public speaking 'occasioned her many severe conflicts and deep inward suffering under a sense of her own unworthyness'. He also hoped that the testimony would 'stand as matter of Instruction to others who may be so favoured'.[71] Furthermore, the Welsh meeting minutes indicate that itinerant woman preachers were not always proscribed. In 1733, Ruth Lewis of Llanfrechfa and Ann Rosser of Trefddyn were granted certificates to visit other Welsh meetings which were 'signed by most if not all that were present'.[72]

Attendance at the Welsh women's meetings gives some indication of their relative strength. The earliest documented meeting attended by women Friends in Wales occurred in April 1747. At the Cardiff Yearly Meeting at least nine women Friends were present and several recommendations were made for the benefit of female members.[73] In tandem, a Women's Quarterly Meeting was instituted.[74] Clearer details of the structure and attendance at these meetings emerge with detailed minutes from 1750 onwards.[75] For example, they reported their efforts to visit Friends' families, and this was encouraged by the Yearly Meeting as it was necessary that 'the strong may help the weak and encourage them to come forward in the Respective Stations and Services in the Truth'.[76] In 1757, the Monmouthshire representatives addressed the problem of finding suitable work for poor women Friends. In spite of their efforts to find appropriate work with Quaker employers, some women were nevertheless forced to work elsewhere.[77] Women Friends throughout Wales were regularly provided with advice from other meetings, especially from London. In 1764, Friends were advised to keep an account of marriages, slave-holding, removals and settlements, tithes, and visiting families.[78]

The women's monthly meetings have been poorly documented, and it is difficult to say with any certainty when they were instituted in each county. There are minutes for north Wales between 1785 and 1815,[79] Monmouthshire from 1801 until 1836,[80] and Carmarthenshire and Glamorganshire between 1839 and 1887.[81] It is possible that earlier meetings were simply meetings for worship, incorporating ad hoc disciplinary meetings.[82] In the winter of 1753, John Player of Herefordshire gives a brief glimpse of the opposition to the establishment of a women's business meeting at Pont-y-Moel. Friends held a conference to discuss the question, as women members were 'desireous to promote it'. Player was not persuaded and observed that 'in this place there is one of an Unsanctified Spirit who can Rule by His means and Speak fair words but Inwardly is full of deceit'.[83] Obviously, his was not a lone voice and the initiative failed.

In time, such hostile attitudes were countermanded by the London Yearly Meeting in 1755 which highlighted the failure to establish Women's Monthly Meetings for Discipline 'in sundry counties'. They called upon Welsh Friends to ensure that such meetings were established,[84] but it was to take several years to change minds and hearts.[85] In 1763, a meeting was established in Carmarthenshire, and by 1783, a women's meeting had been set up in Monmouthshire.[86] Moreover, in a letter to James Lewis of Trosnant in July 1788, Richard Reynolds of Ketley, Salop, advised that a Standing Committee of men and women ought to be established to support Preparative and Monthly Meetings.[87]

Quaker women ministers, unlike their female counterparts in other Nonconformist congregations, tended to be from the middling orders.[88] This was especially true of the late eighteenth and nineteenth centuries when women Quaker representatives tended to be the wives or daughters of industrialists, merchants and shop owners. Table 6.1, which draws upon the minutes of Monmouthshire women Friends between 1801 and 1836, suggests, with one or two exceptions, that representatives clearly followed this pattern.

Table 6.1. Monmouthshire Women Friends c.1801–1836[89]

Name	Year(s)	Occupation of Husband/Father
Sarah James	1801–20	shopkeeper
Ann Cooper	1801–4	mercer
Jane Lloyd Harford	1801–36	ironmaster
Elizabeth Harford	1801–36	ironmaster
Ann Summers Harford	1802–	ironmaster
Sarah Lloyd Harford	1802–	ironmaster
Elizabeth Rees	1801–29	ironmonger
Elizabeth Enoch (neé Harvard)	1801	draper
Elizabeth Ann Parry (neé Chambers)	1801–7	innkeeper
Mary Jones	1802	unspecified
Sarah Gillett	1802–	unspecified (spinster)
Rebecca Edwards	1801	unspecified
Ann Giles	1802–31	poor woman
Mary Lewis	1803–	gentlewoman
Elizabeth Belch	1803–6	ironmonger
Mary Tanner	1803–5	unspecified
Hannah Hughes (neé Jarrett)	1804–5	farmer
Ann Merrefield	1807–	wheelwright/schoolteacher
Mary Merrefield	1807–31	wheelwright/schoolteacher
Deborah Merrefield	1807–	wheelwright/schoolteacher
Elizabeth Bush Rees	1824–	ironmonger
Mary Napper	1824–32	confectioner/shopkeeper
Hannah Napper	1824–36	confectioner/shopkeeper
Martha Lewis	1824–8	yeoman
Amy Harris	1824–31	yeoman
Mary Ann Napper	1825–30	confectioner/shopkeeper
Hannah Merrefield	1826–31	wheelwright/schoolteacher
Deborah Wilmot	1826–31	yeoman
Elizabeth Wilmot	1827–30	yeoman
Margaret Edwards	1829–31	gentlewoman
Martha Harford	1829–36	ironmaster
Susanna M. Napper	1829–	confectioner/shopkeeper
Sophia C. Napper	1829–30	confectioner/shopkeeper

Quaker women were educated to a much higher standard than was usual in the early modern period, as evidenced by their ability to read and discuss the Bible, keep journals and travelogues and correspond with other Friends.[90] Welsh women appointed their own clerks and representatives who took separate minutes, signed relevant documents and attended a plethora of meetings. When appropriate they initiated enquiries into the behaviour of female Friends, and received marriage proposals for investigation. This was particularly necessary in the early years of the Society and during times of intense persecution when their menfolk were in prison or preaching away from home. The practice of announcing marriages separately before a women's meeting was not always welcomed. In the 1670s it was a major issue which contributed to the Wilkinson–Story schism.[91]

Yet, even after the establishment of women's meetings, female members wielded little direct power. The occasional combination of men and women Friends as 'helpmeets' gives a false impression of the role of women members. Although the women's meetings were purportedly calculated to empower women, in reality they constrained their influence by denying them 'an equal share with men'.[92] The work of Gillian Mason demonstrates that the independence of the women's meeting was limited, and that female roles could often be stereo-typical.[93] The gradual transformation of the Society from a sect to a denomination led to a redefinition of the role of men and women Friends. For, although women undertook certain disciplinary and financial tasks, they were subordinate to, and financially dependent upon, their male colleagues. It is notable that women ministers had to seek the approval of the men's meeting before they could embark upon any journeys.[94] In 1758, Martha Williams requested permission from the men's meeting to visit Friends in Bristol. Her journey was successful, but on her return she reported that Bristol Friends were unhappy about her 'certificate' because 'ye womens names was not to it'.[95] Nevertheless, Quakerism offered 'scope for most women's talents – for the literate and numerate, for the born preacher, the adventurer, the teacher, the counsellor and for the woman whose abilities as succourer and organiser had been nurtured in a lifetime of motherhood and domestic labour'.[96]

An epistle written by the Lancashire Women's Meeting between 1675 and 1680 delineated the responsibilities of Quaker women's assemblies. It proposed that overseers should be appointed to ensure that 'backsliders' or 'disorderly' Friends were admonished, and that papers of condemnation were recorded. Overseers were also expected to strengthen the Society by offering helpful advice to erring Friends, and by visiting individual Quakers or families who had lapsed.[97] Women Friends were given a leading role in educating children into the Society's values,[98] and ensuring that Quaker servants were employed in members' households.[99] Knowledge of the Scriptures and the ability to read biblical texts to children and servants were regarded as valuable attributes. George Fox acknowledged that wives would receive religious instruction from their husbands and impart such knowledge to their offspring. This was not controversial. Fox, however, assumed that wives would instruct their husbands if they were new to the faith, for he considered their contribution as preachers and administrators to be extremely important to the growth of Quakerism.[100] Some women were occasionally appointed as teachers. The diary of Lydia Novell, which reflects on her long teaching career at Hambrook, Gloucestershire, in the eighteenth century, provides important insights into the experiences of Quaker women as teachers.[101] In the nineteenth century, Mary and Hannah Merrefield are said to have set up a school at Pontypool. It is unclear when it was inaugurated, or if it was officially recognized. The two women may have been assisting their father, Roger Merrefield, who is listed in the records as a schoolteacher. Notably, both women left the Society in the early 1830s: Mary was disowned for marrying outside the Society in March 1832 and Hannah resigned her membership in March 1833. In her resignation letter, Hannah wrote that she no longer felt able to 'maintain or act exactly in accordance with the rules of the Society of Friends', and wished to join another denomination. She later married a non-member and was subsequently disowned in September 1833.[102]

The code of discipline, especially the requirement to abide by the rule on plainness was primarily directed at women.

The minutes of the Herefordshire Quarterly Meeting for 1697 clearly demonstrate the way that Quaker women were expected to behave. They advised women

> not to fashion themselves after the manner of the world but so goe without Aprons, and not to go with their mantoes open before; nor to go with their Heads hye; nor with Long Strapts at their Hoods: nor with Long Trains at their Mantoe and petticoats ... they are things that ought to be Left off and not worne amongst us ... no Friend should make lace nor sel it.[103]

This can be compared with George Fox's earlier proclamation (*c.*1655) which cautioned women against

> spots on their faces, noses, cheeks, foreheads, having their rings on their fingers, wearing gold, having their cuffs double under and about like unto a butcher with white sleeves, having their ribands tied about their hands, and three or four gold laces about their clothes.[104]

Women Friends were required to ensure that excessive eating or drinking, trivial pursuits, particularly frivolous books, card games and gambling were not permitted in their households. The rejection of trivialities, Sheila Wright has suggested, is more significant than it might otherwise appear. By channelling their efforts into more serious pursuits, Quaker women were undoubtedly raising their own standards as well as making their menfolk aware of their capabilities.[105] Epistles from the Yearly Meetings, or leading Friends, helped to clarify the rules, especially for the young who were told at Swansea in 1690 to cast 'aside all superfluities & needless things'.[106] In the London Yearly Meeting Epistle for 1720 members were informed that they should not 'suffer romances, play-books, or other vain and idle pamphlets in their houses or families, which tend to corrupt the minds of youth, but, instead thereof that they excite them to the reading of the Holy Scriptures and religious books'.[107] Women Friends had a key role in confinements, as midwives and official observers, and were involved in preparing the deceased for burial. In both cases, women ensured that rites of passage were conducted with simple decorum.

The Women's Yearly Meeting held from the mid-eighteenth century onwards called on women Friends, especially mothers, to set an example to their children, 'by walking humbly as becometh their profession, keeping to plainness of speech and habit, and avoiding to give or receive flattering titles, which tend to gratifie a proud mother'.[108] In addition, they had to ensure that young women did not go 'shop keeping or hous keeping' without the approval of their meeting.[109] The rule on plainness was particularly hard on the young, and inevitably some failed to abide by it. This may be related to a wider disaffection with the extreme conservatism of the Society, or to peer pressure. At the Women's Yearly Meeting, Llanidloes, in 1757, Friends admitted that they had 'not been as careful as we ought' and that they hoped to adhere more closely to the rules in the future.[110] As clothing was one of the ways in which status was publicly displayed, wealthy women found the rules on plainness especially challenging. In 1670, the inventory appended to the will of Mary Chapman of St Mellons listed wearing apparel worth £5, while Grace Webley of Shirenewton had clothing worth £8 at her death in 1679.[111] Other eighteenth-century wills reveal that Quaker women owned luxury clothing and accessories. In 1717, Rachel Ellis, formerly of Merionethshire, bequeathed land in Haverford, Pennsylvania, and an array of clothes, including a silk scarf, silk hood and silver buckles,[112] while, in 1724, Cecilia Handley bequeathed to her daughters: her 'best' clothes, her 'best' black scarf and her 'best' beaver hat.[113] Similarly, in 1778, Margaret Bevan of Llantrisant, Glamorganshire, bequeathed to Jennet Watkins her mink gown.[114]

Women were expected to behave in a civilized and dignified manner, and avoid gossiping. In 1705, Monmouthshire Friends reprimanded Mair Daniel for the 'unruly spirit that appeared in her to ye scandall of truth'.[115] Nearly half a century later, in 1750, the Women's Yearly Meeting at Brecon was still actively counselling improvement.[116] In rare cases, where offenders ignored advice and persisted in their bad behaviour, the Society would apply the ultimate sanction: disownment. In 1767, Michel Lewis of Shirenewton was accused of spreading rumours about John Jones, Ambrose

Williams and his wife, but even after counselling she remained stubborn and was disowned for her intransigence.[117] Her quarrelsome behaviour may well have been prompted by the earlier disownment of her husband, Thomas Lewis, in 1763 for refusing to settle a dispute with his sister-in-law.[118]

Female Friends were signatories of removal certificates. If a woman wished to transfer to another meeting both the men's and women's meetings had to be consulted. Only if they agreed that she was of 'good conversation and clearness' would they issue a certificate.[119] Women Friends were responsible for assisting new female members, and supporting their continuing association with the Society. As already noted, responsibility for poor relief rested heavily upon women members. Welsh women Quakers took their responsibilities very seriously and dispensed their own charity as well as that of the Society. In 1669, Mary Erbery gave 20s. to poor Friends of 'Mary Chapman's meeting', and in 1716, Ruth Harris of Christchurch bequeathed £5 to poor Friends at the Pont-y-Moel Meeting, as did Cecilia Handley of Pontypool in 1724.[120] In several cases the Monthly Meeting instigated an investigation by women members into poor relief payments. In 1710, Damaris and Rachel David of Marshfield were requested by the Men's Meeting to decide whether Jenkin Evan's wife ought to receive payment for 'the service shee did to Elizabeth Lewis'. She was duly awarded 10s.[121] In 1795, the charitable endeavours of Abiah Darby were praised in the form of a testimonial to the Welsh Yearly Meeting at Hay. She was

a tender sympathizer with the afflicted whether in body or mind and an Eminent Example of Christian Benevolence to those who are Stewards of the Good things of this life, being rich in good works, ready to distribute, willing to Communicate, feeding the hungry, cloathing the naked, visiting the sick.[122]

Wealthy women contributed to their meeting's general fund ('stock'), which was collected at national and county level to assist any indigent Friends.[123]

Finally, women Friends performed disciplinary duties. Many of their meetings examined and offered counselling to Friends when marriages were proposed, or where cases of immorality were reported. As noted, many of the charges brought against Friends involved sexual impropriety or marriage difficulties.[124] When allegations of a relationship with a non-member, or immorality, were brought before the local assembly it was assumed that leading female members would help to determine the facts of the case. Together with male colleagues, they would investigate the offence, and counsel or censure wrongdoers. The importance of the Society's ruling against mixed marriages is evident in the efforts made by women Friends to deter the development of inappropriate relationships and in their testimonies against those Friends who might infringe the code:

> If there be any that goes out to marry, with priests, or joineth in Marriage with the world, and does not obey the order of the Gospell as it is established amongst friends then for the womens monthly meeting to send to them, to reprove them, and to bear testimony against their acting Contrary to the truth, and if they come to repentance, and sorrow for their offence . . . they must bring in a paper of condemnation, and repentance, and Judgment of their Action . . . And also to carry that paper to the priest, that married them.[125]

Thus, in a letter of confession written in 1711 and read before the members, Barbara Williams of Llanfihangel Llantarnam, condemned 'ye spirit that led her to be married by a Priest'.[126] The full testimony was preserved and may well have been used as an exemplar whenever others broke the Society's rules on marriage. In her testimony, Williams confessed that

> I was prevailed upon to be joyned in marriage by a priest, contrary to ye law of God & ye faithfull in all ages thus I was kept in bondage, & under ye shadow of death for many yeares . . . I shall leave this as a testimony to condemn my disobedience especially that dark spirit wch did lead me to ye priests of Baal.[127]

The following year, leading women were asked to warn female members about the dangers of 'running to ye priests for husbands'.[128] In 1733, Elisha Beadles and Evan Bevan formally counselled Amy Jenkins of Llanfrechfa who had entered into relationship with a non-member, and also discussed it with her parents. At the same time, representatives of the women's meeting talked to both the daughter and the mother to 'endeavour to save ye young woman'.[129] Despite these heavy-handed efforts to persuade her to give up the man, she still refused and was disowned in July 1737.[130] The increasing number of disownments during the eighteenth century suggests that such warnings often went unheeded. Where there were signs of remorse, expressed in papers of condemnation, Quaker women tended to blame themselves or the local clergyman. It was rare for husbands to be accused of wrong-doing. As Barbara Williams acknowledged in 1711, she could not 'charge my dear husband for it was my happiness in that respect to meet with one yt is tender towards me'.[131] Amy Jenkins tendered a confession in which she admitted her failings and expressed deep regret for her actions. Nevertheless, having committed to the marriage, she did not feel able to

> break the bond or covenant I have entered into without due consideration, yet however I desire I may perform my marriage duty with patience and I desire I may find mercy before the throne of grace and that you would assist me with your prayers.[132]

It is clear that many of the responsibilities ascribed to women Friends were a tacit acknowledgment that there were different gender roles. They disciplined other women, and were heavily involved in family matters and poor relief. Yet even these caring duties required the sanction of male Friends. Notwithstanding the limitations outlined in this chapter, the Society gave female members an opportunity to voice their opinions, and allowed them a place in the ministry of the Society. For their part, women valued this measure of autonomy and were mostly valued by the men as 'helpmeets'. The experience gained from their preaching ministries and from involvement in meetings enabled Quaker women to achieve greater independence than most of their contemporaries. This, in turn, helped them to develop organizational and administrative skills which they could then apply to other aspects of their lives. The declining number of women Friends led to the closure of the Women's Yearly

175

Meeting in 1797 and its replacement with a Half-Yearly Meeting which continued until 1832. In spite of new Quaker families moving into Wales, the decline in numbers proved irreversible and amalgamations followed.[133]

Chapter 7

'Letting their minds into the world'?
The Decline of the Welsh Quaker Communities

Within the memory of many, there was here a flourishing congregation. Now the Meeting can hardly be said to exist. One infirm, lame old man, still crosses the hills at the hour of worship to sit there alone with God.[1]

The decline of the Society of Friends in Radnorshire was an all too familiar tale.[2] Mapping the decline of Quakerism in statistical terms is problematic, not least because of the partial survival of some records. However, even without access to precise data, it can still be asserted that the Quaker community in Britain, with some notable exceptions,[3] had significantly declined by the mid-eighteenth century. By 1715, as a result of falling attendance figures and the failure to attract new members, Friends registered only twenty-four congregations in Wales.[4] Notwithstanding the revivals in Cardiff, west Glamorgan and Pembrokeshire, the latter two deriving from the settlement of industrialists and the Quaker-whalers from Nantucket at Milford Haven in the 1790s,[5] other Welsh Quaker communities struggled to maintain their meetings. The last Welsh Yearly Meeting was held at Welshpool in 1797, and thereafter Friends met at a Half-Yearly Meeting[6] Quarterly Meetings in north and south Wales were abandoned at the same time;[7] and the decline in membership is evident in the attendance statistics for meetings. The Monthly Meeting of Merioneth and Montgomery Friends, which had merged in 1769, was represented in 1813 by just twenty-one members,[8] while in 1816 the south Wales Monthly Meetings had a combined membership of 178 (Carmarthenshire and Glamorganshire: 112; Monmouthshire: 36; and Pembrokeshire: 30).[9] By 1836, the membership of the south and central Wales meetings had fallen to 108, and this slumped to 68 members by 1866.[10]

A close scrutiny of the Montgomeryshire, east Glamorgan and Monmouthshire Quaker communities affords a better understanding of the impact of decline at the local level. The ecclesiastical returns for the diocese of St Asaph in 1738 indicated that there were a few Friends in Meifod, Ruabon, and Wrexham, and only a 'poor & obstinate Quaker' in Erbistoc. At Henllan, there was a single Friend who was described as 'an ingenious man very much bigoted to his own opinion'; while at Welshpool and Guilsfield there were three Quakers out of 781 families. Clearly efforts had been made to convert the Friends, but with little success: at Llangyniew, of 102 families there were but two women who had resisted 'the most persuasive argument' of the local vicar.[11] According to the 1749 returns, the few remained faithful, but it is clear that no new members were being recruited. By 1776 there was one solitary Friend recorded at Llangurig and 'a few of low rank' at Trefeglwys.[12] The Tref-y-Rhyg Meeting in Glamorgan, which had briefly revived after the return of John Bevan and his family from Pennsylvania in 1704, was absorbed into the Monmouthshire Quarterly Meeting in 1708. By 1763, of 250 families in Llantrisant and Llantwit Faerdre there was only one Quaker family,[13] and in the following year responsibility for their meeting house was devolved to Monmouthshire Friends.[14] In the mid-1720s meetings were abandoned at Abergavenny (c.1725), Castleton/St Mellons (c.1736) and the Pant (c.1756). John Churchman of Nottingham visited the remaining Monmouthshire meetings in 1753; he found the Shirenewton meeting 'dull' and, while Pont-y-Moel could provide large public meetings for worship, it failed to offer 'a formal ministry'.[15] Twelve years later, John Rule of Llanfair Isgoed observed that Friends in the Pontypool district were very few in number,[16] and this is corroborated by other evidence. The Llandaff ecclesiastical returns for Monmouthshire in 1763 are presented in the table below (see table 7.1),[17] and although they do not include all of the constituent meetings they graphically illustrate the collapse of the Society.[18] In the four parishes where the Pont-y-Moel Meeting had previously drawn its greatest support, namely, Mamheilad, Trefddyn, Pant-Teg and

Table 7.1. Quaker Population in Monmouthshire Parishes *c*.1763

Parish	Population (Families)	Quaker/ Dissenting Families
St Mellons	50	1
Llanfihangel Pont-y-Moel	30	0
Mamheilad	31	2
Trefddyn	320	7
Chepstow	140	1
Llanfrechfa	40	10 (dissenting)
Llanisien (Usk)	11 farmers and 26 cottagers	1
Llantrisaint (Usk)	38	1
Pant-Teg	57	4
Pen-Clawdd (Usk)	7	1

Pont-y-Moel, Friends numbered a mere 13 families out of a total of 438. The numbers were so slight, especially in Pont-y-Moel parish which had no dissenters, that the official recorder, who might have been tempted to play down the statistics, did not even register the existence of the meeting house.[19] In Chepstow, there was one Quaker family among 140,[20] while in Llanisien, there was one solitary Quaker living among 37 farmers and cottagers.[21] One can only speculate the sense of isolation felt by the residuum who would have been under ever-increasing pressure to abandon their faith and make common cause with their neighbours. In other areas where Quakerism had once had a foothold, Friends were no longer in evidence and even other dissenting communities were barely represented. For example, St Mellons parish[22] had only one dissenter out of 50 families, while in Marshfield, out of a total of 60 families, only 5 inhabitants were identified as Dissenters. Apart from signifying the decline of Quakerism, it may, if the figures were accurately recorded, suggest a shift away from older forms of dissent in this part of the county.[23] By 1774, the estimated number of Friends for the whole of Monmouthshire was seven, plus three or four Friends in Mamheilad and Pant-Teg parishes.[24] The returns for 1781 record a Quaker population of just 21 in the county.[25]

In October 1783, Monmouthshire Friends tried to rally members by calling upon them to have 'a godly care' for one another,[26] but two years later there was no improvement and the clerk recorded that 'the state of our meeting is in general low and languid, and increase of zeal and fervency of spirit, being much awanting'.[27] Some slight revival took place in the closing decades of the eighteenth century with the arrival of the Harford family[28] and the leadership of James Lewis of Llanelly, Breconshire. Yet this was not sustained. The Monthly Meeting was adjourned in October 1797 'on account of the smallness of the number present'.[29] In January 1806 Mary Capper, who was a regular visitor to Monmouthshire in this period, was sorry to witness their 'brokenness of spirit', especially as she had celebrated the opening of a new meeting house at Trosnant, Pontypool, in 1802.[30] By 1851, the religious census showed that Friends represented less than 0.01 per cent of the total population of Monmouthshire. This can be compared to the meetings in Herefordshire and Gloucester where Friends represented 1 in 800 and with meetings in adjacent Welsh counties where the ratios were between 1 in 4,800 and 1 in 6,400.[31] The *Pontypool Free Press* reported in July 1868 that two meetings had been held at the 'Old Quaker's chapel' at Trosnant, attended by two Quakers from Leominster and Worcester, and noted that: 'No similar services had been held there for about twenty years, the Society, which once flourished in the neighbourhood, having entirely died out.'[32]

In the 1920s, Thomas Mardy Rees drew attention to the fluctuating fortunes of Welsh Quakerism, and advanced a multi-causal explanation for its subsequent decline. While much of what Rees had to offer has been endorsed by both earlier and later generations of historians, there are notable differences in interpretation.[33] For example, Rees makes very little of the effects of disownment for marrying outside the Society, and, as might be expected, he emphasized instead the passing of the 'heroic age' which left the movement without an effective leadership. For commentators like Rees, leadership was all. In addition, his explanation fails to take into account the remarkable diversity of the Quaker experience in Wales. While it is true that emigration was a key factor in the decline of most Welsh communities, it hardly affected

Monmouthshire. Wales remained a predominantly rural country and so any argument that Quaker landowners became wealthy industrial entrepreneurs, at the expense of their religious beliefs, cannot be universally applied. While Rees rightly homes in on the leadership's preference for English in its communications and how this obstructed the missionary work, he does not register the growth of other Nonconformist congregations, especially Methodists who were so successful in Wales during the period of Quakerism's decline.[34]

Many historians agree that at the end of the 1690s the next generation of Quakers lacked the tenacity and dynamism of the pioneers of the Commonwealth and Restoration years. For Rees, the death of George Fox marked the end of the 'heroic age' of the Society, and his loss was deemed irreplaceable by those who had benefited from his charismatic leadership. Geraint Jenkins points out that an entire generation of Welsh and English religious leaders was lost after 1688. John ap John, Lewis Owen of Tyddyn-y-garreg, Robert Owen of Dolserau, Charles Lloyd II of Dolobran, Richard Davies of Welshpool and key members of the Hanbury and Bevan families in south Wales were all dead by 1708, and were succeeded by devout men like John Kelsall and Evan Bevan. Kelsall, for all his deep spirituality and commitment to Welsh Quakerism, was 'hardly a ball of fire'.[35] Passion gave way to quietism and recruitment suffered.

The early leaders had kept the Society together in the most challenging of circumstances, during the worst years of persecution. Naturally, historians have registered the combined effects of oppression, imprisonment and crippling fines which deterred so many from joining such a beleaguered cause. The imprisonment and death of many of the Society's leaders left a vacuum that was difficult to fill. Although many Quakers endured their hardships with admirable stoicism, they could not always count on the continuing loyalty of all their members, whilst threats of harassment, distraint of property and imprisonment persisted. So long as the Clarendon Code was rigidly applied the Society remained relatively small. Persecution was not an entirely negative force, however, for those who were isolated by their outsider status developed strong coping mechanisms. Perverse though it may appear, toleration not persecution was to prove more damaging in the long term. As Adrian Davies has noted for Essex, after the introduction of toleration 'the Quakers' sense of their own distinctiveness was to a degree removed'.[36]

For some Friends, emigration to the American colonies offered a new way forward,[37] but their departure left their communities sadly depleted and weak. As Jenkins observed,

> If persecution effectively thinned out Quaker ranks in Wales, from 1682 onwards their numbers were further depleted when groups of virile, independent, Welsh-speaking Friends chose to leave the major Quaker bastions in Wales to establish a holy Christian community, under the leadership of William Penn in the 'good and fruitful land' of Pennsylvania.[38]

William Penn was granted the province of Pennsylvania by Royal Charter in March 1681, and twelve prominent Welsh Quakers travelled to London the following May to examine his plans for the new colony. Consequently, seven Welsh companies were established and just over 43,000 acres of land were acquired on the west side of Schuylkill river which variously became known as the 'Welsh barony', 'Cambria', 'New Wales' or the 'Welsh Tract'.[39] This land was then sold in small plots to Welshmen who, it is suggested, came from 'the best social classes'[40] but who, in reality, were a mixture of minor gentry, yeoman and craftsmen.[41]

For many Welsh Quakers who longed for religious freedom the possibility of a 'Quaker colony' was very attractive. Barry Levy has noted that between 1681 and 1695, 37 per cent of emigrants from north Wales had faced imprisonment and 42 per cent had been fined for a variety of reasons.[42] Among them were many of the stalwarts of Quakerism in this part of Wales, including Rowland Ellis, Thomas Lloyd, Thomas Wynne, John Humphrey and Robert Owen. They believed that emigration was in the best interests of their children and a means of safeguarding their own spiritual well-being. For others, the potential to make a good living from the land was the main inducement. In 1685, Thomas Ellis of Is Cregennan, Merionethshire, explained his decision to emigrate thus:

I wish those that have estates of their own . . . may not be offended at the Lords opening a door of mercy to thousands in England, especially in Wales & other nations who had no estates for themselves or children, And that all their industry could not afford them the meanest food & Raymt [raiment] that might properly be sayd to belong even to slaves or servants.[43]

A more circumspect view was provided in 1698 by Rowland Ellis of Bryn Mawr, Pennsylvania. In a letter to Robert Johnson, minister of St Illtyd, near Dolgellau, Merionethshire, he wrote:

I desire yt none may take occasion by any word yt discovers, nor suppose if I do nor did repent of my coming, for be it far from me from encouraging any to venture ymselves, & what they have, furtherly they live comfortable in their native country to ye danger of ye seas and many more inconvenience yt may happen & on ye other hand discourage any yt hath any real inclinations to transport themselves into ye hands of providence. Some cam here might have better staid in their own country, & it is my thought yt great many more would have done better here yt ever they are like to do in their own country.[44]

Significantly, for the Quaker Meetings in south Wales, John Bevan of Tref-y-Rhyg registered an interest in Penn's plan, and in September 1681 eventually bought 2,750 acres.[45] Bevan was largely influenced by his wife, as his journal reveals:

my wife had a great inclination to go thither and thought it might be a good place to train up children amongst sober people and to prevent the corruption of them here, by the loose behaviour of youths, and the bad example of too many of riper years . . . I was sensible her aim was an upright one.[46]

Economic prosperity and religious freedom soon led other Friends to follow the first settlers. It is estimated that for £20 a family of four and a servant could secure passage to America and 500 acres of land.[47] It was cheaper for Welsh meetings to send an entire needy family to the colonies than it was to assist an orphan youth into an apprenticeship in England. In July 1690, north Wales Friends collected £15 to send Robert Ellis, 'a poor friend', and his family to

183

Pennsylvania,[48] where Quakers helped to found the 'Merion' tract and named settlements after their former Welsh homes.[49] However, Penn's 'New Jerusalem' did not remain the preserve of Welsh emigrants as many other European exiles sought sanctuary in the colonies in the eighteenth century. The dream of building a free and vibrant Welsh religious community was far removed from the harsh reality of eking out a living where there was 'neither house nor shelter',[50] and the reorganization of the Welsh barony was a further complication. The abolition of civil authority in 1690 and its replacement with township government was also a disappointment for the Welsh, as it broke the spirit of the understanding between John ap John and William Penn.[51]

Emigration to the Welsh Tract after 1682 had a major impact upon Quaker communities in Wales. Not only did Friends lose some of their key members, but those who remained were ill suited to the task of taking the Society forward. When John Bevan finally left Wales in 1683, the Tref-y-Rhyg Meeting regretted the

> great loss we and others have sustained in the removal of our deare friends John ap Bevan and Barbarah his wife . . . with their tender family in Pennsylvania . . . And further we do certifie that we accounted them as Pillers to this Meeting [and] accounted as nursing father and nursing mother in this place to some weake and young amongst us.[52]

The Welsh Yearly Meeting at Llanidloes in April 1697 was concerned that only 'the remnant' remained, and, therefore, they called on Friends to consult the elders and 'to have their unity afore they resolve to remove to Pensilvania or elsewhere'.[53] Despite their best efforts, the attractions of Pennsylvania proved irresistible. Between 1697 and 1698 the returning migrant Hugh Roberts persuaded William John and Thomas ap Evan from north Wales to buy a further 7,820 acres of land in Pennsylvania. This was again sold in small plots, and by 1698 the second wave of Quaker emigration had begun. The settlement was soon to become known as Gwynedd.[54] Emigration was a significant contributing factor to the decline of the Society throughout many parts of Wales, especially in Montgomeryshire, Merionethshire, Radnorshire and Pembrokeshire. Between 1682 and 1700, 200 Cheshire and Welsh Quaker families settled in the Delaware valley,[55] while there was a further wave of migration from the Quaker communities in north and west Wales between 1700 and 1729.[56] During this latter period, north Wales Friends found themselves in severe financial difficulties, and wrote to Bristol Friends on 2 October 1712 appealing for help.[57]

Some communities were less affected by migration, and their decline must be attributed to other causes. Records for the emigration of Monmouthshire Friends to Pennsylvania are sparse, and therefore it is difficult to offer firm evidence about its scale. Nevertheless, of the 2,000 Quakers who left Wales to settle in Pennsylvania between 1682 and 1700,[58] Monmouthshire Friends represent a very small proportion indeed. This may be because they did not send representatives to the London conference arranged by Penn in 1682.[59] In his examination of Welsh émigrés to Pennsylvania, Thomas Glenn only found six individuals and the family of Lewis Thomas from Monmouthshire and, among them, he mistakenly included Martha Aubrey of Llanelieu, Breconshire.[60] In 1684, these few migrants were joined by James Howell of Pontypool who became a freeholder in the Radnor Township. In September 1691, Friends signed a removal certificate for Rees Thomas of Chepstow,[61] but it was not until 1699 that the records show the loss of more families overseas. It is, of course, still possible that other voyages to Pennsylvania by Monmouthshire Friends occurred during this period, but were not recorded. In the eighteenth century Quaker emigration from the county was negligible, yet it can be argued that even the loss of one family would have some impact upon these fragile communities.[62]

Although persecution and emigration posed considerable problems for Welsh communities, other factors contributed to the decline of the Society. Welsh Quaker meetings began to shun missionary work in favour of introspective and quietist gatherings centred on the application of their code of conduct. John Kelsall feared that 'a spirit of ease has got in amongst many professors of Truth spreading like an hidden leprosie' and had begun to weaken the resolve of the Society.[63] In the mid-nineteenth century commentators such as John S. Rowntree and Thomas Hancock asserted that Friends had lost their passion for spreading the Quaker message as they became increasingly institutionalized. They both judged that the code of conduct had led Quakers to be more inward looking and less pioneering, and this cultural shift was compounded by the loss of the first generation of leaders.[64] These views were endorsed by later generations of Quaker historians, including John W. Rowntree,[65] William Braithwaite and Rufus Jones.[66] They too believed that the organizational structure, which initially supported the Society, put in place an inflexible form of discipline that fostered an unhelpful insularity and a more passive outlook. These explanations were elaborated upon by Brian Wilson, Richard Vann and Christopher Hill, who all related the decline of Quakerism to organizational change and, in particular, to the evolution from a sect to a denomination.[67] In the process, the Society's ethos was said to have fundamentally changed. The desire for respectability and acceptance by their local communities had supposedly fatally weakened the missionary spirit.

Michael Mullett and Nicholas Morgan have challenged some of these explanations. Mullett has revisited the theory that the achievement of denominational status was achieved at the cost of the Society's longevity, and concluded that the transformation was far from complete. Hanoverian Quakers in Lancashire, he maintains, continued to exhibit most of the characteristics of a sect.[68] Nicholas Morgan has supported Mullett's findings, and questions those analyses which view the code of discipline as a negative force.[69] On the contrary, he claims that until the 1760s the code of discipline among Lancashire Friends was 'a tool to stimulate spiritual growth'.[70] While the evidence given by Mullett and Morgan appears to refute the traditional view that the roots of decline can be found in the imposition of discipline after 1690, their arguments apply only to the particular relationship that Lancashire Friends had with the Church and state.

David Scott's study of York Friends between 1650 and 1720 adds further complications. He argues that they relinquished the radical millenarianism which so distinguished them in the early years of the Society, but they still retained a sectarian identity because of their clothing and puritanical lifestyle. Even though Friends strengthened their code of conduct this did not protect them from outside influences. 'Gospel order', he maintains, was primarily 'to confirm Friends' place in the community of the godly'.[71] Nevertheless, he believes that Quakerism in York was becoming an accepted denomination, citing as evidence the Society's accommodation with 'sober people of other persuasions' and improved relationships with the civic authorities.[72] As ever, these English examples merely demonstrate that the experience of Quakerism was diverse and regionally differentiated.

The quest for respectability can be partly located in the wider economic and social changes associated with proto-industrialization.[73] John S. Rowntree highlighted the way that certain wealthy Friends began to privilege their new business interests.[74] As these Quaker businessmen achieved material success which brought them increasingly into association with non-Quakers, they were more reluctant to draw attention to their Quaker identity, and sought to play down the more puritanical aspects of their beliefs. As James Walvin has noted, in the first half of the eighteenth century Quakers controlled between 50 and 75 per cent of the iron industry in England and Wales.[75] Charles Lloyd III of Dolobran who, unlike his predecessors, recklessly 'followed the path of economic self-betterment' and became insolvent in 1727, epitomized everything the Quaker hierarchy counselled against: he was irresponsible, materialist and self-indulgent.[76] The prosperity for which Quakers became renowned created notable stresses and strains.[77] The homes of the Quaker elite, especially in London, were elaborately furnished according to fashionable tastes, and, as these social networks grew stronger, their older solidarities based around the meeting house, became less significant.[78] In 1712, John Kelsall wrote to John Merrick of his fears for the Society: 'the true Church is very much . . . crucifyed between the two thieves Liberty & Carnal Security'.[79] In his analysis, Nicholas Morgan highlighted the differences between Quakers living in urban and rural areas. Urban-dwelling Quakers, notably those from south-east England, were more likely to seek accommodation with their neighbours. Conversely, rural Friends, in the north-west of England, for example, refused to compromise their principles, especially in terms of tithe payments and oaths.[80]

Some historians have proposed that by privileging English in spoken and written communication, the Society alienated the predominantly Welsh-speaking population, especially after the introduction of the Toleration Act in 1689.[81] In the early years, the use of Welsh allowed Quakerism to prosper through many areas of Wales, and as J. Gwynn Williams has observed, Merionethshire Friends were 'securely rooted in the language and culture of Wales'.[82] Even though there were times in the meetings when Welsh was spoken, letters were written in the vernacular or books were translated,[83] for the most part Quakerism was an English movement which paid scant attention to the Welsh language. This was in marked contrast to Welsh Catholic priests who not only produced a significant amount of devotional literature in Welsh in the seventeenth century, but also recognized that using the Welsh language was a 'strict necessity'.[84] Of the 142 Quaker ministers who visited the Dolobran Meeting between 1701 and 1712, only fifteen were from Wales and only eight could communicate in Welsh. This was despite strong evidence that Welsh was highly effective when addressing a non-Quaker audience.[85] H. G. Jones insisted that, 'Quakerism did not blend very successfully with Welsh national life and character in the seventeenth and eighteenth centuries.'[86] Notwithstanding the remarkable vitality of Welsh literature in this period, and the constant requests for Welsh texts made at the Yearly Meetings, the production of indigenous Quaker literature was meagre and infrequent. After the Llanidloes Yearly Meeting in 1702 a subscription was raised and a small number of Welsh translations of well-known Quaker texts were published.[87] Such initiatives were not sustained. According to Jonathan Lloyd, Quakerism was 'never fully Welsh, and the leaders invariably regarded Wales as part of England. Even when the Annual Conferences were held in Wales, most of the meetings were conducted in English.'[88] In 1738, the Yearly Meeting epistle was read out in Welsh 'for the sake of [Monmouthshire] Friends . . . that did not understand English'.[89] However, the situation was compounded by the lack of Welsh Quaker schools and the failure to install the Welsh language as part of the urriculum.[90] The opportunity to sustain their language and cultural identity was a key element in the decision to relocate to Pennsylvania. Once settled, émigrés quickly created their own associational life, developed educational and social institutions and, most notably of all, began to publish Welsh literature.[91] In 1721, the first Welsh-language text was published in America with Ellis Pugh's *Annerch i'r Cymru*, and this was subsequently translated as *A Salutation to the Britons*.[92] It could also be argued that the unemotional and studious nature of eighteenth-century Quakerism was less appealing to the Welsh people than the passionate preaching of the pioneers. The crusade for moral reform and attacks on recreational activities not only struck at the heart of Welsh popular culture, but clearly shows the gulf which existed between Friends and the wider population.

Failure from within was only one part of the story of decline; outside influences must also be taken into account. Mollie Grubb and others have linked the rise of Methodism to the Society's weakening hold on the loyalties of their members.[93] John Kelsall was all too aware that a new religious movement could induce others away from Quakerism. In 1724, he wrote that 'the Lord wearied with waiting for faithfulness from his People will chuse others'.[94] Later, in 1731, he observed that, although many people attended their meetings, few joined the Society. Kelsall questioned the presentation of the Quaker message. He was concerned that Friends were so preoccupied with respectability that they failed to testify 'against the reigning wicked practices in the great & the lifeless superstitious ministry of the Priests'. Rather than focus on dress he thought Friends should direct their energies into opposing the lax spiritual and moral standards:

> it is my belief God will raise in due time a people out of Friends or others who will be commissioned to strike at the Root & Branch of Anti-Christ without regard to the frowns & Favours of High or Low clergy or others & then & not till then I greatly fear it will be that we shall have any considerable addition to the church.[95]

Within four years the vitality of the Methodist Revival had persuaded large numbers to join, while Quaker conversions dried up.[96] Methodism strongly appealed to the Welsh character as it combined spirited preaching with passionate hymn-singing.

Methodist congregations were expanding in Monmouthshire in the mid-eighteenth century with gatherings near Quaker meetings at Pant-Teg (c.1744), Pontypool (c.1749) and New Inn (c.1751).[97] During the early 1750s the Methodist movement was rocked by internal divisions, but the Llangeitho revival of 1762 reinvigorated the movement.[98] By the end of the century, Methodist congregations were sufficiently large to warrant the establishment of new chapels. In Shirenewton, two Wesleyan chapels were built in 1799; the Calvinistic Methodists erected a chapel in St Mellons the following year; and after 1814 several Methodist congregations were established in the Pontypool area.[99] The Methodists were not alone in growing their communities. Before 1780, Congregationalists and Baptists were very successful, particularly in south Wales.[100]

From this investigation into the decline of the Society, it is apparent that there were various factors which led to the disintegration of the Quaker faith in Wales. Some of these concerns, more than others, contributed to the gradual withering away of support until only 'the remnant' remained. Yet, as has been shown, it would be wrong to assume that decline had gathered pace throughout the eighteenth century and quickened in the early decades of the nineteenth century. True, many Friends were disowned, emigrated or resigned their membership during this period, but it is probably more accurate to see the disintegration of the Society as a slow process. Many of the Friends who died in the early nineteenth century had lived long and, for several of them, prosperous lives. What led to the collapse of the Society was the inability to retain the allegiance of younger members, and hence the lifeblood of the Quaker community was lost. The increasing demand by the Society for endogamous marriages in the eighteenth century proved to be unacceptable and indeed wholly impracticable for many Friends, especially those in rural Wales. The shortage of available Quaker marriage partners meant that the only option for many young Friends was a relationship with a non-member. Michael Mullett has suggested that, in the mid-eighteenth century, 'undesirable marriages could not be unmade' and Lancashire Friends had 'little choice but to readmit the exogamously married'.[101] In Wales, such pragmatism seems to have been unusual; membership was not normally reinstated unless those who infringed the code by 'marrying out' publicly admitted the error of their ways. Evidence from Glamorganshire and Monmouthshire shows that exogamous marriage was the cause of more disownments than any other infringement of the code.[102]

The Welsh language was vital to religious and cultural life, and it has been suggested that Quakers, 'stood in complete isolation in Wales – spiritually, as a deliberately Nonconformist body; culturally, as a non-Welsh body; socially, as people who condemned the popular pleasures; economically, as being above the general economic level'.[103] A greater willingness to address the cultural difference would have enabled Friends to breach the communication divide which obstructed their missionary work, especially in rural areas. The social geography of Wales presupposed that there would be many Quakers living in small isolated hamlets and villages, and ministering to their needs presented the Society with notable difficulties. The Society's attitude to exogamous marriage took little account of the realities of Welsh rural life, and it is hardly surprising that so many fled overseas to secure the religious and cultural solidarities that Pennsylvania promised.

Notes

References and the Quaker Records

1 See H. G. Jones, 'John Kelsall: A Study in Religious and Economic History' (unpublished University of Wales, Bangor, MA thesis, 1938), 5–7.

Introduction

1 GAS, D/DSF/353, (28.10.1741). Thomas Lewis's third paper entitled 'A Warning For All Youth'.

2 Ibid. Little is known about Thomas Lewis and there are very few references to him or to members of his family in the minutes of the Quarterly or Monthly meetings of Monmouthshire Friends or in other records. The evidence available does suggest that he had a son called Thomas, a daughter Mary, and lived in or near the village of Shirenewton. On 12 December 1746, Lewis was interred in the Shirenewton burial ground. See NA, SoF Registers. (Monmouthshire). No. 677, fo. 176.

3 GAS, D/DSF/353, (5/8/1741, 28/10/1741, 3/12/1741).

4 R. Pope (ed.), *Religion and National Identity: Wales and Scotland, c.1700–2000* (Cardiff, 2001), p. 3.

5 G. H. Jenkins, *Protestant Dissenters in Wales 1639–1689* (Cardiff, 1992), p. 7.

6 A. Davies, *The Quakers in English Society 1655–1725* (Oxford, 2000), whose study relies upon Colchester and Essex Friends. See also David Scott, *Quakerism in York, 1650–1720*, Borthwick Paper, 80 (York, 1991); N. J. Morgan, *Lancashire Quakers and the Establishment 1660–1730* (Halifax, 1993).

7 GAS, D/DSF/329–31.

8 GAS, DSF/320–2.

[9] GAS, D/DSF/27. This excludes the Women's Meeting minutes which are extant between 1785 and 1815, and the Montgomeryshire Preparative Meeting minutes between 1800 and 1814. See GAS, D/DSF/26; GAS, D/DSF/328.

[10] For details, see bibliography.

[11] From this it has been possible to compile a database of Friends in the county.

[12] For example, John Gough, *A History of the People called Quakers, from their first rise to the present time* (Dublin, 1789); Thomas Clarkson, *A Portraiture of Quakerism* (3 vols, London, 1806).

[13] General studies on the Quaker faith and its history include W. C. Braithwaite, *The Beginnings of Quakerism*, revised H. J. Cadbury (2nd edn, York, 1981), and *The Second Period of Quakerism*, revised H. J. Cadbury (2nd edn, York, 1979); A. Lloyd, *Quaker Social History 1669–1738* (London, 1950).

[14] T. M. Rees, *A History of the Quakers in Wales and their Emigration to North America* (Carmarthen, 1925).

[15] R. T. Vann, *Social Development of English Quakerism 1655–1755* (Cambridge, Mass., 1969); E. Isichei, *Victorian Quakers* (London, 1970); B. Reay, *The Quakers and the English Revolution* (Hounslow, 1985); Rosemary Moore, *The Light in their Consciences: Early Quakers in Britain* (Philadelphia, 2000); K. Peters, *Print Culture and the Early Quakers* (Cambridge, 2005).

[16] Although a considerable amount of work has been published for Wales, much of this offers a county rather than a national perspective. In addition, some texts have a very limited chronological remit. See H. G. Jones, 'John Kelsall: A Study in Religious and Economic History' (unpublished University of Wales, MA thesis, 1938); E. R. Morris, 'Quakerism in West Montgomeryshire', *MC*, 56 (1959–60), 45–65; M. F. Williams, 'The Society of Friends in Glamorgan 1654–1900' (unpublished University of Wales, Aberystwyth, MA thesis, 1950), and her subsequent article 'Glamorgan Quakers 1654–1900', *Morgannwg*, 5 (1961), 49–75; E. R. Morris, 'Llanwddyn Quakers', *MC*, 86 (1978), 46–59; J. G. Williams, 'The Quakers of Merioneth during the seventeenth century', *JMHRS*, 8 (1978–9), 122–56, 312–39; Trevor Macpherson, *Friends in Radnorshire: A Brief History of the Quakers* (Llandrindod Wells, 1999). Other historians have assumed a thematic approach, see G. H. Jenkins, 'Quaker and anti-Quaker literature in Wales from the Restoration to Methodism', *WHR*,

7 (4) (1975), 403–26; C. Trevett, *Quaker Women Prophets in England and Wales 1650–1700* (Lewiston; Queenston and Lampeter, 2000).

17 Larry Ingle, 'The future of Quaker history', *JFHS*, 59 (1) (1997), 1–16.

18 Ibid., 1–2.

19 Ibid., 6.

20 Apart from several standard texts for English Quakerism there is a substantial body of published primary and secondary literature in existence of Quakers for the English border counties and Bristol, including several works by R. S. Mortimer (ed.), *Minute Book of the Men's Meeting of the Society of Friends in Bristol, 1667–1686* (Bristol, 1971); *Minute Book of the Men's Meeting of the Society of Friends in Bristol, 1686–1704* (Bristol, 1977); 'Bristol Quakers and the Oaths', *JFHS*, 43 (1951), 74–7; and *Early Bristol Quakerism: The Society of Friends in the City, 1654–1700* (Bristol, 1967); S. K. Roberts, 'The Quakers in Evesham 1655–1660: a study in religion, politics and culture', *Midland History*, 16 (1991), 63–84; R. G. Lacock, 'The Quakers in Gloucester 1655–1737' (unpublished University of Birmingham, M.Phil. thesis, 2001).

21 More general or county-based studies include articles by Barry Reay: 'The social origins of early Quakerism', *Journal of Interdisciplinary History*, 11 (1) (Summer 1980), 55–72; 'Popular hostility towards Quakers in mid-seventeenth century England', *Social History*, 5 (1980), 387–407; 'Quaker opposition to tithes 1652–1660', *P&P*, 86 (1980), 98–120; and his *The Quakers in the English Revolution* (Hounslow, 1985); Michael A. Mullett (ed.), *Early Lancaster Friends* (Lancaster, 1978); and his 'From sect to denomination: social development in 18th century English Quakerism', *Journal of Religious History*, 13 (2) (1984), 168–91; E. Bell, "Vain unsettled fashions': the early Durham Friends and popular culture, *c.*1660–1725', *QS*, 8 (1) (September 2003), 23–35.

22 Catherine M. Wilcox, *Theology and Women's Ministry in Seventeenth-Century English Quakerism: Handmaids of the Lord* (Lampeter, 1995); C. Trevett, *Women and Quakerism in the Seventeenth Century* (York, 1991); Kay Taylor, 'The role of women in the seventeenth century, and the experiences of the Wiltshire Friends', *Southern History*, 123 (2001), 10–29; Catie Gill, *Women in the Seventeenth-Century Quaker Community: A Literary Study of Political Identities, 1650–1700* (Aldershot, 2005).

23 R. C. Allen, "Taking up her daily cross': women and the early

Quaker movement in Wales, 1653–1689', in Michael Roberts and Simone Clarke (eds), *Women and Gender in Early Modern Wales* (Cardiff, 2000), pp. 104–28; Trevett, *Quaker Women Prophets in England and Wales.*

[24] LSF, Kelsall MS. S.194.2, p. 16 (John Kelsall to John Ecroyd jnr of Lancaster, 8mo 1701).

[25] For the purposes of this study, Welsh Quaker emigration to Pennsylvania has been viewed within the broad context of decline. An exhaustive investigation drawing upon American and British sources is close to completion and will be the subject of my forthcoming book, *Transatlantic Connections: Welsh Quaker Emigrants and Colonial Pennsylvania, 1650–1766.*

Chapter 1 Origins of the Society of Friends in Wales

[1] LSF, E/109 (7 May 1653).

[2] G. F. Nuttall, *The Welsh Saints, 1640–60: Walter Cradock, Vavasor Powell, Morgan Llwyd* (Cardiff, 1957).

[3] H. Barbour, *The Quakers in England* (London, 1964), ch. 1; C. Hill, *The World Turned Upside Down* (Harmondsworth, 1975); M. Watts, *The Dissenter: From the Reformation to the French Revolution* (Oxford, 1978); M. A. Mullett, *Radical Religious Movements in Early Modern Europe* (London, 1980); J. F. MacGregor and B. Reay (eds), *Radical Religion in the English Revolution* (Oxford, 1984); B. Reay, *The Quakers and the English Revolution* (Hounslow, 1985); R. J. Acheson, *Radical Puritans in England, 1550–1660* (London, 1990); N. J. Morgan, *Lancashire Quakers and the Establishment 1660–1730* (Halifax, 1993); A. Davies, *The Quakers in English Society 1655–1725* (Oxford, 2000).

[4] D. Scott, 'Politics, Dissent and Quakerism in York, 1640–1700' (unpublished University of York, Ph.D. thesis, 1990), 7–8; Davies, *Quakers in English Society*, pp. 129–33; R. Moore, *The Light in their Consciences: Early Quakers in Britain* (Philadelphia, 2000), p. 4; C. Gill, *Women in the Seventeenth-Century Quaker Community* (Aldershot, 2005), pp. 12–13, 23–7.

[5] Scott, 'Politics, Dissent and Quakerism in York', 8–10.

[6] Richard Davies, *An Account of the Convincement, Exercises and Services and Travels of . . . Richard Davies* (London, 1877), pp. 26–7. See also T. A. Glenn, *Merion in the Welsh Tract* (Morriston, Pa, 1896), p. 224; J. G. Williams, 'The Quakers of Merioneth during the Seventeenth Century', *JMHRS*, 8 (1978–9), 147, for further examples of family divisions.

7   B. Hall, 'Puritanism – the problem of definition', in G. Cuming (ed.), *Studies in Church History*, 2 (London, 1965), pp. 283–96; Melvin B. Endy, 'Puritans, Spiritualist and Quakerism: An Historiographical Essay', in Richard S. Dunn and Mary Maples Dunn (eds), *The World of William Penn* (Philadelphia, 1986), pp. 281–301.

8   J. W. Frost, 'The Dry Bones of Quaker Theology', *Church History*, 39 (1970), 504.

9   Kevin Sharpe, *The Personal Rule of Charles I* (New Haven and London, 1992).

10 Kenneth Fincham (ed.), *The Early Stuart Church, 1603–1642* (Basingstoke, 1993); C. Hill, 'Archbishop Laud and the English Revolution', in G. J. Schochet, P. E. Tatspaugh and C. Brobeck (eds), *Religion, Resistance, and Civil War* (Washington, DC, 1990), pp. 127–49.

11 R. L. Greaves, 'The Puritan-Nonconformist Tradition in England, 1560–1700: Historiographical Reflections', *Albion*, 17 (4) (Winter 1985), 449–86.

12 W. C. Braithwaite, *The Beginnings of Quakarism* (York, 1981), ch. 2; H. L. Ingle, *First Among Friends: George Fox and the creation of Quakerism* (New York and Oxford, 1994). For Margaret Fell, see I. Ross, *Margaret Fell: Mother of Quakerism* (London; New York, 1949).

13 Based upon John 1: 9.

14 J. W. Frost, 'From Plainness to Simplicity: Changing Quaker Ideals for Material Culture', in E. J. Lapsansky and A. A. Verplanck (eds), *Quaker Aesthetics: Reflections on a Quaker ethic in American design and consumption* (Philadelphia, 2003), pp. 16–17.

15 Thomas Wynne, *An Antichristian Conspiracy detected and Satans champion defeated . . .* (London, 1679), ch. 1 (pp. 8, 9, 24). Wynne had been severely criticized for the views he expressed in *The Antiquity of the Quakers* (1677) by an anonymous writer, possibly William Jones of Rhuddlan, in *Work for a Cooper* (London, 1679). See also William MacLean, 'Dr. Thomas Wynne's account of his early life', *PMHB*, 25 (1901), 104–8; G. H. Jenkins, 'From Ysgeifiog to Pennsylvania: The rise of Thomas Wynne, Quaker barber-surgeon', *Flintshire Historical Society Journal*, 28 (1977–8), 39–40, 46–8.

16 G. F. Nuttall, 'Puritan and Quaker Mysticism', *Theology*, LXXVIII (October 1975), 518–31; Frost, 'Dry Bones of Quaker Theology', 503–23; B. Reay, 'Quakerism and society', in MacGregor and Reay (eds), *Radical Religion*, pp. 141–64.

17 Walter Jenkins, *The Law given forth out of Sion* (London, 1661), p. 3.

[18] J. F. Maclear, 'Quakerism and the end of the Interregnum', *Church History*, 19 (1950), 240. See also E. B. Underhill and N. Haycroft (eds), *The Records of a Church of Christ Meeting at Broadmead, Bristol* (London, 1865), pp. 515–17; D. F. Durnbaugh, 'Baptists and Quakers – Left wing Puritans?', *Quaker History*, 62 (2) (Autumn 1973), 67–82.

[19] An Independent Minister empowered by the Commission for the Propagation of the Gospel in Wales (CPGW) to 'preach the gospel in the highlands of Monmouth'. See T. Richards, *A History of the Puritan Movement in Wales 1639–1653* (London, 1920), pp. 150, 161; T. Richards, *Religious Developments in Wales 1654–1662* (London, 1923), pp. 197–8, 202.

[20] Edmund Jones, *A Geographical, Historical and Religious Account of the Parish of Aberystruth in the county of Monmouth* (Trefecca, 1779), pp. 120–1.

[21] 'Ateb Philo-Evangelius i Martha Philopur', in G. H. Hughes, *Gweithiau William Williams Pantycelyn* (2 vols, Cardiff, 1967), II, pp. 15–16, and translated in G. T. Hughes, *Williams Pantycelyn* (Cardiff, 1983), p. 5. Llandaff diocese was one of the most impoverished areas of England and Wales with a revenue in 1559 of only £141. 3s. 4d. See G. Williams, 'Injunctions of the Royal Visitation of 1559 for the Diocese of Llandaff', *NLWJ*, IV, 3–4 (Summer 1946), 189–97; F. Pugh, 'Recusancy in the diocese of Llandaff during the late sixteenth and early seventeenth centuries' (unpublished, University of Wales, MA thesis 1953), 7–12; Glanmor Williams, *The Welsh and Their Religion* (Cardiff, 1991), p. 43.

[22] C. Hill, 'Puritans and 'the Dark Corners of the Land'', *TRHS*, XIII (1963), 83.

[23] T. Rees, *History of Protestant Nonconformity in Wales* (2nd edn, London, 1883), p. 41.

[24] Walter Cradock, *The Saints Fulnesse of Joy* (London, 1646), p. 34. See also Lloyd Bowen, 'Representations of Wales and the Welsh during the Civil Wars and Interregnum', *Historical Research*, 77 (197) (2004), 367–9, 372–5 (for alternative assessments of the spiritual state of Wales).

[25] Gwenllian Jones, 'Bywyd a gwaith Edward Morris, Perthi Llwydion' (unpublished University of Wales, Bangor, MA thesis, 1941), 325–6; NLW MS. 11440D, fo. 14. Both are cited in Williams, 'Quakers of Merioneth', 124–5.

[26] BL, Harleian MS. 280, fo. 157; Harleian MS 595, fo. 1; NA, E 112/223/21; Pugh, 'Recusancy in the Diocese of Llandaff', 9–10, 330–4.

27 For the efforts of William Blethin of Llandaff to improve the quality of preachers in the diocese see Pugh, 'Recusancy in the Diocese of Llandaff', 12; Williams, *Welsh and their Religion*, pp. 51–2.

28 Williams, *Welsh and their Religion*, pp. 44–5.

29 Richards, *Puritan Movement in Wales*, pp. 10–12; Hill, 'Puritans and "the Dark Corners of the Land"', 81–2.

30 Pugh, 'Recusancy in the Diocese of Llandaff', ch. 4–6, 8; J. Kenyon, *The Popish Plot* (London, 1972), p. 226ff; J. Bossy, *The English Catholic Community 1570–1850* (London, 1975), pp. 97–100; J. P. Jenkins, '"A Welsh Lancashire"? Monmouthshire Catholics in the Eighteenth Century', *Recusant History*, 15 (3) (May, 1980), 176–88; R. P. Matthews, 'Roman Catholic Recusancy in Monmouthshire 1608–89. A demographic and morphological analysis' (unpublished University of Wales, Cardiff, Ph.D. thesis, 1996).

31 R. G. Gruffydd, *'In that Gentile Country': The Beginnings of Puritan Nonconformity in Wales* (Bridgend, 1976), pp. 6–9.

32 NRL, MS. px.mooo.900.MON. *A General Description of the county of Monmouth*, [*c*.seventeenth century].

33 B. P. Jones, *Sowing Besides All Waters. The Baptist Heritage of Gwent* (Cwmbrân, 1985), p. 1. See also Richards, *Puritan Movement in Wales*, p. 25.

34 T. Watts, 'William Wroth (1570–1641). Piwritan ac Apostol Cymru', *Y Cofiadur*, 44 (1979), 5–13; Gruffydd, *In that Gentile Country*, pp. 9–21.

35 B. Ll. James, 'The Evolution of a Radical: The life and career of William Erbery 1605–54', *JWEH*, 3 (1986), 31–48.

36 N. Gibbard, *Walter Cradock: A New Testament Saint* (Bridgend, 1977).

37 M. Wynn Thomas, *Morgan Llwyd* (Cardiff, 1984).

38 R. T. Jones, *Vavasor Powell* (Swansea, 1971), and his English summary, *Vavasor Powell* (Leominster, 1975).

39 J. E. Southall, 'Morgan Llwyd and his times', *Friends Quarterly Examiner*, 53 (1919), 33. See also Williams, 'Quakers of Merioneth', 132–3, 153 n. 104.

40 J. Conway Davies, 'Records of the Church in Wales', *NLWJ*, IV (Summer 1945), 25.

41 Pugh, 'Recusancy in the Diocese of Llandaff', 17–26, 41–57; M. M. C. O'Keefe, 'The Popish Plot in South Wales and the Marches of Hereford and Gloucester' (unpublished University of Galway, MA thesis, 1969), 13–18. The Monmouthshire Catholic population is said to have doubled between 1603 (550 Catholics) and 1641–2 (1,100 Catholics), and it continued to

rise over the course of the next thirty years. See Matthews, 'Roman Catholic Recusancy', 144.

42 NA, E 377/11–18, 21, 26–8, 34–6, 39–40, 42–3, 45, 48; Matthews, 'Roman Catholic Recusancy', 127–8, 373–6.

43 C. Hibbard, *Charles I and the Popish Plot* (Chapel Hill, 1983), pp. 152–7, 186–93; K. J. Lindley, 'The part played by the Catholics', in B. Manning (ed.), *Politics, Religion and the Civil War* (London, 1973), pp. 139–46; 157–8, 162–4; Matthews, 'Roman Catholic Recusancy', 59–69. Matthews questions the belief that gentry Catholic families continued after the Civil War years to be the focal point of the Catholic community in Monmouthshire. See Matthews, 'Roman Catholic Recusancy', 5–6; ch. 5.

44 NA, SP 16/450/260; *CSPD. Charles I.* 1640 (London, 1880), p. 52.

45 T. Royle, *Civil War: The Wars of the Three Kingdoms, 1638–1660* (London, 2004), pp. 143–7; Nicholas P. Canny, 'What really happened in Ireland in 1641?', in J. H. Ohlmeyer (ed.), *Ireland from Independence to Occupation, 1641–1660* (Cambridge, 1995), pp. 24–42.

46 Details of these returns and the reasons for the survey are provided in Matthews, 'Roman Catholic Recusancy', 129–30, 135–6; Pugh, 'Recusancy in the Diocese of Llandaff', 163.

47 Matthews, 'Roman Catholic Recusancy', 3.

48 NA, E 377/28, 34–6, 39–43, 45, 48. These Rolls cover the years 1625–8, 1632–4, 1636, 1639–42; Matthews, 'Roman Catholic Recusancy', 373–6.

49 NA, E 377/61; Matthews, 'Roman Catholic Recusancy', 72–3, 373–6.

50 Matthews, 'Roman Catholic Recusancy', ch. 2, 4 and 5. See also Herbert Croft, *A Short Narrative of the Discovery of a College of Jesuits, at a Place called the Come* (London, 1679); Paul P. Murphy, 'The Jesuit College of the Cwm, Llanrothall', *Severn and Wye Review*, 1 (6) (1970–2), pp. 135–9; O'Keefe, 'Popish Plot in South Wales', 27–8.

51 Matthews, 'Roman Catholic Recusancy', 69.

52 N. Penney (ed.), 'The First Publishers of Truth', *JFHS* Supplements 1–5 (1904–7), II, 124.

53 NLW, MS. 17743E.

54 Lambeth Palace, MS. 639, fo. 186.

55 In 1669, James Adams was recorded as a 'teacher' of the Friends in south-east Wales. Ibid., fo. 187.

56 Matthews, 'Roman Catholic Recusancy', 71 (23 and 35 Elizabeth I).

57 Lambeth Palace, MS. 943. According to Bishop Murray, Cradock was 'a bold, ignorant young fellow'. See Rees, *Protestant Nonconformity in Wales*, p. 46.

58 King James I had issued an earlier version in 1618. See L. Racaut, 'The 'Book of Sports' and Sabbatarian legislation in Lancashire, 1579–1616', *Northern History*, 33 (1997), 73–87.

59 Richards, *Puritan Movement in Wales*, pp. 26–7; James, 'Evolution of a Radical', 38.

60 Rees, *Protestant Nonconformity in Wales*, pp. 44, 47; Gruffydd, *In that Gentile Country*, pp. 13–14.

61 R. T. Jones, 'Puritan Llanvaches', *Presenting Monmouthshire*, 15 (1963), 36–9; Gruffydd, *In that Gentile Country*, pp. 14–18.

62 Edward Whiston, *Life and Death of Mr. Henry Jessey* (London, 1671), pp. 9–10; Richards, *Puritan Movement in Wales*, pp. 28–30.

63 Cradock, *Saints Fulnesse of Joy*, p. 12; Richards, *Puritan Movement in Wales*, p. 28; Gruffydd, *In that Gentile Country*, pp. 14–15.

64 Quoted in Idris Davies, 'Dyddiau Cynnar Annibyniaeth ym Mrycheiniog a Maesyfed', *Y Cofiadur*, 16 (March 1946), 8–9, 52.

65 Edward Harris, *A True Relation of a Company of Brownists* . . . (London, 1641), p. 1.

66 *Journal of the House of Commons*, II (26 June 1641), 189.

67 J. A. Bradney (ed.), *The Diary of Walter Powell of Llantilio Crossenny, Gent., 1603–1654* (Bristol, 1907), p. 28. For attacks upon church rituals see J. Morrill, 'The Church in England 1643–49', in J. Morrill (ed.), *Reactions to the English Civil War* (London, 1992), pp. 103–14.

68 Richards, *Puritan Movement in Wales*, ch. 5.

69 Underhill and Haycroft (eds), *Records*, pp. 25–30.

70 Ibid., p. 30ff.

71 Jones, *A Geographical, Historical and Religious Account* . . . *of Aberystruth*, p. 93.

72 Established in July 1643, and proposed a Presbyterian ministry to halt absenteeism and the growth of sectarianism. See R. B. Knox, 'The Westminster Assembly of Divines', *Bulletin of the Presbyterian Historical Society of Ireland*, 22 (1993), 5–15.

73 Richards, *Puritan Movement in Wales*, p. 51.

74 *Journal of the House of Lords*, X (6 October 1648), 531; Richards, *Puritan Movement in Wales*, pp. 57–72 (p. 67).

75 G. H. Jenkins, *Protestant Dissenters in Wales 1639–1689* (Cardiff, 1992), p. 15.

[76] Richards, *Puritan Movement in Wales*, p. 76.

[77] Walter Cradock, *Glad Tydings from Heaven* (London, 1648), pp. 49–50; W. T. Pennar Davies, 'Episodes in the History of Brecknock Dissent', *Brycheiniog*, 3 (1957), 23.

[78] *Journal of the House of Commons*, VII (11 February 1652), 258.

[79] J. H. Davies and T. E. Ellis (eds), *Gweithiau Morgan Llwyd o Wynedd* (2 vols, Bangor, 1899, and London, 1908), I, pp. 207–8 (*Llyfr y Tri Aderyn)*; Richards, *Puritan Movement in Wales*, p. 167.

[80] E. K. L. Quine, 'The Quakers in Leicestershire' (unpublished University of Nottingham, Ph.D. thesis, 1968), vii.

[81] *Journal*, p. 290; LSF, Swarthmore MS. I. 196, (Thomas Holme to Margaret Fell, Llanfihangel Ystum Llywern, 16 April [1657]). See also Gill, *Women in the Seventeenth-Century*, pp. 23–7.

[82] Acheson, *Radical Puritans*, ch. 6; J. MacGregor, 'Seekers and Ranters', in MacGregor and Reay (eds), *Radical Religion*, ch. 4.

[83] Joshua Thomas, *Hanes Y Bedyddwyr* (Carmarthen, 1778), pp. 209–10; Richards, *Puritan Movement in Wales*, pp. 159, 165, 167–9, 202–4, 211; T. M. Bassett, *The Welsh Baptists* (Swansea, 1977), ch.1; B. R. White, 'John Miles and the structures of the Calvinist Baptist Mission to South Wales 1649–1660', in M. John (ed.), *Welsh Baptist Studies* (Cardiff, 1976), pp. 35–76; Jenkins, *Protestant Dissenters*, pp. 12, 29–33.

[84] Richards, *Religious Developments*, pp. 183–90; Underhill and Haycroft (eds), *Records*, p. 516.

[85] A. L. Morton, *The World of the Ranters* (London, 1970); J. F. MacGregor, 'Ranterism and the Development of Early Quakerism', *Journal of Religious History*, 9 (1977), 349–63.

[86] Richards, *Religious Developments*, ch. 10; G. F. Nuttall, *The Holy Spirit in Puritan Faith and Experience* (Oxford, 1946); B. S. Capp, *The Fifth Monarchy Men: A Study in Seventeenth-Century Millenarianism* (London, 1972); B. R. Vandevelde, 'Quakers and Fifth Monarchy Men: Problems of Public Order *c.*September 1654-January 1657' (unpublished University of Exeter, MA thesis, 1978).

[87] C. Hill, 'Propagating the Gospel', in H. E. Bell and R. L. Ollard (eds), *Historical Essays, 1600–1750* (London, 1963), pp. 35–59; A. M. Johnson, 'Politics and Religion 1649–60', in G. Williams (ed.), *Glamorgan County History*, IV (Cardiff, 1974), pp. 283–92; G. Williams, 'Wales during the Commonwealth and Protectorate', in D. H. Pennington and K.

Thomas (eds), *Puritans and Revolutionaries* (Oxford, 1978), pp. 233–56; S. K. Roberts, 'Godliness and Government in Glamorgan, 1647–1660', in C. Jones, M. Newitt and S. Roberts (eds), *Politics and People in Revolutionary England* (London, 1986), pp. 225–51; S. K. Roberts, 'Propagating the Gospel in Wales: the making of the 1650 Act', *THSC*, 10 (2004), 57–75.

88 Richards, *Puritan Movement in Wales*, pp. 115–33, 135.
89 Rees, *Protestant Nonconformity in Wales*, p. 78; Richards, *Puritan Movement in Wales*, ch. 12–13.
90 Richards, *Puritan Movement in Wales*, pp. 148–50, 154, 160–1; Richards, *Religious Developments*, ch. 9.
91 Bradney, *Diary of Walter Powell*, pp. 41–3; Richards, *Puritan Movement in Wales*, pp. 151, 153, 159–61.
92 Johnson, 'Politics and Religion', pp. 288–90, 297–8; Roberts, 'Godliness and Government', pp. 238–40.
93 L. C. Martin (ed.), *The Works of Henry Vaughan* (2nd edn, Oxford, 1957), p. 166, and cited in Jenkins, *Protestant Dissenters*, p. 80 (Document VIII).
94 D. Walker, 'The Reformation in Wales', in D. Walker (ed.), *A History of the Church in Wales* (Penarth, 1976), pp. 76–7; J. E. Southall, 'The Society of Friends in Wales', *Friends Quarterly Examiner*, 14 (1880), 87.
95 John Cragge, *Public Dispute touching Infant baptism . . .* (London, 1654), and *Arraignment and Conviction of Anabaptism* (London, 1656), pp. 25–7; Richards, *Puritan Movement in Wales*, pp. 153, 170ff.
96 Richards, *Religious Developments*, p. 216.
97 Davies, 'Episodes in the History of Brecknockshire Dissent', 18.
98 Ibid., 21.
99 C. L. Leachman, 'From an "unruly sect" to a society of "strict unity": The development of English Quakerism c.1650–1689' (unpublished University of London, Ph.D. thesis, 1998), 8–34.
100 LSF, Box 19/3; William Dewsbury, *The Discovery of Mans Returne to his First Estate* (London, 1654); C. Horle, 'Quakers and Baptists 1647–1660', *Baptist Quarterly*, 26 (1976), 346.
101 M. F. Williams, 'Glamorgan Quakers 1654–1900', *Morgannwg*, 5 (1961), 54; Horle, 'Quakers and Baptists', 354; G. H. Jenkins, 'James Owen versus Benjamin Keach: a controversy over Infant Baptism', *NLWJ*, XIX (1975), 57–66.
102 T. L. Underwood, *Primitivism, Radicalism and the Lamb's War: The Baptist–Quaker Conflict in Seventeenth-Century England* (Oxford, 1997); A. Hughes, 'The Pulpit Guarded: Confrontations between Orthodox and Radicals in Revolutionary England', in A. Laurence, W. R. Owens and

S. Sim (eds), *John Bunyan and his England 1628–1688* (London, 1990), pp. 30–50; G. H. Jenkins, *Foundations of Modern Wales, 1642–1780* (Oxford, 1987) p. 80.

103 LSF, GBS II (Breconshire), fo. 9; Horle, 'Quakers and Baptists', 346ff. See also Wynne, *Antiquity of the Quakers,* where Thomas Wynne accused 'Papists, Protestants, Presbyterians, Independents and Anabaptists' of 'scoffing at Quaking and Trembling' when it was 'of greater Antiquity' than their own beliefs.

104 Thomas, *Morgan Llwyd*, p. 12.

105 J. G. Jones and G. W. Owen (eds), *Gweithiau Morgan Llwyd o Wynedd*, III (Caerdydd, 1994), pp. 57–65; A. H. Dodd, 'A Remonstrance from Wales, 1655', *BBCS*, 17 (4) (1958), 279–92.

106 Jones and Owen (eds), *Gweithiau Morgan Llwyd*, p. 161.

107 Ibid., pp. 69–77.

108 Ibid., pp. 78–9; Dodd, 'A Remonstrance from Wales', 282; Thomas, *Morgan Llwyd*, pp. 14–15.

109 Richards, *Religious Developments*, p. 136; Thomas, *Morgan Llwyd*, p. 15.

110 On 27 June 1659, Powell proposed reconciliation between the two men. However, his letter to Llwyd arrived after his former colleague had died. See Jones and Owen (eds), *Gweithiau Morgan Llwyd*, p. 148.

111 G. F. Nuttall, 'A Parcel of Books for Morgan Llwyd', *JFHS*, 56 (3) (1992), 180–7; G. F. Nuttall, 'A New Letter to George Fox', *JFHS*, 57 (3) (1996), 221–7; Jones and Owen (eds), *Gweithiau Morgan Llwyd*, pp. 196–7. For the conversion process, see Gill, *Women in the Seventeenth-Century*, pp. 17–23.

112 LSF, Swarthmore MS. IV. 66, (John Lawson to Margaret Fell, Chester *c.*1653); Nuttall, 'New Letter', p. 224.

113 Jones and Owen (eds), *Gweithiau Morgan Llwyd*, p. 196.

114 Nuttall, 'New Letter', 225; Nuttall, *Welsh Saints*, pp. 56–7.

115 Nuttall, 'A Parcel of Books', 180–1; Jones and Owen (eds), *Gweithiau Morgan Llwyd*, p. 54; Nuttall, 'New Letter', 221–2.

116 N. H. Keeble and G. F. Nuttall (eds), *Calendar of Correspondence of Richard Baxter* (2 vols, London, 1991), I, pp. 168–70, 208–10, 218–19, 234, 248–9; Davies and Ellis (eds), *Gweithiau Morgan Llwyd*, I, p. 57; II, pp. 270–5; Jones and Owen (eds), *Gweithiau Morgan Llwyd*, pp. 104–5.

117 R. T. Jones, *Hanes Annibynwyr Cymru* (Swansea, 1966), p. 63; Nuttall, 'Parcel of Books', 185.

118 Llwyd to Erbery, Wrexham 29.4.1652; Llwyd to Erbery, Wrexham 3mo. 1652 (mispr. for 1653); Llwyd to Erbery concerning Erbery's *The Babe of Glory* (London, 1653). All

passages are quoted in Nuttall, 'Parcel of Books', 183–4. See also Davies (ed.), *Gweithiau Morgan Llwyd*, II, pp. 256–63; Jones and Owen (eds), *Gweithiau Morgan Llwyd*, pp. 108–20.

[119] Nuttall, 'Parcel of Books', 184–5; Nuttall, 'Overcoming the World: The early Quaker programme', in D. Baker (ed.), *Studies in Church History, 10: Sanctity and Secularity: the church and the world* (Oxford, 1973), pp. 145–64.

[120] See Davies, *Account*, pp. 69–70.

[121] Jenkins, *Protestant Dissenters*, p. 34; Davies, *Account*, pp. 69–71 (Thomas Ellis, a former deacon of the Independents), 71–84 (James Parkes).

[122] Jenkins, *Law given forth out of Sion*, p. 11. See also Wynne, *An Antichristian Conspiracy Detected*, pp. 25–31.

[123] Braithwaite, *Beginnings*, pp. 59, 63–4, 93, 120; Richards, *Puritan Movement in Wales*, p. 218; H. L. Ingle, 'From Mysticism to Radicalism: Recent Historiography of Quaker Beginnings', *QH*, 76 (1987), 79–94.

[124] Lambeth Palace, MS. 639, fo. 186 – Episcopal Returns, 1669; Bradney, *Diary of Walter Powell*, p. 37.

[125] *Journal*, p. 222.

[126] Richards, *Puritan Movement in Wales*, ch. 12; Nuttall, *Welsh Saints*, ch. 1–3.

[127] Extracted from their probates in 1686. See Williams, 'Quakers of Merioneth', 134.

[128] For the convincement of Robert Owen of Fron-goch, Penllyn, and John Roberts of Llyn, see ibid., 134–5.

[129] John Miles, *An Antidote against the Infection of the Times* (London, 1656), and reprinted in T. Shankland (ed.), *Transactions of the Welsh Baptist Historical Association* (Cardiff, 1904), pp. 1, 6, 19–20, 25.

[130] Morgan Watkins, *The Perfect Life* (London, 1659), pp. 11, 34.

[131] Richards, *Religious Developments*, pp. 256–7; G. F. Nuttall, *The Holy Spirit in Puritan Faith and Experience* (Oxford, 1946), pp. 157–9, 161; Horle, 'Quakers and Baptists', 345, 358; M. Watts, *The Dissenters: From the Reformation to the French Revolution* (Oxford, 1978); pp. 189–93. For a sympathetic treatment of Fox's testimony, see Ingle, *First Among Friends*, ch. 8.

[132] William Erbery, *Apocrypha* (London, 1625), p. 2; Rees, *Protestant Nonconformity in Wales*, pp. 44, 47. See also Richards, *Puritan Movement in Wales*, pp. 26, 162, 205, 218; James, 'The Evolution of a Radical', 44–5.

[133] R. M. Jones, *Spiritual Reformers in the Sixteenth and Seventeenth Centuries* (London, 1914), pp. 28, 243; Horle, 'Quakers and Baptists', 352–3.

[134] Hill, *World Turned Upside Down*, ch. 10; Nuttall, *The Holy Spirit*, pp. 110–12, 151; Horle, 'Quakers and Baptists', 44; Maclear, 'Quakerism and the end of the Interregnum', 246; T. L. Underwood, 'Early Quaker Eschatology', in P. Toon (ed.), *Puritans, The Millennium and the Future of Israel* (London, 1970), pp. 91–103.

[135] Quine, 'Quakers in Leicestershire', xii.

[136] Anon., *An Alarum to Corporations* . . . (London, 1659), p. 8.

[137] Quoted in Rees, *Protestant Nonconformity in Wales*, p. 93. See also Watts, *Dissenters*, pp. 191–2, 203–7; Moore, *Light in their Consciences*, pp. 3–13, 21, 26–7, 116.

[138] E. H. Milligan, *Brittanica on Quakerism* (London, 1965), p. 5. For early Quaker meetings see Moore, *Light in their Consciences*, pp. 142–54.

[139] Horle, 'Quakers and Baptists', p. 353, and citing P. Oliver, 'The Quakers and Quietism' (unpublished University of Melbourne, MA thesis, 1972), 12. See also Milligan, *Brittanica on Quakerism*, pp. 3, 5, 15–20.

[140] Hill, *World Turned Upside Down*, pp. 231–41.

[141] Richards, *Puritan Movement in Wales*, ch. 10; Richards, *Religious Developments*, ch. 7.

[142] Richards, *Puritan Movement in Wales*, pp. 162–5; Richards, *Religious Developments*, pp. 155, 177ff.

[143] Johnson, 'Politics and Religion', pp. 286–7.

[144] William Erbery, 'The Grand Oppressor, Or, The Terror of Tithes; First Felt, and now Confest. The Sum of a Letter to one of the Commissioners in South Wales, April 19, 1652', in *The Testimony of William Erbery* (London, 1658), pp. 50–1.

[145] Jones and Owen (eds), *Gweithiau Morgan Llwyd*, p. 146.

[146] Ibid., p. 79.

[147] M. James, 'The Political Importance of the Tithes Controversy in the English Revolution 1640–60', *History*, 26 (June 1941), 1–18; E. J. Evans, *The Contentious Tithe* (London, 1976); B. Reay, 'Quaker Opposition to Tithes 1652–1660', *P&P*, 86 (1980), 100–5; Jonathan Harlow, 'Preaching for Hire: Public issues and private concerns in a skirmish of the Lamb's War', *QS*, 10 (1) (September 2005), 31–45.

[148] Roberts, 'Godliness and Government', p. 249; J. P. Jenkins, '"The Sufferings of the Clergy": The Church in Glamorgan during the Interregnum', *JWEH*, 4 (1987), 13.

[149] Horle, 'Quakers and Baptists', 354.

[150] LSF, Swarthmore MS. IV. 247, (Thomas Holme to George Fox, Cardiff, 27 February 1655). See also Richards, *Religious Developments*, p. 256ff ; Rees, *Quakers in Wales*, p. 3; R. T.

Vann, *Social Development of English Quakerism* (Cambridge, Mass., 1969), pp. 23–7; J. F. MacGregor, 'The Baptists: Fount of all heresy', in MacGregor and Reay (eds), *Radical Religion in the English Revolution*, p. 34; Horle, 'Quakers and Baptists', 345–8; Vavasor Powell's congregations and the Independents also lost members to the Quaker movement. See Rees, *Quakers in Wales*, pp. 72, 133, 146; Nuttall, *Welsh Saints*, ch. 4.

151 Originally published in London, 1656, reprinted in *Transactions of the Welsh Baptist Historical Association* (1904), 1–52. For Fox's reply see George Fox, *The Great Mystery*, originally published in London, 1656, reprinted in the same volume, pp. 214–16. See also G. H. Jenkins, 'Quaker and anti-Quaker literature in Welsh from the Restoration to Methodism', *WHR*, 7 (1975), 403–26. Another Welsh Quaker was Edward Edwards of Denbighshire who was convinced while in Yorkshire. See C. Trevett, *Quaker Women Prophets in England and Wales 1650–1700* (Lewiston; Queenston and Lampeter, 2000), p. 118 n. 25.

152 *Journal*, p. 172; J. Gough, *A History of the People called Quakers* (4 vols, Dublin, 1789), I, pp. 287–8.

153 LSF, Swarthmore MS. IV. 66; W. G. Norris and N. Penney, 'John ap John, and early records of Friends in Wales', *JFHS* Supplement, 6 (1907); Rees, *Quakers in Wales*, pp. 16–22; R. C. Allen, 'John ap John', *Oxford Dictionary of National Biography* (Oxford, 2004).

154 M. F. Williams, 'The Society of Friends in Glamorgan 1654–1900' (unpublished University of Wales, Aberystwyth, MA thesis, 1950), 17–19.

155 *Journal*, p. 174; LSF, Swarthmore MS. I. 189, 190, 191, 192, 193 and IV. 249. See also E. Vipont, *George Fox and the Valiant Sixty* (London, 1975).

156 LSF, Swarthmore MS. IV. 66.

157 LSF, Swarthmore MS. VII. 4, (John Audland to George Fox, Bristol, 8.3.1654); Swarthmore MS. VII. 18, (Journal of John Audland 27.4 – 30.7.1654).

158 LSF, Swarthmore Ms. I. 194, (Thomas Home to Margaret Fell, 10.10.1654); Penney (ed.), 'First Publishers of Truth', p. 321.

159 LSF, Swarthmore MS. IV. 247.

160 Ibid.

161 LSF, Swarthmore MS. IV. 244 (Thomas Holme to George Fox, Palace of West Chester, 6 August 1655).

162 LSF, Swarthmore MS. I. 203 (Thomas Holme to Margaret Fell, Newport, 30 April 1656).

[163] LSF, Swarthmore MS. IV. 247. Jenkins was the son of Thomas Jenkins, an Episcopalian minister of the Pant, Llanfihangel Ystum Llywern, and served as a magistrate for the Skenfrith Hundred from 18 July 1653 to 8 July 1656. See Bradney, *Diary of Walter Powell*, p. 37 n. 2.

[164] Williams, 'Quakers of Merioneth', 128, 131, 134 who suggests that Owen was convinced in 1660. See also *A Collection of Memorials . . . of the People called Quakers* (Philadelphia, 1808), p. 31; C. H. Browning, *The Welsh Settlement of Pennsylvania* (Philadelphia, 1912), p. 594; B. E. Howells (ed.), *A Calendar of Letters relating to North Wales* (Cardiff, 1967), p. 111.

[165] *Journal*, pp. 289–90; LSF, Swarthmore MS. IV. 219, (Francis Gawler to George Fox. Cardiff, 26 January 1659/60); IV. 221, (Francis Gawler to George Fox. Cardiff, 5 May 1661); Penney (ed.), 'First Publishers of Truth', p. 324; Williams, 'Glamorgan Quakers', 54; Williams, 'Quakers of Merioneth', 127. For further details of Quaker magistrates see J. R. S. Phillips, *The Justices of the Peace in Wales and Monmouthshire, 1541–1689* (Cardiff, 1975).

[166] Scott, 'Politics, Dissent and Quakerism', 13.

[167] Penney (ed.), 'First Publishers of Truth', pp. 323–5.

[168] Davies, *Account*, p. 8.

[169] Ibid., p. 9ff.

[170] For example, Mary Chapman bequeathed half a Welsh acre of her Tîr Pant Annos estate 'as a place of burial for the dead especially those who are called Quakers or should be of their faith and persuasion'. See NLW, LL/1670/176 (Mary Chapman of St Mellons, 1670). For further details of Quaker burial grounds see ch. 3 of this present study and Rees, *Quakers in Wales*, ch. 4.

[171] *Journal*, p. 290.

[172] Ibid., pp. 290–1.

[173] Ibid., pp. 291–3.

[174] Ibid., pp. 293–4.

[175] Ibid., pp. 297–307.

[176] Ibid., pp. 298–9.

[177] Ibid., pp. 299–300.

[178] Ibid., pp. 300–1.

[179] Ibid., pp. 301–2.

[180] Ibid., pp. 302–4.

[181] Ibid., p. 304.

[182] Ibid., pp. 304–5.

[183] Ibid., p. 306.

[184] See Davies, *Account*, pp. 31, 36.

[185] Ibid., p. 38.

[186] Durnbaugh, 'Baptists and Quakers', 67ff; J. J. Hurwich, "A Fanatick Town': The political influence of Dissenters in Coventry 1660–1720', *Midland History*, 4 (1977–78), 15–47; K. L. Carroll, 'Early Quakers and 'going naked as a sign', *Quaker History*, 67 (2) (Autumn 1978), 69–87; C. L. Cherry, 'Enthusiasm and Madness: Anti-Quakerism in the seventeenth century', *Quaker History*, 73 (2) (Autumn 1984), 1–24.

[187] Davies, *Account*, pp. 42–3.

[188] Anon, *For the King and both Houses of Parliament being a short declaration of the cruelty inflicted* . . . (1661), pp. 1–2; Williams, 'Quakers of Merioneth', 136.

[189] LSF, Swarthmore MS. IV. 219.

[190] LSF, Swarthmore MS. IV. 253, (Thomas Holme to George Fox, Cardiff, 1657).

[191] Davies, *Account*, p. 33.

[192] F. Gawler, *A Record of some Persecutions* . . . *in South Wales* (London, 1659), p. 9ff.

[193] LSF, Swarthmore MS. IV. 257, (Thomas Holme to George Fox, Kendal, March 1663).

[194] Penney (ed.), 'First Publishers of Truth', p. 260.

[195] NA, SoF Registers (Monmouthshire). No.677, p. 42; G. E. Evans, 'Llandovery, Friends' Burial Ground', *TCASFC*, 4 (1906), 47.

[196] *Journal*, pp. 514, 515–16.

[197] Ibid., pp. 516–17.

[198] Ibid., pp. 520–2.

[199] Ibid., p. 521.

[200] Ellis's conversion to Quakerism and subsequent persecution was later told in a fictional work. See Marion Eames, *Y Staffell Ddirgel* (Llandybïe, 1969) and translated as *The Secret Room* (Llandysul, 1995).

[201] GAS, D/DSF/2, p. 490.

Chapter 2 Social Composition of Monmouthshire Friends

1   G. H. Jenkins, *Protestant Dissenters in Wales, 1639–1689* (Cardiff, 1992), p. 21.

2   R. T. Vann and D. Eversley, *Friends in Life and Death: The British and Irish Quakers in the demographic transition, 1650–1900* (Cambridge, 1992).

3   Extant registers are held in the National Archives.

[4] F. Emery, 'The Farming Regions of Wales', in J. Thirsk (ed.), *The Agrarian History of England and Wales* (8 vols, Cambridge, 1967–90), IV (1500–1640), pp. 142–7. It has been shown that the population was 29,200 by the eighteenth century. See M. Watts, *The Dissenters: From the Reformation to the French Revolution* (Oxford, 1978), p. 509.

[5] W. C. Braithwaite, *The Beginnings of Quakerism* (York, 1981), p. 512; B. Reay, *Quakers and the English Revolution* (Hounslow, 1985), pp. 11, 26; Watts, *Dissenters*, p. 270. See also T. Underhill, *Hell Broke Loose* (London, 1660), p. 14.

[6] A. Davies, *The Quakers in English Society, 1655–1725* (Oxford, 2000), p. 156.

[7] This acted as a precursor to the Second Conventicle Act of 1670. See Lambeth Palace, MS. 639; G. L. Turner, *Original Records of Early Nonconformity under Persecution and Indulgence* (3 vols, London, 1911); T. Richards, *Wales under the Penal Code, 1622–1687* (London, 1925), pp. 124–31, and his 'The Religious Census of 1676', *THSC* Supplement (1925–6).

[8] Lambeth Palace, MS. 639, fo. 186; Turner, *Original Records*, III, p. 113; Richards, *Wales under the Penal Code*, p. 62.

[9] Lambeth Palace, MS. 639, fo. 186; Turner, *Original Records*, II, p. 1224.

[10] Lambeth Palace, MS. 639, fo.186; Richards, *Wales under the Penal Code*, p. 63.

[11] Lambeth Palace, MS. 639, fo. 186b; Turner, *Original Records*, II, p. 1227.

[12] Lambeth Palace, MS. 639, fo. 186; Richards, *Wales under the Penal Code*, p. 63.

[13] T. Rees, *Protestant Nonconformity in Wales* (2nd edn, London, 1883), p. 172.

[14] Richards, *Wales under the Penal Code*, p. 66; See also Richard Davies, *An Account of the Convincement, Exercises and Services and Travels of ... Richard Davies* (London, 1877), p. 9ff.

[15] NA, SoF Registers (Monmouthshire). No. 677, p. 42.

[16] Ibid., p. 175.

[17] A former Commissioner for the Propagation of the Gospel in Wales. See Lambeth Palace, MS. 1027, No. 23; NA, E 112/481/2; Richards, *Wales under the Penal Code*, p. 67.

[18] Lambeth Palace, MS. 639, fos 186b, 188b; Richards, *Wales under the Penal Code*, pp. 66–7.

[19] Lambeth Palace, MS. 639, fo. 188; Richards, *Wales under the Penal Code*, pp. 93–4.

[20] Lambeth Palace, MS. 639, fo. 187.

21 Ibid., fos 187, 187b.
22 Ibid., fo. 139; Richards, 'Religious Census of 1676', 53. Fifty Quakers, as well as 'abettors' or supporters of the conventicle, were recorded at Meifod, including Thomas Lloyd, Cadwallader Edwards and William Evans.
23 NLW, SD/CCB/G, 57, 547e, and cited in Walter T. Morgan, 'The Prosecution of Nonconformists in the Consistory Courts of St Davids, 1681–88', *Journal of the Historical Society of the Church in Wales*, 12 (1962), 36–7.
24 Bodleian Library, Tanner MS. CXLVI, 138, and cited in Morgan, 'Prosecution of Nonconformists', 41–2.
25 *Journal*, p. 521.
26 Welsh diocesan entries are held in the William Salt Library, Stafford. Salt MS. 2112. See also Anne Whiteman (ed.), *The Compton Census of 1676: A Critical Edition* (London, 1986).
27 Richards, 'Religious Census of 1676', 14–16 (minimum age), 16–32 (population anomalies), 32–46 (miscalculations and revised totals), 47–63 (underestimates); Whiteman (ed.), *Compton Census*, pp. xxxii–xlvii, li–liv, lxxvi–lxxix; 511ff (Llandaff Diocese).
28 Richards, 'Religious Census', 3–7; Whiteman (ed.), *Compton Census*, pp. xxiv-xxxii.
29 Jenkins, *Protestant Dissenters*, p. 58.
30 Whiteman (ed.), *Compton Census*, pp. cxxiii-cxxiv (Appendix F). Bangor (247), Llandaff (905), St Asaph (643), St David's (2,401). To this figure an additional 52 Welsh Dissenters who lived in the diocese of Hereford can be added.
31 G. H. Jenkins, *The Foundations of Modern Wales, 1642–1780* (Oxford, 1987), p. 88.
32 William Salt Library, Salt MS. 2112, fo. 415, 418–22. The inaccuracies are exposed by Richards who compared the findings of the 1669 ecclesiastical returns for Llandaff, Llanfihangel Ystum Llywern, Llanwenarth and Pant-Teg (total: 190 Friends) with that of the total number of Nonconformists in 1676 for the same areas (38 Nonconformists). See Lambeth Palace, MS. 639, fos 186–7; William Salt Library, Stafford. Salt MS. 2112, fos 421–2, 424; Richards, 'Religious Census', 53.
33 N. Penney (ed.), 'The First Publishers of Truth', *JFHS* Supplements 1–5 (1904-7), IV, 324; T. M. Rees, *A History of the Quakers in Wales and their emigration to North America* (Carmarthen, 1925), pp. 90, 130, 136–7, 142–3, 151, 153–5, 168, 171.
34 Dr Williams Library, London, MS. 38.4; Watts, *Dissenters*, pp. 267–89, 491–510.

35 Michael Watts used surviving Episcopal visitation returns and records kept in LSF. See Watts, *Dissenters*, pp. 268–9, 505–6.

36 Ibid., p. 269, table I. Monmouthshire is calculated among the English counties which represented a total of 672 congregations and Wales the remaining 24.

37 Ibid., p. 270, table II. Watts was able to calculate the overall dissenting population for Wales (17,770 out of a total population of 309,750 or 5.74 per cent), but the loss of many registers meant that only the major dissenting groups in Wales were included. Ibid., table III.

38 A. E. Jones, 'Protestant Dissent in Gloucestershire: A Comparison between 1676 and 1735', *Bristol and Gloucestershire Archaeological Transactions*, 51 (1983), 131–45.

39 Gaps in the registers occur between 1668 and 1710 (Births); 1663 and 1710 (Marriages); 1676 and 1709 (Burials). See NA, SoF Registers (Monmouthshire). No. 677, pp. 207, 226, 247.

40 Vann and Eversley, *Friends in Life and Death*, pp. 65-8. See also B. Levy, *Quakers and the American Family: British Settlement in the Delaware Valley* (Oxford, 1988), pp. 88-9 based on the transcripts of Friends' registers.

41 Births (37.5 per cent): marriages (41.5 per cent).

42 NA, SoF Registers (Monmouthshire), No. 677, pp. 4–6.

43 For example, William Morgan of St Brides was buried in Cardiff. See NA, SoF Registers (Monmouthshire). No. 677, p. 247.

44 The registers for Cardiff Friends are lost. However, the lease of Sowdrey burial ground in 1667 indicated that six Glamorgan Friends were still alive including Mary Erbery, Francis Gawler, John Mayo and Tobias Hodges. A later deed of ownership dated 30 November 1695 was made between the sole surviving trustee, Tobias Hodges, and several Monmouthshire Friends, including Samuel David of Marshfield and Howell Thomas of St Brides as well as Rowland Thomas of Cardiff. It is obvious, therefore, that between 1667 and 1695 the first generation of Cardiff Quakers had died out and that membership was not sufficiently large to warrant the appointment of trustees.

45 For instance, Phillip Morgan, the son of William Morgan of St Brides, appears only in the births register. An administration on 9 June 1720 for Phillip Morgan of St Brides would, however, suggest that the family remained in the area after his death in 1668. See NLW, LL/1720/164.

46 For example, Nathan and Elizabeth Chapman, the son and daughter of Mary Chapman. See NLW, LL/1670/176.

47 R. C. Allen, 'The Society of Friends (Quakers) in Wales: The Case of Monmouthshire c.1654–1836' (unpublished University of Wales, Aberystwyth, Ph.D. thesis, 1999), 509–25 (Appendix A). This topic is further discussed in N. Tadmor, 'The Concept of the Household-Family in Eighteenth-Century England', P&P, 151 (May 1996), 111–40; E. A. Wrigley and R. S. Schofield, 'English Population History from Family Reconstitution: Summary Results 1600–1799', Population Studies, 37 (1983), 157–84.

48 Occasionally, the husband/wife is not named or the date of marriage given. There is also the difficulty of ascertaining dates of death/burial. Moreover, many individuals are not recorded as having partners but may nevertheless have been married.

49 NA, SoF Registers (Monmouthshire). No. 677, p. 21.

50 Ibid., p. 24.

51 Ibid., pp. 3–4.

52 Ibid., p. 68.

53 Ibid., p. 111.

54 Ibid., p. 5.

55 See comments made by John Gillis which suggest that in the early modern period the average duration of marriage was less than twenty years. See J. R. Gillis, For Better, For Worse: British Marriages, 1600 to the Present (New York and Oxford, 1985), p. 11.

56 Allen, 'Society of Friends in Wales', 526–7 (Appendix B).

57 Vann and Eversley, Friends in Life and Death, ch. 5. See also B. M. Willmott Dobbie, 'An attempt to Estimate the True Rate of Maternal Mortality, Sixteenth to Eighteenth Centuries', Medical History, XXVI (1982), 79–90; W. Coster, 'Tokens of Innocence: Infant baptism, death and burial in early modern England', in B. Gordon and P. Marshall (eds), The Place of the Dead: Death and Remembrance in Late Medieval and Early Modern Europe (Cambridge, 2000), pp. 266–87; Jean Wilson, 'Dead Fruit: The commemoration of still-born and unbaptized children in early modern England', Church Monuments, 17 (2002), 89–106; Garthine Walker, 'Just Stories: Telling Tales of Infant Death in Early Modern England', in M. Mikesell and A. F. Seeff (eds), Culture and Change: Attending to Early Modern Women (Newark and London, 2003), pp. 98–115.

58 NA, SoF Registers (Monmouthshire). No. 677, p. 50.

59 Thurston Beadles died after three months in 1741; Handley Beadles died aged two and a half in 1742; Fowler Beadles died after three months in 1743. Ibid., pp. 24–5, 50.

60 L. M. Beier, 'In Sickness and in Health: A seventeenth century family's experience', in R. Porter (ed.), *Patients and Practitioners: Lay Perceptions of Medicine in Pre-Industrial Society* (Cambridge, 1985), pp. 101–28; R. Porter, *Disease, Medicine and Society in England 1550–1860* (Basingstoke, 1987); M. J. Dobson, *Contours of Death and Disease in Early Modern England* (Cambridge, 1997); P. Griffiths, J. Landers, M. Pelling and R. Tyson, 'Population and Disease, Estrangement and Belonging 1540–1700', in P. Clark (ed.), *The Cambridge Urban History of Britain* (3 vols, Cambridge, 2000), II, ch. 6.

61 NA, SoF Registers (Monmouthshire). No. 677, p. 42.

62 NA, SoF Registers (Monmouthshire). No. 680, p. 76.

63 Ibid.

64 NA, SoF Registers (Monmouthshire). No. 677, p. 48.

65 Vann and Eversley, *Friends in Life and Death*, pp. 115–16, 203–4, 228–32.

66 NA, SoF Registers (Monmouthshire). No. 677, pp. 43, 111.

67 Ibid., p. 49; A. A. Locke, *The Hanbury Family* (2 vols, London, 1916) II, pp. 244, 289.

68 NA, SoF Registers (Monmouthshire). No. 677, p. 46.

69 Ibid., p. 47.

70 Ibid., p. 53.

71 J. J. Hurwich, 'The Social Origins of Early Quakers', *P&P*, 48 (1970), 158–9; R. T. Vann, *Social Development of English Quakerism, 1655–1755* (Cambridge, Mass., 1969), pp. 163–4; Reay, *Quakers and the English Revolution*, p. 25; Davies, *Quakers in English Society*, pp. 159–62.

72 Llanfihangel Pont-y-Moel; Trefddyn; Pant-Teg and Mamheilad parishes.

73 This figure does not take into consideration the parishes near to these market towns or from those within easy reach of Pontypool, notably Betws Bassaleg (1); Christchurch (5); Goldcliffe (18); Llanbadog (3); Llanddewi Fach (2); Llandeilo Bertholau (1); Llanelen (1); Llanfihangel Llantarnam (4); Llanfrechfa (21); Llangybi (14); Llanhiledd (6); Llanwenarth (2); Malpas (18); Mynyddislwyn (5); and Rhisga (1). These 102 Friends would have substantially increased the Quaker presence in these market towns and many would have been involved in agricultural work.

74 E. T. Davies, 'Richard Hanbury and the Early Industrial History of Pontypool', *Pontypool and District Review*, 3 (February 1970), 1–3; R. Hanbury-Tenison, 'The Hanburys of Pontypool', *Pontypool and District Review*, 7 (June 1971), 1–8.

75 NRL, MS. qm.350.739.15 (unpublished MS. by J. K. Fletcher entitled 'Pontypool Japan 1728–1822' written *c*.1920), p. 2; R. Nichols, *Pontypool and Usk Japan Ware* (Pontypool, 1981), p. 7.

76 NA, E 377/14; R. P. Matthews, 'Roman Catholic Recusancy in Monmouthshire 1608–89: A Demographic and Morphological Analysis' (unpublished University of Wales, Cardiff, Ph.D. Thesis, 1996), 101 n. 23, 250, 374.
77 Matthews, 'Roman Catholic Recusancy', 101, 110–11.
78 Michael A. Mullett, 'Catholic and Quaker Attitudes to Work, Rest, and Play in Seventeenth- and Eighteenth-Century England', in R. N. Swanson (ed.), *Studies in Church History*, 37: *The Use and Abuse of Time in Christian History* (Woodbridge, 2002), pp. 185–209.
78 Matthews, 'Roman Catholic Recusancy', 91–3, 99, 105–14, 137, 178–9.
80 Ibid., 247.
81 Ibid., 115, 373.
82 R. C. Allen, 'Catholic Records in the Attic: Details of everyday life found in the seventeenth century Catholic household of the Gunter family of Abergavenny', *Gwent Local History*, 86 (Spring 1999), 17–30; J. P. Jenkins, 'Anti-Popery on the Welsh Marches in the Seventeenth Century', *Historical Journal*, 23 (2) (1980), 275–93.
83 Matthews, 'Roman Catholic Recusancy', 122.
84 Ibid., 115.
85 Between 1679 and 1684, 133 Catholics were prosecuted for recusancy. Ibid., 374.
86 F. Gawler, *A Record of some Persecutions . . . in South Wales* (London, 1659), p. 28.
87 NA, E 377/73,74,75,77,78,79. Recusant Rolls for 1679–84.
88 Matthews, 'Roman Catholic Recusancy', 375–6.
89 *Journal of the House of Commons*, IX (1678), p. 468; Matthews, 'Roman Catholic Recusancy', 124–6, 174–5, 238–40.
90 *Journal of the House of Commons*, IX (1678), pp. 466, 468.
91 Notably Henry, 3rd Marquis of Worcester and Henry Milborne.
92 Matthews, 'Roman Catholic Recusancy', 243–6.
93 W. A. Cole, 'The Quakers and Politics 1654–1660' (unpublished University of Cambridge, Ph.D. thesis, 1955). See also his 'The Social Origins of Early Friends', *JFHS*, 48 (3) (1957), 99–118.
94 R. T. Vann, 'Quakerism and the Social Structure in the Interregnum', *P&P*, 43 (1969), 71–91; Vann, *Social Development*, ch. 2; Hurwich, 'Social Origins of Early Quakers', 156–62; A. Anderson, 'Lancashire Quakers and Persecution 1652–1670' (unpublished University of Lancaster, MA thesis, 1971), 74–80 (Appendix 1); M. Spufford, 'The Social Status of some Seventeenth-Century Rural Dissenters', in G. J. Cuming and

D. Baker (eds), *Studies in Church History, 8: Popular Belief and Practice* (Cambridge, 1972), pp. 203–11; H. Forde, 'Derbyshire Quakers 1650–1761' (unpublished University of Leicester, Ph.D. thesis, 1977), ch. 3; A. Anderson, 'The Social Origins of the Early Friends', *QH*, 68 (1) (1979), 33–40; B. Reay, 'The Social Origins of Early Quakerism', *Journal of Interdisciplinary History*, 11 (1980), 55–72; Reay, *Quakers and the English Revolution*, pp. 20–6; D. Scott, 'Politics, Dissent and Quakerism in York' (unpublished University of York, D.Phil. thesis, 1990), 34–41; Davies, *Quakers in English Society*, pp. 141–55.

95   Cf. Forde, 'Derbyshire Quakers', 81.

96   This excludes Friends from other counties who married Monmouthshire members and settled outside the county. The majority of this evidence has been derived from Friends' records of sufferings, deeds, probate evidence and other title deeds held in NLW and GwRO; Cole, 'Social Origins', 107.

97   Further discussions on the reliability of sources and questions of rank are given in Vann, *Social Development*, pp. 54, 63–70; Reay, 'Social Origins', 59–60; Vann and Eversley, *Friends in Life and Death*, pp. 11–31, 68–72; Davies, *Quakers in English Society*, pp. 140–1. See also K. Wrightson, '"Sorts of People" in Tudor and Stuart England', in J. Barry and C. Brooks (eds), *The Middling Sorts of People: Culture, Society and Politics in England, 1500–1800* (London, 1994), pp. 28–30, 33–40; K. Wrightson, *Earthly Necessities: Economic Lives in Early Modern Britain* (New Haven, 2000).

98   The decline of the traditional landed gentleman in eighteenth-century Wales probably reflects a tendency which had begun during the previous century. See J. P. Jenkins, 'The Demographic Decline of the Landed Gentry in the Eighteenth Century: A South Wales study', *WHR*, 11 (1982–3), 31–49.

99   This is commented upon by Geraint H. Jenkins who suggests that the distraints for non-payment of tithes which Roger Jenkin suffered would indicate that he was a fairly wealthy husbandman. He adds that Jenkin was 'a good deal more prosperous than most Welsh husbandmen', and underlines the danger of using elastic terms like 'husbandman' and 'yeoman'. See G. H. Jenkins, *Literature, Religion and Society in Wales, 1660–1730* (Cardiff, 1978), p. 212. Further comments on the links between social status and agriculture are given in M. I. Williams, 'The Economic and Social History of Glamorgan, 1660–1760', in G. Williams (ed.), *Glamorgan County History* (6 vols, Cardiff, 1938–90), IV, ch. 7.

100   NLW, LL/1674/96.

101 NLW, LL/1698/61.

102 John Beadles who came from Kempton Hardwick in Bedfordshire was the grandson of Sir Capel Beadles of Hamerton, Huntingtonshire. See R. Nichols, 'Elisha Beadles: An Apothecary, 1670–1734', *Pontypool and District Review*, 8 (October, 1971), 1.

103 A map book in the possession of Sir Richard Hanbury-Tenison indicates that John Handley held over 113 acres in Pant-Teg parish. See Pontypool Park Estate. E. Folio Map Book of Hanbury Estate Farms. (*c.*1715), p. 19.

104 H. Barbour, *The Quakers in Puritan England* (London and New Haven, 1964), p. 92.

105 For example, the Lloyds of Dolobran and Robert Vaughan of Hendre Mawr, Penllyn. For details of the Lloyd family see H. Lloyd, *The Quaker Lloyds in the Industrial Revolution* (London, 1975), and, for a brief overview based largely on correspondence, see G. H. Jenkins, 'The Friends of Montgomeryshire in the Heroic Age', *MC*, 76 (1988), 22–3.

106 Davies, *Account*, pp. 59–60.

107 Jenkins, 'Friends of Montgomeryshire', 23.

108 Others, of course, were to take important civic positions in Penn's colony, particularly Thomas Lloyd of Dolobran who became president of the Provincial Council in 1684 and deputy governor until 1693, and Thomas Wynne, who was Penn's physician and speaker of the Provincial Assembly.

109 Swarthmore College MS. MR-Ph.532. Radnor Monthly Meeting Memorials, 1683–1697, p. 9. Details are also provided in J. G. Williams, 'The Quakers of Merioneth during the Seventeenth Century', *JMHRS*, 8 (1978–9), 318.

110 Jenkins, 'Friends of Montgomeryshire', 23. For additional examples see E. R. Morris, 'Quakerism in West Montgomeryshire', *MC*, 56 (1959–60), 47–8; M. F. Williams, 'The Society of Friends in Glamorgan 1654–1990' (unpublished University of Wales, Aberystwyth, MA thesis, 1950), 199, 251–4, 333 (for Welsh Quaker emigrants); Jenkins, *Protestant Dissenters*, p. 65.

111 Lewis Owen III was nevertheless referred to as an esquire and left over £830 in his will in 1699. See J. J. Levick, 'An old Welsh Pedigree', *PMHB*, 4 (1880), 477; Williams, 'Quakers of Merioneth', 122, 318, 319.

112 Williams, 'Quakers of Merioneth', 319; HSP, MS. 898 (J. J. Levick Collection) for details of these seventeen Friends and the purchase of the land in Pennsylvania; B. Levy, *Quakers and the American Family: British Settlement in the Delaware Valley* (Oxford, 1988),

p. 26. This structure of the economy life in mid and north-Wales is further discussed by Williams, 'Quakers of Merioneth', 122–4; Levy, *Quakers and the American Family*, ch. 1.

113 Williams, 'Quakers of Merioneth', 122, 320, and citing NA, E179/351/94.

114 Details of Llanfihangel Ystum Llywern parish, c.1680–1720, and the nature of agriculture during this period are given in N. T. Fryer, 'Some Aspects of the Agricultural History of a Monmouthshire Parish', *Presenting Monmouthshire*, 19 (Spring 1965), 22–9.

115 Jenkins, *Protestant Dissenters*, p. 60.

116 NRL, MS. px.mooo.900.Mon. A General Description of the county of Monmouth [c.seventeenth century].

117 W. P. Wyndham, *A Gentleman's Tour Through Monmouthshire and Wales. June and July 1774* (London, 1781), p. 20.

118 GAS, D/DSF/28.

119 See Jenkins, *Protestant Dissenters*, p. 68.

120 Cole, 'Social Origins of Early Friends', 107–8.

121 Reay, 'Social Origins', 62, 69–72 (Appendix 2).

122 See chapter 7 of this present study.

123 For an in-depth examination into the Harford family business interests in Monmouthshire, see NLW, Maybery MS. I and II; GwRO, D.2472.1. Ebbw Vale Memorandum Book. c.1796–1819; GwRO, D.2472.2. Ebbw Vale Letter Book. c.1824–7; GwRO, D.2472.3. Ebbw Vale Steel, Iron and Coal Company Accounts c.1791–1796. See also J. Elliott, *The Industrial Development of the Ebbw Valleys, 1780–1914* (Cardiff, 2004); Cf. the development of the Neath Abbey ironworks in the late 1790s and the central role of the Fox and Price families from Cornwall. See Williams, 'Society of Friends in Glamorgan', 204–10.

Chapter 3 The Organization of the Society

1 Rufus Jones, introduction in W. C. Braithwaite, *The Second Period of Quakerism* (2nd edn, York, 1979), pp. xxix–xxx.

2 C. L. Leachman, 'From an 'unruly sect' to a society of 'strict unity'' (unpublished University of London, Ph.D. thesis, 1998), ch. 2.

3 Details of the importance of Swarthmore Hall are provided in W. C. Braithwaite, *The Beginnings of Quakerism* (2nd edn, York, 1981), ch. 5; B. Y. Kunze, *Margaret Fell and the Rise of Quakerism* (Stanford, 1994).

4   Table reproduced with Welsh meetings added from E. K. Quine, 'Quakers in Leicestershire' (unpublished University of Nottingham, Ph.D. thesis, 1968), 21.

5   M. Brailsford, *Quaker Women 1650–1690* (London, 1915), p. 270; Braithwaite, *Second Period*, p. 275; Leachman, 'From an "unruly sect"', 73–101.

6   K. Peters, *Print Culture and the Early Quakers* (Cambridge, 2005).

7   C. W. Horle, *The Quakers and the English Legal System 1660–1688* (Philadelphia, 1988), pp. 175–6.

8   C. W. Horle, 'Changing Quaker Attitudes towards Legal Defense: The George Fox Case, 1673–75, and the establishment of the Meeting for Sufferings', in J. W. Frost and J. M. Moore (eds), *Seeking the Light: Essays in Quaker History* (Wallingford, Pa, 1986), pp. 17–18.

9   GAS, D/DSF/2, pp. 483, 485, 489, 492, 495, 498, 501, 504. Richard Davies also documents his attendance at the London Yearly Meeting and appeals to Charles II and James II's government, particularly to Lord Hyde and Lord Powis, on behalf of persecuted Friends. See Richard Davies, *An Account of the Convincement, Exercises and Services and Travels of . . . Richard Davies* (London, 1877), pp. 147–9, 153–5, 162, 166–7.

10 T. Richards, *Wales under the Penal Code, 1622–1687* (London, 1925), pp. 30–3, 36–7; Horle, *Quakers and the English Legal System*, ch. 4–5; R. L. Greaves, 'Shattered Expectations? George Fox, the Quakers, and the Restoration State, 1660–1685', *Albion*, 2 (2) (1992), 243–4.

11 T. M. Rees, *A History of the Quakers in Wales and their Emigration to North America* (Carmarthen, 1925), p. 214.

12 See *Journal*, p. 294; Rees, *Quakers in Wales*, p. 42.

13 R. S. Mortimer, 'Quakerism in Seventeenth Century Bristol' (unpublished University of Bristol, MA thesis, 1946), ch. 3.

14 Non-members were welcomed.

15 Silent meetings were normally held on the first day of the week and are often referred to as 'first day meetings'.

16 J. Lloyd, *The Quakers in Wales* (London, 1947), p. 6.

17 GAS, D/DSF/325 (3.2.1695).

18 Ibid., (3.5.1706). Cf. Pembrokeshire where two first day meetings were common practice. See David Salmon, 'The Pembrokeshire Quakers' Monthly Meeting', *THSWW*, 12 (1927), 4.

19 GAS, D/DSF/379 (27.10.1698).

20 GAS, D/DSF/324 (last day.5.1693); GAS, D/DSF/379 (27.6.1695);
GAS, D/DSF/325 (7.8.1696, 4.11.1698–9, 4.2.1705, 31.1.1708).
See also GAS, D/DSF/364 (16.11.1701/2, 15.4.1705,
17.11.1713).
21 GAS, D/DSF/325 (27.1.1710).
22 Ibid., (1.8.1711, 2.5.1712); GAS, D/DSF/351 (3.7.1712,
5.9.1712, 7.10.1715).
23 Owen Parry, 'Welsh Quakerism in the light of the Joseph Wood
Papers', *BBCS*, 25 (2) (1972–4), 177–8. See also A. Lloyd,
Quaker Social History 1669–1738 (London, 1950), pp. 121–3.
24 Cambridge University Library. Add. MS. 5716, pp. 174–5, and
cited in C. R. Kerkham, 'An Anglican's observations on a
Sunday evening Meeting at an Inn in Radnorshire, 1799', *JFHS*,
54 (2) (1977), 68–9.
25 GAS, D/DSF/325 (3.5.1695). For evidence of meetings held in
Friends' houses in mid and north Wales in the 1690s, a practice
which continued well into the eighteenth century, see GAS,
D/DSF/379 (30.3.1693, 27.4.1693, 26.7.1693, 28.9.1693,
27.1.1694, 29.3.1694, 26.4.1694, 27.9.1694, 25.10.1694,
28.3.1695, 31.1.1696, 26.3.1696, 30.4.1696, 25.6.1696,
29.10.1696, 23.12.1696, 26.3.1697, 29.4.1697, 28.7.1697,
29.1.1698, 31.3.1698, 28.4.1698, 30.6.1698, 27.4.1699,
26.7.1699, 26.10.1699).
26 Particular Meetings or local gatherings.
27 Other Monthly Meetings were held at the Pant (1708, 1710,
1712, 1720, 1724, 1726, 1734, 1737, 1742); Castleton (1728,
1730), Newport (1729); Monmouth (1734, 1736, 1737). In the
nineteenth century, Trosnant was the main centre. See NLW,
MS. 4859C.
28 Rees, *Quakers in Wales*, p. 215. A Welsh translation is included
in GAS, D/DSF/351. Preface to Monthly Meeting minutes, and
an English version is provided in GAS, D/DSF/325 (preface to
Quarterly Meeting minutes).
29 GAS, D/DSF/380 (14.12.1747); GAS, D/DSF/356 (6.2.1799,
6.3.1799); GAS, D/DSF/19 (14.12.1814, 14.2.1816); GAS,
D/DSF/20 (8.11.1820).
30 GAS, D/DSF/325 (27.1.1710); GAS, D/DSF/351 (4.6.1714); GAS,
D/DSF/352 (1.11.1723, 7.2.1725); GAS, D/DSF/355 (3.9.1794);
GAS, D/DSF/356 (11.11.1801, 10.3.1802, 11.9.1805); GAS,
D/DSF/19 (13.3.1816); GAS, D/DSF/20 (11.6.1818, 8.9.1819,
10.5.1820).
31 M. F. Williams, 'Glamorgan Quakers 1654–1900', *Morgannwg*,
5 (1961), 64.
32 GAS, D/DSF/325 (2.5.1707, 1.8.1707, 7.11.1707–8, 7.5.1708).

33 LSF, Portfolio MS. 24.190. The testimony of John Jones of Llanfrechfa read in a public meeting at Pont-y-Moel and dated 2.4.1668. Copy also provided in GAS, D/DSF/325.

34 GAS, D/DSF/320 for North Wales Quarterly Meeting minutes 1668–1752; D/DSF/1 for details of the Pembrokeshire Entry Book, 1660–1794; Mortimer, 'Quakerism in Seventeenth Century Bristol', 146.

35 GAS, D/DSF/325 (6.8.1697).

36 Mortimer, 'Quakerism in Seventeenth Century Bristol', 159–62.

37 GAS, D/DSF/352 (4.11.1720)

38 GAS, D/DSF/92–122. Answers to Queries (Miscellaneous 1737–69) from the Meetings of Elders and Ministers, Monthly Meetings, Quarterly and Yearly Meetings in Monmouthshire.

39 GAS, D/DSF/363. These minutes date from 1.12.1789 to 13.9.1791; 31.1.1800 to 8.4.1800; 7.8.1804. Various pages that relate to the period c.1791–6 had been torn out before the book was deposited with Neath Friends in 1869.

40 Ibid., (9.3.1791).

41 Ibid., (13.9.1791, 5.9.1796, 20.8.1798, 7.8.1804).

42 GAS, D/DSF/23. These minutes date from 1784–97.

43 Ibid., (26.6.1785, 2.10.1785, 7.5.1786, 31.12.1786, 28.4.1787, 12.4.1788, 27.12.1789, 24.9.1792).

44 Ibid., (18.9.1791).

45 GAS, D/DSF/315.

46 Mortimer, 'Quakerism in Seventeenth Century Bristol', 162.

47 Davies, Account, pp.143–5; W. G. Norris and N. Penney, 'John ap John, and early records of Friends in Wales', JFHS Supplement, 6 (1907), 29–32; E. S. Whiting, 'The Yearly Meeting for Wales 1682–1797', JFHS, 47 (Spring 1955), 57–70.

48 GAS, D/DSF/23. The Enquiries for Ministers and Elders c.1789.

49 GAS, D/DSF/320, p. 35. Communication from Devonshire House to the Quarterly Meeting for north Wales at Dolobran, 26.5.1681.

50 LSF, Kelsall MS. S.187, p. 89 (8.2.1724).

51 Benjamin Holme, A Collection of the Epistles and Works of . . . (London, 1754), p. 66.

52 'The Journal of John Player', cited in Rees, Quakers in Wales, pp. 274–5.

53 GAS, D/DSF/2, pp. 498, 503, 509.

54 Ibid., pp. 505–6.

55 Ibid., p. 504.

56 E. R. Morris, 'Quakerism in West Montgomeryshire', MC, 56 (1959–60), 53.

57 Ibid., 53–4.
58 H. G. Jones, 'John Kelsall: A Study in Religious and Economic History' (unpublished University of Wales, Bangor, MA thesis, 1938), 117.
59 GAS, D/DSF/2, pp. 494–5, 501. See also GAS, D/DSF/320, p. 70.
60 GAS, D/DSF/2, p. 709.
61 Ibid., p. 511.
62 Ibid., p. 540.
63 Ibid., p. 573.
64 Ibid., pp. 763–4.
65 Ibid., p. 943.
66 Ibid., p. 976.
67 Ibid., pp. 1049–53.
68 Mortimer, 'Quakerism in Seventeenth Century Bristol', 146–59; C. M. Wilcox, *Theology and Women's Ministry in Seventeenth-Century English Quakerism* (Lampeter, 1995), pp. 249–53l; C. Gill, *Women in the Seventeenth-Century Quaker Community* (Aldershot, 2005), pp. 164–71.
69 GAS, D/DSF/380. Women's Quarterly Meeting minute book, 1747–88; GAS, D/DSF/382. Women's Yearly Meeting minute book, 1748–56.
70 GAS, D/DSF/379 (28.9.1693).
71 Ibid., (30.2.1695).
72 A. Davies, *The Quakers in English Society 1655–1725* (Oxford, 2000), pp. 79–81.
73 Lloyd, *Quaker Social History*, p. 2.
74 Llangelynnin Parish Register, and cited in J. G. Williams, 'The Quakers of Merioneth during the Seventeenth Century', *JMHRS*, 8 (1978–9), 127.
75 Williams, 'Glamorgan Quakers', 56–7.
76 For other examples see Rees, *Quakers in Wales*, ch. 4; Williams, 'Quakers of Merioneth', 320; R. Nichols, 'Friends Meeting houses and Burial Grounds in Monmouthshire', *Gwent Local History*, 48 (1980), 25–32; 49 (1980), 6–17. See also David M. Butler, *The Quaker Meeting Houses of Britain . . . and 900 burial grounds* (2 vols, London, 1999).
77 T. Wakeman, *Antiquarian Excursion in the Neighbourhood of Monmouth* (Newport, 1867), pp. 54–5.
78 Francis Gawler, *The Children of Abraham's Faith who are blessed, being found in Abraham's practice of burying their dead in their own purchased grounds* (London, 1663), p. 7.
79 NA, PROB 11.446. Will of Richard Clarke of Parc Gras Dieu, Treworgan, 8 May 1697; GAS, D/DSF/227.

80 GAS, D/DSF/279–80 (deeds dated 3.3.1712).
81 GAS, D/DSF/354 (22.7.1751).
82 Edward Lewis of Tre'r Gaer, 10.3.1771. See NA, SoF Registers (Monmouthshire). No. 680, p. 77. A total of 66 interments were conducted altogether. See Norris and Penney, 'John ap John', 35 n. 24.
83 GAS, D/DSF/254, deed dated 2 March 1660.
84 NA, SoF Registers. (Monmouthshire). No. 677, p. 42.
85 Ibid., p. 53.
86 GAS, D/DSF/423; D/DSF/21, (26.12.1841); Nichols, 'Friends Meeting houses', 29.
87 NA, SoF Registers (Monmouthshire). No. 677, pp. 43, 44, 50 (23.11.1695–6, 22.4.1714, 11.11.1745); No. 678, p. 4 (8.5.1716).
88 NA, SoF Registers (Wales). No. 644, p. 92 (15.4.1817).
89 GAS, D/DSF/325 (4.11.1698/9).
90 Ibid., (5.2.1704).
91 Ibid., (2.5.1707).
92 GAS, D/DSF/351 (1.12.1715).
93 GAS, D/DSF/423; GAS, D/DSF/226.
94 GAS, D/DSF/221 (F. W. Gibbins to the clerk of the South Wales Monthly Meeting, 23.11.1909).
95 Ibid. For example, plot 5 contained the bodies of William Merrefield; Jemima Napper (aged 12), John Chorley Napper (aged 10 months); Ann Merrefield (aged 67); Roger Merrefield; Arthur Peters Napper (aged 4).
96 GAS, D/DSF/38 (5.4.1870); 39 (26.6.1873).
97 Nichols, 'Friends Meeting houses', 9.
98 The first interment took place in February 1669. See NA, SoF Registers (Wales). No. 677, p. 175 (Morgan George of Llanfihangel Roggiet, 12mo 1668). See also R. Nichols, 'The Shirenewton Quaker Meeting house', Severn and Wye Review, 1–2 (Winter 1972–3), 61–2.
99 GAS, D/DSF/325 (2.8.1700).
100 GwRO, D.1243.0001. Lease of Shirenewton Meeting burial ground, 7 October 1700.
101 GwRO, D.1243.0003. Assignment of Shirenewton burial ground and meeting house, 23 September 1745; GwRO, D.1243.0004; D.1243.0006. Lease and Declaration of Uses for Shirenewton properties, 21 July 1815, 9 July 1817; GAS, D/DSF/28, pp. 22–5 (transcriptions). See also GAS, D/DSF/19 (13.9.1815).
102 NA, SoF Registers (Monmouthshire). No. 701, p. 5.
103 In 1861, the Preparative Meeting considered a request to build a chapel over the burial ground but this was rejected. Later, the

dilapidated state of the property led Friends to consider selling
it. See GAS, D/DSF/21 (8.9.1861, 23.3.1862, 22.3.1863).
104 Davies, *Quakers in English Society*, pp. 76–9.
105 Davies, *Account*, pp. 57–8.
106 Ibid., pp. 58–9, 64–5.
107 See Rees, *Quakers in Wales*, ch. 4; Davies, *Quakers in English Society*, p. 78.
108 *Journal*, pp. 520–1.
109 GAS, D/DSF/354 (4.8.1756); LSF, Western General Meeting 15 b 14; NLW, Church in Wales Records. LL/QA/7.
110 NA, SoF Registers (Monmouthshire). No. 677, p. 42. He was buried at Pont-y-Moel, 23.6.1685.
111 For brief details of the Aubreys and Elizabeth's frequent Quarter Sessions appearances, see *JFHS*, 1 (3) (October, 1904), 129–30; R. T. Jones, 'Religion in Post-Restoration Brecknockshire 1660–1688', *Brycheiniog*, 8 (1962), 62.
112 GAS, D/DSF/2, p. 489.
113 Ibid., p. 500.
114 Morris, 'Quakerism in West Montgomeryshire', 56.
115 A. Davies, *Quakers in English Society*, p. 79; H. Lidbetter, *The Friends Meeting House* (2nd edn, York, 1979).
116 GAS, D/DSF/325 (26.10.1723).
117 GAS, D/DSF/2, p. 598 (7–9.2.1724); D. M. Butler, 'Meeting Houses Built and Meetings Settled. Answers to the Yearly Meeting Queries, 1688–1791', *JFHS*, 51 (1967), 174–211 (199: Shirenewton).
118 GwRO, D1243.0009 (4 June 1724).
119 GAS, D/DSF/195.
120 GAS, D/DSF/2, p. 647.
121 GAS, D/DSF/258–9. See also A. A. Locke, *The Hanbury Family* (2 vols, London, 1916), p. 242 n. 56. The trustees were two generations of the Hanbury family, Rose Taylor of Pant-Teg, William Howell of Pont-y-Moel, Rowland Thomas and Howell James of Llanfrechfa, George White of Llanfihangel-y-Gofion and Thomas Wisdom of Malpas.
122 GAS, D/DSF/261–2.
123 GAS, D/DSF/356 (1.1.1800).
124 GAS, D/DSF/423.
125 GAS, D/DSF/266–8.
126 GAS, D/DSF/88–9.
127 GAS, D/DSF/356 (11.5.1808).
128 Other donors were Deborah and Rebecca Darby, George Braithwaite Junior, Samuel Southall and Priscilla Gurney. Ibid.
129 GAS, D/DSF/20 (3.4.1818).

130 The Trosnant meeting house was already in decline by 1814. It was rented out to local Anglicans until St James's Church was completed in 1821, and thereafter it was used by the Baptists c.1836–47. See R. Nichols, 'Friends Meeting house, Trosnant', *Monmouthshire Medley* (4 vols, Cwmbrân, 1985), IV, 26–8.

131 GAS, D/DSF/21 (20.3.1842).

132 Preparative Meetings were nevertheless held at Newport and at Llanddewi until at least 1867.

133 GwRO, D.1243.0001.

134 GwRO, D.1243.0003.

135 The other trustees were Francis Gawler, John Mayo, Jenkin Evan and Miles Jones.

136 GAS, D/DSF/28, p. 1.

137 Ibid., p. 4.

138 Ibid., pp. 15–17, 37.

139 Ibid., p. 7.

140 Ibid., pp. 9, 10–11.

141 GAS, D/DSF/353 (5.7.1739).

142 For example, see GAS, D/DSF/364 (15.3.1702, 15.9.1706, 16.3.1707, 16.8.1713: Puncheston); GAS, D/DSF/353 (2.7.1741: Shirenewton).

143 GAS, D/DSF/354 (3.3.1749).

144 GAS, D/DSF/214 (letter dated 27.5.1868).

145 GAS, D/DSF/351 (2.7.1713).

146 GAS, D/DSF/354 (19.4.1745).

147 For example, see GAS, D/DSF/351 (1.9.1704, 7.9.1705, 6.12.1705–6, 4.7.1706; GAS, D/DSF/353 (last day [31].10.1739).

148 NLW, LL/1709/119. Will of Richard Lewis of Llanhilledd, 13 January 1709.

149 GAS, D/DSF/325 (6.2.1698, 2.2.1707, 27.10.1708–9, 2.11.1711); GAS, D/DSF/351 (5.12.1706–7); GAS, D/DSF/354 (25.4.1759).

150 GAS, D/DSF/19 (10.4.1816).

151 GAS, D/DSF/20 (13.12.1820); NLW, Maybery MS. II. 2803–3A (letter from Richard Summers Harford to John Jones, Solicitor, Brecon, 9.11.1821).

152 GAS, D/DSF/20 (9.1.1822).

153 Ibid., (12.6.1822); NLW, Maybery MS. II. 2804–5 (letters from R. S. Harford to Powell, Jones and Powell, Solicitors, Brecon, 21 and 25 May 1822).

154 GAS, D/DSF/20 (13.10.1824). The outcome is not known.

155 Ibid., (7.11.1701/2).

156 GAS, D/DSF/351 (2.4.1703).

157 GAS, D/DSF/325 (5.11.1703/4).
158 Ibid., (5mo.1704; 4.5.1705).
159 Ibid., (3.2.1706).
160 GAS, D/DSF/351, (4.10.1706).
161 GAS, D/DSF/325, (2.2.1707).
162 NLW, Church in Wales Records, LL/QA/7, 9.
163 GAS, D/DSF/352 (5.2.1727). He died two years later and was buried in the Pont-y-Moel burial ground (27.5.1729). See NA, SoF Registers (Monmouthshire). No. 677, p. 47.
164 GAS, D/DSF/354 (1.1.1770).
165 GAS, D/DSF/356 (11.12.1805).
166 GAS, D/DSF/357 (13.1.1813; 17.3.1813).
167 J. Taylor, *Joseph Lancaster: The Poor Child's Friend. Educating the Poor in the Early Nineteenth Century* (Campanile, 1996).
168 GAS, D/DSF/19 (14.7.1813).
169 Ibid., (11.8.1813, 13.10.1813).
170 Ibid., (8.12.1813). The tenants had to avoid the use of liturgies and catechisms if it was to be used as a school, and Friends were to have unrestrained access to the burial ground.
171 Ibid.
172 Ibid., (20.9.1840; 3.6.1856, 15.3.1857).
173 GAS, D/DSF/21 (20.9.1840; 20.9.1846); Rees, *Quakers in Wales*, p. 78.
174 There would be a male clerk for the meeting and a female clerk who would deal specifically with the women's meetings but liaise with her male counterpart.
175 GAS, D/DSF/351 (2.12.1708/9, 3.5.1717).
176 GAS, D/DSF/325 (1.5.1696: marriage certificate; 6.8.1697: testimony; 5.11.1703/4: treasurer).
177 Ibid., (6.11.1713/4: correspondence with London); GAS, D/DSF/351, (2.4.1703: marriage certificate).
178 Such a system was not unique to the Quakers for the Seekers had used a similar method to reach decisions at their meetings.
179 GAS, D/DSF/325 (27.10.1725, 5.8.1726).
180 GAS, D/DSF/351 (7.9.1711, 5.10.1711).
181 Anon., 'Financial Statements sent to Swarthmore, 1655 and 1656', *JFHS*, 6 (1–3) (1909), 49–52, 82–85, 127–8.
182 Ibid., 49–50.
183 A. C. Dudley, 'Nonconformity under the "Clarendon Code"', *American Historical Review*, 18 (1913), 66 n. 7.
184 GAS, D/DSF/325 (3.5.1695).
185 For early Quaker finance, see Leachman, 'From an "unruly sect"', 69–73, 144–5.

186 GAS, D/DSF/389. Included in Women's Half Yearly Committee minute book *c*.1802–17 there is a list of accounts *c*.1803–17 of payments made to Friends and a list of Committee members.
187 Lloyd, *Quaker Social History*, ch. 9.
188 GAS, D/DSF/2, p. 672 (5–7.2.1743).
189 All denominations undertook social visits to ensure continued allegiance. See B. Wilson, 'Time, Generations and Sectarianism', in B. Wilson (ed.), *The Social Impact of the New Religious Movements* (New York, 1981), p. 232.
190 GAS, D/DSF/2, p. 561.
191 LSF, Kelsall MS. S.185, p. 38 (18.5.1705).
192 GAS, D/DSF/325 (2.11.1705/6).
193 LSF, Kelsall MS. S.185, pp. 123, 125 (6.10.1710).
194 Jones, 'John Kelsall', 114.
195 GAS, D/DSF/352 (1.4.1720).
196 W. J. Allisson (ed.), *Memorials of Rebecca Jones* (2nd edn, London, 1849), pp. 124, 127–8.
197 GAS, D/DSF/325 (5.2.1699, 4.8.1699).
198 GAS, D/DSF/351 (2.12.1714).

Chapter 4 Persecution and Tolerance of Friends

1 LSF, GBS, II (Glamorganshire), fo. 6.
2 Exception to this include, A. Anderson, 'A Study in the Sociology of Religious Persecution: The First Quakers', *Journal of Religious History*, 9 (3) (June 1977), 260–1; A. Davies, *The Quakers in English Society 1655–1725* (Oxford, 2000), pp. 28–30, 70–2, 184–90; John Miller, "A Suffering People': English Quakers and Their Neighbours *c*.1650–*c*.1700', *P&P*, 188 (2005), 87–94.
3 A. P. Hampshire and J. A. Beckford, 'Religious Sects and the Concept of Deviance: The Mormons and the Moonies', *British Journal of Sociology*, 34 (2) (1983), 208–29; J. M. Chu, *Neighbors, Friends or Madmen: The Puritan adjustment to Quakerism in Seventeenth-Century Massachusetts Bay* (Westport, Conn., Greenwood Press, 1985); Kai T. Erikson, *Wayward Puritans: A Study in the Sociology of Deviance* (New York, 1966), ch. 1.
4 J. T. Rutt (ed.), *Diary of Thomas Burton* (4 vols, London, 1828) I, pp. 25, 96, 126; *Publick Intelligencer*, 10–17 November 1656, p. 974.
5 P. Jenkins, '"The Old Leaven": The Welsh Roundheads after

1660', *Historical Journal*, 24 (4) (1981), 808–10, 813; J. F. Maclear, 'Quakerism and the end of the Interregnum: A Chapter in the Domestication of Radical Puritanism', *Church History*, 19 (1950), 245–6, 263–6. See also F. Gawler, *A Record of some Persecutions . . . in South Wales* (London, 1659), pp. 7, 18, 25; Richard Davies, *An Account of the Convincement, Exercises and Services and Travels of . . . Richard Davies* (London, 1877), p. 37.

6   William Prynne, *The Quakers Unmasked* (2nd edn, London, 1655), p. 36.

7   *A Proclamation prohibiting the Disturbing of Ministers* (1655).

8   G. H. Jenkins, *Protestant Dissenters in Wales, 1639–1689* (Cardiff, 1992), p. 36; C. Horle, *The Quakers and the English Legal System, 1660–1688* (Philadephia, 1988), pp. 7–10.

9   Joshua Miller, *Antichrist in Man: The Quakers Idol* (London, 1655), p. 29.

10 M. F. Williams, 'The Society of Friends in Glamorgan 1654–1900' (unpublished University of Wales, Aberystwyth, MA thesis, 1950), 53.

11 Miller, *Antichrist in Man*, p. 1.

12 N. Penney, 'Going Naked for a Sign', in N. Penney (ed.), 'The First Publishers of Truth', *JFHS* Supplements 1–5 (1904–7), V, 366, 368; K. L. Carroll, 'Early Quakers and "Going Naked as a Sign"', *QH*, 67 (2) (Autumn 1978), 69–87; R. Bauman, *Let your words be few: Symbolism of Speaking and Silence among Seventeenth-Century Quakers* (Cambridge, 1983), ch. 6.

13 Penney (ed.), 'First Publishers of Truth', V, 366, 368.

14 *Journal*, p. 407.

15 Carroll, 'Early Quakers', 77; W. C. Braithwaite, *The Beginnings of Quakerism* (2nd edn, York, 1981), pp. 158–9.

16 LSF, Swarthmore MS. I. 197, (Thomas Holme to Margaret Fell, Chester, 28 August 1655); Penney (ed.), 'First Publishers of Truth', V, 366, 368.

17 H. Barbour, *The Quakers in Puritan England* (London and New Haven, 1964), pp. 199–204; Carroll, 'Early Quakers', 84–5;

18 Thomas Briggs, *An Account of Some of the Travels and Sufferings of that Faithful Servant of the Lord, Thomas Briggs* (London, 1685), p. 8; Carroll, 'Early Quakers', 80; Bauman, *Let your words be few*, pp. 89, 91.

19 Briggs, *Account of Some of the Travels and Sufferings*, p. 8.

20 J. Miles, *An Antidote against the Infection of the Times* (London, 1656), p. 1 (Original Preface); D. F. Durnbaugh, 'Baptists and Quakers – Left wing Puritans', *QH*, 62 (2)

(Autumn 1973), 67–82; C. W. Horle, 'Quakers and Baptists 1647–1660', *Baptist Quarterly*, 26 (1976), 344–62; T. L. Underwood, *Primitivism, Radicalism and the Lamb's War* (Oxford, 1997).

21 For Nayler see W. G. Bittle, *James Nayler: 1618–1660. The Quaker Indicted by Parliament* (York, 1986); L. Damrosch, *The Sorrows of the Quaker Jesus: James Nayler and the Puritan crackdown on the free spirit* (Cambridge, Mass.; London, 1996); R. Moore, *The Light in their Consciences: Early Quakers in Britain* (Philadelphia, 2000), pp. 35–48; K. Peters, *Print Culture and the Early Quakers* (Cambridge, 2005), pp. 233–51.

22 *Journal*, p. 290; T. M. Rees, *A History of the Quakers in Wales and their Emigration to North America* (Carmarthen, 1925), pp. 32–3; Bittle, *James Nayler*, pp. 95, 104, 116, 142. For the relationship between Quakers and Ranters see J. F. MacGregor, 'Ranterism and the Development of Early Quakerism', *Journal of Religious History*, 9 (1977), 351–4.

23 LSF, Swarthmore MS. I. 196; M. F. Williams, 'Glamorgan Quakers 1654–1900', *Morgannwg*, 5 (1961), 53–4. Meredith Edward may have exhibited 'ranter' characteristics at Redstone in Pembrokeshire in 1663–4. Richard Davies stated that: 'I could not call him a Friend, because he was not guided by the right spirit.' See Davies, *Account*, pp. 99, 100.

24 B. R. Vandevelde, 'Quakers and Fifth Monarchy Men' (unpublished University of Exeter, MA thesis, 1978), 113; B. Reay, *The Quakers and the English Revolution* (Hounslow, 1985), pp. 68–71.

25 Davies, *Account*, 36; J. E. Southall (ed.), *Leaves from the History of Welsh Nonconformity . . . Autobiography of Richard Davies* (Newport, 1899), pp. 28, 36; J. G. Williams, 'Quakers of Merioneth during the Seventeenth Century', *JMHRS*, 8 (1978–9), 136.

26 Miller, *Antichrist in Man*, p. 29.

27 Gawler, *Record*, p. 9; Rees, *Quakers in Wales*, p. 28. See also Peter Elmer, '"Saints or sorcerers": Quakerism, Demonology and the Decline of Witchcraft in Seventeenth-Century England', in J. Barry, M. Hester and G. Roberts (eds), *Witchcraft in Early Modern Europe: Studies in Culture and Belief* (Cambridge, 1996), 145–79; C. Trevett, *Women and Quakerism in the Seventeenth Century* (York, 1991), pp. 25–7.

28 LSF, GBS, II (Glamorganshire), fo. 4; Gawler, *Record*, p. 26.

29 B. Reay, 'The Authorities and Early Restoration Quakerism', *Journal of Ecclesiastical History*, 34 (1) (January 1983), 69–84.

30 Arise Evans, *To the Most High and Mighty Prince Charles the II ... an Epistle* (London, 1660), p. 64. For Welsh Quaker soldiers see Gawler, *Record*, pp. 7, 17–18, 25. See also M. G. F. Bitterman, 'Early Quaker Literature of Defence', *Church History*, 42 (June 1973), 214–7; Reay, *Quakers and the English Revolution*, pp. 18–20, 64–5, 83, 88–91, 98–9, 107–10.

31 *CSPD* (1659–60), pp. 192, 563; Williams, 'Quakers of Merioneth', 128.

32 Details of the alleged conspiracy and Owen's role are recounted in Williams, 'Quakers of Merioneth', 129–30.

33 Davies, *Account*, pp. 46–7.

34 LSF, GBS, II (Monmouthshire), fo. 1.

35 Matthew 5: 44. See also M. B. Weddle, *Walking in the Way of Peace* (Oxford, 2000); G. H. Jenkins, 'The Early Peace Testimony in Wales', *Llafur*, 4 (1985), 10–19.

36 Morgan Watkins, *Swearing denyed in the new covenant ...* (London, 1660); Davies, *Quakers in English Society*, pp. 192–4.

37 T. Richards, *Religious Developments in Wales 1654–1662* (London, 1923), pp. 250–1; Penney (ed.), 'First Publishers of Truth', V, 346; R. Clifton, 'The Popular Fear of Catholics during the English Revolution', *P&P*, 52 (1971), 23–55; Reay, *Quakers and the English Revolution*, pp. 59–60; S. A. Kent, 'The "Papist" Charges Against the Interregnum Quakers', *Journal of Religious History*, 12 (1982), 180–90; G. DesBrisay, 'Catholics, Quakers and religious persecution in Restoration Aberdeen', *Innes Review*, 47 (1996), 136–68.

38 Anon, *For the King and both Houses of Parliament being a short declaration of the cruelty inflicted ...* (London, 1661), pp. 2–3; Anon, 'John Humphrey's Narrative', in H. M. Jenkins, *Historical Collections of Gwynedd* (Philadelphia, 1897), p. 97; GAS, D/DSF/313, pp. 15–17. They were denied food and were beaten by the gaoler who confiscated their bibles, inkhorns, knives and money, and forced them to carry heavy loads.

39 W. Jenkins, *The Law given forth out of Sion* (London, 1661), p. 8; LSF, GBS, II (Monmouthshire), fo. 1; GAS, D/DSF/313, p. 3.

40 W. Prynne, *The Quakers Unmasked* (2nd edn, London, 1655), title page.

41 E. B. Underhill and N. Haycroft (eds), *The Records of a Church of Christ Meeting at Broadmead, Bristol* (London, 1865), pp. 44–6.

42 Moore, *Light of their Consciences*, pp. 21, 92, and citing Thomas Weld, *A further discovery of that generation of men called Quakers* (Gateshead, 1654).

43 Miller, *Antichrist in Man*, p. 4.

44 Ibid., pp. 25, 30–1. See also Anon, 'John Humphrey's Narrative', p. 101 where Merionethshire Friends were questioned about the 'Ffydd Gatholig'.
45 Richards, *Religious Developments in Wales*, pp. 296, 396.
46 Gawler, *Record*, p. 28.
47 Morgan Watkins in F. Gawler, *The Children of Abraham's Faith* . . . (London, 1663), p. 3.
48 J. P. Jenkins, 'Anti-popery on the Welsh Marches in the Seventeenth Century', *Historical Journal*, 23 (2) (1980), 290–1.
49 R. P. Matthews, 'Roman Catholic Recusancy in Monmouthshire 1608–89: A Demographic and Morphological Analysis' (unpublished University of Wales, Cardiff, Ph.D. thesis, 1996), 205, 208–9, 219–29.
50 J. H. Matthews, 'Mass in Penal Times', *SPM*, 9 (1929), 322–6; Matthews, 'Roman Catholic Recusancy', 231–2, 291–9.
51 Matthews, 'Roman Catholic Recusancy', 74.
52 *Journal of the House of Commons*, IX (1678), pp. 464–7; Matthews, 'Roman Catholic Recusancy', 118, 257–9.
53 Matthews, 'Roman Catholic Recusancy', 83.
54 D. Scott, 'Politics, Dissent and Quakerism in York, 1640–1700' (unpublished University of York, D. Phil. thesis, 1990), 8–9.
55 Ibid., 9.
56 E. K. L. Quine, 'The Quakers in Leicestershire' (unpublished University of Nottingham, Ph.D. thesis, 1968), 277–316.
57 Gawler, *Record*, p. 11.
58 Bodleian Library, Oxford. Tanner MS. 37. fo. 119r. (5 mo.17.1680).
59 Gawler, *Record*, p. 27.
60 NA, E 112/322/Monm. 15.
61 Ibid., E 112/322/Monm. 17.
62 Gawler, *Record*, pp. 17–18. See also B. Reay, 'Quaker Opposition to Tithes 1652–1660', *P&P*, 86 (1980), 105–20; N. J. Morgan, *Lancashire Quakers and the Establishment 1660–1730* (Halifax, 1993), ch. 5; Davies, *Quakers in English Society*, pp. 30–4, 69–70; L. Brace, *The Idea of Property in Seventeenth-Century England: Tithes and the Individual* (Manchester, 1999); C. Gill, *Women in the Seventeenth-Century Quaker Community* (Aldershot, 2005), pp. 87–108.
63 George Fox, *The Great Mystery* (London, 1659), and reprinted in T. Shankland (ed.), *Transactions of the Welsh Baptist Historical Association* (Cardiff, 1904), 56.
64 S. K. Roberts, 'Godliness and Government in Glamorgan, 1647–1660', in C. Jones, M. Newitt, S. Roberts (eds), *Politics and People in Revolutionary England* (London, 1986), p. 236.

65 Jenkins, *Protestant Dissenters*, p. 21; Roberts, 'Godliness and Government', pp. 240–51.

66 NA, E 112/481/Monm. 14; Richards, *Religious Developments in Wales*, p. 345; T. Richards, *Wales under the Indulgence 1672–1675* (London, 1928), pp. 19–20.

67 NA, E 112/481/Monm. 9; Richards, *Wales under the Indulgence*, p. 20.

68 Roberts, 'Godliness and Government', p. 245; T. Richards, *A History of the Puritan Movement in Wales, 1639–53* (London, 1920), pp. 238–9.

69 NA, E 112/322/Monm. 5; Richards, *Religious Developments in Wales*, p. 283; Richards, *Puritan Movement in Wales*, pp. 1–2, 237–8, 251. In Wales tithes were offered direct to the parishioners. As a consequence parish 'tithe farming' in Breconshire was conducted in 5 parishes or more in 1650, 22 in 1651 and 22 in 1652; in Monmouthshire, the figures were higher: 26 parishes in 1650, 38 in 1651 and 47 in 1652. See Richards, *Puritan Movement in Wales*, pp. 238–9; Roberts, 'Godliness and Government', pp. 242–3.

70 Gawler, *Record*, p. 20.

71 Ibid.

72 *The Copie of a paper presented to the Parliament and read the 27th of the fourth Moneth*, (London, 1659), p. 8; *Journal of the House of Commons*, VII (June 1659), p. 694.

73 *These several papers was sent to the Parliament the twentieth day of the fifth month 1659. Being above seven thousand of the Names of the Hand-maids and Daughters of the Lord* (London, 1659).

74 NA, E 112/481/Monm.21; Richards, *Religious Developments in Wales*, pp. 255, 285.

75 NA, E 112/482/Monm.138.

76 NLW, MS. 7563D, and citing an excommunication order in Cwmcarfan Parish for March 1663. See also Davies, *Account*, pp. 147–8; NLW, SA/Misc/1452; J. Besse, *A Collection of the Sufferings* (2 vols, London, 1753), I, p. 757, for seventeenth-century Quaker excommunicants in Montgomeryshire.

77 Other evidence, for example Montgomeryshire gaol files, can be used to corroborate cases of persecution. See R. Williams, 'Montgomeryshire Nonconformity: Extracts from Gaol Files', MC, 24 (1890), 201–32; 25 (1891), 41–72; 26 (1892), 49–78; 27 (1893), 57–76; 28 (1894), 81–106.

78 GAS, D/DSF/313, p. 4; Besse, *Sufferings*, I, p. 745.

79 Anon., *For the King and both Houses of Parliament for you (who have known sufferings)* . . . (London, 1660), p. 16.

80 LSF, GBS, II (Glamorganshire), fo. 7; GAS, D/DSF/313, pp. 4–5; Anon, *For the King and both Houses of Parliament being a short declaration of the cruelty inflicted* . . ., p. 4.

81 LSF, Swarthmore MS. IV. 252, (Thomas Holme to George Fox, Pont-y-Moel, 25 March [1660]).

82 LSF, GBS, II (Radnorshire), fo. 8.

83 Ibid., IV. 245, (Thomas Holme to George Fox, Swansea, 11.4.1663).

84 Lambeth Palace, MS.639.

85 Miles, *Antidote*, p. 31.

86 Jenkins, *Protestant Dissenters*, p. 38.

87 Davies, *Account*, p. 85; Rees, *Quakers in Wales*, pp. 63–4.

88 Anon., 'The Bishop and the Peasant' (Yr Esgob a'r Gwladwr). See *JFHS*, 9 (1912), 171–2; *Cylchgrawn Cymdeithas Alawon Gwerin Cymru (Journal of Welsh Folk Song Society)*, II (1910), 45.

89 Gawler, *Record*, p. 14; Rees, *Quakers in Wales*, pp. 28–9.

90 LSF, GBS, II (Carmarthenshire), fo. 6; Anon, *For the King and both Houses of Parliament being a short declaration of the cruelty inflicted* . . ., p. 7.

91 GAS, D/DSF/353 (28.10.1741).

92 R. Darnell, 'The Second Person Singular Pronoun in English: The Society of Friends', *Western Canadian Journal of Anthropology*, I (1970), 1–11; R. Bauman, 'Aspects of 17th Century Quaker Rhetoric', *Quarterly Journal of Speech*, 56 (1970), 67–74; Bauman, *Let your words be few*, pp. 44–6; Reay, *Quakers and the English Revolution*, pp. 44–5; M. P. Graves, 'Functions of Key Metaphor in Early Quaker Sermons', *Quarterly Journal of Speech*, 69 (1983), 364–78.

93 Gawler, *Record*, p. 27.

94 Davies, *Account*, p. 21. See also pp. 22, 23–4: 'I was now first called a Quaker, because I said to a single person thee and thou, and kept on my hat, and did not go after the customs and fashions of the world . . . For obeying this voice we came to be mocked and derided.'

95 Jenkins, *Law Given Forth*, p. 9. See also Davies, *Account*, p. 68, when in 1662 Thomas Lloyd of Dolobran met with Baron Cherbury and other gentleman but 'went not in their complimenting posture'.

96 B. Reay, 'The Quakers, 1659, and the Restoration of the Monarchy', *History*, 63 (1978), 193–213.

97 Miller, 'A Suffering People', 94–100.

98 Jenkins, *Law Given Forth*, p. 8.

99 *A Collection of Acts of Parliament, Clauses of Acts of Parliament relative to those Protestant Dissenters who are*

usually called by the name of Quakers (London, 1777); M. Watts, *The Dissenters: From the Reformation to the French Revolution* (Oxford, 1978), pp. 221–38; Horle, *Quakers and the English Legal System*, pp. 101–49.

100 Quaker Act. 13 & 14 Car II. C.1. (1662). The Act allowed no more than five people above the age of sixteen to assemble for worship. The first two offences incurred fines and/or imprisonment, while a third made Friends liable for transportation.

101 For further details see GAS, D/DSF/1, pp. 740–2; Davies, *Account*, pp. 118–31; Williams, 'Quakers of Merioneth', 142–8; A. W. Braithwaite, 'Early Friends and Informers', *JFHS*, 51 (2) (1966), 107–14; A. Fletcher, 'The Enforcement of the Conventicle Acts 1664–1679', in W. J. Sheils (ed.), *Studies in Church History*, 21: *Persecution and Toleration* (Oxford, 1984), pp. 235–46; Horle, *Quakers and the English Legal System*, pp. 120–5.

102 Besse, *Sufferings*, I, pp. 753–4; Jenkins, *Protestant Dissenters*, pp. 50, 95–6; Davies, *Account*, pp. 118–21; 128–31 (128).

103 Besse, *Sufferings*, I, pp. 755–6.

104 Ibid., I, p. 756; Davies, *Account*, pp. 137–8. For other examples of the prosecution of Merionethshire Friends in the 1670s and 1680s see HSP, MS. 898.

105 Itinerants were punished for disturbing ministers (1 Mar. Cap. 2 & 3 c.1553), and this was strengthened by *A Proclamation prohibiting the Disturbing of Ministers* (1655). For disputations see Richards, *Wales under the Indulgence*, pp. 6–7; A. Hughes, 'The Pulpit Guarded: Confrontations between Orthodox and Radicals in Revolutionary England', in A. Laurence, W. R. Owens and S. Sim (eds), *John Bunyan and his England 1628–1688* (London, 1990), pp. 30–50.

106 Gawler, *Record*, p. 5.

107 LSF, GBS, II (Monmouthshire, Glamorganshire, Pembrokeshire), fos 2–4, 11.

108 Miller, *Antichrist in Man*, pp. 6–11; Gawler, *Record*, pp. 13–14; Williams, 'Glamorgan Quakers', 51–3.

109 Gawler was a milliner.

110 LSF, Swarthmore MS. I. 201, (Thomas Holme to Margaret Fell, Newport, 3 March 1657).

111 LSF, GBS, II (Breconshire), fo. 9; Gawler, *Record*, p. 7.

112 LSF, GBS, II (Monmouthshire), fo. 2; Gawler, *Record*, p. 6.

113 P. Toon (ed.), *Puritans, The Millennium and the Future of Israel* (London, 1970), p. 94; B. Reay, 'Popular hostility towards Quakers in mid-seventeenth-century England', *Social History, 5* (1980), 387–407; Reay, *Quakers and the English Revolution*, ch. 4.

114 *Journal*, pp. 290–1.

115 LSF, GBS, II (Monmouthshire), fo. 2; Gawler, *Record*, pp. 16–17.

116 LSF, GBS, II (Glamorganshire), fo. 4; Gawler, *Record*, pp. 17–18. In 1661, John Gawler was arrested as a Quaker and later described as 'a Notorious Malefactor'. See LSF, GBS, II (Glamorganshire), fo. 4, 6; Reay, 'The Authorities and Early Restoration Quakerism', 71.

117 LSF, GBS, II (Glamorganshire), fo. 3; Gawler, *Record*, p. 13.

118 Gawler, *Record*, p. 26.

119 The first Vagrancy Act of 1569 was extended in 1655 and 1657. See Reay, *Quakers and the English Revolution*, pp. 56–7.

120 LSF, GBS, II (Glamorganshire), fo. 6.

121 Ibid. (Monmouthshire), fo. 2; Gawler, *Record*, pp. 7–8.

122 LSF, GBS, II (Glamorganshire), fo. 7; GAS, D/DSF/313, p. 20. *An order given to the Constables of Glamorgan 2 February 1660. Appendix for Wales. No.55.*

123 Anon, *For the King and both Houses of Parliament being a short declaration of the cruelty inflicted . . .*, pp. 4–5.

124 LSF, GBS, II (Glamorganshire), fo. 5; GAS, D/DSF/313, pp. 11–12.

125 LSF, GBS, II (Carmarthenshire), fo. 10; NLW, Gaol Files. co. Carmarthen, Wales 4/723/5, no. 59. Autumn Assize.

126 Richards, *Wales under the Indulgence*, pp. 99, 171–2. For additional examples see Davies, *Account*, pp. 68, 96. Under a charge of *praemunire* an individual was accused of acknowledging the supremacy of a power other that of the English Crown. This Statute was originally applied in the fourtheenth century to curb the power of the papacy in England and Wales, but was subsequently used against Quakers when they refused to swear the oaths of allegiance and supremacy, or attend divine service. In both cases, the Quakers were judged to be rejecting the authority of the Church and the State.

127 LSF, GBS, II (Monmouthshire), fo. 1; Gawler, *Record*, p. 20.

128 LSF, GBS, II (Monmouthshire), fo. 2; Gawler, *Record*, pp. 20–1.

129 A. Lloyd, *Quaker Social History 1669–1738* (London, 1950), p. 82; R. S. Mortimer, 'Bristol Quakers and the Oaths', *JFHS*, 43 (1951), 74–7.

130 LSF, GBS, II (Glamorganshire), fo. 6; GAS, D/DSF/313, pp. 3–4, 19–20.

131 LSF, GBS, II (Monmouthshire), fo. 1; GAS, D/DSF/313, p. 3, Williams, 'Quakers of Merioneth', 141–2. For the consequences of the Venner uprising, see A. D. Selleck, 'The

NOTES

History of the Society of Friends in Plymouth and West Devon from 1654 to the early Nineteenth Century' (unpublished University of London, MA thesis, 1959), 69–70; Reay, 'Authorities and Early Restoration Quakerism', 72–3.

132 LSF, GBS, II (Carmarthenshire), fo. 10; Anon, *For the King and both Houses of Parliament being a short declaration of the cruelty inflicted* . . ., pp. 7–8.

133 LSF, GBS, II (Monmouthshire), fo. 1; GAS, D/DSF/313, p. 3. Cf. the attitude of several Merionethshire magistrates who, in 1660, arrested various Merionethshire Quakers. John Humphrey recalled that they made 'merry over us . . . [and] sent in their Parasite to force us to drink the King's Health . . . They sent the fiddler to Play and sing over us and so Continued Tormenting us almost all night, pouring drink in our faces and committed an Indecency hardly fit to be mentioned.' See Anon, 'John Humphrey's Narrative', pp. 101–2.

134 LSF, GBS, II (Monmouthshire), fo. 1; GAS, D/DSF/313, p. 3.

135 LSF, GBS, IV (2), fo. 347 (William Dawson to John Marrock, 29.10.1668).

136 Horle, *Quakers and the English Legal System*, p. 161. See also GAS, D/DSF/367, p. 121 ('Sufferers by Informers').

137 LSF, GBS, IV (Wales), fos 348–50 (William David to George Fox, Talgarth, September 1668).

138 J. B. Little, *The Law of Burial* (London, 1902), pp. 41, 45. See also, Davies, *Quakers in English Society*, pp. 40–1.

139 LSF, GBS, IV (Wales), fos 348–50.

140 Gawler, *Record*, p. 24.

141 Ibid., p. 5.

142 Ibid., p. 23.

143 LSF, Swarthmore MS. I. 201.

144 LSF, Swarthmore MS. IV. 219; Penney (ed.), 'First Publishers of Truth', IV, 324.

145 These included Robert Owen, Owen Lewis, Owen Humphreys, Thomas Ellis and Richard Jones. See Rees, *Quakers in Wales*, p. 65; Reay, 'The Quakers, 1659, and the Restoration of the Monarchy', 201–2; Southall (ed.), *Leaves from the History of Welsh Nonconformity*, pp. 56–7, 62.

146 LSF, Swarthmore MS. IV. 252. See Davies, *Account*, pp. 46–7. Further examples of 'sympathy' are provided in J. P. Jenkins, '"The Old Leaven": The Welsh Roundheads after 1660', *History Journal*, 24 (4) (1981), 815–23; Horle, *Quakers and the English Legal System*, p. 256ff.

147 Davies, *Account*, pp. 46–7, 107–8. Lord Cherbury, Thomas Corbett, a magistrate of Welshpool, and Lord Herbert also

235

showed leniency in the early 1660s. Ibid., pp. 67–8, 84–90, 120–1. See also Williams, 'Quakers of Merioneth', 139, 147–50; Jenkins, '"The Old Leaven"...', 815–23; Horle, *Quakers and the English Legal System*, p. 256ff.

148 Davies, *Account*, p. 125.

149 Jenkins, *Protestant Dissenters in Wales*, p. 49.

150 Rondl Davies, *Profiad yr Ysprydion* (Oxford, 1675), and cited in G. H. Jenkins, 'The Friends of Montgomeryshire in the Heroic Age' *MC*, 76 (1988), 19 which provides further evidence of the deep divisions in Davies's own household after his daughter Prudence became a Quaker.

151 Swarthmore College MS. MR-Ph. 352, p. 5 (testimony of Hugh Roberts concerning John Thomas of Llaithgwm, 1683).

152 NLW, Flintshire Gaol Files, Wales 4/988/6–10, 4/988/1–8, 4/990/1–3, and cited in G. H. Jenkins, 'From Ysgeifiog to Pennsylvania: the rise of Thomas Wynne, Quaker Barber-Surgeon', *Flintshire Historical Society Journal*, 28 (1977–8), 44.

153 Davies, *Account*, pp. 145, 165.

154 Bodleian Library, Tanner MS. fo. 162; NLW, Lloyd-Baker MS. (Facsimile 125), letter no. 5; NLW MS. 18018D; HSP, Humphreys Papers, letter dated 8.12.1681–2, and also cited in Jenkins, 'From Ysgeifiog to Pennsylvania', 48–9.

155 Davies, *Account*, pp. 145–7, 149–52; Haverford College, Pennsylvania. Vaux Collection MS. 1167, Document Box 3; HSP, Norris MS, Family Letters 1, 94–6. Davies also recounts the imprisonment of Bishop Lloyd in 1688, his visit to the Tower of London where Lloyd was being held and the way the bishop acted on Friends' behalf afterwards. See Davies, *Account*, pp. 168–73.

156 GAS, D/DSF/2, p. 485.

157 Ibid., p. 487.

158 GAS, D/DSF/320, p. 54.

159 Davies, *Account*, pp. 166–8.

160 Ibid., p. 8; Anderson, 'A Study in the Sociology of Religious Persecution', 258–9; Horle, *Quakers and the English Legal System*, pp. 265–6.

161 Jenkins, *Protestant Dissenters*, p. 50. See also G. H. Jenkins, *Literature, Religion and Society in Wales 1660–1730* (Cardiff, 1978), p. 183; H. Lloyd, *The Quaker Lloyds in the Industrial Revolution* (London, 1975).

162 Besse, *Sufferings*, I, pp. 743, 746, 755, 761. For other examples see R. C. Allen, 'The Society of Friends (Quakers) in Wales' (University of Wales, Aberystwyth, Ph.D. thesis, 1999), 244–8.

163 LSF, GBS, II (Merionethshire), fos 17–18; Williams, 'Quakers of Merioneth', 130–1.

[164] Williams, 'Montgomeryshire Nonconformity'; E. R. Morris, 'Llanwddyn Quakers', *MC*, 86 (1978), 51–4; Jenkins, 'The Friends of Montgomeryshire in the Heroic Age', 19.

[165] NA, E 178/6743; NA, E 377/73, 74, 75, 77, 78, 80–1; A. A. Locke, *The Hanbury Family* (2 vols, London, 1916), I, pp. 241–2. For Quaker recusants, see Horle, *Quakers and the English Legal System*, pp. 143–4.

[166] NA, E 377/80; Locke, *Hanbury Family*, I, p. 241.

[167] NA, E 178/6743.

[168] A. W. Braithwaite, 'Early Tithe Prosecutions: Friends as Outlaws', *JFHS*, 49 (3) (Autumn 1960), 148–56; Horle, *Quakers and the English Legal System*, pp. 134–5.

[169] LSF, Meeting for Sufferings, 2, p. 136 (14.5.682); GAS, D/DSF/194–5; NA, E 178/6743.

[170] Williams, 'Quakers of Merioneth', 128–31.

[171] Jenkins, *Law given forth out of Sion*, p. 9.

[172] Braithwaite, *Beginnings*, p. 472.

[173] Davies, *Account*, p. 60.

[174] GAS, D/DSF/313, pp. 10–11; Besse, *Sufferings*, I, pp. 747–8.

[175] LSF, GBS, II (Monmouthshire), fo. 1; GAS, D/DSF/313, p. 3; Besse, *Sufferings*, I, p. 745.

[176] Anon, *For the King and both Houses of Parliament being a short relation of the sad estate and sufferings of the innocent people of God . . .* (London, 1661), pp. 4–5.

[177] See Davies, *Account*, p. 61.

[178] Jenkins, *Protestant Dissenters*, p. 55.

[179] GBS, II (Montgomeryshire), fo. 15; Davies, *Account*, p. 65; Jenkins, 'Friends of Montgomeryshire', 18.

[180] Gawler, *Record*, pp. 21–2.

[181] GAS, D/DSF/313, pp. 3–4. See also Richards, *Wales under the Penal Code*, pp. 61, 71–2.

[182] GAS, D/DSF/313, p. 11.

[183] LSF, GBS, II (Monmouthshire), fo. 2; GAS, D/DSF/313, p. 2.

[184] For early Quaker eschatological and apocalyptic beliefs see Toon (ed.), *Puritans*, ch. 5; K. L. Carroll, 'John Perrot, Early Quaker Schismatic', *JFHS* Supplement, 33 (1971); Carroll, 'Early Quakers', 72–6; A. B. Anderson, 'Lancashire Quakers and Persecution 1652–1670' (unpublished University of Lancaster, MA thesis, 1971), 23–4.

[185] Gawler, *Record*, p. 28.

[186] C. Trevett, *Quaker Women Prophets in England and Wales, 1650–1700* (Lewiston; Queenston and Lampeter, 2000), pp. 81–94.

[187] Davies, *Account*, p. 60,

188 Gawler, *Record*; Thomas Briggs, *Account of some of the Travels and Sufferings* (London, 1685).
189 *Journal*, pp. 290–1; *Acts of the Apostles* 19: 21–41.
190 GAS, D/DSF/2, p. 491.
191 GAS, D/DSF/194–5.
192 Anon, 'John Humphrey's Narrative', p. 107; GBS, II (Merionethshire), fo. 18. See also GAS, D/DSF/320, pp. 7, 8 (28.5.1668: 'judgments . . . yt falls on ye heads of persecutors'; 26.11.1668: 'Register of most remarkable things').
193 Gawler, *Record*, pp. 9–12.
194 W. C. Braithwaite, *The Second Period of Quakerism* (2nd edn, York, 1979), p. 248; Carroll, 'Early Quakers', 86.
195 MacGregor, 'Ranterism and the Development of Early Quakerism', 359.
196 Davies, *Account*, pp. 94–5, 101–4. For further details of the John Perrot, William Mucklow, John Wilkinson and John Story schisms, see MacGregor, 'Ranterism and the Development of Early Quakerism', 360–3; Carroll, 'John Perrot'; C. J. L. Martin, 'Controversy and Disagreement in 17th-Century Quakerism' (unpublished Open University, Ph.D. thesis, 2003).
197 LSF, Meetings for Sufferings, 3, p. 71 (23.9.1683). See also A. W. Braithwaite, 'Thomas Rudyard: Early Friends' "Oracle of Law"', *JFHS*, 27 (1956), 1–19.
198 LSF, Meetings for Sufferings, 17, pp. 177, 182, 258 (5.12.1704, 9.12.1704, 22.4.1705).
199 A. W. Braithwaite, 'Early Friends' Experience with Juries', *JFHS*, 50 (4) (1964), 217–27; C. Horle, 'Judicial Encounters with Quakers 1660–1688', *JFHS*, 54 (2) (1977), 85–100; Horle, *Quakers and the English Legal System*, ch. 3.
200 LSF, Meetings for Sufferings, 14, pp. 229, 244 (4.7.1700, 5.5.1700).
201 Ibid., 17, p. 55 (4.10.1704).
202 Ibid., p. 316 (2.9.1705).
203 Miller, 'A Suffering People', 100–3.
204 GAS, D/DSF/324 (2.9.1694) where a 'lewd people' disrupted a Quaker burial in Pembrokeshire.
205 Jenkins, *Protestant Dissenters*, p. 49; GAS, D/DSF/2, pp. 494, 495 (Haverfordwest, 14.2.1691).
206 GAS, D/DSF/325 (6.8.1697).
207 Ibid.
208 M. Clement (ed.), *Correspondence and Minutes of the S.P.C.K. relating to Wales 1699–1740* (Cardiff, 1952), p. 265.
209 Thomas Andrews, *A Serious Expostulation . . .* (London, 1708), p. iii.
210 Ibid., p. iv.

211 LSF, Meetings for Sufferings, 18, p. 359 (19.10.1707).

212 Ibid.

213 Andrews, *Serious Exposition*, p. iii.

214 R. C. Allen, "Turning hearts to break off the yoke of oppression.' The travels and sufferings of Christopher Meidel *c.*1659–*c.*1715', QS (forthcoming).

215 Thomas Andrews, *A Modest Enquiry* ... (London, 1709), p. 53.

216 Theodore Eccleston, *A Reply to Tho. Andrews letter* ... (London, 1708), pp. iv–v.

217 LSF, Meeting for Sufferings, 18, pp. 66, 85, 90, 150 (9.2.1706, 10.3.1706, 24.3.1706, 27.7.1706); LSF, C. Horle unpublished 'Transcripts of the original records of Suffering', II, p. 253 (no. 669).

218 LSF, 'Transcripts of the original records of Suffering', II, pp. 255 (no. 673), 256 (no.674).

219 GAS, D/DSF/2, p. 671.

220 GAS, D/DSF/354, (17.6.1746).

221 E. J. Evans, 'Tithing Customs and Disputes: The Evidence of Glebe Terriers, 1698–1850', *Agricultural History Review*, 18 (1970), 17–35.

222 GAS, D/DSF/353 (5.8.1741: 2nd paper).

223 Braithwaite, *Second Period*, p. 181; Lloyd, *Quaker Social History*, p. 101.

224 GAS, D/DSF/351 (5.7.1705); LSF, Tract Box 78. A.46.

225 LSF, Tract Box 78. A.46.

226 Ibid.

227 GAS, D/DSF/325 (4.5.1711).

228 Ibid. (5.8.1736: *An Application to Parliament for relief to our Friends ... for recovering tythes and other Ecclesiastical demands*).

229 GAS, D/DSF/352 (19.1.1732–3).

230 GAS, D/DSF/353 (4.10.1734).

231 E. J. Evans, '"Our Faithful Testimony." The Society of Friends and Tithe Payments, 1690–1730', *JFHS*, 52 (2) (1969), 106–21; H. Forde, 'Friends and Authority: A Consideration of Attitudes and Expedients with Particular Reference to Derbyshire', *JFHS*, 54 (3) (1978), 115–25.

232 GAS, D/DSF/320, pp. 61–2, 65, 70; GAS, D/DSF/2, pp. 496, 510, 513 (29.1.1692, 6–7.2.1697, 26.2.1698).

233 GAS, D/DSF/2, pp. 535–6 (11.2.1705); LSF, Portfolio MS. 24.194; T. Clark (ed.), *Autobiographical Narrations* (London, 1848), pp. 93–4.

234 GAS/DSF/325 (2.5.1712).

235 GAS, D/DSF/2, p. 684 (1–3.2.1746).
236 Ibid., p. 841 (30.4.1765–1–2.5.1765). See also GAS, D/DSF/324 (12.3.1703, 10. 12. 1704); GAS, D/DSF/330 (14.6.1759) for the case of John Owen of Carmarthenshire who was censured for non-attendance at the Monthly Meeting and for paying tithes.
237 Information extracted from the Yearly Meeting accounts c.1720–7 (excl. 1721–2 for which no data was supplied) and Monthly Meeting entries for 1728–9. See GAS, D/DSF/2, pp. 153–4, 176, 189, 194, 199, 201; GAS, D/DSF/352 (8.2.1729, 28.1.1730).
238 Morgan, *Lancashire Quakers*, p. 199 (table 5).
239 Ibid.
240 GAS, D/DSF/2, p. 68.
241 Ibid., p. 588.
242 Roger Jenkin served 11 years and his brother served 14 years.
243 NLW, Picton Castle MS. 577.
244 GAS, D/DSF/354 (2.8.1745).
245 GAS, D/DSF/206–7. Militia case and counsel's opinion (c.1759 and 1778).
246 GAS, D/DSF/164 (16.4.1760: Monmouthshire answers to Yearly Meeting); LSF, Meetings for Sufferings, 30, pp. 405, 406–7 (4.4.1760, 1.8.1760).
247 GAS, D/DSF/2, p. 361.
248 NA, SP 32/13/11.
249 Anon, 'A Friend's Journal: Brief Journal of Hugh Roberts 1682–1702', *Wales*, 3 (1896), 336.
250 LSF, Kelsall MS. S.194.2, pp. 145–7 (Kelsall to George Lewis, 14.7.1722).
251 LSF, Meeting for Sufferings, 25, pp. 83–4, 144, 153, 159, 178 (5.9.1731, 19.3.1732, 23.4.1732, 7.5.1732, 15.7.1732).
252 GAS, D/DSF/325 (6.8.1735).
253 NA, SoF Registers (Monmouthshire). No. 677, p. 176.
254 R. T. W. Denning (ed.), *The Diary of William Thomas of Michaelston-super-Ely . . . 1762–1795* (Cardiff, 1995), pp. 181, 236.
255 GAS, D/DSF/88.

Chapter 5 The Quaker Code of Discipline

1 Thomas Clarkson, *A Portraiture of Quakerism* (3 vols, 2nd edn, London, 1806), I, pp. ii–iii.
2 D. J. Hall, 'The Discipline of the Society of Friends' (unpublished University of Durham, MA thesis, 1972), ch. 2.

3   GAS, D/DSF/353 (5.8.1741).
4   See Patrick Collinson, *The Religion of Protestants* (Oxford, 1983).
5   NLW, LL/1674/96.
6   G. H. Jenkins, *Literature, Religion and Society in Wales, 1660–1730* (Cardiff, 1978), pp. 29–30, ch. 4.
7   R. T. Vann, *Social Development of English Quarkerism 1655–1755* (Cambridge, Mass., 1969), pp. 128–43.
8   GAS, D/DSF/325 (3.5.1695: back of volume; 1.11.1706–7).
9   Anon, 'The Journal of John Churchman (1753)', *Friends Library*, 6 (1842), 229.
10 GAS, D/DSF/2, pp. 897–98.
11 Vann, *Social Development*, pp. 138–9. See also M. A. Mullett, 'From Sect to Denomination?', *Journal of Religious History*, 13 (2) (1984), 178–9; A. Davies, *The Quakers in English Society 1655–1725* (Oxford, 2000), pp. 252–60.
12 NA, SoF Registers (Monmouthshire). No. 677, p. 24. See also Davies, *Quakers in English Society*, pp. 37–8, 203; C. Trevett, *Women and Quakerism in the Seventeenth Century* (York, 1991), p. 60; T. R. Forbes, 'The Regulation of English Midwives in the Sixteenth and Seventeenth Centuries', *Medical History*, 8 (1964), 235–44; Jean Towler and Joan Bramall, *Midwives in History and Society* (London, 1986); H. Marland (ed.), *The Art of Midwifery: Early Modern Midwives in Europe and North America* (London, 1993).
13 *Cambrian*, 11 August 1832.
14 *Extracts*, pp. 223–4.
15 LSF, MS. S.187, pp. 77–8 (16.12.1723). See also W. Coster, 'Purity, Profanity and Puritanism: The Churching of Women, 1500–1700', in W. J. Sheils and D. Wood (eds), *Studies in Church History, 27: Women in the Church* (Oxford, 1990), pp. 377–87; David Cressy, 'Purification, Thanksgiving and the Churching of Women in post-Reformation England', *P&P*, 141 (1993), 106–46.
16 M. F. Williams, 'The Society of Friends in Glamorgan 1654–1900' (unpublished University of Wales, Aberystwyth, MA thesis, 1950), 147 n. 3.
17 D. G. B. Hubbard, 'Early Quaker Education, 1650–1780' (unpublished University of London, MA thesis, 1940); L. J. Stroud, 'The History of Quaker Education in England, 1647–1903' (unpublished University of Leeds, M.Ed. thesis, 1944); R. S. Mortimer, 'Quaker Education', *JFHS*, 39 (1947), 66–70; Williams, 'Society of Friends in Glamorgan', 48–50, 174–7; R. Randles, '"Faithful Friends and Well Qualified": The Early Years of the Friends' School at Lancaster', in M. Mullett

(ed.), *Early Lancaster Friends* (Lancaster, 1978), pp. 33–42; G. Mason, 'Quaker Women and Education 1642–1840' (unpublished University of Lancaster, MA thesis, 1987).

18 *Extracts*, pp. 48, 219. See also Richard Davies, *An Account of the Convincement, Exercises and Services and Travels of . . . Richard Davies* (London, 1877), p. 189.

19 Bodleian Library, Tanner Ms. 146, fo. 138 *r-v*; G. H. Jenkins, *Protestant Dissenters in Wales, 1639–1689* (Cardiff, 1992), pp. 93–4.

20 Hubbard, 'Early Quaker Education', ch. 6–7; Stroud, 'Quaker Education', ch. 3.

21 GAS, D/DSF/2, pp. 1015, 1019.

22 LSF, Kelsall MS. S.193.3 (1 mo. [March] 1703); S.193.4, pp. 1, 89 (21.4.1701, 13.4.1708); H. C. Jones, 'John Kelsall: A Study in Religious and Economic History' (unpublished University of Wales, Bangor, MA thesis, 1938), 15–17. Kelsall recorded in his diary that in 1703 among the scholars were several sons 'of note in the County, as two that had been High-Sheriffs of ye County'. See LSF, Kelsall MS. 194.1, p. 21.

23 GAS, D/DSF/364 (17.11.1700/1); GAS, D/DSF/324 (11.12.1701/2).

24 GAS, D/DSF/351 (3.6.1709).

25 GAS, D/DSF/325 (30.7.1719).

26 NLW, SD/1685/61; NLW, LL/1719/82.

27 GAS, D/DSF/352 (7.12.1721).

28 Ibid. (2.4.1725).

29 For his career see E. R. Morris, 'Quakerism in West Montgomeryshire', *MC*, 56 (1959–60), 64.

30 LSF, TCMD, I (1728–58), p. 265.

31 LSF, Gibson MS. I, p. 29.

32 LSF, TCMD, I, p. 265.

33 GAS, D/DSF/326 (30.1.1747, 4.8.1748, 25.1.1750); GAS, D/DSF/126–93.

34 J. C. Lettersom, *Memoirs of John Fothergill M.D.* (4th edn, London, 1786), p. 137.

35 NLW, LL/1710/158.

36 GAS, D/DSF/352 (2.8.1734).

37 GAS, D/DSF/354 (5.9.1746).

38 Ibid. (10.12.1747).

39 Ibid. (3.2.1762).

40 Ibid. (6.7.1763).

41 GAS, D/DSF/2, p. 797.

42 Hubbard, 'Early Quaker Education', ch. 10; E. Vipont Foulds, *Ackworth School* (London, 1959). For details of Welsh subscriptions see GAS, D/DSF/356 (3.12.1801).

43 GAS, D/DSF/356 (13.1.1808). See also V. Leimdorfer, *Quakers at Sidcot 1690–1990* (Sidcot, 1990).
44 W. A. Campbell-Stewart, 'Punishment in Friends' Schools, 1779–1900', *JFHS*, 42 (2) (1950), 51–6.
45 L. W. Evans, *Education in Industrial Wales 1700–1900* (Cardiff, 1971), pp. 39–41, 43, 71–4, 84, 158. Evans discusses the roles of Joseph Tregelles Price of Neath and John Harford.
46 Cardiff Central Library, Bute MS.4.999, Whitchurch School, Melingriffith, Subscription Book (1807) and Admission Tickets (1808–9); Evans, *Education in Industrial Wales*, pp. 30, 158–9; A. Raistrick, *Quakers in Science and Industry* (York, 1993), p. 150.
47 Evans, *Education in Industrial Wales*, pp. 158–9.
48 E. Chappelle, *Historic Melingriffith* (Cardiff, 1940), pp. 48–50; Raistrick, *Quakers in Science and Industry*, p. 150.
49 Mary Phillips, *Memoirs of Richard Phillips* (London, 1841), p. 140; Williams, 'Society of Friends in Glamorgan', 174–5.
50 Evans, *Education in Industrial Wales*, p. 84 (Appendix 21).
51 Ibid., p. 30 (Appendix 2).
52 Ibid., p. 19, and quoting Rhys William Jones's findings for the *First Report of Commissioners for Inquiring into the Employment of children in mines and manufactories, 1842*, XV, p. 343. Four schools were established by the Ebbw Vale Company and Darby & Co. See Evans, *Education in Industrial Wales*, p. 31 (Appendix 4).
53 GAS, D/DSF/354 (7.8.1771).
54 L. Wright, *The Literary Life of the Early Friends, 1650–1725* (New York, 1932); D. Cressy, *Literacy and the Social Order: Reading and Writing in Tudor and Stuart England* (Cambridge, 1980); M. Spufford, *Small Books and Pleasant Histories: Popular Fiction and its Readership in Seventeenth-Century England* (London, 1981).
55 NA, SoF Registers (Monmouthshire). No. 677, p. 2.
56 NLW, LL/1709/152; NLW, LL/1758/50.
57 GAS, D/DSF/324 (10.12.1702/3, 12.3.1703); GAS, D/DSF/353 (5.3.1742). For apprenticeships see C. Brooks, 'Apprenticeship, Social Mobility and the Middling Sort, 1550–1800', in J. Barry and C. Brooks (eds), *The Middling Sort of People* (London, 1994), p. 73ff.
58 NLW, LL/1707/33.
59 NA, PROB 11/446.
60 GAS, D/DSF/353 (6.4.1739); GAS, D/DSF/354, (25.4.1759).
61 GAS, D/DSF/351 (6.8.1708).
62 GAS, D/DSF/354 (28.1.1748, 5.8.1748).

63 GAS, D/DSF/353 (2.12.1742).
64 GAS, D/DSF/20 (13.10.1819). See also M. A. Mullett, *Radical Religious Movements in Early Modern Europe* (London, 1980), pp. 41–2.
65 GAS, D/DSF/325 (5.2.1704, 5 mo. 1704, 4.8.1704).
66 GAS, D/DSF/2, pp. 620–1 (1–2.2.1730); Jones, 'John Kelsall', 121–2; E. R. Morris, 'The Dolobran Family in Religion and Industry in Montgomeryshire', *MC*, 56 (1959–60), 142–4.
67 GAS, D/DSF/21 (19.3.1835).
68 GAS, D/DSF/20 (12.3.1823, 18.6.1823). For Welsh bankruptcies see Williams, 'Society of Friends in Glamorgan', 242–9.
69 GAS, D/DSF/353 (4.6.1742).
70 GAS, D/DSF/352 (3.9.1731).
71 A. Lloyd, *Quaker Social History 1669–1738* (London, 1950), p. 2.
72 GAS, D/DSF/352 (5.5.1721, 2.6.1721).
73 GAS, D/DSF/351 (4.1.1712/3).
74 GAS, D/DSF/354 (7.7.1762, 3.10.1763, 1.12.1763, 18.4.1764).
75 GAS, D/DSF/326 (27.4.1743); GAS, D/DSF/354 (28.10.1747).
76 GAS, D/DSF/1, p. 270.
77 GAS, D/DSF/356 (1.6.1796, 3.9.1800); Williams, 'Society of Friends in Glamorgan', 167–8.
78 HSP, Records (transcripts) of Radnor Monthly Meeting, Pennsylvania, 1680–1788, pp. 4–5.
79 Anon, 'John Roberts of Merion', *PMHB*, 19 (1895), 263.
80 Swarthmore College Library, Pennsylvania. RG5, folder 119. Ser.3 (July 1686). For other examples, see GAS, D/DSF/325 (1.8.1717: testimony for William Walters of Merion). See also B. Levy, 'Tender Plants: Quaker Farmers and Children in the Delaware Valley 1681–1735', *Journal of Family History*, 3 (June 1978), 118–19.
81 GAS, D/DSF/326 (5.8.1741).
82 GAS, D/DSF/2, p. 492.
83 Ibid.
84 A. M. Gummere, *The Quaker: A Study in Costume* (Philadelphia, 1901); J. Kendall, 'The Development of a Distinctive Form of Quaker Dress', *Costume*, 19 (1985), 58–74; D. J. Hall, 'Plainness of Speech, Behaviour and Apparel in Eighteenth-Century English Quakerism', in W. J. Sheils (ed.), *Studies in Church History*, 22: *Monks, Hermits and the Ascetic Tradition* (Oxford, 1985), pp. 307–18.
85 LSF, Box. C1.5. Elisha Beadles's testimony of Barbara Bevan Junior *c*.1705; cf. the testimony of Dorothy Owen of

Dewispren, near Dolgellau (Tyddyn-y-garreg Meeting) in 1794 who 'contented herself with the least expensive manner of living & of Dress in order to have the more to distribute to the necessities of others'. See GAS, D/DSF/2, p. 1028.

86 GAS, D/DSF/2, p. 569; *Extracts*, pp. 185–6; GwRO, D.2200.20. John Cash of Coventry to Mary Lewis of Trosnant, 27.6.1808, regarding drab poplin for the poor.

87 GAS, D/DSF/356 (12.7.1809); Kendall, 'Distinctive form of Quaker dress', 69–71.

88 Kendall, 'Distinctive form of Quaker dress', 58–9.

89 NLW, SD/1685/61.

90 NLW, LL/1693/41. See also NLW, LL/1692/80 (John Jones of Llanfrechfa, 27 May 1692); NLW, LL/1708/191 (Rowland Thomas of Pant-Teg, 5 June 1708); NLW, LL/1709/105 (Samuel Lewis of Llanfihangel Ystum Llywern, 1709).

91 J. A. Bradney (ed.), *Registrum Antiquum de Llanfihangel Ystern Llewern 1685–1812* (London, 1920), p. 2.

92 NLW, LL/1674/96.

93 NLW, LL/1679/177.

94 NLW, LL/1692/80.

95 References to wigs and wig-making in the minutes are rare. One surviving tract is John Mulliner, *A Testimony Against Perriwigs and Perriwig Making* (London, 1677). See also Gummere, *Quaker: A Study in Costume*, ch. 3; M. Pointon, *Hanging the Head: Portaiture and Social Formation in Eighteenth-Century England* (New Haven, 1992), pp. 116–17; E. Bell, 'Vain unsettled fashions', *QS*, 8 (1) (September 2003), 31–2.

96 GAS, D/DSF/353 (4.3.1737).

97 For example, see GAS, D/DSF/2, p. 922 (22–4.4.1777). See also Owen Parry, 'Welsh Quakers in the Light of the Joseph Wood Papers', *BBCS*, 25 (2) (1972–4), 162–3.

98 GAS, D/DSF/324 (14.6.1705, 7.9.1705).

99 At a Quaker wedding at Neath between Mary Eliza Richardson and Henry Habberley Price Junior, 'the dresses of the ladies of the bridal party were chaste and elegant, but not gaudy. The bride was dressed in a white silk bonnet and lace fall, and bore in her hand a beautiful bouquet.' The children of Charles S. Price were also elegantly dressed in their 'knickerbocker dress of blue with white cashmere caps and feathers'. See *Neath Gazette*, 12 March 1864; Williams, 'Society of Friends in Glamorgan', 141–2.

100 B. Reay, *The Quakers and the English Revolution* (Hounslow, 1985), p. 120.

101 Ibid., p. 118. Michael Mullett suggested that a gulf existed between the 'middling sorts' and the better-educated and wealthy

members who consequently abandoned their association with the Quaker faith. See Mullett, *Radical Religious Movements*, p. 44.

102 G. R. Cragg (ed.), *The Works of John Wesley* (Oxford, 1975), pp. 254–7.

103 J. Howells, 'Quakerism in Wales', *Red Dragon*, 4 (1883), 38.

104 For consumerism and Quakers see P. Langford, *A Polite and Commercial People: England, 1727–1783* (Oxford, 1989); J. Brewer, *The Pleasures of the Imagination: English Culture in the Eighteenth Century* (London, 1997); R. C. Allen, 'An Alternative Community in North-East England: Quakers, Morals and Popular Culture in the Long Eighteenth Century', in H. Berry and J. Gregory (eds), *Creating and Consuming Culture in North-East England, 1660–1830* (Aldershot, 2004), pp. 98–119.

105 Joseph Pike, *Some Account of the Life of Joseph Pike of Cork* (London, 1837), pp. 147–8. See also R. S. Mortimer, 'Quakerism in Seventeenth Century Bristol' (unpublished University of Bristol, MA thesis, 1946), 223–6.

106 Matthew 5: 34–7.

107 In 1696, Parliament granted Friends the right to affirm in courts or to attest to wills rather than to swear. Thereafter, wills were generally acknowledged in the following manner: 'I am a dissenter commonly called a Quaker . . . do declare', 'I do solemnly declare'.

108 H. Forde, 'Derbyshire Quakers, 1650–1761' (unpublished University of Leicester, Ph.D. thesis, 1977), 145–51; Davies, *Quakers in English Society*, pp. 194–5.

109 NLW, LL/1669/151.

110 NLW, LL/1677/35.

111 NLW, LL/1692/90.

112 GAS, D/DSF/320, pp. 148–9; GAS, D/DSF/379 (31.1.1713); T. G. Jones, 'Parish of Meifod. Sketch of the History of Nonconformity', *MC*, 11 (1878), 121.

113 GAS, D/SF/352 (6.9.1723, 4.10.1723).

114 Mullett, 'From Sect to Denomination?', 182; N. J. Morgan, *Lancashire Quakers and the Establishment, 1660–1730* (Halifax, 1993), ch. 4; D. Scott, *Quakerism in York, 1650–1720* (York, 1991), pp. 25–9.

115 Scott, *Quakerism in York*, pp. 28–9.

116 GAS, D/DSF/379, p. 69; LSF, S. 193.1, pp. 50–1 (24.6.1721); GAS, D/DSF/320, p. 172. See also Jenkins, *Literature, Religion and Society*, pp. 100, 212.

117 GAS, D/DSF/352 (2.10.1730, 4.7.1734).

118 Thomas Wynne, *An Antichristian Conspiracy Detected* (London, 1679), p. 24.

119 GAS, D/DSF/379 (31.5.1705).

[120] Anon, 'A Letter from Hugh Roberts to William Penn', *Wales*, 3 (1896), 371–3.
[121] GAS, D/DSF/324 (31.5.1694).
[122] Mary Clement (ed.), *Correspondence and Minutes of the S.P.C.K. relating to Wales 1699–1740* (Cardiff, 1952), p. 1; G. H. Jenkins, 'Quaker and anti-Quaker literature in Welsh from the Restoration to Methodism', *WHR*, 7 (1975), 420.
[123] GAS, D/DSF/351 (6 mo. 1711, 3.8.1711, 3.1.1714, 1.4.1715); GAS, D/DSF/352, (6.10.1727); GAS, D/DSF/353 (31.3.1736).
[124] GAS, D/DSF/364 (19.2.1700, 21.4.1701, 15.3.1702, 18.7.1702, 16.2.1703, 19.9.1703, 17.1.1703/4, 20.8.1704, 17.9.1704, 17.7.1708, 19.9.1708, 17.4.1709); D. Salmon, 'The Pembrokeshire Quakers' Monthly Meeting', *THSWW*, 12 (1927), 11–12.
[125] W. W. Comfort, 'Quaker Marriage Certificates', *Quaker History*, 40 (2) (Autumn 1951), 67–80; R. G. Burtt, 'The Quaker Marriage Declaration', *JFHS*, 46 (1955), 53–9; R. S. Mortimer, 'Marriage Discipline in Early Friends', *JFHS*, 48 (4) (Autumn 1957), 175–95; C. L. Leachman, 'From an "unruly sect" to a Society of "strict unity"' (unpublished University of London, Ph.D. thesis, 1998), pp. 148–50.
[126] *Extracts*, p. 98. See also L. Stone, *The Family, Sex and Marriage in England, 1500–1800* (Harmondsworth, 1977), ch. 7–8; C. Durston, *The Family in the English Revolution* (Oxford, 1989), ch. 4–5; L. Stone, *The Road to Divorce: England 1530–1987* (Oxford, 1990); R. A. Houlbrooke, *The English Family, 1450–1700* (London, 1983), ch. 4–5; J. Gillis, *For Better, For Worse* (Oxford, 1985), ch. 1–3; A. MacFarlane, *Marriage and Love in England, Modes of Reproduction 1300–1840* (pbk edn, Oxford, 1993), ch. 8–9.
[127] GAS, D/DSF/351, preface to volume; trans. T. M. Rees, *A History of the Quakers in Wales and their Emigration to North America* (Carmarthen, 1925), p. 214; cf. the courting procedures provided in Gillis, *For Better, For Worse*, p. 23ff; MacFarlane, *Marriage and Love in England*, ch. 13.
[128] Davies, *Account*, pp. 39–41.
[129] T. Woods (ed.), *The Registers of Glasbury, Breconshire, 1660–1836* (London, 1904), p. 13; R. T. Jones, 'Religion in Post-Restoration Brecknockshire 1660–1688', *Brycheiniog*, 8 (1962), 48; R. W. McDonald, 'The Parish Registers of Wales', *NLWJ*, 19 (4) (1976), 424.
[130] GAS, D/DSF/354 (6.11.1747: Letter 'C' 10 mo.1741).
[131] George Fox, *A Collection of Many Select and Christian Epistles* (London, 1698), no. 317, p. 359; W. C. Braithwaite, *The*

Beginnings of Quakerism (2nd edn, York, 1981), p. 146; Mortimer, 'Marriage Discipline', 175.

132 The Lord Campbell Marriage Act (1847) recognized Quaker marriage ceremonies.

133 Davies, *Account*, pp. 41–2.

134 GAS, D/DSF/325, (7.3.1675: London Yearly Meeting epistle; 4.8.1704).

135 R. S. Mortimer (ed.), *Minute Book of the Men's Meeting . . . 1686–1704* (Bristol, 1977) p. 163.

136 GAS, D/DSF/365 (2.8.1774, 15.2.1774, 5.2.1777, 3.3.1779); Salmon, 'Pembrokeshire Quakers', 17.

137 GAS, D/DSF/353 (26.1.1739, 4.2.1739, 18.2.1739).

138 GAS, D/DSF/354 (3.6.1752, 3.1.1753). See also Mortimer, 'Quakerism in Seventeenth Century Bristol', 195, 204, 206, 467 n. 1.

139 Lloyd, *Quaker Social History*, p. 51.

140 Comfort, 'Quaker Marriage Certificates', 70–1.

141 GAS, D/DSF/2, p. 510.

142 GAS, D/DSF/382 ('Queries').

142 GAS, D/DSF/325 (1.8.1701, 7.11.1701/2).

144 GAS, D/DSF/351 (6.6.1712).

145 Ibid., (7.3.1718).

146 GAS, D/DSF/351 (7.3.1718).

147 NA, SoF Registers. (Monmouthshire). No. 677, p. 49.

148 GAS, D/DSF/326 (30.12.1754).

149 GAS, D/DSF/325 (2.11.1711).

150 GAS, D/DSF/354 (9.4.1786).

151 Ibid., (6.6.1746, 5.9.1746).

152 Ibid., (4.2.1761).

153 Ibid., (5.12.1754, 12.10.1764).

154 See R. S. Mortimer (ed.), *Minute Book of the Men's Meeting . . . 1667–1686* (Bristol, 1971), pp. 78, 80–2, 84; Mortimer, 'Quakerism in Seventeenth Century Bristol', 167, 182. A letter to Pont-y-Moel Friends is in the Bristol Archives Office, SF/A7/3, 21. For an additional example, GAS, D/DSF/320, p. 11 when in 1670 Humphrey and Katherine Overton were censured by north Wales Friends for their 'disorderly marriage'.

155 J. Tual, 'Sexual Equality and Conjugal Harmony: The way to celestial bliss. A view of early Quaker matrimony', *JFHS*, 55 (6) (1988), 161–74.

156 'John Bevan's *Journal*', and cited in T. A. Glenn, *Merion in the Welsh Tract* (Norristown, Pa., 1896), p. 174.

157 This was common, see NLW, LL/1709/4 (William Lewis of Abergavenny, 8 October 1709); NLW, LL/1726/151 (Joseph John

of Trefddyn, 3 May 1726); NLW SD/1732/60 (Lewis Musgrave of Haverfordwest, 2 January 1732); NLW SD/1732/64 (Thomas Cornock of Haverfordwest, 1732); cf. Davies, *Quakers in English Society*, p. 220.

158 LSF, Swarthmore MS. I. 195.

159 M. R. Brailsford, *Quaker Women 1650–1690* (London, 1915), p. 150; N. Penney (ed.), 'The First Publishers of Truth', *JFHS* Supplements 1–5 (1904–7), IV, 260.

160 Cf. the clear affection between Thomas Lloyd of Dolobran and his wife provided in a letter written *c.*1675. He wrote to his 'Dear & Lo[ving] Wife', and specified 'my dear love is to thy selfe', and 'Thy Truely lo[ving] Husband'. See HSP, Etting Collection 37, no. 4.

161 GAS, D/DSF/325 (4.11.1692, 5.2.1693). For illegitimacy statistics see Stone, *Family, Sex and Marriage in England*, pp. 385–95.

162 GAS, D/DSF/325 (2.2.1701, 2.5.1701). See also P. Laslett, *Family Life and Illicit Love in Earlier Generations* (Cambridge, 1977); G. R. Quaife, *Wanton Wenches and Wayward Wives: Peasants and Illicit Sex in Seventeenth Century England* (London, 1979).

163 GAS, D/DSF/364 (17.10.1703, 17.1.1703/4); GAS, D/DSF/351 (7.1.1704–5, 5.10.1705).

164 GAS, D/DSF/353 (5.2.1738).

165 GAS, D/DSF/354 (6.8.1760, 13.8.1760, 10.9.1760).

166 Ibid. (13.9.1775).

167 M. Wiesner, *Women and Gender in Early Modern Europe* (Cambridge, 1993), pp. 49–50.

168 C. Stevens, *Welsh Courting Customs* (Llandysul, 1993), pp. 7, 83, 97–9, 105.

169 M. A. Mullett, 'The Assembly of the People of God: The Social Organisation of Lancashire Friends', in M. A. Mullett, *Early Lancaster Friends* (Lancaster, 1978), p. 15.

170 LSF, Portfolio MS. 26.198 (7.10.1712).

171 *Journal*, p. 37. See also Mullett, 'From Sect to Denomination?', 171–4; Reay, *Quakers and the English Revolution*, pp. 118–20; Scott, *Quakerism in York*, pp. 14–5, 21–2.

172 NLW, MS. 17743E. See also Jenkins, *Literature, Religion and Society in Wales*, p. 111; R. W. Malcolmson, *Popular Recreations in English Society, 1700–1850* (Cambridge, 1973); Eamon Duffy, 'The Godly and the Multitude in Stuart England', *The Seventeenth Century*, 1 (1) (1986), 31–55; D. Underdown, *Revel, Riot and Rebellion: Popular Politics and Culture in England 1603–1660* (pbk edn, Oxford, 1987), ch.

3–4, 9–10; P. Burke, *Popular Culture in Early Modern Europe* (revised edn, Cambridge, 1994), pp. 238–40; R. Hutton, *The Rise and Fall of Merry England: The Ritual Year 1400–1700* (Oxford, 1994), ch. 2, 4.

173 LSF, Swarthmore MS. I. 247.

174 Margaret Fell, *Touch-stone, or a perfect tryal by the Scriptures, of all the Priests, Bishops and Ministers* (London, 1667), p. 30.

175 Davies, *Account*, p. 32.

176 GAS, D/DSF/379 (27.12.1704–5, 27.1.1705); Jenkins, 'Quaker and anti-Quaker literature', 413.

177 Reay, *Quakers and the English Revolution*, p. 118. See also K. Wrightson, 'The Puritan Reformation of Manners' (unpublished University of Cambridge, Ph.D. thesis, 1973); Hutton, *Rise and Fall of Merry England*, ch. 4.

178 Mullett, *Radical Religious Movements*, p. 90. See also M. Spufford, *Contrasting Communities: English Villagers in the Sixteenth and Seventeenth Centuries* (Cambridge, 1974), pp. 346–9; Underdown, *Revel, Riot and Rebellion*, pp. 254–5; Davies, *Quakers in English Society*, ch. 14.

179 Reay, *Quakers and the English Revolution*, p. 120.

180 LSF, Kelsall MS. S.193.1, pp. 114, 117 (18.5.1722, 9.6.1722).

181 *Gloster Journal*, 13 April 1731, p. 2.

182 GAS, D/DSF/353 (28.10.1741: 'A Warning to all Youth').

183 GAS, D/DSF/354 (7.3.1746, 4.4.1746).

184 GAS, D/DSF/2, pp. 823–4, 897–8 (8–10.5.1764, 28–30.4.1773). See also Jenkins, *Literature, Religion and Society*, pp. 92–7; P. Clark, 'The Alehouse and the Alternative Society', in D. Pennington and K. Thomas (eds), *Puritans and Revolutionaries* (Oxford, 1978), pp. 47–72; L. Davison, 'Experiments in the Social Regulation of Industry: Gin Legislation, 1729–1751', in in L. Davison, T. Hitchcock, T. Keirn and R. B. Shoemaker (eds), *Stilling the Grumbling Hive: The Response to Social and Economic Problems in England, 1689–1750* (Stroud, 1992), ch. 2.

185 GAS, D/DSF/2, p. 498. For additional examples and comments see GAS, D/DSF/325 (1.11.1700, 2.2.1700–1, 7.11.1701); *Extracts*, pp. 25–6, 115; Reay, *Quakers and the English Revolution*, pp. 118–19.

186 GAS, DSF/324 (14.6.1706, 13.9.1706). See also GAS, D/DSF/329 (1.3.1734) for the case of William Lewis of the Pen-y-Banc Meeting.

187 GAS, D/DSF/351 (6.9.1706, 4.10.1706).

188 NA, SoF Registers (Monmouthshire). No. 677, p. 247.

189 GAS, D/DSF/351 (7.3.1707); GAS, D/DSF/325 (2.5.1707: his recantation).

[190] GAS, D/DSF/354 (22.3.1775, 9.4.1786).

[191] GwRO, D.2472.1, pp. 3, 39 (28 March 1796, 20 July 1796).

[192] GwRO, D.2472.1, p. 9 (22 April 1796).

[193] K. Peters, *Print Culture and the Early Quakers* (Cambridge, 2005), ch. 1–2

[194] Jenkins, *Literature, Religion and Society*, pp. 179–83, ch. 10.

[195] The situation was later exacerbated by the issuing of *An Act for preventing the frequent abuses in printing seditious, treasonable, and unlicensed books and pamphlets and for regulating of printing and printing presses* (13–14 Car.II. c.XXXIII). See Lloyd, *Quaker Social History*, pp. 148–55, Peters, *Print Culture and the Early Quakers*, ch. 2, 4, 6–7.

[196] Jenkins, 'Quaker and Anti-Quaker Literature', 403–26.

[197] Probates list a considerable number of books and maps. See NLW, LL/1692/80; NLW, LL/1728/141; NLW, LL/1709/105; NLW, LL/1707/33; NLW SD/1732/60.

[198] For eighteenth-century Quaker literature, see R. G. Burtt, 'Quaker Books in the 18th Century', *JFHS*, 38 (1946), 7–18.

[199] NA, SoF Registers. (Monmouthshire). No. 677, p. 201.

[200] Ibid., p. 232.

[201] Jenkins, *Literature, Religion and Society*, pp. 134–45; P. Aries, *The Hour of our Death* (Harmondsworth, 1983); C. Gittins, *Death, Burial and the Individual in Early Modern England* (London, 1984); K. Wrightson, 'Love, Marriage and Death', in L. Smith (ed.), *The Making of Britain: The Age of Expansion* (London, 1986), pp. 111–12; M. J. Dobson, *Contours of Death and Disease in Early Modern England* (Cambridge, 1997); David Cressy, *Birth, Marriage and Death: Ritual, Religion, and the Life-Cycle in Tudor and Stuart England* (Oxford, 1999).

[202] F. Godlee, 'Aspects of Non-Conformity: Quakers and the lunatic fringe', in W. F. Bynum, R. Porter and M. Stephens (eds), *The Anatomy of Madness: Essays in the History of Psychiatry: Institution and Society* (2 vols, London, 1986), II, pp. 73–85; M. MacDonald, *Mystical Bedlam: Madness, Anxiety and Healing in Seventeenth Century England* (Cambridge, 1981), pp. 106–7; M. Glover and J. R. Glover, *The Retreat, York: An Early Quaker Experiment in the Treatment of Mental Illness* (York, 1984).

[203] GAS, D/DSF/320, p. 71, 125; GAS, D/DSF/325 (4/11/1692, 5/2/1693); LSF, Portfolio 24/193 (1731).

[204] GAS, D/DSF/324 (20.6.1707); GAS, D/DSF/325 (27.10.1708–9, 4.5.1711). In the will of John Jones of Llanfrechfa in 1692 there is this terse reminder of the need to prepare for death: 'well knowing the certainety of death, and being uncertaine of the

tyme thereof'. See NLW, LL/1692/80. See also J. Goody, J. Thirsk and E. P. Thompson (eds), *Family and Inheritance: Rural Society in Western Europe 1200–1800* (Cambridge, 1976).

205 NA, PROB 11/424 (John Beadles, 5 December 1693, proved *c.*1695).
206 NLW, LL/1720/103 (Isaac Lawrence of Llanfrechfa, 28 July 1720); GAS, D/DSF/325 (26.10.1724, 5.8.1726).
207 Braithwaite, *Beginnings*, p. 313.
208 NA, SoF Registers (Carmarthenshire and Glamorganshire). No. 690, p. 15.
209 In 1666 Thomas Holme was interred at Pont-y-Moel, 26 miles from St Fagans where he died.
210 Davies, *Quakers in English Society*, p. 90; P. Mack, *Visionary Women: Ecstatic Prophecy in Seventeenth-Century England* (Oxford, 1992), pp. 393–402.
211 Francis Gawler, *The Children of Abraham's Faith* . . . (London, 1663); GAS, D/DSF/352 (5.7.1722); cf. J. Hitchcock, 'Early Separatist Burial Practice', *Transactions of the Congregational Historical Society*, 20 (1966), 105–6; Gittins, *Death, Burial and the Individual*, ch. 2, 6–7.
212 C. E. Whiting, *Studies in English Puritanism from the Restoration to the Revolution 1660–1688* (London, 1968), pp. 449–50.
213 George Fox, *An Encouragement to Trust in the Lord* (London, 1682); See also *JFHS*, 10 (1918), 12.
214 Gawler, *Children of Abraham's Faith*, p. 3.
215 GAS, D/DSF/352 (3.8.1722). See also GAS, D/DSF/320, p. 95.
216 GAS, D/DSF/320, p. 94; GAS, D/DSF/2, p. 506 (14.2.1696).
217 GAS, D/DSF/2, p. 523 (22.5.1701).
218 GAS, D/DSF/325 (7.8.1702).
219 Ibid.
220 Ibid., (4.8.1704).
221 GAS, D/DSF/2, pp. 569–70 (19–21.2.1715).
222 GAS, D/DSF/364 (19.2.1700).
223 LSF, Box C 1.5.
224 LSF, Portfolio MS. 24.195.
225 *A Collection of Testimonies concerning Several Ministers of the Gospel* (London, 1760), p. 200. His funeral was later attended 'by a great Number of most Perswasions and Degrees'. Ibid., p. 201.
226 Mullett, *Radical Religious Movements*, p. 67.
227 Davies, *Quakers in English Society*, pp. 201–14.

Chapter 6 Women Friends and their Role in the Quaker Community

1   A letter from a Royalist messenger, October 1647. Bodleian Library, Oxford. Clarendon MS. 30, fo. 140; A. Laurence, 'A Priesthood of She-Believers: Women and Congregations in Mid-Seventeenth-Century England', in W. J. Sheils and D. Wood (eds), *Studies in Church History*, 27: *Women in the Church* (Oxford, 1990), p. 355.

2   C. Trevett, *Quaker Women Prophets in England and Wales* (Lewiston; Queenston and Lampeter, 2000), pp. 87–90, 110–16, 168–70; C. Gill, *Women in the Seventeenth-Century Quaker Community* (Aldershot, 2005), pp. 153–64.

3   Swarthmore College MS. Mr–Ph. 352, p. 9.

4   For example, Elaine Hobby, "Come to Live a Preaching Life': Female Community in Seventeenth-Century Radical Sects', in R. D'Monté and N. Pohl (eds), *Female Communities 1600–1800: Literary Visions and Cultural Realities* (Basingstoke, 2000), pp. 76–92; C. Gill, "Women's Speaking Justified': The Feminine Quaker Voice 1662–1797', *Tulsa Studies in Women's Literature*, 9 (2) (2002), 61–83.

5   S. D. Amussen, 'Gender, Family and the Social Order 1560–1735', in A. Fletcher and J. Stevenson (eds), *Order and Disorder in Early Modern England* (Cambridge, 1985), pp. 196–217; C. Durston, *The Family in the English Revolution* (Oxford, 1989), ch. 5–6; P. Crawford, *Women and Religion in England 1500–1720* (London, 1993), ch. 2; R. O'Day, *The Family and Family Relationships, 1500–1900* (Basingstoke, 1994), ch. 1–2; B. Capp, 'Separate Domains? Women and Authority in Early Modern England', in P. Griffiths, A. Fox and S. Hindle (eds), *The Experience of Authority in Early Modern England* (Basingstoke, 1996), pp. 117–45; W. Coster, *Family and Kinship in England 1450–1800* (Harlow, 2001).

6   Keith Thomas, 'Women and the Civil War Sects', *P&P*, 13 (1958), 43.

7   L. Charles and L. Duffin (eds), *Women and Work in Pre-industrial England* (London, 1985); M. E. Wiesner, *Women and Gender in Early Modern Europe* (Cambridge, 1993), ch. 3; A. Laurence, *Women in England 1500–1760* (pbk. edn, London, 1995), ch. 8–9.

8   A. Lloyd, *Quaker Social History 1669–1738* (London, 1950), p. 119; A. L. Erikson, *Women and Property in Early Modern England* (pbk edn, London, 1995), pp. 156–61.

9 P. Crawford, 'Historians, Women and Civil War Sects, 1640–1660', *Parergon*, 6 (1988), 19–32; A. M. McEntee, "The [un]civill-sisterhood of oranges and lemons': Female Petitioners and Demonstrators, 1642–1653', in J. Holstun (ed.), *Pamphlet Wars: Prose in the English Revolution* (London, 1992), pp. 92–111; A. Plowden, *Our Women all on Fire: The Women of the English Civil War* (Stroud, 1998); S. Davies, *Unbridled Spirits: Women of the English Revolution, 1640–1660* (London, 1998); R. Hudson (ed.), *The Grand Quarrel: Women's Memoirs of the English Civil War* (Stroud, 2000).

10 C. Cross, '"He-Goats before the flocks": A Note on the Part Played by Women in the Founding of some Civil War Churches', in G. J. Cuming and D. Baker (eds), *Studies in Church History, 8: Popular Belief and Practice* (Cambridge, 1972), pp. 195–8; Crawford, *Women and Religion in England*, ch. 6; J. Briggs, 'She-Preachers, widows and Other Women: The Feminine Dimension in Baptist Life since 1600', *Baptist Quarterly*, 31 (July 1986), 337–52; Laurence, 'A Priesthood of She-Believers', pp. 345–63; Trevett, *Quaker Women Prophets*, pp. 151–77.

11 Phyllis Mack has calculated that there were over 300 women visionaries of which Quaker prophetesses numbered 200. See P. Mack, 'Women as Prophets during the English Civil War', *Feminist Studies*, 8 (1982), 24, 41 n. 26. For early Quaker women preachers and prophets see M. Brailsford, *Quaker Women 1650–1690* (London, 1915); R. Smith, "Female Intransigence' in the Early Quaker Movement' (unpublished University of Lancaster, MA thesis, 1990), ch. 2–3; C. Trevett, *Women and Quakerism in the Seventeenth Century* (York, 1991), pp. 16–41; Trevett, *Quaker Women Prophets*; Gill, *Women in the Seventeenth-Century Quaker Community*, ch. 4.

12 E. C. Huber, 'A Woman Must Not Speak: Quaker Women in the English Left Wing', in R. R. Ruether and E. McLaughlin (eds), *Women of Spirit: Female Leadership in the Jewish and Christian Traditions* (New York, 1979), pp. 153–82; Mack, 'Women as Prophets', 20–45; K. O. Sprunger, "God's powerful army of the weak': The Anabaptist Women of the Radical Reformation', in R. L. Greaves (ed.), *Triumph over Silence: Women in Protestant History* (London, 1985), pp. 45–74; D. P. Ludlow, 'Shaking Patriarchy's Foundation: Sectarian Women in England 1641–1700', in Greaves (ed.), *Triumph over Silence*, pp. 93–123; P. Mack, *Visionary Women* (Berkley, Ca. and Oxford, 1992); C. M. Wilcox, *Theology and Women's Ministry in Seventeenth-Century English Quakerism: Handmaids of the Lord* (Lampeter, 1995), pp. 236–44; Trevett, *Quaker Women Prophets*.

13 G. Keith, *The Woman Preacher of Samaria* (London, 1674), p. 9; Mack, *Visionary Women*, p. 58

14 Smith, 'Female Intransigence', pp. 4–6, 28–33.

15 P. Crawford, 'The Challenge to patriarchalism', in J. Morrill (ed.), *Revolution and Restoration: England in the 1650s* (London, 1992), pp. 114–16; Gill, *Women in the Seventeenth-Century*, p. 60.

16 R. Baxter, *One sheet against the Quakers* (London, 1657), p. 11; Trevett, *Quaker Women Prophets*, p. 153.

17 Ludlow, 'Shaking Patriarchy's Foundations', pp. 93–4. See also Crawford, *Women and Religion in England*, pp. 142–3.

18 Hugh Barbour, 'Quaker Prophetesses and Mothers in Israel', in J. W. Frost and J. M. Moore (eds), *Seeking the Light* (Wallingford, Pa., 1986), p. 41.

19 This letter is attributed to Sarah Fell, the daughter of Margaret Fell of Swarthmore Hall. See M. D. Spiezman and J. C. Kronick, 'A Seventeenth-Century Quaker Women's Declaration', *Signs. Journal of Women in Culture and Society*, I (1975), 236, 244. See also J. C. Gadt, 'Women and Protestant Culture: The Quaker Dissent from Protestantism' (unpublished University of California, Los Angeles, Ph.D. thesis, 1974); G. Mason, 'Quaker Women and Education 1642' (unpublished University of Lancaster, MA thesis, 1987), ch.1.

20 Trevett, *Quaker Women Prophets*, pp. 155–7. See also Crawford, *Women and Religion in England*, pp. 161–2.

21 LSF, Swarthmore MS. I. 195, (Thomas Holme to Margaret Fell, Frandley, 1654); LSF, Swarthmore MS. I. 203; M. F. Williams, 'Society of Friends in Glamorgan 1654–1900' (unpublished University of Wales, Aberystwyth, MA thesis, 1950), 31–2; Trevett, *Women and Quakerism*, pp. 98–9. See also W. C. Braithwaite, *The Beginnings of Quakerism* (2nd edn, York, 1981), pp. 236–7; Brailsford, *Quaker Women*, pp. 148–56; Mack, *Visionary Women,* pp. 182–3; B. Y. Kunze, *Margaret Fell and the Rise of Quakerism* (Stanford, Ca., 1994), pp. 107–8.

22 LSF, Swarthmore MS. I. 203.

23 Ibid.

24 LSF, Swarthmore MS. I. 205, (Thomas Holme to Margaret Fell, Cardiff, 4 June 1656). By 1664, Elizabeth Holme had two children, but had relocated to Westmoreland. See LSF, GBS, IV (part 2), p. 427; Mack, *Visionary Women*, pp. 178–83. On two occasions, Elizabeth Lloyd of Dolobran joined her husband, Charles, in prison. On the second occasion in February 1663 she was forced to leave her four-month-old son behind. See

Richard Davies, *An Account of the Convincement, Exercises and Services and Travels of . . . Richard Davies* (London, 1877), p. 60; LSF, Lloyd MS. 1/1–1/16 (letters to Charles Lloyd II, no. 21); G. H. Jenkins, 'The Friends of Montgomeryshire in the Heroic Age', *MC*, 76 (1988), 17.

25 LSF, Swarthmore MS. I. 196.

26 NA, Society of Friends Registers (Monmouthshire). No. 677, p. 52.

27 GAS, D/DSF/2, p. 992.

28 J. Miller, *Anti-Christ in Man* (London, 1655), p. 27.

29 George Fox, *The Woman Learning in Silence* (London, 1654); cf. Margaret Fell, *Womens Speaking Justified* (London, 1666). See also Trevett, *Women and Quakerism*, ch. 2.

30 *Journal*, pp. 8–9.

31 B. Carré, 'Early Quaker Women in Lancaster and Lancashire', in M. A. Mullett (ed.), *Early Lancaster Friends* (Lancaster, 1978), p. 43.

32 Mack, *Visionary Women*, pp. 134–7.

33 LSF, G. E. Nuttall, 'Early Quaker Letters', 'Introduction'.

34 Trevett, *Women and Quakerism*, pp. 41–2.

35 Mack, 'Women as Prophets', 25–6, 30. See also P. Mack, 'Gender and Spirituality in Early English Quakerism 1650–1665', in E. Potts Brown and S. Mosher Stuard (eds), *Witnesses for Change* (London, 1989), p. 37.

36 B. Reay, *The Quakers and English Revolution* (Hounslow, 1985), p. 26.

37 Mack, 'Women as Prophets', 28.

38 A. Cohen, 'Prophecy and Madness: Women Visionaries during the Puritan Revolution', *Journal of Psychohistory*, 11 (Winter 1984), 411–30.

39 Mack, 'Women as Prophets', 35–6; Trevett, *Women and Quakerism*, pp. 25–6.

40 M. R. Brailsford, *A Quaker from Cromwell's Army: James Nayler* (London, 1927), pp. 122–54; Braithwaite, *Beginnings*, pp. 247, 252–6, 266; W. G. Bittle, *James Nayler* (York, 1986), p. 142; Crawford, *Women and Religion in England*, pp. 166–72.

41 F. Gawler, *A Record of Some Persecutions . . . in South Wales* (1659), p. 16.

42 Trevett, *Quaker Women Prophets*, pp. 122–32; J. Besse, *A Collection of the Sufferings* (2 vols, London, 1753), I, pp. 365, 740; B. Ll. James, 'The Evolution of a Radical: the Life and Career of William Erbery', *JWEH*, 3 (1986), 47–8.

43 Trevett, *Quaker Women Prophets*, p. 137.

44 LSF, GBS, II (Monmouthshire) p. 3; Gawler, *Record*, p. 8.

45   LSF, GBS, II (Glamorganshire) p. 3; Gawler, *Record*, p. 8; cf.
      the example of Catherine Graves of Barnard Castle in the
      eighteenth century where people pricked her with pins to 'draw
      blood and immunise themselves from her magic'. See J. D.
      Walsh, 'Methodism and the mob in the eighteenth century' in
      G. J. Cuming and D. Baker (eds), *Studies in Church History*, 8:
      Popular Belief and Practice (Cambridge, 1972), p. 225; P.
      Elmer, '"Saints or sorcerers": Quakerism, Demonology and the
      Decline of Witchcraft in Seventeenth-Century England', in B. P.
      Levack (ed.), *New Perspectives on Witchcraft, Magic and
      Demonology: Vol. I: Demonology, Religion, and Witchcraft*
      (New York and London, 2002), pp. 145–79.

46   Gawler, *Record*, p. 15.

47   LSF, GBS, II (Glamorganshire), p. 3; Gawler, *Record*, p. 21.

48   Gawler, *Record*, p. 6.

49   GAS, D/DSF/2, p. 501 (10.2.1694).

50   Cf. Catholic Recusants. See NA, E179.6743.

51   See the example of John ap Evan's wife in Society of Friends, *A
      Collection of Memorials concerning divers deceased ministres
      and others of the people called Quakers, in Pennsylvania*
      (Philadelphia, 1824), p. 67; Williams, 'Society of Friends in
      Glamorgan', 68–9.

52   GAS, D/DSF/2, pp. 991–4. Other testimonies to Welsh women
      Friends who emigrated to Pennsylvania can be found in HSP,
      Records (transcripts) of Radnor Monthly Meeting,
      Pennsylvania, 1680–1788.

53   GAS, D/DSF/2, pp. 992–3.

54   Ibid., pp. 928–9, 1027–8, 1041–2. Young Quaker ministers are
      referred to in the Yearly Meeting minutes. Ibid., pp. 538
      (Barbara Bevan Junior of Tref-y-Rhyg, *c.*1706,), 565 (Elizabeth
      Lloyd of Radnorshire, *c.*1714).

55   W. C. Braithwaite, *The Second Period of Quakerism* (2nd edn,
      York, 1979), p. 286.

56   Ibid., p. 252; Brailsford, *Quaker Women*, pp. 268–9; I. Ross,
      Margaret Fell, Mother of Quakerism (London and New York,
      1949), pp. 284–5; I. Edwards, 'The Women Friends of London.
      The Two Weeks and Box Meetings', *JFHS*, 47 (1955), 3–21;
      Kunze, *Margaret Fell and the Rise of Quakerism*, pp. 145–7.
      Arnold Lloyd identifies 1671 as the date when Women's
      Meetings first began. See Lloyd, *Quaker Social History*, p. 112.

57   John Banks, *To all the Women's Meetings* (London, 1674),
      pp. 181–2.

58   The schism is clearly set out in Trevett, *Women and Quakerism*,
      pp. 80–5; Smith, 'Female Intransigence', 33–6.

59 See Carré, 'Early Quaker Women in Lancaster', p. 43.
60 There were 43 Women's Meetings, 13 Quarterly Meetings and 15 Preparatory Meetings, see E. K. L. Quine, 'The Quakers in Leicestershire' (unpublished University of Nottingham, Ph.D. thesis, 1968), 65 n.1.
61 Trevett, *Quaker Women Prophets*, p. 169.
62 Ibid.
63 Braithwaite, *Second Period*, p. 287.
64 Ibid.
65 Laurence, 'A Priesthood of She-Believers', pp. 356–7.
66 NA, SoF Registers. (Monmouthshire). No. 677, p. 49.
67 Ibid., p. 50. See also Mack, 'Women as Prophets', 34, nn. 72, 74.
68 C. L. Cherry, 'Enthusiasm and Mandes: Anti-Quakerism in the Seventeenth Century', *QH*, 73 (2) (Autumn 1984), 9.
69 GAS, D/DSF/326 (29.6.1752).
70 GAS, D/DSF/2, pp. 991–2.
71 Ibid. See also Haverford College MS. 975B where Margaret Ellis of Montgomeryshire provided a full account of her convincement and missionary work.
72 GAS, D/DSF/352 (1.8.1733).
73 GAS, D/DSF/382. Back of volume. Letters from constituent Meetings to the Yearly Meeting held at Cardiff, 21–23.2.1747; cf. English Women's Yearly Meeting which began *c*.1784. See Trevett, *Women and Quakerism*, p. 81.
74 GAS, DSF/380 (1747–88).
75 In 1750, ten women attended the Brecon Yearly Meeting. See GAS, D/DSF/382, (1–3.3.1750).
76 Ibid.
77 GAS, D/DSF/383, p. 15 (28.4.1757).
78 GAS, D/DSF/384 (opening pages of the volume).
79 GAS, D/DSF/26.
80 GAS, D/DSF/361–2; GAS, D/DSF/22.
81 GAS, D/DSF/391–2.
82 GAS, D/DSF/320, p. 66 (29.5.1690); GAS, D/DSF/364 (19.9.1703); GAS, D/DSF/324 (10.12.1703/4, 1.9.1704); GAS, D/DSF/325 (2.8.1706, 1.8.1707); GAS, D/DSF/351 (6.2.1709, 1.10.1714).
83 'The Journal of John Player' and cited in T. M. Rees, *A History of the Quakers in Wales and their Emigration to North America* (Carmarthen, 1925), p. 275 (11.11.1753).
84 GAS, D/DSF/354 (1.10.1755).
85 GAS, D/DSF/26.
86 There are no separate minutes for either meeting; details are taken from the Men's meeting. See GAS, D/DSF/331 (17.5.1763); GAS, D/DSF/354 (20.10.1783).

NOTES

87 GwRO, D.2200.17.
88 Cf. Wesleyan and Primitive Methodists who came from working-class backgrounds. For details, see S. Wright, 'Quakerism and its Implications for Quaker Women: The Women Itinerant Ministers of York Meeting, 1780–1840', in Sheils and Wood (eds), Women in the Church, pp. 403–14.
89 Based on minutes c.1801–8, 1825–36 (1808 and 1824 are missing). See GAS, D/DSF/361–2; GAS, D/DFSF/22.
90 For the education of women and literacy levels in the early modern period see D. Cressy, Literacy and the Social Order: Reading and Writing in Tudor and Stuart England (Cambridge, 1980), ch. 6; P. Stock, Better Than Rubies: A History of Women's Education (New York, 1978); R. O'Day, Education and Society 1500–1800: The Social Foundations of Education in Early Modern Britain (London, 1982); Mason, 'Quaker Women and Education', ch. 4; R. A. Houston, Literacy in Early Modern England: Culture and Education 1500–1800 (London, 1988); Wilcox, Theology and Women's Ministry, pp. 132–5; A. Laurence, Women in England, ch. 11; Wiesner, Women and Gender, ch. 4.
91 Braithwaite, Second Period, ch. 11; C. J. L. Martin, 'Tradition versus Innovation: The Hat, Wilkinson-Story and Keithian Controversies', QS, 8 (1) (September 2003), 15–18.
92 Braithwaite, Second Period, p. 273.
93 Mason, 'Quaker Women and Education', 8–9. For example, see GAS, D/DSF/351 (8.1.1710).
94 GAS, D/DSF/324 (5.12.1699/1700); GAS, D/DSF/354 (4.10.1758). Other examples are provided in GAS, D/DSF/361 (14.9.1803); GAS, D/DSF/362 (12.9.1804, 1.5.1805).
95 GAS, D/DSF/354 (5.1.1785).
96 Trevett, Women and Quakerism, p. 86.
97 Spiezman and Kronick, 'A Seventeenth-Century Quaker Women's Declaration', 242; Kunze, Margaret Fell and the Rise of Quakerism, pp. 158–65.
98 Brailsford, A Quaker from Cromwell's Army, p. 110; Wright, 'Quakerism and its Implications for Quaker women', 407.
99 London Women's Quarterly Meeting (4 January 1675); R. S. Mortimer, 'Quakerism in Seventeenth Century Bristol' (unpublished University of Bristol, MA thesis, 1946), 148 n. 2. See also R. S. Mortimer, Minute Book of the Men's Meeting 1667–1686 (Bristol, 1971), pp. 121, 210.
100 Carré, 'Early Quaker Women in Lancaster', pp. 43–4.
101 LSF, Seventeenth Century Diaries. Box Q; Mason, 'Quaker Women and Education', 21–2, 40–6; Trevett, Women and Quakerism, pp. 124–6.

259

102 *Pontypool and District Review*, 18 (February 1975), p. 13; GAS, D/DSF/21 (30.3.1832, 21.3.1833, 18.7.1833, 19.9.1833); GAS, D/DSF/22 (9.5.1832, 21.3.1833, 19.9.1833).

103 NLW, MS. 17743E.

104 *Journal*, pp. 205–6.

105 Wright, 'Quakerism and its Implications for Quaker Women', pp. 412–13.

106 GAS, D/DSF/2, p. 493.

107 London Yearly Meeting *Epistles [from the Yearly Meeting of Friends . . . from 1681 to 1857]* (2 vols, London, 1858), I, pp. 157–8; D. J. Hall, 'Plainness of Speech, Behaviour and Apparel', in W. J. Sheils (ed.), *Studies in Church History, 22: Monks, Hermits and the Ascetic Tradition* (Oxford, 1985), p. 314.

108 GAS, D/DSF/382. Women Yearly Meeting minute book 'Queries'.

109 Ibid.

110 GAS, D/DSF/383, p. 6 (28.4.1757).

111 NLW, LL/1670/176; NLW, LL/1679/177. For additional examples see NLW LL/1710/158; J. Kendall, 'The Development of a Distinctive Form of Quaker Dress', *Costume*, 19 (1985), 62–3.

112 HSP, transcript of Philadelphia and Pennsylvania Wills 1681–1825. Book D, 76.

113 GwRO, D8A.0826 (Cecilia Handley of Pontypool, 5 November 1724). See also A. M. Gummere, *The Quaker: A Study in Costume* (Philadelphia, 1901), pp. 193–4.

114 NLW, LL/1778/71 (Margaret Bevan of Llantrisant, 26 September 1778).

115 GAS, D/DSF/351 (5.7.1705).

116 GAS, D/DSF/382 (1–3.3.1750). For 'gossip-mongers' or 'scolds' see J. Addy, *Sin and Society in the Seventeenth Century* (London, 1989), ch. 8; D. Underdown, 'The Taming of the Scold: The Enforcement of Patriarchal Authority in Early Modern England', in Fletcher and Stevenson (eds), *Order and Disorder*, pp. 116–36; Irmgard Maassen, 'Whoring, Scolding, Gadding About: Threats to Family Order in Early Modern Conduct Literature', *Journal for the Study of British Cultures*, 9 (2) (2002), 159–72.

118 GAS, D/DSF/382 (1.12.1763).

119 For an early example see the certificate of Katherine Robert of Llaithgwm who emigrated to Pennsylvania in July 1683, endorsed by the Men's and Women's meetings. HSP, MS. 898.

120 NLW, LL/1669/27; NLW, LL/1716/127; GwRO, D8A.0826.

121 GAS, D/DSF/351 (7.4.1710, 2.6.1710).
122 GAS, D/DSF/2, p. 1042 (27–9.4.1795).
123 GAS, D/DSF/361 (8.9.1802).
124 See also Smith, 'Female Intransigence', 71–80.
125 Epistle from the Lancaster Women's Meeting c.1675–80, and cited in Spiezman and Kronick, 'A Seventeenth-Century Quaker Women's Declaration', 241–2.
126 GAS, D/DSF/351 (7.1.1711).
127 GAS, D/DSF/325 (back of the minute book).
128 GAS, D/DSF/351 (6.12.1711–2).
129 GAS, D/DSF/352 (5.10.1733).
130 GAS, D/DSF/353 (6.5.1737).
131 GAS, D/DSF/325 (Back of minute book).
132 GAS, D/DSF/353 (7.7.1737). Cf. examples given in Carré, 'Early Quaker Women in Lancaster', 50.

Chapter 7 The Decline of the Welsh Quaker Communities

1 Henry Newman, Memories of Stanley Pumphrey (London, 1883), p. 23.
2 See T. Macpherson, 'A Measure of Grace: Quakers in Radnorshire', Transactions of the Radnorshire Society, 69 (1999), 8–33.
3 Sheila Wright, Friends in York: The Dynamics of Quaker Revival 1780–1860 (Keele, 1995), p. 133; A. Davies, The Quakers in English Society (Oxford, 2000), p. 163.
4 M. Watts, The Dissenters: From the Reformation to the French Revolution (Oxford, 1978), p. 269.
5 M. F. Williams, 'The Society of Friends in Glamorgan 1654–1900' (unpublished University of Wales, Aberystwyth, MA thesis, 1950), 108–36, 204–29; R. C. Allen, "A most industrious well-disposed people', Milford Haven Quakers and the Pembrokeshire Whaling Industry c.1791–1821', in P. O'Neill (ed.), Nation and Federation in the Celtic World (Sydney, 2003), pp. 64–94.
6 GAS, D/DSF 2, 1049–54.
7 North Wales (including Shropshire) Quarterly Meeting ended in 1797; Monmouthshire and Radnorshire Quarterly Meeting closed in 1791; while the Quarterly Meeting of Cardiganshire, Carmarthenshire, Pembrokeshire and Glamorgan was abandoned much earlier in 1710. See GAS, D/DSF/322; GAS, D/DSF/327; GAS, D/DSF/324.

8   E. R. Morris, 'Quakerism in West Montgomeryshire', *MC*, 56 (1959–60), 54, 61.
9   T. M. Rees, *A History of the Quakers in Wales and their Emigration to North America* (Carmarthen, 1925), p. 216.
10   Ibid.
11   NLW, Church in Wales, SA/QA/1.
12   Morris, 'Quakerism in West Montgomeryshire', 54.
13   NLW, LL/QA/1; J. R. Guy (ed.), *The Diocese of Llandaff in 1763* (Cardiff, 1991), pp. 59, 63.
14   It was eventually sold in 1821. See GAS, D/DSF/16; Williams, 'Society of Friends in Glamorgan', 80–1, 84–8, 96–7, 138.
15   Anon., 'Journal of John Churchman (1753)', *The Friends' Library*, 6 (1842), 229.
16   J. J. Green, 'Joseph Rule, The Quaker in White', *JFHS*, 2 (2) (1905), 66.
17   NLW, LL/QA/1–2.
18   For example, Shirenewton was not specifically referred to. See Guy, *Diocese of Llandaff*, p. 117. Later references to Shirenewton, Caldicot and Newchurch do appear in the 1771 returns: Caldicot: one Quaker couple who kept 'an alehouse and they have a meeting house in the parish of Shirenewton'; Newchurch: 3 Quakers; Shirenewton: 6 Quakers and 'a place of worship. The teacher is Seth Thomas. Their number is not increased, since I have been acquainted with ye parish.' NLW, LL/QA/5.
19   NLW, LL/QA/2; Guy, *Diocese of Llandaff*, pp. 89, 101, 104, 144, 152.
20   NLW, LL/QA/2; Guy, *Diocese of Llandaff*, p. 111.
21   There was an additional Quaker family who lived at Llantrisaint with one Friend dwelling at Pen-y-Clawdd among a small community of seven families. Guy, *Diocese of Llandaff*, pp. 148, 151, 154.
22   Including Llanedeyrn.
23   NLW, LL/QA/2; Guy, *Diocese of Llandaff*, p. 128.
24   NLW, LL/QA/7.
25   NLW, LL/QA/9: Chepstow (1); Llanfihangel Ystern Llywern (1); Llanfrechfa (3); Mamheilad (1); Llanfihangel-y-Fedw (2); Shirenewton (3); and Trefddyn (10).
26   GAS, D/DSF/354 (20.10.1783).
27   Ibid., (6.4.1785).
28   They can be compared with that of other prosperous Quaker families, including the Price, Bath, Millwyn, Bigg, Gibbins, Eaton families who migrated into south Wales at the end of the eighteenth century. See Williams, 'Society of Friends in Glamorgan', 109–14.

29 GAS, D/DSF/355 (4.10.1797).

30 K. Backhouse (ed.), *A Memoir of Mary Capper* (Philadelphia, 1882), pp. 124, 143.

31 E. A. Isichei, *Victorian Quakers* (London, 1970), p. 170.

32 *Pontypool Free Press*, 26 July 1868.

33 J. S. Rowntree, *Quakerism Past and Present: being an Inquiry Into the Causes of its Decline in Great Britain and Ireland* (London, 1859); Thomas Hancock, *The Peculium: An Endeavour to throw some light on some of the causes of the Decline of the Society of Friends* (London, 1859); H. G. Jones, 'John Kelsall: A Study in Religious and Economic History' (unpublished University of Wales, Bangor, MA thesis, 1938), 123ff; G. H. Jenkins, 'The Friends of Montgomeryshire in the Heroic Age', *MC*, 76 (1988), 24–30; D. Scott, *Quakerism in York* (York, 1991), pp. 1–2 31–2; N. J. Morgan, *Lancashire Quakers and the Establishment* (Halifax, 1993), ch. 7.

34 Rees, *Quakers in Wales*, pp. 269–71.

35 Jenkins, 'Friends of Montgomeryshire', 28.

36 Davies, *Quakers in English Society*, p. 165.

36 C. H. Browning, *Welsh Settlement of Pennsylvania* (Philadelphia, 1912); Howard M. Jenkins, 'The Welsh Settlement of Gwynedd', *PMHB*, 8 (1884), 174–83; John E. Pomfret, 'The First Purchasers of Pennsylvania, 1681–1700', *PMHB*, 80 (1956), pp. 137–63; T. A. Glenn, *The Welsh Founders of Pennsylvania* (Baltimore edn, 1970); J. G. Williams, 'The Quakers of Merioneth During the Seventeenth Century' *JMHRS*, 8 (1978–9), 324–35; Jenkins, 'Friends of Montgomeryshire', 22, 25–6; B. Levy, *Quakers and the American Family: British Settlement in the Delaware Valley* (Oxford, 1988); R. C. Allen, 'In search of a New Jerusalem: A Preliminary Investigation into the Causes and Impact of Welsh Quaker Emigration to Pennsylvania, c.1660–1750', *QS*, 9 (1) (September 2004), 31–53.

38 G. H. Jenkins, *Literature, Religion and Society in Wales, 1660–1730* (Cardiff, 1978), pp. 178–9.

39 T. A. Glenn, *Merion in the Welsh Tract* (Norristown, Pa., 1896), p. 21; Browning, *Welsh Settlement of Pennsylvania*, pp. 33–248. For Penn's relations with the Welsh, see Levy, *Quakers and the American Family*, pp. 111, 279–80.

40 C. M. Andrews, *The Colonial Period of American History* (3 vols, New Haven, 1934), III, p. 302.

41 A statistical analysis of 300 emigrant families calculated that yeomen constituted 50 per cent; gentlemen 28 per cent; artisans 11 per cent; and shopkeepers and others about 5 per cent. This

data did not include servants or other settlers who had no property rights. See Glenn, *Welsh Founders of Pennsylvania*, pp. 152–219; A. H. Dodd, 'The Background of the Welsh Quaker Migration to Pennsylvania', *JMHRS*, 3 (2) (1958), 123.

42 Levy, *Quakers and the American Family*, pp. 112–13.

43 A letter from Thomas Ellis to George Fox, 13.4mo. [July] 1685, and cited in Anon., 'Pioneers in Pennsylvania, 1685', *JFHS*, 6 (4) (November 1909), 174.

44 Anon., 'Philadelphia in 1698', *PMHB*, 18 (1894), 247–8.

45 Browning, *Welsh Settlement of Pennsylvania*, pp. 33, 163ff; Glenn, *Merion in the Welsh Tract*, pp. 34–5.

46 'The Journal of John Bevan', quoted in J. J. Levick, 'The Early Welsh Quakers and their Emigration to Pennsylvania', *PMHB*, 17 (4) (1893), 404.

47 Jenkins, 'Friends of Montgomeryshire', 25.

48 GAS, D/DSF/320, p. 66.

49 Radnor, Haverford, Montgomery and Gwynedd.

50 Browning, *Welsh Settlement of Pennsylvania*, p. 310.

51 Allen, 'In Search of a New Jerusalem', p. 39.

52 Tref-y-Rhyg Meeting (10.7.1683), and cited in Levick, 'Early Welsh Quakers', 405.

53 GAS, D/DSF/2, p. 511.

54 See Howard M. Jenkins, *Historical Collections relating to Gwynedd: A Township of Montgomery County, Pennysylvania, settled, 1698* (Philadelphia, 1884).

55 Levy, *Quakers and the American Family*, pp. 13–14.

56 Jones, 'John Kelsall', 134–58.

57 GAS, D/DSF/320, p. 146.

58 G. H. Jenkins, *Protestant Dissenters in Wales, 1639–1689* (Cardiff, 1992), p. 67.

59 Representatives from north Wales numbered 10: Merioneth [5], Flintshire [2], Montgomeryshire [2], Denbighshire [1]; and Glamorganshire and Pembrokeshire, 1 each.

60 Glenn, *Welsh Founders of Pennsylvania*, pp. 155, 173, 178, 212, 218–19.

61 NLW, MS. 1116D, p. 130.

62 For details see Allen, 'In Search of a New Jerusalem', 44–5.

63 LSF, Kelsall MS. S.194.2, p. 16; Jenkins, *Literature, Religion and Society*, p. 179.

64 Rowntree, *Quakerism Past and Present*, pp. 55–65, 77–88, 92–6, 167–86; Hancock, *Peculium*, pp. 166–7. See also Morgan, *Lancashire Quakers*, pp. 244–6.

65 Joshua Rowntree (ed.), *John Wilhelm Rowntree, Essays and Addresses* (2nd edn, London, 1906). See also D. J. Hall,

'Membership Statistics of the Society of Friends, 1800–1880', *JFHS*, 52 (1969), 97–100; Morgan, *Lancashire Quakers*, pp. 247–9.

66 W. C. Braithwaite, *The Beginnings of Quakerism* (2nd edn, York, 1981), p. 309; W. C. Braithwaite, *The Second Period of Quakerism* (2nd edn, York, 1979), pp. 630–47; R. M. Jones, *The Later Periods of Quakerism* (2 vols, London, 1921). See also Morgan, *Lancashire Quakers*, pp. 249–52.

67 B. Wilson, *Sects and Society* (London, 1961); B. Wilson, 'An Analysis of Sect Development', *American Sociological Review*, 24 (February 1959), 3–15; R. T. Vann, *Social Development of English Quakerism 1655–1755* (Cambridge, Mass., 1969), ch. 6; C. Hill, *The World Turned Upside Down* (Harmondsworth, 1975), pp. 231–58. Further research into the evolution from sect to denomination includes D. A. Martin, 'The Denomination', *British Journal of Sociology*, 13 (March 1962), 1–14; E. A. Isichei, 'From Sect to Denomination among English Quakers', in B. R. Wilson (ed.), *Patterns of Sectarianism* (London, 1967), pp. 161–81.

68 M. A. Mullett, 'From Sect to Denomination', *Journal of Religious History*, 13 (2) (1984), 190–1.

69 Morgan, *Lancashire Quakers*, p. 244.

70 Ibid., p. 269.

71 Scott, *Quakerism in York*, p. 31.

72 Ibid.

73 H. Lloyd, *The Quaker Lloyds in the Industrial Revolution* (London, 1975); R. Floud and D. McCloskey (eds), *The Economic History of Britain since 1700* (2nd edn, London, 1994).

74 Rowntree, *Quakerism Past and Present*, p. 94.

75 J. Walvin, *The Quakers. Men and Morals* (London, 1997), p. 88.

76 GAS, D/DSF/320, pp. 186–90; GAS, D/DSF/2, p. 621 (disownment *c*.1730); Lloyd, *Quaker Lloyds*, pp. 52–63; Jenkins, 'Friends of Montgomeryshire', 29.

77 A. Prior and M W. Kirby, 'The Society of Friends and Business Culture, 1700–1830', in D. J. Jeremy (ed.), *Religion, Business, and Wealth in Modern Britain* (London, 1998), pp. 121–9.

78 Walvin, *Quakers*, pp. 89–90.

79 LSF, Kelsall MS. S.194.2, pp. 99–100.

80 Morgan, *Lancashire Quakers*, pp. 280–1.

81 Rees, *Quakers in Wales*, p. 221; Morris, 'Quakerism in West Montgomeryshire', 54; G. H. Jenkins, 'Quaker and Anti-Quaker literature in Welsh from the Restoration to Methodism', *WHR*, 7 (1975), 403–8, 414–5.

82 Williams, 'Quakers of Merioneth', 321.
83 Richard Davies, *An Account of the Convincement, Exercises and Services and Travels of . . . Richard Davies* (London, 1877), pp. 100, 110–11, 116; GAS, D/DSF/320, pp. 7, 109, 110, 112–13, 115, 171; GAS, D/DFSF/364 (20.6.1703, 15.8.1703); Rees, *Quakers in Wales*, ch. 7; Williams, 'Quakers of Merioneth', 321–2, 324. In Monmouthshire, there was also a Welsh translation of the Society's regulations for the good behaviour of members. See GAS, D/DSF/351; GAS, D/DSF/325 (4.11.1698–99, 1.11.1700, 7.5.1703). Elisha Beadles, *Y gyfraith a roddwyd allan o Sion . . .* (Amwythig, 1715). See also Jenkins, 'Quaker and Anti-Quaker literature', 413–14.
84 R. P. Matthews, 'Roman Catholic Recusancy in Monmouthshire 1608–89: A Demographic and Morphological Analysis' (unpublished University of Wales, Cardiff, Ph.D. thesis, 1996), 235–6.
85 Jones, 'John Kelsall', 115, 117.
86 Ibid., 107.
87 GAS, D/DSF/2, pp. 483, 525 (17.2.1682, 7.2.1702); Jenkins, 'Quaker and Anti-Quaker Literature', 409–10.
88 J. Lloyd, *The Quakers in Wales* (London, 1947), p. 5.
89 GAS, D/DSF/326 (26.4.1738). See also GAS, D/DSF/325 (1.11.1732).
90 M. F. Williams, 'Glamorgan Quakers 1654–1900', *Morgannwg*, 5 (1961), 67.
91 R. C. Allen, 'The Making of a Holy Christian Community: Welsh Quaker Emigrants to Pennsylvania, c.1680–1750', in T. Kirk and Lud'a Klusáková (eds), *Cultural Conquests* (Prague, forthcoming).
92 Ellis Pugh, *Annerch ir Cymru . . .* (Philadelphia, 1721); Ellis Pugh, *A Salutation to the Britons . . . Translated from the British language by Rowland Ellis, revised and corrected by David Lloyd* (Philadelphia, 1727).
93 M. Grubb, 'Tensions in the Religious Society of Friends in England in the Nineteenth Century', *JFHS*, 56 (1) (1990), 1–14; Mullett, 'From Sect to Denomination', 175.
94 LSF, Kelsall MS. S.194.2, p. 162 (Kelsall to Richard Lewis of Pennsylvania, 21.1.1723–4).
95 LSF, Kelsall MS. S.190, pp. 250–1 (31.3.1731).
96 David C. Jones, *'A Glorious Work in the World': Welsh Methodism and the International Evangelical Revival, 1735–1750* (Cardiff, 2004).
97 G. M. Roberts (ed.), *Hanes Methodistiaeth Galfinaidd Cymru* (2 vols, Caernarfon, 1973–8), I, pp. 229–34, 451.

98 G. H. Jenkins, *The Foundations of Modern Wales, 1642–1780* (Oxford, 1988), pp. 365–6.
99 I. G. Jones and D. Williams (eds), *The Religious Census of 1851: A Calendar of the Returns relating to Wales* (2 vols, Cardiff, 1976), I (south Wales); D. L. Morgan, *The Great Awakening in Wales* (London, 1988).
100 Jenkins, *Foundations of Modern Wales*, p. 367.
101 Mullett, 'From Sect to Denomination', 177.
102 An exhaustive trawl of the Monmouthshire minutes (1692–1836) shows that disownments for 'marrying out' were substantially greater in number than those for other stated causes. For Glamorganshire see Williams, 'Society of Friends in Glamorgan', 167–8, 322–4.
103 Jones, 'John Kelsall', 106–7.

Bibliography

Manuscripts

Bodleian Library, Oxford
Tanner MSS

British Library, London
Harleian MSS

Cardiff Central Library
Bute MS.4.999. Whitchurch School, Melingriffith, Subscription Book (1807) and Admission Tickets (1808–9)

Glamorgan Record Office, Cardiff

Society of Friends Records

[a] Wales

[i] Men's

D/DSF/2 Welsh Yearly Meeting, 1682–1797; Sufferings 1682–1797

D/DSF/53 Yearly Meeting, 1797; Half-Yearly Meeting, 1797

D/DSF/316 Half-Yearly Meeting, 1828; General Meeting for Wales, Herefordshire and Worcestershire, 1833–49

D/DSF/54–66 Half-Yearly Meeting, 1803, 1807, 1811, 1813–16, 1818, 1827–29

D/DSF/3 Quarterly Meeting, 1793–7

[ii] Women's

D/DSF/382–6	Yearly Meeting, 1749–56, 1757–63, 1764–77, 1778–84, 1785–97
D/DSF/388, 319	Half-Yearly Meeting, 1797–1807, 1808–32
D/DSF/389	Half-Yearly Committee, 1802–17
D/DSF/390	Half-Yearly Meeting, 1803–11 (rough minutes)
D/DSF/380–1	Quarterly Meeting, 1747–88, 1789–96
D/DSF/387	Epistles from the Women's Yearly Meeting for Wales, 1788–9

[iii] Ministers and Elders

D/DSF/314	Yearly Meeting, 1759–97
D/DSF/315	Half-Yearly Meeting, 1806–32
D/DSF/323	Quarterly Meeting, 1789–1832

[iv] Sufferings

D/DSF/313	Accounts of Sufferings, c.1660–5
D/DSF/318	Half-Yearly Meeting Register, 1800–28

[v] Correspondence

D/DSF/333	Epistles received, 1685 (abstract); 1746–78
D/DSF/92–122	Answers to Queries from Welsh Meetings, 1737–69
D/DSF/123–93	Answers to Yearly Meeting Queries from Welsh Meetings, 1755–71

[vi] Accounts

D/DSF/317	Half-Yearly Meeting Treasurers' Account Book, 1825–45

[vii] Friends' Registers

D/DSF/29	Registers of Marriages, Births and Burials of the General Meeting of Herefordshire, Worcestershire and Wales, 1694–1837 (transcripts)

[viii] Miscellaneous

D/DSF/206	Militia case and Counsel's opinion, 1759, 1778

[b] Counties

[i] Cardiganshire, Carmarthenshire, Glamorgan and Pembrokeshire

D/DSF/324	Quarterly Meeting of Cardiganshire, Carmarthenshire, Pembrokeshire and Glamorgan c.1692–1710
D/DSF/329–31	Carmarthenshire Monthly Meeting, 1724–44, 1756–68
D/DSF/332–5	Glamorgan Monthly Meeting, 1748–87, 1787–1811 (Carmarthenshire and Glamorganshire)
D/DSF/4–5	Glamorgan (Swansea and Neath) Monthly Meeting, 1812–47
D/DSF/348	Glamorgan Women Ministers and Elders Monthly Meeting, 1806–19
D/DSF/10–11	Glamorgan (Swansea and Neath) Women Monthly Meeting, 1802–39
D/DSF/247–8	Deeds of 'Sowdrey' burial ground, Cardiff, 1695 and 1745
D/DSF/1	Pembrokeshire Entry Book, 1660–1794
D/DSF/364–6	Pembrokeshire Monthly Meeting, 1700–1829
D/DSF/367	Pembrokeshire Sufferings, 1660–84

[ii] Monmouthshire (inc. Breconshire, East Glamorgan and Radnorshire)

D/DSF/325	Monmouthshire Quarterly Meeting, 1692–1737
D/DSF/326	Monmouthshire and East Glamorganshire Quarterly Meeting, 1738–56
D/DSF/327	Monmouthshire and Radnorshire Quarterly Meeting, 1757–91
D/DSF/351–7, 19–21	Monmouthshire Men's Monthly Meeting, 1703–19, 1720–34, 1734–44, 1745–91, 1791–8, 1791–1809, 1808–13, 1813–17, 1817–27, 1827–36
D/DSF/361–2, 22	Monmouthshire Women's Monthly Meeting, 1801–8, 1809–23, 1824–36
D/DSF/23	Monmouthshire and Radnorshire Ministers and Elders Quarterly Meeting, 1784–97
D/DSF/363	Monmouthshire Monthly Meeting of Ministers and Elders, 1789–91, 1796–1800, 1804
D/DSF/194–199	Accounts of Sufferings, Monmouthshire, 1662 and 1682; Carmarthenshire, 1737; Carmarthenshire, Radnorshire and Shropshire, 1762

D/DSF/24–5	Monmouthshire Treasurer's Accounts *c.*1846–63
D/DSF/254–294	Monmouthshire Deeds, 1660/1–1923
D/DSF/300–7	Breconshire Deeds, 1705–46
D/DSF/28, 308–11	Abstracts and transcripts of Glamorganshire, Monmouthshire and Breconshire property deeds, 1785–1838
D/DSF/16	Monmouthshire Monthly Meeting Entry Book, 1802
D/DSF/70, 88–9	Monmouthshire Licences, 1698, 1803
D/DSF/200	Monmouthshire Legacies, 1695–1773
D/DSF/34, 45–7	Monmouthshire Certificates of Birth, 1822–37
D/DSF/92–122	Monmouthshire answers to Elders and Ministers, Monthly, Quarterly and Yearly Meetings, 1737–1769
D/DSF/123–63	Monmouthshire answers to Yearly Meetings 'Queries', 1755–63
D/DSF/216–17	Monmouthshire Correspondence, 1801–74
D/DSF/226	Monmouthshire Correspondence, 1811–68

[iii] **North Wales (inc. Shropshire)**

D/DSF/320–2	Quarterly Meeting, 1668–1752, 1753–85, 1786–97
D/DSF/379	Shropshire and Montgomeryshire Monthly Meeting, 1693–1714
D/DSF/27	Monthly Meeting, 1815–29
D/DSF/328	Montgomeryshire Preparative Meeting minutes, 1800–14
D/DSF/26	Women's Monthly Meeting (Merionethshire and Montgomeryshire), 1785–1815

Gwent Record Office, Cwmbrân

Edlogan Manor Records
Evans and Evill Deeds and Documents
John Capel Hanbury Collection (D8A)
Newport Collection (D43)
Williams and Tweedy Deeds and Document

D.1243.0001–11	Shirenewton property deeds, 1700–1924
D.25.0271	Shirenewton meeting house deed, 1822
D. D.2200.27	Account of deeds 1635–1790
D8A. 0062	Quaker marriage settlement, 31 December 1690
D8A. 0825	Will (copy) of John Handley of Pontypool, 1719

D. 2200.12	Quaker Marriage settlement, Brecon, 1764
D. 2200.21	Will and Codicil of James Lewis of Trosnant, 1810
D. 2472.1	Ebbw Vale Steel, Iron and Coal Company Memorandum Book, 1796–1819
D. 2472.2	Ebbw Vale Steel, Iron and Coal Company Letter Book c.1824–27
D. 2472.3	Ebbw Vale Steel, Iron and Coal Company Accounts c.1791–6
D. 2200.17, 20	Correspondence, 1788, 1808

Hanbury Estate Papers, Pontypool

Bundle 7, nos. 2–5 Wills and administrations of Anthony and Elizabeth Ridley, 1714–55

Haverford College, Pennsylvania

Allinson Collection
Ms. 975B. Diary of Margaret Ellis
Vaux Collection

Historical Society of Pennsylvania

Etting Collection
J. J. Levick Collection
Norris Family Collection
Radnor Monthly Meeting, Pennsylvania, 1680–1788 (transcripts)
Society Collection
Transcripts of Philadelphia and Pennsylvania Wills 1681–1825.

Lambeth Palace Library, London

| MS. 639 | Episcopal Returns, 1669 |
| MS. 997 | Certificates to livings granted by the Commissioners for Approbation of Public Preachers, 28 April–23 June 1654 |

Library of the Society of Friends, London

Gibson MSS
Kelsall Papers
Lloyd of Dolobran MSS
Meeting for Sufferings
Morning Meeting minutes
Seventeenth Century Diaries (Box Q)
Swarthmore Collection

Testimonials (Box C, Portfolio, Testimonies Concerning Ministers
    Deceased)
The Great Book of Sufferings
Tract Book 78
Unpublished transcripts of the original records of Suffering
    (compiled by C. Horle)
Yearly meeting Minutes

The National Archives

Chancery Proceedings
Canterbury Probate
Exchequer Bills and Answers
Recusancy Rolls
Original Registers of the Births, Marriage and Burials of the Society
    of Friends

National Library of Wales

Abergavenny Manuscripts
Badmington Manuscripts
Church in Wales
Cwrt Mawr MSS
Gaol Files
J. R. Hughes MSS and Papers
Llangibby Castle Collection
Lloyd-Baker MSS
Maybery MS. I & II
Milborne Manuscripts
NLW Minor Lists (1992: Evelyn Whiting Papers)
NLW MSS
Picton Castle MSS
Tredegar Park MSS

Newport Reference Library

px.mooo.900.MON.   A General Description of the county of
                   Monmouth, [c.seventeenth century].
qm.350.739.15   Unpublished MS. by J. K. Fletcher entitled
                   'Pontypool Japan 1728–1822' (written
                   c.1920)
Southall Collection

Pontypool Park Estate
E. Folio Map Book of Hanbury Estate Farms. (*c*.1715)

William Salt Library, Stafford
MS. 2112   Compton Census of 1676

Swarthmore Library, Pennsylvania
MR-Ph. 352.   Radnor (Pennsylvania) Monthly Meeting
                              Memorials, 1683–1697
RG5, folder 119   (George Family Collection). Ser.3

Dr Williams's Library, London
MS.38.4   Dr John Evans's List of Dissenting
                              Congregations in England and Wales,
                              1715–18

Printed Sources and Calendars
[*published in London unless otherwise stated*]

A Collection of Acts of Parliament, Clauses of Acts of Parliament relative to those Protestant Dissenters who are usually called by the name of Quakers (1777)
A Collection of Memorials . . . *of the People called Quakers* (Philadelphia, 1808)
A Collection of Testimonies concerning Several Ministers of the Gospel amongst the People called Quakers (1760)
A Declaration of the Present Sufferings of 140 Persons of the People of God (who are now in prison) called Quakers (1659)
An Act for the Propagation of the Gospel in Wales, 1650 (rept., Cardiff, 1908)
Andrews, Thomas, *A Serious Expostulation with the People call'd Quakers: by way of a letter to a Parishioner of that persuasion at Pontypool* . . . (1708)
——, *A Modest enquiry into the weight of Theodore Eccleston's 'Reply' to 'A Serious Expostulation with the People call'd Quakers' in a second letter to a Parishioner at Pontypool, Monmouthshire* (1709)
Anon, *An Alarum to Corporations* . . . (1659)
——, *For the King and both Houses of Parliament being a short declaration of the cruelty inflicted upon some of the servants of the Lord now called Quakers, by some barbarous & bloudy men inhabitants in Merionyth shire in North Wales, the 3d month, 1660, and in part of South Wales* (1661)

——, *For the King and both Houses of Parliament being a short relation of the sad estate and sufferings of the innocent people of God called Quakers for worshipping God and exercising a good conscience towards God and man* (1661)

——, *For the King and both Houses of Parliament for you (who have known sufferings) now (in this the day of your prosperity) in the fear and wisdom of God, to read over and consider these sufferings of the people of God in scorn called Quakers, which they have suffered in the dayes of the Commonwealth, and of Oliver and Richard Cromwel, and which they now suffer in your day for conscience sake, and bearing testimony to the truth, as it is in Jesus* . . . (1660)

——, *The Copie of a paper presented to the Parliament and read the 27th of the fourth Moneth, 1659* (1659)

——, *These several papers was sent to the Parliament the twentieth day of the fifth month 1659. Being above seven thousand of the Names of the Hand-maids and Daughters of the Lord* (1659)

——, *Work for a Cooper* (1679)

Banks, John, *To all the Women's Meetings* (1674)

Baxter, Richard, *One sheet against the Quakers* (1657)

Beadles, Elisha, *Y gyfraith a roddwyd allan o Sion* . . . (Amwythig, 1715)

Besse, Joseph, *A brief account of many of the prosecutions of the People called Quakers in the Exchequer, Ecclesiastical and other courts* (1736)

——, *A Collection of the Sufferings of the People called Quakers, 1650–1689* (2 vols, 1753)

Briggs, Thomas, *An Account of Some of the Travels and Sufferings of that Faithful Servant of the Lord, Thomas Briggs* (1685)

Cradock, Walter, *The Saints Fulnesse of Joy* (1646)

——, *Glad Tydings from Heaven* (1648)

Cragge, John, *Public Dispute touching Infant baptism* . . . (1654)

——, *Arraignment and Conviction of Anabaptism* (1656)

Croft, Herbert, *A Short Narrative of the Discovery of a College of Jesuits, at a Place called the Come* (1679)

Davies, Richard, *An Account of the Convincement, Exercises and Services and Travels of that Ancient Servant of the Lord, Richard Davies* (1877 edn)

Davies, Rondl, *Profiad yr Ysprydion* (Oxford, 1675)

Dewsbury, William, *The Discovery of Mans Returne to his First Estate* (1654)

Eccleston, Theodor, *A Reply to Tho. Andrews letter to parishioner of Pontypool, called 'A Serious Expostulation with the people call'd Quakers'* (1708)

——, *Remarks upon Thos Andrews book, miscalled, 'A Modest Enquiry'* (1709)

Erbery, William, *Apocrypha* (1625)

——, *The Babe of Glory . . .* (1653)

——, *The Grand Oppressor, Or, The Terror of Tithes . . .* (1658)

——, *The Testimony of William Erbery* (1658)

Evans, Arise, *To the Most High and Mighty Prince Charles the II . . . an Epistle* (1660)

Fell, Margaret, *Touch-Stone, or a perfect tryal by the Scriptures, of all the Priests, Bishops and Ministers* (1667)

——, *Womens Speaking Justified* (1666)

Fox, George, *The Woman Learning in Silence* (1654)

——, *The Great Mystery* (1659), and reprinted in T. Shankland (ed.), *Transactions of the Welsh Baptist Historical Association* (Cardiff, 1904)

——, *An Encouragement to Trust in the Lord* (1682)

——, *A Collection of Many Select and Christian Epistles, Letters, Testimonies Written on Sundry Occasions, by that Ancient, Eminent, Faithful Friend, and Minister of Christ Jesus, George Fox* (1698)

Gawler, Francis, *A Record of some Persecutions inflicted upon some of the Servants of the Lord in South-Wales, with the sufferings of many for not paying Tithes . . . in South Wales* (1659)

——, *The Children of Abraham's Faith who are blessed, being found in Abraham's practice of burying their dead in their own purchased grounds* (1663)

Gough, J., *A History of the People called Quakers, from their first rise to the present time* (Dublin, 1789)

Harris, Edward, *A True Relation of a Company of Brownists, Separatists and Non-conformists in Monmouth in Wales* (1641)

Holme, Benjamin, *A Collection of the Epistles and Works of . . .* (1754)

Hookes, Ellis, *For the King and both Houses of Parliament* (1675)

Jenkins, Walter, *The Law Given Forth out of Sion* (1661)

Jones, Edmund, *A Geographical, Historical and Religious Account of the Parish of Aberystruth in the county of Monmouth* (Trefecca, 1779)

Journal of the House of Commons

Journal of the House of Lords

Keith, George, *The Woman Preacher of Samaria* (1674)

Laurence, Thomas and Fox, George, *Concerning Marriage* (1663)

London Yearly Meeting, *Extracts from the Minutes and Advices of the Yearly Meeting of Friends held in London from its first institution* (2nd edn, 1802)

——, *Epistles from the Yearly Meeting of Friends, Held in London, to the Quarterly and Monthly Meetings in Great Britain, Ireland and Elsewhere, from 1681 to 1857* (2 vols, 1858)

Miles, John, *An Antidote against the Infection of the Times. A faithfull watchword from Mount Sion, to prevent the ruine of Soules* (1656), and reprinted in T. Shankland (ed.), *Transactions of the Welsh Baptist Historical Association* (Cardiff, 1904)

Miller, Joshua, *Antichrist in Man: The Quakers Idol* (1655)

Mulliner, John, *A Testimony Against Perriwigs and Perriwig Making* (1677)

Prynne, William, *The Quakers Unmasked* (2nd edn, 1655)

——, *A Proclamation prohibiting the Disturbing of Ministers* (1655)

Pugh, Ellis, *Annerch ir Cymru* . . . (Philadelphia, 1721)

——, *A Salutation to the Britons . . . Translated from the British language by Rowland Ellis, revised and corrected by David Lloyd,* (Philadelphia, 1727)

Society of Friends, *A Collection of Memorials concerning divers deceased ministres and others of the people called Quakers, in Pennsylvania* (Philadelphia, 1824)

Thomas, Joshua, *Hanes Y Bedyddwyr* (Carmarthen, 1778)

Underhill, T., *Hell Broke Loose* (1660)

Watkins, Morgan, *The Perfect Life* (1659)

——, *Swearing denied in the New Covenant: and its pretended foundation Rased* . . . (1660)

Weld, Thomas, *A further discovery of that generation of men called Quakers* (Gateshead, 1654)

Whiston, Edgard, *Life and Death of Mr. Henry Jessey* (1671)

Williams, Thomas, *To the Society of People called Baptists, who formerly did meet at Llwinah* . . . (1745)

Wyndham, W. P., *A Gentleman's Tour Through Monmouthshire and Wales. June and July 1774* (1781)

Wynne, Thomas, *The Antiquity of the Quakers* (1677)

——, *An Antichristian Conspiracy detected and Satans champion defeated* . . . (1679)

Newspapers

Cambrian
Gloster Journal
Monmouthshire Merlin
Neath Gazette
Pontypool Free Press. The Local Register or Chronology of Pontypool and the Neighbourhood (2nd edn, Pontypool, 1870)
Publick Intelligencer

Secondary Works

Acheson, R. J., *Radical Puritans in England, 1550–1660* (London, 1990)

Addy, J., *Sin and Society in the Seventeenth Century* (London, 1989)

Allen, R. C., 'Catholic Records in the Attic: Details of everyday life found in the seventeenth century Catholic household of the Gunter family of Abergavenny', *GLH*, 86 (Spring 1999), 17–30

——, '"Taking up her daily cross": Women and the early Quaker movement in Wales, 1653–1689', in Michael Roberts and Simone Clarke (eds), *Women and Gender in Early Modern Wales* (Cardiff, 2000)

——, '"A most industrious well-disposed people." Milford Haven Quakers and the Pembrokeshire Whaling Industry *c*.1791–1821', in P. O'Neill (ed.), *Nation and Federation in the Celtic World* (Sydney: University of Sydney Press, 2003)

——, 'An Alternative Community in North-East England: Quakers, Morals and Popular Culture in the Long Eighteenth Century', in H. Berry and J. Gregory (eds), *Creating and Consuming Culture in North-East England, 1660–1830* (Aldershot, 2004)

——, 'In search of a New Jerusalem: A preliminary Investigation into the Causes and Impact of Welsh Quaker Emigration to Pennsylvania, *c*.1660–1750', *QS*, 9 (1) (September 2004), 31–53

——, 'John ap John', *Oxford Dictionary of National Biography* (Oxford, 2004)

——, 'The making of a Holy Christian Community: Welsh Quaker emigrants to Pennsylvania, c.1680–1750', in Tim Kirk and Lud'a Klusáková (eds), *Cultural Conquests* (Prague, forthcoming)

——, '"Turning hearts to break off the yoke of oppression." The travels and sufferings of Christopher Meidel *c*.1659–*c*.1715', *QS* (forthcoming)

Allisson, W. J. (ed.), *Memorials of Rebecca Jones* (2nd edn, London, 1849)

Amussen, S. D., 'Gender, Family and the Social Order 1560–1735', in A. Fletcher and J. Stevenson (eds), *Order and Disorder in Early Modern England* (Cambridge, 1985)

——, *An Ordered Society: Gender and Class in Early Modern England* (Oxford, 1988)

Anderson, Alan, 'A Study in the Sociology of Religious Persecution: The First Quakers', *Journal of Religious History*, 9 (3) (June 1977), 247–62

——, 'The Social Origins of the Early Friends', *QH*, 68 (1) (Spring 1979), 33–40

Andrews, C. M., *The Colonial Period of American History* (3 vols, New Haven, 1934)

Anon., 'Journal of John Churchman (1753)', *The Friends' Library*, 6 (1842), 229

——, 'Philadelphia in 1698', *PMHB*, 18 (1894), 247–8

——, 'John Roberts of Merion', *PMHB*, 19 (1895), 262–3

——, 'A Friend's Journal: A Brief Journal of Hugh Roberts', *Wales*, 3 (1896), 335–6, 370–3

——, 'A Letter from Hugh Roberts to William Penn', *Wales*, 3 (1896), 371–3

——, 'John Humphrey's Narrative', in H. M. Jenkins, *Historical Collections of Gwynedd* (Philadelphia, 1897)

——, 'Financial Statements sent to Swarthmore, 1654 to 1656', *JFHS*, 6 (1–3) (1909), 49–52, 82–5, 127–8

——, 'Pioneers in Pennsylvania, 1685', *JFHS*, 6 (4) (November 1909), 174

——, 'Yr Esgob a'r Gwladwr', *Cylchgrawn Cymdeithas Alawon Gwerin Cymru (Journal of Welsh Folk Song Society)*, II (1910), 45; trans. 'The Bishop and the Peasant', *JFHS*, 9 (1912), 171–2

Aries, P., *The Hour of our Death* (Harmondsworth, 1983)

Aylmer, G. E., *The Interregnum: The Quest for Settlement 1646–1660* (London, 1971)

Ayoub, Raymond, 'The Persecution of "an Innocent People" in Seventeenth-Century England', *QS*, 10 (1) (September 2005), 46–66

Backhouse, K. (ed.), *A Memoir of Mary Capper, late of Birmingham, a Minister of the Society of Friends* (Philadelphia, 1882)

Baker, D. (ed.), *Studies in Church History, 10: Sanctity and Secularity: The Church and the World* (Oxford, 1973)

Barbour, H., *The Quakers in Puritan England* (London and New Haven, 1964)

——, 'Quaker Prophetesses and Mothers in Israel', in J. W. Frost and J. M. Moore (eds), *Seeking the Light* (London, 1986)

Barbour, H. and Frost, J. W., *The Quakers* (Connecticut, 1988)

Barbour, H. and Roberts, A. O. (eds), *Early Quaker Writings, 1650–1700* (Grand Rapids, Michigan, 1973)

Barry, J. and Brooks, C. (eds), *The Middling Sort of People: Culture, Society and Politics in England 1550–1800* (London, 1994)

Barry, J., Hester, M. and Roberts, G. (eds), *Witchcraft in Early Modern Europe: Studies in Culture and Belief* (Cambridge, 1996)

Bassett, T. M., *The Welsh Baptists* (Swansea, 1977)

Bauman, R., 'Aspects of 17th Century Quaker Rhetoric', *The Quarterly Journal of Speech*, 56 (1970), 67–74

——, *Let your words be few. Symbolism of Speaking and Silence among Seventeenth-Century Quakers* (Cambridge, 1983)

Beckford, J. A. and Hampshire, A. P., 'Religious Sects and the Concept of Deviance', *British Journal of Sociology*, XXXIV (2) (June 1983), 208–29

Beier, L. M., 'In Sickness and in Health: A seventeenth century family's experience', in R. Porter (ed.), *Patients and Practitioners: Lay Perceptions of Medicine in Pre-Industrial Society* (Cambridge, 1985)

Bell, E., '"Vain unsettled fashions": The early Durham Friends and Popular Culture, *c*.1660–1725', *QS*, 8 (1) (September 2003), 23–35

Bell, H. E. and Ollard, R. L (eds), *Historical Essays, 1600–1750* (London, 1963)

Berry, H. and Gregory, J. (eds), *Creating and Consuming Culture in North-East England, 1660–1830* (Aldershot, 2004)

Bitterman, M. G. F., 'The Early Quaker Literature of Defence', *Church History*, 42 (1973), 203–28

Bittle, W. G., *James Nayler: 1618–1660. The Quaker Indicted by Parliament* (York, 1986)

Bonfeld, L., Smith, R. M. and Wrightson, K. (eds), *The World We Have Gained* (London, 1986)

Booy, David (ed.), *Autobiographical Writings by Early Quaker Women* (Aldershot, 2004)

Bossy, J., *The English Catholic Community 1570–1850* (London, 1975)

Bowen, Lloyd, 'Representations of Wales and the Welsh during the Civil Wars and Interregnum', *Historical Research*, 77 (197) (2004), 358–76

Brace, L., *The Idea of Property in Seventeenth-Century England: Tithes and the Individual* (Manchester, 1999)

Bradney, J. A. (ed.), *The Diary of Walter Powell of Llantilio Crossenny, Gent., 1603–1654* (Bristol, 1907)

—— (ed.), *Registrum Antiquum de Llanfihangel Ystern Llewern 1685–1812* (London, 1920)

Brailsford, M. R., *Quaker Women 1650–1690* (London, 1915)

——, *A Quaker from Cromwell's Army: James Nayler* (London, 1927)

Braithwaite, A. W., 'Thomas Rudyard: Early Friends' 'Oracle of Law'', *JFHS*, 27 (1956), 1–19

——, 'Early Tithe Prosecutions: Friends as Outlaws', *JFHS*, 49 (3) (1960), 148–56

——, 'Early Friends' Experiences with Juries', *JFHS*, 50 (4) (1964), 217–27

——, 'Early Friends and Informers', *JFHS*, 51 (2) (1966), 107–14

——, 'Early Friends' Testimony against Carnal Weapons', *JFHS*, 52 (2) (1969), 101–5

Braithwaite, W. C., *The Beginnings of Quakerism*, revised H. J. Cadbury (2nd edn, York, 1981)

——, *The Second Period of Quakerism*, revised H. J. Cadbury (2nd edn, York, 1979)

Brewer, J., *The Pleasures of the Imagination: English Culture in the Eighteenth Century* (London, 1997)

Briggs, J., 'She-Preachers, Widows and Other Women: The feminine dimension in Baptist life since 1600', *Baptist Quarterly*, 31 (July 1986), 337–52

Brooks, C., 'Apprenticeship, Social Mobility and the Middling Sort, 1550–1800', in J. Barry and C. Brooks (eds), *The Middling Sort of People* (London, 1994)

Brown, E. Potts and Stuard, S. Mosher (eds), *Witnesses for Change* (London, 1989)

Browning, C. H., *Welsh Settlement of Pennsylvania* (Philadelphia, 1912)

Burke, P., *Popular Culture in Early Modern Europe* (revised edn, Cambridge, 1994)

Burtt, R. G., 'The Quaker Marriage Declaration', *JFHS*, 46 (1955), 53–9

——, 'Quaker Books in the 18th Century', *JFHS*, 38 (1946), 7–18

Butler, D. M., 'Meeting Houses Built and Meetings Settled. Answers to the Yearly Meeting Queries, 1688–1791', *JFHS*, 51 (1967), 174–211

——, *The Quaker Meeting Houses of Britain: An Account of the 1,300 meeting houses and 900 burial grounds in England, Wales and Scotland, from the start of the movement in 1652 to the present time* (2 vols, London, 1999)

Bynum, W. F., Porter, R. and Stephens, M. (eds), *The Anatomy of Madness: Essays in the History of Psychiatry: Institution and Society* (2 vols, London, 1986)

Campbell-Stewart, W. A., 'Punishment in Friends' Schools, 1779–1900', *JFHS*, 42 (2), (1950), 51–6

Canny, Nicholas P., 'What really happened in Ireland in 1641?', in J. H. Ohlmeyer (ed.), *Ireland from Independence to Occupation, 1641–1660* (Cambridge, 1995)

Capp, B. S., *The Fifth Monarchy Men: A Study in Seventeenth-Century Millenarianism* (London, 1972)

——, 'Separate Domains? Women and Authority in Early Modern England', in P. Griffiths, A. Fox and S. Hindle (eds), *The Experience of Authority in Early Modern England* (Basingstoke, 1996)

Carré, B., 'Early Quaker Women in Lancaster and Lancashire', in M. A. Mullett (ed.), *Early Lancaster Friends* (Lancaster, 1978)

Carroll, K. L., 'John Perrot, Early Quaker Schismatic', *JFHS* Supplement, 33 (1971)

——, 'Sackcloth and Ashes and other Signs and Wonders', *JFHS*, 53 (1975), 314–25

——, 'Quaker Attitudes towards Signs and Wonders', *JFHS*, 54 (2) (1977), 70–84

——, 'Early Quakers and "going naked as a sign"', *QH*, 67 (2) (Autumn 1978), 69–87

Chappelle, E., *Historic Melingriffith* (Cardiff, 1940)

Charles, L. and Duffin, L. (eds), *Women and Work in Pre-industrial England* (London, 1985)

Cherry, C. L., 'Enthusiasm and Madness: Anti-Quakerism in the Seventeenth Century', *QH*, 73 (2) (Autumn 1984), 1–24

Chu, J. M., *Neighbors, Friends or Madmen: The Puritan Adjustment to Quakerism in Seventeenth-Century Massachusetts Bay* (Westport, Conn., 1985)

Clark, P., 'The Alehouse and the Alternative Society', in D. Pennington and K. Thomas (eds), *Puritans and Revolutionaries* (Oxford, 1978)

—— (ed.), *The Cambridge Urban History of Britain* (3 vols, Cambridge, 2000)

Clark, P. and Souden, D. (eds), *Migration and Society in Early Modern England* (London, 1987)

Clark, R., "The gangreen of Quakerism': An Anti-Quaker Anglican Offensive in England after the Glorious Revolution', *Journal of Religious History*, 11 (1981), 404–29

Clark, T., (ed.), *Autobiographical Narrations* (London, 1848)

Clarkson, T., *A Portraiture of Quakerism* (3 vols, 2nd edn, London, 1807)

Clement, M. (ed.), *Correspondence and Minutes of the S.P.C.K. relating to Wales 1699–1740* (Cardiff, 1952)

Clifton, Robin, 'The Popular Fear of Catholics during the English Revolution', *P&P*, 52 (1971), 23–55

Cohen, A., 'Prophecy and Madness: Women Visionaries during the Puritan Revolution', *Journal of Psychohistory*, 11 (Winter 1984), 411–30

Cole, A., 'The Quakers and the English Revolution', *P&P*, 10 (1956), 39–54

——, 'The Social Origins of the Early Friends', *JFHS*, 48 (3) (Spring 1957), 99–118

Collinson, P., *The Religion of Protestants* (Oxford, 1983)

Comfort, W. W., 'Quaker Marriage Certificates', *QH*, 40 (2) (Autumn 1951), 67–80

Corley, T. A. B., 'Changing Quaker Attitudes to Wealth, 1690–1950', in D. J. Jeremy (ed.), *Religion, Business, and Wealth in Modern Britain* (London, 1998)

Coster, W., 'Purity, Profanity and Puritanism: The Churching of Women 1500–1700', in W. J. Sheils and D. Woods (eds), *Studies in Church History*, 27: *Women in the Church* (Oxford, 1990)

——, *Family and Kinship in England 1450–1800* (Harlow, 2001)

——, 'Tokens of Innocence: Infant baptism, death and burial in early modern England', in B. Gordon and P. Marshall (eds), *The Place of the Dead: Death and Remembrance in Late Medieval and Early Modern Europe* (Cambridge, 2000)

Cragg, G. R. (ed.), *The Works of John Wesley* (Oxford, 1975)

Crawford, P., 'Historians, Women and Civil War Sects, 1640–1660', *Parergon* (Bulletin of the Australian and New Zealand Association for Medieval and Renaissance Studies), 6 (new series, 1988), 19–32

——, 'The Challenge to Patriarchalism: How did the Revolution Affect Women?', in J. Morrill (ed.), *Revolution and Restoration: England in the 1650s* (London, 1992)

——, *Women and Religion in England 1500–1720* (London, 1993)

Cressy, D., *Literacy and the Social Order: Reading and Writing in Tudor and Stuart England* (Cambridge, 1980)

——, 'Purification, Thanksgiving and the Churching of Women in post-Reformation England', *P&P*, 141 (1993), 106–46

——, *Birth, Marriage and Death: Ritual, Religion, and the Life-Cycle in Tudor and Stuart England* (Oxford, 1999)

Cross, C., '"He-Goats Before the Flocks": A note on the part played by women in the founding of some Civil War churches', in G. J. Cuming and D. Baker (eds), *Studies in Church History*, 8: *Popular Belief and Practice* (Cambridge, 1972)

Cuming, G. J. (ed.), *Studies in Church History*, 2 (London, 1965)

Cuming, G. J. and Baker, D. (eds), *Studies in Church History*, 8: *Popular Belief and Practice* (Cambridge, 1972)

Damrosch, L., *The Sorrows of the Quaker Jesus: James Nayler and the Puritan Crackdown on the Free Spirit* (Cambridge, Mass., 1996)

Darnell, R., 'The Second Person Singular Pronoun in English: The Society of Friends', *Western Canadian Journal of Anthropology*, I (1970), 1–11

Davies, A., *The Quakers in English Society 1655–1725* (Oxford, 2000)

Davies, E. T., 'Richard Hanbury and the Early Industrial History of Pontypool', *Pontypool and District Review*, 3 (February 1970), 1–3

Davies, Idris, 'Dyddiau Cynnar Annibyniaeth ym Mrycheiniog a Maesyfed' (The early days of Independency (Congregationalism) in Breconshire and Radnorshire, *Y Cofiadur*, 16 (March 1946), 3–64

Davies, J., *A History of Wales* (pbk edn, Harmondsworth, 1994)

Davies, J. Conway, 'Records of the Church in Wales', *NLWJ*, IV (Summer 1945), 1–34

Davies, J. H. and Ellis, T. E. (eds), *Gweithiau Morgan Llwyd o Wynedd* (2 vols, Bangor, 1899; London, 1908)

Davies, S., *Unbridled Spirits: Women of the English Revolution, 1640–1660* (London, 1998)

Davies, W. T. Pennar, 'Episodes in the History of Brecknock Dissent', *Brycheiniog*, 3 (1957), 11–65

Davison, L., 'Experiments in the Social Regulation of Industry: Gin Legislation, 1729–1751', in L. Davison, T. Hitchcock, T. Keirn and R. B. Shoemaker (eds), *Stilling the Grumbling Hive: The Response to Social and Economic Problems in England, 1689–1750* (Stroud, 1992)

Davison, L., Hitchcock, T., Keirn, T. and Shoemaker, R. B. (eds), *Stilling the Grumbling Hive: The Response to Social and Economic Problems in England, 1689–1750* (Stroud, 1992)

Denning, R. T. W. (ed.), *The Diary of William Thomas of Michaelston-super-Ely, near St. Fagans, Glamorgan, 1762–1795* (Cardiff, 1995)

DesBrisay, G., 'Catholics, Quakers and religious persecution in Restoration Aberdeen', *Innes Review*, 47 (1996), 136–68

D'Monté, R. and Pohl, N. (eds), *Female Communities 1600–1800: Literary Visions and Cultural Realities* (Basingstoke, 2000)

Dobbie, B. M. Willmott, 'An attempt to Estimate the True Rate of Maternal Mortality, Sixteenth to Eighteenth Centuries', *Medical History*, XXVI (1982), 79–90

Dobson, M. J., *Contours of Death and Disease in Early Modern England* (Cambridge, 1997)

Dodd, A. H., 'The background of the Welsh Quaker migration to Pennsylvania', *JMHRS*, 3 (2) (1958), 111–27

——, 'A Remonstrance from Wales, 1655', *BBCS*, 17 (4) (1958), 279–92

Dudley, A. C., 'Nonconformity under the "Clarendon Code"', *American Historical Review*, 18 (1913), 65–78

Duffy, Eamon, 'The Godly and the Multitude in Stuart England', *The Seventeenth Century*, 1 (1) (1986), 31–55

Dunn, R. S. and Dunn, M. M. (eds), *The World of William Penn* (Philadelphia, 1986)

Durnbaugh, D. F., 'Baptists and Quakers – Left wing Puritans?', *QH*, 62 (2) (Autumn 1973), 67–82

Durston, C., *The Family in the English Revolution* (Oxford, 1989)

Durston, C. and Eales, J. (eds), *The Culture of English Puritanism, 1560–1700* (Basingstoke, 1996)

Eames, M., *Y Staffell Ddirgel* (Llandybïe, 1969) and translated as *The Secret Room* (Llandysul, 1995)

Edwards, G. W., 'The London Six Weeks Meeting: Some of its work and records over 200 years', *JFHS*, 50 (4) (1964), 228–45

Edwards, I., 'The Women Friends of London. The Two Weeks and Box Meetings', *JFHS*, 47 (1955), 3–21

Elliott, J., *The Industrial Development of the Ebbw Valleys, 1780–1914* (Cardiff, 2004)

Ellis, S. G. and Barber, S. (eds), *Conquest and Union: Fashioning a British State, 1485–1725* (London, 1995)

Elmer, P., "'Saints or sorcerers': Quakerism, demonology and the decline of witchcraft in seventeenth-century England', in J. Barry, M. Hester and G. Roberts (eds), *Witchcraft in Early Modern Europe: Studies in Culture and Belief* (Cambridge, 1996); reprinted in B. P. Levack (ed.), *New Perspectives on Witchcraft, Magic and Demonology: Vol. I: Demonology, Religion, and Witchcraft* (New York & London, 2002)

Emery, F., 'The Farming Regions of Wales', in J. Thirsk (ed.), *The Agrarian History of England and Wales* (8 vols, Cambridge, 1967–90), IV (1500–1640)

Endy, M. B., 'Puritans, Spiritualist and Quakerism: An Historiographical Essay', in R. S. Dunn and M. M. Dunn (eds), *The World of William Penn* (Philadelphia, 1986)

Erikson, A. L., *Women and Property in Early Modern England* (London, 1995)

Erikson, K. T., *Wayward Puritans: A Study in the Sociology of Deviance* (New York, 1966)

Evans, E. J., '"Our Faithfull Testimony". The Society of Friends and Tithe Payments 1690–1730', *JFHS*, 52 (2) (1969), 106–21

——, 'Tithing Customs and Disputes: The Evidence of Glebe Terriers, 1698–1850', *Agricultural History Review*, 18 (1970), 17–35

Evans, E. L., 'Morgan Llwyd and the Early Friends', *Friends Quarterly*, 8 (1) (1954), 48–57

Evans, G. E., 'Llandovery Friends' Burial Ground', *TCASFC*, 4 (1906), 47

Evans, L. W., *Education in Industrial Wales 1700–1900* (Cardiff, 1971)

Fincham, K. (ed.), *The Early Stuart Church, 1603–1642* (Basingstoke, 1993)

Fischer, D. H., *Albion's Seed: Four British Folkways in America* (Oxford, 1989)

Fletcher, A., 'The Enforcement of the Conventicle Acts 1664–1679', in W. J. Sheils (ed.), *Studies in Church History*, 21: *Persecution and Toleration* (Oxford, 1984)

——, *Gender, Sex and Subordination* (New Haven, 1995)

Fletcher, A. and Stevenson, J. (eds), *Order and Disorder in Early Modern England* (Cambridge, 1985)

Floud, R. and McCloskey, D. (eds), *The Economic History of Britain since 1700* (2nd edn, London, 1994)

Forbes, T. R., 'The Regulation of English Midwives in the Sixteenth and Seventeenth Centuries', *Medical History*, 8 (1964), 235–44

Forde, Helen, 'Friends and Authority: A Consideration of Attitudes and Expedients, with particular reference to Derbyshire', *JFHS*, 54 (3) (1978), 115–25

Foulds, E. Vipont, *Ackworth School* (London, 1959)

Frost, J. W., 'The Dry Bones of Quaker Theology', *Church History*, 39 (1970), 503–23

——, 'From Plainness to Simplicity: Changing Quaker Ideals for Material Culture', in E. J. Lapsansky and A. A. Verplanck (eds), *Quaker Aesthetics: Reflections on a Quaker ethic in American design and consumption* (Philadelphia, 2003)

Frost, J. W. and Moore, J. M. (eds), *Seeking the Light: Essays in Quaker History* (Wallingford, Pa., 1986)

Fryer, N. T., 'Some Aspects of the Agricultural History of a Monmouthshire Parish', *Presenting Monmouthshire*, 19 (Spring 1965), 22–9

Gibbard, N., *Walter Cradock: A New Testament Saint* (Bridgend, 1977)

Gill, C., 'Identities in Quaker Women's Writing, 1652–60', *Women's Writing*, 9 (2) (2002), 267–83

——, '"Women's Speaking Justified": The Feminine Quaker Voice 1662–1797', *Tulsa Studies in Women's Literature*, 9 (2) (2002), 61–83

——, *Women in the Seventeenth-Century Quaker Community* (Aldershot, 2005)

Gilley, S. and Sheils, W. J., *A History of Religion in Britain: Practice and Belief from pre-Roman Times to the Present* (Oxford, 1994)

Gillis, J., *For Better, For Worse: British Marriages, 1600 to the Present* (New York and Oxford, 1985)

Gittins, C., *Death, Burial and the Individual in Early Modern England* (London, 1984)

Glenn, T. A., *Merion in the Welsh Tract* (Norristown, Pa., 1896)

——, *The Welsh Founders of Pennsylvania* (2 vols, Oxford, 1911–13; reprinted Baltimore, 1970)

Glover, M. and Glover, J. R., *The Retreat, York: An Early Quaker Experiment in the Treatment of Mental Illness* (York, 1984)

Godlee, F., 'Aspects of Non-Conformity: Quakers and the lunatic fringe', in W. F. Bynum, R. Porter and M. Stephens (eds), *The Anatomy of Madness: Essays in the History of Psychiatry: Institution and Society* (2 vols, London, 1986)

Goody, J., Thirsk, J. and Thompson, E. P. (eds), *Family and Inheritance: Rural Society in Western Europe 1200–1800* (Cambridge, 1976)

Gordon, B. and Marshall, P. (eds), *The Place of the Dead: Death and Remembrance in Late Medieval and Early Modern Europe* (Cambridge, 2000)

Graves, M. P., 'Functions of Key Metaphor in Early Quaker Sermons', *Quarterly Journal of Speech*, 69 (1983), 364–78

Greaves, R. L., 'The Early Quakers as Advocates of Educational Reform', *QH*, 58 (1) (Spring 1969), 22–30

——, 'The Puritan-Nonconformist Tradition of England, 1650–1700: Historiographical Reflections', *Albion*, 17 (4) (Winter 1985), 449–86

——, *Deliver Us From Evil: The Radical Underground in Britain, 1660–1663* (Oxford, 1986)

——, *Enemies Under His Feet: Radicals and Nonconformists in Britain, 1664–1667* (Stanford, 1990)

——, 'Shattered Expectations. George Fox, The Quakers and the Restoration State', *Albion*, 24 (2) (1992), 237–59

——, 'Seditious sectaries or 'sober and useful inhabitants'? Changing conceptions of the Quakers in early modern Britain', *Albion*, 33 (1) (2001), 24–50

—— (ed.), *Triumph Over Silence: Women in Protestant History* (London, 1985)

Green, J. J., 'Joseph Rule, The Quaker in White', *JFHS*, 2 (2) (1905), 64–8

Griffith, S., *History of the Quakers in Pembrokeshire* (Haverfordwest, 1990)

Griffiths, P., Fox, A. and Hindle, S. (eds), *The Experience of Authority in Early Modern England* (Basingstoke, 1996)

Griffiths, P., Landers, J., Pelling M., and Tyson, R., 'Population and Disease, Estrangement and Belonging 1540–1700', in P. Clark (ed.), *The Cambridge Urban History of Britain* (3 vols, Cambridge, 2000)

Grubb, M., 'Tensions in the Religious Society of Friends in England in the Nineteenth Century', *JFHS*, 56, 1 (1990), 1–14

Gruffydd, R. G., *In that Gentile Country: The Beginnings of Puritan Nonconformity in Wales* (Bridgend, 1976)

Grundy, I. and Wiseman, S. (eds), *Women, Writing, History, 1640–1740* (London, 1992)

Gummere, A. M., *The Quaker: A Study in Costume* (Philadelphia, 1901)

——, *Witchcraft and Quakerism: A Study in Social History* (Philadelphia, 1908)

Guy, J. R. (ed.), *The Diocese of Llandaff in 1763: The Primary Visitation of Bishop Ewer* (Cardiff, 1991)

Hall, B., 'Puritanism – the problem of definition', in G. Cuming (ed.), *Studies in Church History*, 2 (London, 1965)

Hall, D. J., 'Membership Statistics of the Society of Friends, 1800–1880', *JFHS*, 52 (1969), 97–100

——, 'Plainness of Speech, Behaviour and Apparel in Eighteenth-Century English Quakerism', in W. J. Sheils (ed.), *Studies in Church History, 22: Monks, Hermits and the Ascetic Tradition* (Oxford, 1985)

Hampshire, A. P. and Beckford, J. A., 'Religious Sects and the concept of deviance: The Mormons and the Moonies', *British Journal of Sociology*, 34 (2) (1983), 208–29

Hanbury-Tenison, R., 'The Hanburys of Pontypool', *Pontypool and District Review*, 7 (June 1971), 1–8

Hancock, T., *The Peculium: An Endeavour to throw light on some of the Causes of the Decline of the Society of Friends* (London, 1859)

Hardy, D., *Alternative Communities in Nineteenth Century England* (London, 1979)

Harlow, Jonathan, 'Preaching for Hire: Public Issues and Private Concerns in a Skirmish of the Lamb's War', *QS*, 10 (1) (September 2005), 31–45

Hayden, R. (ed.), *The Records of a Church of Christ Meeting at Broadmead, Bristol* (Bristol, 1974)

Hibbard, C., *Charles I and the Popish Plot* (Chapel Hill, 1983)

Hill, C., 'Propagating the Gospel', in H. E. Bell and R. L. Ollard (eds), *Historical Essays, 1600–1750* (London, 1963)

——, 'Puritans and the "Dark Corners of the Land"', *TRHS*, 13 (1963), 77–102

——, *Change and Continuity in 17th Century England* (London, 1974)

——, *The World Turned Upside Down: Radical Ideas during the English Revolution* (pbk edn, Harmondsworth, 1975)

——, *The Experience of Defeat* (London, 1984)

——, 'Archbishop Laud and the English Revolution', in G. J. Schochet, P. E. Tatspaugh and C. Brobeck, (eds), *Religion, Resistance, and Civil War* (Washington, DC., 1990)

——, 'Quakers and the English Revolution' *JFHS*, 56 (3) (1992), 165–79

Hinds, H., *God's Englishwomen: Seventeenth-Century Radical Sectarian Writing and Feminist Criticism* (Manchester, 1996)

Hitchcock, J., 'Early Separatist Burial Practice', *Transactions of the Congregational Historical Society*, 20 (1966), 105–6

Hobby, Elaine, '"Discourse so Unsavoury": Women's Published Writings of the 1650s', in I. Grundy and S. Wiseman (eds), *Women, Writing, History, 1640–1740* (London, 1992)

——, '"Come to Live a Preaching Life": Female Community in Seventeenth-Century Radical Sects', in R. D'Monté and N. Pohl (eds), *Female Communities 1600–1800: Literary Visions and Cultural Realities* (Basingstoke, 2000)

——, 'Prophecy, Enthusiasm and Female Pamphleteers', in N. H. Keeble (ed.), *The Cambridge Companion to Writing of the English Revolution* (Cambridge, 2001)

Holstun, J. (ed.), *Pamphlet Wars: Prose in the English Revolution* (London, 1992)

Horle, C. W., 'Quakers and Baptists 1647–1660', *Baptist Quarterly*, 26 (1976), 344–62

——, 'Changing Quaker Attitudes towards Legal Defense: The George Fox Case, 1673–75, and the establishment of the Meeting for Sufferings', in J. W. Frost and J. M. Moore (eds), *Seeking the Light: Essays in Quaker History* (Wallingford, Pa, 1986)

——, 'Judicial Encounters with Quakers, 1660–1688', *JFHS*, 54 (2) (1977), 85–100

——, *The Quakers and the English Legal System, 1660–1688* (Philadelphia, 1988)

Houlbrooke, R. A., *The English Family 1450–1700* (London, 1983)

Houston, R. A., *Literacy in Early Modern England: Culture and Education 1500–1800* (London, 1988)

Howells, B. E. (ed.), *A Calendar of Letters relating to North Wales* (Cardiff, 1967)

Howells, J., 'Quakerism in Wales', *Red Dragon*, 4 (1883), 37–43

Huber, E. C., 'A Woman Must Not Speak: Quaker Women in the English Left Wing', in R. R. Ruether and E. McLaughlin (eds), *Women of Spirit: Female Leadership in the Jewish and Christian Traditions* (New York, 1979)

Hudson, R. (ed.), *The Grand Quarrel: Women's Memoirs of the English Civil War* (Stroud, 2000)

Hughes, A., 'The Pulpit Guarded: Confrontations between Orthodox and Radicals in Revolutionary England', in A. Laurence, W. R. Owens and S. Sim (eds), *John Bunyan and his England 1628–1688* (London, 1990)

Hughes, G. H., *Gweithiau William Williams Pantycelyn* (2 vols, Cardiff, 1967)

——, *Williams Pantycelyn* (Cardiff, 1983)

Hurwich, J. J., '"A Fanatick Town": The political influence of Dissenters in Coventry 1660–1720', *Midland History*, 4 (1977–78), 15–47

——, 'The Social Origins of Early Quakers', *P&P*, 48 (1970), 156–62

Hutton, R., *The British Republic, 1649–1660* (Basingstoke, 1990)

——, *The Rise and Fall of Merry England: The Ritual Year, 1400–1700* (Oxford, 1994)

Ingle, H. L., 'From Mysticism to Radicalism: Recent Historiography of Quaker Beginnings', *QH*, 76 (1987), 79–94

——, *First Among Friends: George Fox and the creation of Quakerism* (Oxford, 1994)

——, 'The Future of Quaker History', *JFHS*, 59 (1) (1997), 1–16

Irwin, J. L., *Womanhood in Radical Protestantism 1525–1675* (New York, 1979)

Isichei, E. A., 'From Sect to Denomination in English Quakerism, with special reference to the nineteenth century', *British Journal of Sociology*, 15 (1964), 207–22

——, 'From Sect to Denomination among English Quakers', in B. R. Wilson (ed.), *Patterns of Sectarianism: Organisation and Ideology in Social and Religious Movements* (London, 1967)

——, *Victorian Quakers* (London, 1970)

James, B. Ll., 'The Evolution of a Radical: The Life and Career of William Erbery (1604–54)', *JFHS*, 3 (1986), 31–48

James, M., 'The Political Importance of the Tithes Controversy in the English Revolution 1640–60', *History*, 26 (June 1941), 1–18

Jenkins, G. H., 'James Owen versus Benjamin Keach: a controversy over Infant Baptism', *NLWJ*, XIX (1975), 57–66

——, 'Quaker and anti-Quaker literature in Welsh from the Restoration to Methodism', *WHR*, 7 (1975), 403–26

——, 'Popular beliefs in Wales from the Restoration to Methodism', *BBCS*, 27 (1977), 440–62

——, 'From Ysgeifiog to Pennsylvania: the Rise of Thomas Wynne, Quaker Barber-Surgeon', *Flintshire Historical Society Journal*, 28 (1977–8), 39–61

——, *Literature, Religion and Society in Wales, 1660–1730* (Cardiff, 1978)

——, 'Llythyr Olaf Thomas Wynne o Gaerwys: A farewell of endeared love to ould England and Wales, 1686', *BBCS*, 29 (1980), 91–110

——, 'The Early Peace Testimony in Wales', *Llafur*, 4 (1985), 10–19

——, 'Rhyfel yr Oen: y mudiad heddwch yn Nghymru 1653–1816', *Cof Cenedl*, I (1986), 65–94

——, 'The Friends of Montgomeryshire in the Heroic Age', *MC*, 76 (1988), 17–30

——, *The Foundations of Modern Wales, 1642–1780* (Oxford, 1987)

——, *Protestant Dissenters in Wales, 1639–1689* (Cardiff, 1992)

Jenkins, H. M., 'The Welsh Settlement of Gwynedd', *PMHB*, 8 (1884), 174–83

——, *Historical Collections relating to Gwynedd: A Township of Montgomery County, Pennysylvania, settled 1698* (Philadelphia, 1884)

Jenkins, J. P., 'A Welsh Lancashire? Monmouthshire Catholics in the Eighteenth Century', *Recusant History*, 15 (3) (May 1980), 176–88

——, 'Anti-Popery on the Welsh Marches in the Seventeenth Century', *Historical Journal*, 23 (2) (1980), 275–93

——, '"The Old Leaven": The Welsh Roundheads after 1660', *Historical Journal*, 24 (4) (1981), 807–23

——, 'The Demographic Decline of the Landed Gentry in the Eighteenth Century: A South Wales study', *WHR*, 11 (1) (1982–3), 31–49

——, 'The Sufferings of the Clergy: The Church in Glamorgan during the Interregnum', *JWEH*, 3 (1986), 1–17; 4 (1987), 9–41; 5 (1988), 74–80

——, 'The Anglican Church and the Unity of Britain: The Welsh Experience, 1560–1714', in S. G. Ellis and S. Barber (eds), *Conquest and Union: Fashioning a British State, 1485–1725* (London, 1995)

Jeremy, D. J. (ed.), *Religion, Business, and Wealth in Modern Britain* (London, 1998)

John, M. (ed.), *Welsh Baptist Studies* (Cardiff, 1976)

Johnson, A. M., 'Politics and Religion 1649–60', in G. Williams (ed.), *Glamorgan County History* IV (Cardiff, 1974)

——, 'Wales during the Commonwealth and Protectorate', in D. Pennington and K. Thomas (eds), *Puritans and Revolutionaries* (Oxford, 1978)

Jones, A. E., 'Protestant Dissent in Gloucestershire: A Comparison between 1676 and 1735', *Bristol and Gloucestershire Archaeological Transactions*, 51 (1983), 131–45

Jones, A. G., *A History of Ebbw Vale* (Risca, 1970)

Jones, B. P., *Sowing Besides All Waters. The Baptist Heritage of Gwent* (Cwmbrân, 1985)

Jones, C., Newitt, M. and Roberts, S. (eds), *Politics and People in Revolutionary England* (London, 1986)

Jones, D. C., *'A Glorious Work in the World': Welsh Methodism and the International Evangelical Revival, 1735–50* (Cardiff, 2004)

Jones, I. G. and Williams, D. (eds), *The Religious Census of 1851: A Calendar of the Returns relating to Wales* (2 vols, Cardiff, 1976), I (south Wales)

Jones, J. G. and Owen, G. W. (eds), *Gweithiau Morgan Llwyd o Wynedd*, III (Caerdydd, 1994)

Jones, R. M., *Spiritual Reformers in the Sixteenth and Seventeenth Centuries* (London, 1914)

——, *The Later Periods of Quakerism* (2 vols, London, 1921)

Jones, R. T., 'Religion in Post-Restoration Brecknockshire 1660–1688', *Brycheiniog*, 8 (1962), 11–65

——, 'Puritan Llanvaches', *Presenting Monmouthshire*, 15 (1963), 36–9

——, *Hanes Annibynwyr Cymru* (Swansea, 1966)

——, *Vavasor Powell* (Swansea, 1971)

——, *Vavasor Powell* (Leominster, 1975)

Jones, T. G., 'Parish of Meifod. Sketch of the History of Nonconformity', *MC*, 11 (1878), 61–124

Keeble, N. H. (ed.), *The Cambridge Companion to Writing of the English Revolution* (Cambridge, 2001)

Keeble, N. H. and Nuttall, G. F. (eds), *Calendar of Correspondence of Richard Baxter* (2 vols, London, 1991)

Kendall, J., 'The development of a Distinctive Form of Quaker Dress', *Costume*, 19 (1985), 58–74

Kent, S. A., 'The "Papist" Charges Against the Interregnum Quakers', *Journal of Religious History*, 12 (1982), 180–90

Kenyon, J., *The Popish Plot* (London, 1972)

Kerkham, C. R., 'An Anglican's observations on a Sunday evening meeting at an inn in Radnorshire, 1799', *JFHS*, 54 (2) (1977), 67–9

Kim, C., 'The Diggers, the Ranters and the Early Quakers', *American Benedictine Review*, 25 (4) (1974), 460–75

Knox, R. B., 'The Westminster Assembly of Divines', *Bulletin of the Presbyterian Historical Society of Ireland*, 22 (1993), 5–15

Kunze, B. Y., *Margaret Fell and the Rise of Quakerism* (Stanford, Ca., 1994)

Langford, P., *A Polite and Commercial People: England, 1727–1783* (Oxford, 1989)

Lapsansky, E. J. and Verplanck, A. A. (eds), *Quaker Aesthetics: Reflections on a Quaker Ethic in American Design and Consumption* (Philadelphia, 2003)

Laslett, P., *Family Life and Illicit Love in Earlier Generations* (Cambridge, 1977)

——, *The World We Have Lost* (revised edn, London, 1983)

Laurence, A., 'A Priesthood of She-Believers: Women and Congregations in Mid-Seventeenth-Century England', in W. J Sheils and D. Wood (eds), *Studies in Church History*, 27: *Women in the Church* (Oxford, 1990)

——, *Women in England 1500–1760. A Social History* (pbk edn, London, 1995)

Laurence, A., Owens, W. R. and Sim, S. (ed.), *John Bunyan and his England 1628–1688* (London, 1990)

Leimdorfer, V., *Quakers at Sidcot 1690–1990* (Sidcot, 1990)

Lettersom, J. C., *Memoirs of John Fothergill M.D.* (4th edn, London, 1786)

Levack, B. P. (ed.), *New Perspectives on Witchcraft, Magic and Demonology: Vol. I: Demonology, Religion, and Witchcraft* (New York and London, 2002)

Levick, J. J., 'John ap Thomas and his Friends', *PMHB*, 4 (1880), 301–28

——, 'An old Welsh Pedigree', *PMHB*, 4 (1880), 471–83

——, 'The Early Welsh Quakers and their Emigration to Pennsylvania', *PMHB*, 17 (4) (1893), 385–413

Levy, B., 'Tender Plants: Quaker Farmers and Children in the Delaware Valley 1681–1735', *Journal of Family History*, 3 (June 1978), 116–35

——, *Quakers and the American Family: British Settlement in the Delaware Valley* (Oxford, 1988)

Lidbetter, H., *The Friends Meeting House* (2nd edn, York, 1979)

Lindley, K. J., 'The part played by the Catholics', in B. Manning (ed.), *Politics, Religion and the Civil War* (London, 1973)

Little, J. B., *The Law of Burial* (London, 1902)

Lloyd, A., *Quaker Social History 1669–1738* (London, 1950)

Lloyd, H., *The Quaker Lloyds in the Industrial Revolution* (London, 1975)

Lloyd, J., *The Quakers in Wales* (London, 1947)

Locke, A. A., *The Hanbury Family* (2 vols, London, 1916)

Ludlow, D. P., '"Shaking Patriarchy's Foundations": Sectarian Women in England 1641–1700', in R. L. Greaves (ed.), *Triumph Over Silence* (London, 1985)

Maassen, Irmgard, 'Whoring, Scolding, Gadding About: Threats to Family Order in Early Modern Conduct Literature', *Journal for the Study of British Cultures*, 9 (2) (2002), 159–72

MacDonald, M., *Mystical Bedlam: Madness, Anxiety and Healing in Seventeenth Century England* (Cambridge, 1981)

MacFarlane, A., *Marriage and Love in England: Modes of Reproduction 1300–1840* (pbk edn, Oxford, 1993)

MacGregor, J. F., 'Ranterism and the Development of Early Quakerism', *Journal of Religious History*, 9 (1977), 349–63

——, 'The Baptists: Fount of all heresy', in J. F. MacGregor and B. Reay (eds), *Radical Religion in the English Revolution* (Oxford, 1984)

MacGregor, J. F. and Reay, B. (eds), *Radical Religion in the English Revolution* (Oxford, 1984)

Mack, P., 'Women as Prophets during the English Civil War', *Feminist Studies*, 8 (1982), 20–45

——, 'Gender and Spirituality in Early English Quakerism 1650–1665', in E. Potts Brown and S. Mosher Stuard (eds), *Witnesses for Change* (London, 1989)

——, *Visionary Women: Ecstatic Prophecy in Seventeenth-Century England* (Berkeley, Ca and Oxford, 1992)

MacLean, William, 'Dr. Thomas Wynne's account of his early life', *PMHB*, 25 (1901), 104–8

Maclear, J. F., 'Quakerism and the end of the Interregnum', *Church History*, 19 (1950), 240–70

Macpherson, T., *Friends in Radnorshire: A Brief History of the Quakers* (Llandrindod Wells, 1999)

——, 'A measure of grace: Quakers in Radnorshire', *Transactions of the Radnorshire Society*, 69 (1999), 8–33

Malcolmson, R. W., *Popular Recreations in English Society, 1700–1850* (Cambridge, 1973)

Manning, B. (ed.), *Politics, Religion and the Civil War* (London, 1973)

Marland, H. (ed.), *The Art of Midwifery: Early Modern Midwives in Europe and North America* (London, 1993)

Martin, C. J. L., 'Tradition Versus Innovation: The Hat, Wilkinson-Story and Keithian Controversy', *QS*, 8 (1) (September 2003), 5–22

Martin, D. A., 'The Denomination', *British Journal of Sociology*, 13 (March 1962), 1–14

Martin, L. C. (ed.), *The Works of Henry Vaughan* (2nd edn, Oxford, 1957)

Matthews, J. H., 'Mass in Penal Times', *SPM*, 9 (1929), 322–6

McDonald, R. W., 'The Parish Registers of Wales', *NLWJ*, 19 (4) (1976), 399–429

McEntee, A. M., "The [un]civill-sisterhood of oranges and lemons': Female Petitioners and Demonstrators, 1642–1653', in J. Holstun (ed.), *Pamphlet Wars: Prose in the English Revolution* (London, 1992)

Mendelson, S. and Crawford, P., *Women in Early Modern England 1550–1720* (Oxford, 1998)

Mikesell, M. and Seeff, A. F. (eds), *Culture and Change: Attending to early Modern Women* (Newark and London, 2003)

Miller, John, "A Suffering People': English Quakers and Their Neighbours *c*.1650–*c*.1700', *P&P*, 188 *(2005)*, 71–103

Milligan, E. H., *Brittanica on Quakerism* (London, 1965)

Moore, R., 'Reactions to Persecution in Primitive Quakerism', *JFHS*, 57 (1995), 123–31

——, *The Light in their Consciences: Early Quakers in Britain* (Philadelphia, 2000)

Morgan, D. L., *The Great Awakening in Wales* (London, 1988)

Morgan, N. J., 'Lancashire Quakers and the Oath, 1660–1772', *JFHS*, 54 (5) (1980), 235–54

——, 'Lancashire Quakers and the Tithe, 1660–1730', *Bulletin of the John Rylands University Library of Manchester*, 70 (1988), 61–75

——, *Lancashire Quakers and the Establishment 1660–1730* (Halifax, 1993)

Morgan, S. (ed.), *Women, Religion and Feminism in Britain, 1750–1900* (Basingstoke, 2002)

Morgan, W. T., 'The Prosecution of Nonconformists in the Consistory Courts of St Davids, 1681–88', *Journal of the Historical Society of the Church in Wales*, 12 (1962), 28–54

Morrill, J., 'The Church in England 1643–49', in J. Morrill (ed.), *Reactions to the English Civil War* (London, 1992)

—— (ed.), *Revolution and Restoration: England in the 1650s* (London, 1992)

—— (ed.), *Reactions to the English Civil War* (London, 1992)

Morris, E. R., 'Quakerism in West Montgomeryshire', *MC*, 56 (1959–60), 45–65

——, 'The Dolobran Family in Religion and Industry in Montgomeryshire', *MC*, 56 (1959–60), 124–47

——, 'Llanwddyn Quakers', *MC*, 86 (1978), 46–59

Mortimer, J., 'Quaker women in the eighteenth century: opportunities and constraints', *JFHS*, 57 (3) (1996), 228–59

Mortimer, R. S., 'Quaker Education', *JFHS*, 39 (1947), 66–70

——, 'Bristol Quakers and the Oaths', *JFHS*, 43 (1951), 72–7

——, 'Marriage Discipline in Early Friends', *JFHS*, 48 (Autumn 1957), 175–95

——, *Early Bristol Quakerism: The Society of Friends in the City, 1654–1700* (Bristol, 1967)

—— (ed.), *Minute Book of the Men's Meeting of the Society of Friends in Bristol, 1667–1686* (Bristol, 1971)

—— (ed.), *Minute book of the Men's Meeting of the Society of Friends in Bristol, 1686–1704* (Bristol, 1977)

Morton, A. L., *The World of the Ranters* (London, 1970)

Mullett, M. A., 'The Assembly of the People of God: The Social Organisation of Lancashire Friends' in M. A. Mullett (ed.), *Early Lancaster Friends* (Lancaster, 1978)

——, *Radical Religious Movements in Early Modern Europe* (London, 1980)

——, 'From Sect to Denomination? Social Developments in Eighteenth-Century English Quakerism', *Journal of Religious History*, 13 (2) (1984), 168–91

——, 'Radical Sects and Dissenting Churches, 1600–1750', in S. Gilley and W. J. Sheils (eds), *A History of Religion in Britain: Practice and Belief from pre-Roman Times to the Present* (Oxford, 1994)

——, 'Catholic and Quaker Attitudes to Work, Rest, and Play in Seventeenth- and Eighteenth-Century England', in R. N. Swanson (ed.), *Studies in Church History, 37: The Use and Abuse of Time in Christian History* (Woodbridge, 2002)

—— (ed.), *Early Lancaster Friends* (Lancaster, 1978)

—— (ed.), *New Light on George Fox* (York, 1991)

Murphy, Paul P., 'The Jesuit College of the Cwm, Llanrothall', *Severn and Wye Review*, 1 (6) (1970–2), 135–9

Newman, H., *Memories of Stanley Pumphrey* (London, 1883)

Nichols, R., 'Elisha Beadles: An Apothecary 1670–1734', *Pontypool and District Review*, 8 (October 1971), 1–8

——, 'The Shirenewton Quaker Meeting house', *Severn and Wye Review*, 1–2 (Winter 1972–3), 61–2

——, 'Early Quakers in Gwent', *Anglo-Welsh Review*, 22 (49) (Spring 1973), 88–97

——, 'More about Early Quakers in Monmouthshire', *Anglo-Welsh Review*, 25 (56) (Spring 1976), 97–113

——, 'Friends Meeting-Houses and Burial Grounds in Monmouthshire', *GLH*, 48 (1980), 25–32; 49 (1980), 6–17

——, *Pontypool and Usk Japan Ware* (Pontypool, 1981)

——, 'Friends Meeting house, Trosnant', *Monmouthshire Medley* (4 vols, Cwmbrân, 1985), IV, 26–8

Nickalls, J. L. (ed.), *The Journal of George Fox* (Cambridge, 1952; pbk edn, Philadelphia, 1997)

Norris, W. G. and Penney, N., 'John ap John, and early records of Friends in Wales', *JFHS* Supplement, 6 (1907)

Nuttall, G. F., *The Holy Spirit in Puritan Faith and Experience* (Oxford, 1946)

——, *The Welsh Saints 1640–1660* (Cardiff, 1957)

——, 'Overcoming the World: the Early Quaker Programme', in D. Baker (ed.), *Studies in Church History, 10: Sanctity and Secularity: The Church and the World* (Oxford, 1973)

——, 'Puritan and Quaker Mysticism', *Theology*, LXXVIII (October 1975), 518–31

——, 'A Parcel of Books for Morgan Llwyd', *JFHS*, 56 (3) (1992), 180–8

——, 'A New Letter to George Fox', *JFHS*, 57 (3) (1996), 221–7

O'Day, R., *Education and Society 1500–1800: The Social Foundations of Education in Early Modern Britain* (London, 1982)

——, *The Family and Family Relationships, 1500–1900* (Basingstoke, 1994)

Ohlmeyer, J. H. (ed.), *Ireland from Independence to Occupation, 1641–1660* (Cambridge, 1995)

O'Malley, T. P., 'The Press and Quakerism, 1653–59', *JFHS*, 54 (4) (1979), 169–84

——, '"Defying the powers and tempering the spirit." A review of Quaker Control over their Publications 1672–1689', *Journal of Ecclesiastical History*, 33 (1) (January 1982), 72–88

Owen, J. E. (ed.), *The History of Aberystruth by Edmund Jones* (Bridgend, 1988)

Parry, Owen, 'Welsh Quakers in the light of the Joseph Wood papers', *BBCS*, 25 (2) (1972–4), 157–85

Penney, N., *Extracts from State Papers relating to Friends 1654–1672* (London, 1913)

——, 'John ap John, and early records of Friends in Wales', *JFHS* Supplement, 6 (1907)

—— (ed.), 'The First Publishers of Truth', *JFHS* Supplements 1–5 (1904–7)

Pennington, D. and Thomas, K. (eds), *Puritans and Revolutionaries* (Oxford, 1978)

Peters, K., '"Women's Speaking Justified": Women and Discipline in the early Quaker Movement, 1652–1656', in R. N. Swanson (ed.), *Studies in Church History, 34: Gender and Christian Religion* (Woodbridge, 1998)

——, *Print Culture and the Early Quakers* (Cambridge, 2005)

Phillips, J. R. S., *The Justices of the Peace in Wales and Monmouthshire, 1541–1689* (Cardiff, 1975)

Phillips, Mary, *Memoirs of Richard Phillips* (London, 1841)

Pike, Joseph, *Some Account of the Life of Joseph Pike of Cork* (London, 1837)

Plowden, A., *Our Women All on Fire: The Women of the English Civil War* (Stroud, 1998)

Pointon, M., *Hanging the Head: Portaiture and Social Formation in Eighteenth-Century England* (New Haven, 1992)

Pomfret, J. E., 'The First Purchasers of Pennsylvania, 1681–1700', *PMHB*, 80 (1956), 137–63

Pope, R. (ed.), *Religion and National Identity: Wales and Scotland, c.1700–2000* (Cardiff, 2001)

Porter, R., *Disease, Medicine and Society in England 1550–1860* (Basingstoke, 1987)

Porter, R. (ed.), *Patients and Practitioners: Lay Perceptions of Medicine in Pre-Industrial Society* (Cambridge, 1985)

Prior, Ann and Kirby, Maurice W., 'The Society of Friends and business culture, 1700–1830', in D. J. Jeremy (ed.), *Religion, Business, and Wealth in Modern Britain* (London, 1998)

Prior, M. (ed.), *Women in English Society, 1500–1800* (London, 1985)

Quaife, G. R., *Wanton Wenches and Wayward Wives: Peasants and Illicit Sex in Seventeenth Century England* (London, 1979)

Racaut, L., 'The "Book of Sports" and Sabbatarian Legislation in Lancashire, 1579–1616', *Northern History*, 33 (1997), 73–87

Raistrick, A., *Quakers in Science and Industry* (York, 1993)

Rakenshaw, J., 'A Memoir of Evan Bevan', *Friends Library*, 13 (1849), 174–8

Randles, R., '"Faithful Friends and Well Qualified": The Early Years of the Friends' School at Lancaster', in M. A. Mullett (ed.), *Early Lancaster Friends* (Lancaster, 1978)

Reay, B., 'The Quakers and 1659: Two newly discovered broadsides by Edward Burrough', *JFHS*, 54 (2) (1977), 101–11

——, 'The Quakers, 1659, and the Restoration of the Monarchy', *History*, 63 (1978), 193–213

——, 'The Social Origins of Early Quakerism', *Journal of Interdisciplinary History*, XI (1) (Summer 1980), 55–72

——, 'Quaker Opposition to Tithes 1652–1660', *P&P*, 86 (1980), 98–120

——, 'Popular Hostility towards Quakers in Mid-Seventeenth Century England', *Social History*, 5 (1980), 387–407

——, 'The Authorities and Early Restoration Quakerism', *Journal of Ecclesiastical History*, 34 (1) (1983), 69–84

——, 'Quakerism and society', in J. F. MacGregor and B. Reay (eds), *Radical Religion in the English Revolution* (Oxford, 1984)

——, *The Quakers and the English Revolution* (Hounslow, 1985)

—— (ed.), *Popular Culture in Seventeenth Century England* (London, 1985)

Rees, T., *History of Protestant Nonconformity in Wales* (2nd edn, London, 1883)

Rees, T. M., *A History of the Quakers in Wales and their Emigration to North America* (Carmarthen, 1925)

Richards, T., *A History of the Puritan Movement in Wales, 1639–53* (London, 1920)

——, *Religious Developments in Wales 1654–1662* (London, 1923)

——, *Wales under the Penal Code, 1622–1687* (London, 1925)

——, 'The Religious Census of 1676', *THSC*, Supplement (1925–6)

——, *Wales under the Indulgence 1672–1675* (London, 1928)

Roberts, G. M. (ed.), *Hanes Methodistiaeth Galfinaidd Cymru* (2 vols, Caernarfon, 1973–8)

Roberts, M. and Clarke, S. (eds), *Women and Gender in Early Modern Wales* (Cardiff, 2000)

Roberts, S. K., 'Godliness and Government in Glamorgan, 1647–1660', in C. Jones, M. Newitt and S. Roberts (eds), *Politics and People in Revolutionary England* (London, 1986)

——, 'The Quakers in Evesham 1655–1660: A Study in Religion, Politics and Culture', *Midland History*, 16 (1991), 63–84

——, 'Propagating the Gospel in Wales: The making of the 1650 Act', *THSC*, ns, 10 (2004 for 2003), 57–75

Ross, I., *Margaret Fell: Mother of Quakerism* (London and New York, 1949)

Rowntree, J. (ed.), *John Wilhelm Rowntree, Essays and Addresses* (2nd edn, London, 1906)

Rowntree, J. S., *Quakerism Past and Present: being an Inquiry into the causes of its decline in Great Britain and Ireland* (London, 1859)

Royle, T., *Civil War: The Wars of the Three Kingdoms, 1638–1660* (London, 2004)

Ruether, R. R. and McLaughlin, E. (eds), *Women of Spirit: Female Leadership in the Jewish and Christian Traditions* (New York, 1979)

Rutt, J. T. (ed.), *Diary of Thomas Burton* (4 vols, London, 1828)

Salmon, David, 'The Quakers of Pembrokeshire', *THSWW*, IX (1920–3), 1–32

——, 'The Pembrokeshire Quakers' Monthly Meeting', *THSWW*, 12 (1927), 1–24

Saul, A. R. Lewis, 'Cloddiau Cochion and the Welsh Quakers', *MC*, 55 (1957–8), 202–5

Schochet, G., Tatspaugh, J. P. E. and Brobeck, C. (eds), *Religion, Resistance, and Civil War* (Washington, DC, 1990)

Scott, D., *Quakerism in York, 1650–1720*, Borthwick Paper, 80 (York, 1991)

Sharpe, K., *The Personal Rule of Charles I* (New Haven and London, 1992)

Sheils, W. J. (ed.), *Studies in Church History, 21: Persecution and Toleration* (Oxford, 1984)

—— (ed.), *Studies in Church History, 22: Monks, Hermits and the Ascetic Tradition* (Oxford, 1985)

Sheils, W. J. and Wood, D. (eds), *Studies in Church History, 27: Women in the Church* (Oxford, 1990)

Smith, L. (ed.), *The Making of Britain: The Age of Expansion* (London, 1986)

Southall, J. E., 'Morgan Llwyd and his times', *Friends Quarterly Examiner*, 53 (1919), 23–35

——, 'The Society of Friends in Wales', *Friends Quarterly Examiner*, 14 (1880), 86–97

—— (ed.), *Leaves from the History of Welsh Nonconformity ... Autobiography of Richard Davies* (Newport, 1899)

Speizman, M. D. and Kronick, J. C., 'A Seventeenth Century Quaker Women's Declaration', *Signs. Journal of Women in Culture and Society*, 1 (1975), 231–45

Sprunger, K. O., "God's powerful army of the weak': The Anabaptist Women of the Radical Reformation', in R. L. Greaves (ed.), *Triumph over Silence: Women in Protestant History* (London, 1985)

Spufford, M., 'The Social Status of some Seventeenth-Century Rural Dissenters', in G. J. Cuming and D. Baker (eds), *Studies in Church History, 8: Popular Belief and Practice* (Cambridge, 1972)

——, *Contrasting Communities: English Villagers in the Sixteenth and Seventeenth Centuries* (Cambridge, 1974)

——, *Small Books and Pleasant Histories: Popular Fiction and its Readership in Seventeenth-Century England* (London, 1981)

Stevens, C., *Welsh Courting Customs* (Llandysul, 1993)

Stock, P., *Better than Rubies: A History of Women's Education* (New York, 1978)

Stone, L., *The Family, Sex and Marriage in England, 1500–1800* (Harmondsworth, 1977)

——, *The Road to Divorce: England 1530–1987* (Oxford, 1990)

Swanson R. N. (ed.), *Studies in Church History, 37: The Use and Abuse of Time in Christian History* (Woodbridge, 2002)

Tadmor, N., 'The Concept of the Household-Family in Eighteenth-Century England', *P&P*, 151 (May 1996), 111–40

Taylor, J., *Joseph Lancaster: The Poor Child's Friend. Educating the Poor in the Early Nineteenth Century* (Campanile, 1996)

Taylor, Kay S., 'The Role of Quaker Women in the Seventeenth Century, and the Experiences of the Wiltshire Friends', *Southern History*, 23 (2001), 10–29

Thirsk, J. (ed.), *The Agrarian History of England and Wales* (8 vols, Cambridge, 1967–90)

Thomas, Keith, 'Women and the Civil War Sects', *P&P*, 13 (1958), 42–62

Thomas, M. Wynn, *Morgan Llwyd* (Cardiff, 1984)

Toon, P. (ed.), *Puritans, The Millennium and the Future of Israel* (London, 1970)

Towler, J. and Bramall, J., *Midwives in History and Society* (London, 1986)

Trevett, C., 'The Women Around James Nayler, Quaker: A Matter of Emphasis', *Religion*, 20 (1990), 249–73

——, *Women and Quakerism in the Seventeenth Century* (York, 1991)

——, 'William Erbery and his daughter Dorcas: Dissenter and Resurrected Radical', *Journal of Welsh Religious History*, 4 (1996), 23–50

——, 'Women and the Coming of Quakerism to Wales', *Journal of Welsh Religious History*, 7 (1999), 38–53

——, *Quaker Women Prophets in England and Wales, 1650–1700* (Lewiston, Queenston and Lampeter, 2000)

Tual, J., 'Sexual Equality and Conjugal Harmony: The way to celestial bliss. A view of early Quaker matrimony', *JFHS*, 55 (6) (1988), 161–74

Turner, G. L., *Original Records of Early Nonconformists under Persecution and Indulgence* (3 vols, London, 1911–14)

Underdown, D., 'The Taming of the Scold: The Enforcement of Patriarchal Authority in Early Modern England', in A. Fletcher and J. Stevenson (eds), *Order and Disorder in Early Modern England* (Cambridge, 1985)

——, *Revel, Riot, and Rebellion: Popular Politics and Culture in England 1603–1660* (pbk edn, Oxford, 1987)

Underhill, E. B. and Haycroft, N. (eds), *The Records of a Church of Christ Meeting at Broadmead, Bristol* (London, 1865)

Underwood, T. L., 'Early Quaker Eschatology', in P. Toon (ed.), *Puritans, The Millennium and the Future of Israel* (London, 1970)

——, *Primitivism, Radicalism, and the Lamb's War: The Baptist-Quaker conflict in seventeenth-century England* (Oxford, 1997)

Vann, R. T., 'Quakerism and the Social Structure in the Interregnum', *P&P*, 43 (1969), 71–91

——, *Social Development of English Quakerism 1655–1755* (Cambridge, Mass., 1969)

Vann, R. T. and Eversley, D., *Friends in Life and Death – the British and Irish Quakers in the demographic transition, 1650–1900* (Cambridge, 1992)

Vipont, E., *George Fox and the Valiant Sixty* (London, 1975)

Wakeman, T., *Antiquarian Excursion in the Neighbourhood of Monmouth* (Newport, 1867)

Walker, D., 'The Reformation in Wales', in D. Walker (ed.), *A History of the Church in Wales* (Penarth, 1976)

——, (ed.), *A History of the Church in Wales* (Penarth, 1976)

Walker, Garthine, 'Just Stories: Telling Tales of Infant Death in Early Modern England', in M. Mikesell and A. F. Seeff (eds), *Culture and Change: Attending to Early Modern Women* (Newark and London, 2003)

Walsh, J. D., 'Methodism and the mob in the eighteenth century', in G. J. Cuming and D. Baker (eds), *Studies in Church History, 8: Popular Belief and Practice* (Cambridge, 1972)

Walvin, J., *The Quakers. Men and Morals* (London, 1997)

Watts, M., *The Dissenters: From the Reformation to the French Revolution* (Oxford, 1978)

Watts, T., 'William Wroth (1570–1641). Piwritan ac Apostol Cymru', *Y Cofiadur*, 44 (1979), 5–13

Weddle, M. B., *Walking in the Way of Peace: Quaker Pacifism in the Seventeenth Century* (Oxford, 2000)

White, B. R., 'John Miles and the structures of the Calvinist Baptist Mission to South Wales 1649–1660', in M. John (ed.), *Welsh Baptist Studies* (Cardiff, 1976)

Whiteman, A. (ed.), *The Compton Census of 1676: A Critical Edition* (London, 1986)

Whiting, C. E., *Studies in English Puritanism from the Restoration to the Revolution 1660–1688* (London, 1968),

Whiting, E. S., 'The Yearly Méeting for Wales, 1682–1797', *JFHS*, 47 (Spring 1955), 57–70

Whiting, E. S., Morris, E. R. and Hughes, J. R., *The Background of Quakerism in Wales and the Border* (Malvern, 1952)

Wiesner, M. E., *Women and Gender in Early Modern Europe* (Cambridge, 1993)

Wilcox, C. M., *Theology and Women's Ministry in seventeenth-century English Quakerism: Handmaids of the Lord* (Lampeter, 1995)

Williams, D. (ed.), *A History of the Church in Wales* (Penarth, 1976)

Williams, G., 'Injunctions of the Royal Visitation of 1559 for the Diocese of Llandaff', *NLWJ*, IV (3–4) (Summer 1946), 189–97

——, 'Wales during the Commonwealth and Protectorate', in D. H. Pennington and K. Thomas (eds), *Puritans and Revolutionaries* (Oxford, 1978)

——, *The Welsh and Their Religion* (Cardiff, 1991)

—— (ed.), *Glamorgan County History*, IV (Cardiff, 1974)

Williams, J. G., 'The Quakers of Merioneth during the Seventeenth Century', *JMHRS*, 8 (1978–9), 122–56, 312–39

Williams, M. F., 'Glamorgan Quakers 1654–1900', *Morgannwg*, 5 (1961), 49–75

Williams, M. I., 'The Economic and Social History of Glamorgan, 1660–1760', in G. Williams (ed.), *Glamorgan County History* (6 vols, Cardiff, 1938–90), IV: (1974)

Williams, R., 'Montgomeryshire Nonconformity: Extracts from the Gaol Files', *MC*, 24 (1890), 201–32; 25 (1891), 41–72; 26 (1892), 49–78; 27 (1893), 57–76; 28 (1894), 81–106

Wilson, B., 'An Analysis of Sect Development', *American Sociological Review*, 24 (February 1959), 3–15

——, *Sects and Society* (London, 1961)

——, 'Time, Generations and Sectarianism', in B. Wilson (ed.), *The Social Impact of the New Religious Movements* (New York, 1981)

—— (ed.), *Patterns of Sectarianism: Organisation and Ideology in Social and Religious Movements* (London, 1967)

—— (ed.), *The Social Impact of the New Religious Movements* (New York, 1981)

Wilson, Jean, 'Dead Fruit: The Commemoration of Still-born and Unbaptized Children in Early Modern England', *Church Monuments*, 17 (2002), 89–106

Woods, T., (ed.), *The Registers of Glasbury, Breconshire, 1660–1836* (London, 1904)

Worden, B., 'Toleration and the Cromwellian Protectorate', in W. J. Sheils (ed.), *Studies in Church History*, 21: *Persecution and Toleration* (Oxford, 1984)

Wright, L., *The Literary Life of the Early Friends, 1650–1725* (New York, 1932)

Wright, Sheila, 'Quakerism and its Implications for Quaker Women: The Women Itinerant Ministers of York Meeting, 1780–1840', in W. J. Sheils and D. Wood (eds), *Studies in Church History*, 27: *Women in the Church* (1990)

——, *Friends in York: The Dynamics of Quaker Revival, 1780–1860* (Keele, 1995)

——, '"Every good woman needs a companion of her own sex": Quaker Women and Spiritual Friendship 1750–1850', in S. Morgan (ed.), *Women, Religion and Feminism in Britain, 1750–1900* (Basingstoke, 2002)

Wrightson, K., *English Society, 1500–1600* (London, 1982)

——, 'Love, Marriage and Death', in L. Smith (ed.), *The Making of Britain: The Age of Expansion* (London, 1986)

——, '"Sorts of People" in Tudor and Stuart England', in J. Barry and C. Brooks (eds), *The Middling Sorts of People: Culture, Society and Politics in England, 1500–1800* (London, 1994)

——, *Earthly Necessities: Economic Lives in Early Modern Britain* (New Haven, 2000)

Wrigley, E. A. and Schofield, R. S., 'English Population History from Family Reconstitution: Summary Results 1600–1799', *Population Studies*, 37 (1983), 157–84

——, 'Love, Marriage and Death', in L. Smith (ed.), *The Making of Britain: The Age of Expansion* (London, 1986)

Unpublished Theses and Dissertations

Allen, R. C., 'The Society of Friends (Quakers) in Wales: The case of Monmouthshire c.1654–1836' (University of Wales, Aberystwyth, Ph.D. thesis, 1999)

Anderson, A. B., 'Lancashire Quakers and Persecution 1652–1670' (University of Lancaster, MA thesis, 1971)

Bell, A. E., 'Discipline and Manhood in the Society of Friends: a study with particular reference to Durham, c.1650–1750' (University of York, D.Phil. thesis, 2003)

Cole, W. A., 'The Quakers and Politics 1654–1660' (University of Cambridge, Ph.D. thesis, 1955)

Forde, H., 'Derbyshire Quakers, 1650–1761' (University of Leicester, Ph.D. thesis, 1977)

Gadt, J. C., 'Women and Protestant Culture: The Quaker Dissent from Protestantism' (University of California, Los Angeles, Ph.D. thesis, 1974)

Hall, D. J., 'The Discipline of the Society of Friends' (University of Durham, MA thesis, 1972)

Hubbard, D. G. B., 'Early Quaker Education' (University of London M.Ed. thesis, 1940)

Jones, G., 'Bywyd a gwaith Edward Morris, Perthi Llwydion' (University of Wales, Bangor, MA thesis, 1941)

Jones, H. G., 'John Kelsall: A Study in Religious and Economic History' (University of Wales, Bangor, MA thesis, 1938)

Lacock, R. G., 'The Quakers in Gloucester 1655–1737' (University of Birmingham, M.Phil. thesis, 2001)

Leachman, C. L., 'From an "unruly sect" to a Society of "strict unity": The Development of English Quakerism c.1650–1689' (University of London, Ph.D. thesis, 1998)

O'Keefe, M. M. C., 'The Popish Plot in South Wales and the Marches of Hereford and Gloucester' (University of Galway, MA thesis, 1969)

Oliver, P., 'The Quakers and Quietism' (University of Melbourne, MA thesis, 1972)

Martin, C. J. L., 'Controversy and Disagreement in 17th-Century Quakerism' (Open University, Ph.D. thesis, 2003)

Mason, G., 'Quaker Women and Education 1642–1840' (University of Lancaster, MA thesis, 1987)

Matthews, R. P., 'Roman Catholic Recusancy in Monmouthshire 1608–89: A Demographic and Morphological Analysis' (University of Wales, Cardiff, Ph.D. thesis, 1996)

Mortimer, R. S., 'Quakerism in Seventeenth Century Bristol' (University of Bristol, MA thesis, 1946)

Pugh, F., 'Recusancy in the Diocese of Llandaff during the Late Sixteenth and Early Seventeenth Centuries' (University of Wales, Cardiff, MA thesis, 1953)

Quine, E. K. L., 'The Quakers in Leicestershire' (University of Nottingham, Ph.D. thesis, 1968)

Scott, D., 'Politics, Dissent and Quakerism in York, 1640–1700' (University of York, Ph.D. thesis, 1990)

Selleck, A. D., 'The History of the Society of Friends in Plymouth and West Devon from 1654 to the early Nineteenth Century' (University of London, MA thesis, 1959)

Smith, R., 'Female "Intransigence" in the early Quaker movement from the 1650s to about 1700, with particular reference to North West of England' (University of Lancaster, MA thesis, 1990)

Stroud, L. J., 'The History of Quaker Education in England 1647–1903' (University of Leeds, M.Ed. thesis, 1944)

Vandevelde, B. R., 'Quakers and Fifth-Monarchy Men: Problems of Public Order c.September 1654–January 1657' (University of Exeter, MA thesis, 1978)

Williams, M. F., 'The Society of Friends in Glamorgan 1654–1900' (University of Wales, Aberystwyth, MA thesis, 1950)

Wrightson, K., 'The Puritan Reformation of Manners' (University of Cambridge, Ph.D. thesis, 1973)

Index